Moral Panic and the Politics of Anxiety

Moral Panic and the Politics of Anxiety is a collection of original essays written by some of the world's leading social scientists. It seeks to provide unique insight into the importance of moral panic as a routine feature of everyday life, whilst also developing an integrated framework for moral panic research by widening the scope of scholarship in the area.

Many of the key twenty-first century contributions to moral panic theory have moved beyond the parameters of the sociology of deviance to consider the importance of moral panic for identity formation, national security, industrial risk, and character formation. Reflecting this growth, the book brings together recognized moral panic researchers with prominent scholars in moral regulation, social problems, cultural fear, and health risks, allowing for a more careful and critical discussion around the cultural and political significance of moral panic to emerge.

This book will prove valuable reading for both undergraduate and postgraduate students on courses such as politics and the media, regulatory policy, the body and identity, theory and political sociology, and sociology of culture.

Sean P. Hier is Associate Professor and Chair of Sociology at the University of Victoria, British Columbia, Canada. He has authored several articles on moral panic, and he is recognized for his efforts to link moral panic to moral regulation/social problems.

Moral Panic and the Politics of Anxiety

Edited by
Sean P. Hier

Routledge
Taylor & Francis Group
LONDON AND NEW YORK

First published 2011
by Routledge
2 Park Square, Milton Park, Abingdon, Oxon, OX14 4RN

Simultaneously published in the USA and Canada
by Routledge
711 Third Avenue, New York, NY 10017

Routledge is an imprint of the Taylor & Francis Group, an informa business

© 2011 Sean P. Hier; individual chapters the contributors

The right of Sean P. Hier to be identified as editor of this work has been asserted by him in accordance with the Copyright, Designs and Patent Act 1988.

All rights reserved. No part of this book may be reprinted or reproduced or utilized in any form or by any electronic, mechanical, or other means, now known or hereafter invented, including photocopying and recording, or in any information storage or retrieval system, without permission in writing from the publishers.

Trademark notice: Product or corporate names may be trademarks or registered trademarks, and are used only for identification and explanation without intent to infringe.

British Library Cataloguing in Publication Data
A catalogue record for this book is available from the British Library

Library of Congress Cataloging in Publication Data
Moral panic and the politics of anxiety / edited by Sean Hier.
p. cm.
1. Moral panics. 2. Deviant behavior. 3. Anxiety. I. Hier, Sean P. (Sean Patrick), 1971-
HM811.M67 2011
302'.17--dc22
2010048557

ISBN13: 978-0-415-55555-5 (hbk)
ISBN13: 978-0-415-55556-2 (pbk)
ISBN13: 978-0-203-86972-7 (ebk)

Typeset in Bembo and Stone Sans
by Integra Software Services Pvt. Ltd, Pondicherry, India

Printed and bound in Great Britain by
CPI Antony Rowe, Chippenham, Wiltshire

Contents

Foreword vii
  Kenneth Thompson
Contributors xii

1   Introduction: Bringing moral panic studies into focus 1
    Sean P. Hier

Part 1: Conceptualizing moral panic studies 17

2   Grounding and defending the sociology of moral panic 20
    Erich Goode and Nachman Ben-Yehuda

3   Locating moral panics within the sociology of social problems 37
    Joel Best

4   Fractious rivals? Moral panics and moral regulation 53
    Alan Hunt

5   Shifting the focus?: Moral panics as civilizing and decivilizing processes 71
    Amanda Rohloff

Part 2: Examining moral panic studies 87

6   The objectification of fear and the grammar of morality 90
    Frank Furedi

7	How emotions matter to moral panics *Kevin Walby and Dale Spencer*	104
8	Folk devils reconsidered *Mary deYoung*	118
9	The duality of the devil: Realism, relationalism and representation *James Meades*	134

Part 3: Applying moral panic studies   153

10	Panic, regulation, and the moralization of British law and order politics *Dan Lett, Sean P. Hier, Kevin Walby, and André Smith*	155
11	Drunken antics: The gin craze, binge drinking and the political economy of moral regulation *Chas Critcher*	171
12	The artful creation of global moral panic: Climatic folk devils, environmental evangelicals, and the coming catastrophe *Sheldon Ungar*	190
13	When harm is done: Panic, scandal and blame *Graham Knight and Juliet Roper*	208
14	The unhealthy risk society: Health scares and the politics of moral panic *Daniel Béland*	224

Index 236

FOREWORD

Kenneth Thompson

Almost 40 years have passed since Stanley Cohen (1972) launched the career of the moral panic concept. In this time period, the concept enjoyed a greater level of acceptance in popular usage than almost any other sociological concept since Max Weber's conception of bureaucracy. The introduction of the moral panic concept, like bureaucracy, was symptomatic of problematical trends in the age in which it emerged, and it has excited critical reactions within the academic community. Some of the criticisms of moral panic studies have been concerned with a suspected negative bias inherent in the concept and with its heuristic value. The ensuing debates are often cogent and productive of clarifications and theoretical developments, as can be seen in the scholarly contributions appearing in this volume.

The initial success of moral panic in the 1970s was due to public and academic interest in problems concerning youth subcultures. Cohen's (1972) study was sparked off by sensationalistic media accounts of clashes between rival youth subcultures—the Mods and Rockers. In terms of sociological interest, it was mainly within the area of studies of deviancy and labeling theory. As Cohen (2003) pointed out in his introduction to the third edition of *Folk Devils and Moral Panics*, the term moral panic arose from social reaction theory in the 1960s and from concern with the media's role in stereotyping and misrepresenting deviance. Demands for increased social control or regulation could lead to intensified deviance through an interactive process of psychological adjustment and self-fulfilling social action. It may have been significant that this new generation of deviancy theorists in Britain—including Stanley Cohen (1972), Jock Young (1971), and Jason Ditton (1979), as well as Leslie Wilkins (1964)—were themselves very much closer to the youth subcultures than to the controllers (Garland 2008). This is true regardless of the fact that the new generation drew on the American interactionism of Edwin Lemert (1967) and the ideas about moral boundaries and 'collective conscience' derived from Durkheim by Kai Erikson (1966).

The critique of exaggerated moral reaction was about relatively minor deviancy and delinquency. It was not difficult to show that sensationalist media accounts of youth subcultures, leading to public outrage and calls for greater control, fitted very well the ideal type of moral panic. The concept became more controversial when Stuart Hall and his colleagues used it to refer to reactions to 'muggings'—street robberies entailing violence (Hall et al. 1978). Critics began to claim that the moral panic concept was ideologically biased towards tolerance of deviants and against the maintenance of social order (Waddington 1986). For a time in the 1970s and 1980s, the term lost its earlier precision and heuristic value and became caught up in ideological battles about deviance, crime, and social control. This happened not only within academic debates, but also in national politics (Garland 2008). The mounting criticisms led to the concept's falling into relative disfavor in both British and American sociology.

At the same time, from the 1980s onwards, popular usage of moral panic increased and media commentators began to make self-conscious and even ironical use of the term, just as supposed deviant groups were happy to generate actual or simulated moral panics in order to gain attention (Thompson 1998; Garland 2008; McRobbie and Thornton 1995). It is only within the last 20 years that there has been a serious and positive reappraisal of the concept within sociology (beginning with Jenkins 1992 and Goode and Ben-Yehuda 1994), supplemented with a sustained attempt to relate the concept to other theoretical developments, such as Risk Society, discourse analysis and moral regulation (Thompson 1997 and 1998; Critcher 2003; Hier 2002).

There are a number of possible lessons to be learned from studying the debates about moral panic. The first one stems from its 'symptomatic' character—the fact that its rise and development in specific times and locations focused attention on underlying socio-cultural trends that were a source of growing anxiety. Second, analyses of the institutional and cultural processes involved in moral panic events can yield valuable information about changing mechanisms of control and regulation. Third, comparative sociology has much to gain from comparing the content and effects of moral panics in different societies. Fourth, the sociology of knowledge (and sociology in general) can learn from the differences of emphasis in the treatment of the concept within national sociologies and from the efforts to relate this concept to other concepts and theories.

Moral panics provide a prime example of the kind of symptomatic social phenomena that Emile Durkheim recommended sociologists take as their central object of enquiry (Thompson 1998:142). They alert us to possible underlying social trends that may be a cause of individual anxiety and social pathology, just as Durkheim showed that apparently unrelated acts of suicide were symptomatic of changes in factors affecting moral regulation and social integration (Durkheim 1897; Thompson 1982:119–20). It has sometimes seemed that the moral dimension and the symptomatic quality of moral panics are neglected in favor of focusing on other aspects such as immediate causes and consequences or secondary characteristics like 'disproportionality' (the extent to which the conduct or threat it poses are exaggerated), as part of an argument about whether an episode of social drama fitted the ideal type of a moral panic. Attention to such questions can only be a starting point, a 'means of beginning an analysis' of larger social conditions' of a particular type, 'not the entire analysis in itself' (Critcher 2008:1138). This would respond to the criticism that sometimes the use of the concept of moral panic seems to oblige the user to contrast 'representations' to the arbitration of the 'real' and is therefore unable to develop a full theory concerning the operations of ideology within systems of representation (Watney 1987: 42). As pointed out previously (Thompson 1998: 77), Watney was not so much denying that certain episodes constitute moral panics, but rather wished to broaden the discussion to place the particular panic over AIDS within the broader framework of ideological contestation about how certain groups are represented by the mass media as threats to the cohesion of a unified general public with shared values and characteristics.

In reading these latest scholarly contributions to the literature on moral panics, it is worth considering how they can help to build more rigor into the analysis of moral panics. One criterion might be how far they suggest ways of strengthening the evidential basis by drawing on multiple sources of data, perhaps ranging beyond mainstream media reports to include other documentary sources and even ethnographic work with relevant groups. Of course, broadening the spread of data sources should not come at the cost of carrying out rigorous investigation of the operations of the mainstream media, drawing on the work of media sociologists and others who can reveal the workings of the media complex, with its various pressures and preferences. The tabloid press, especially in Britain, still plays a major role in forming public opinion, and competition within the Press has been a factor leading to a rapid succession of moral panic episodes. However, the proliferation of new and more publically accessible forms of media, such as blogs and Twitter, as well as media representing minorities, are bringing about changes that will radically alter the familiar pathways that were mapped by the sociology of moral panics.

Rival voices putting forward conflicting views make the targeting of folk devils and consensual expressions of concern much more difficult. There may be 'a shift away from moral panics as traditionally conceived (involving a vertical relation between society and a deviant group) towards something more closely resembling American-style "culture wars" (which involve a more horizontal conflict between social groups)' (Garland 2008: 17). Conflicts over same-sex marriage or Muslim girls wearing the hijab in school may have resembled moral panics at one stage, but eventually turned into politically contested culture wars, as the deviant minority resisted their deviant identity labels. When there is a sufficiently strong majority outrage, it can still take on some of the characteristics of a moral panic, even if sociologists are understandably reluctant to use that term about a sensitive issue, as was the case in the immediate aftermath of the terrorist attacks in New York and Washington on 11 September 2001. Subsequently some sociologists were prepared to use the term (Rothe and Muzzatti 2004), and in 2010 the outcry against a proposed Islamic community center near New York's Ground Zero was poised between turning into a moral panic or becoming another battle in the culture wars. This may be another example where the moral panic concept cannot stand alone and needs to be related to other relevant concepts and theories, such as neo-Durkheimian concepts of 'collective effervescence and social solidarity' (Tiryakian 2005) and 'cultural trauma' (Alexander et al. 2004).

As in the case of the history of the concept of 'bureaucracy' (Albrow 1970; Thompson 1980), so too with 'moral panic': a highly serviceable and popular sociological concept can stimulate new insights into contemporary social problems and lead to productive theoretical developments. But there has to be a continuing effort to refine the concept and to revise it to fit in with other relevant theoretical developments. The contents of this volume represent the latest contributions to achieve that goal.

References

Albrow, M. (1970) *Bureaucracy*. London: Macmillan.
Alexander, J., R. Eyerman, B. Giesen, N. Smelser and P. Sztompka (2004) *Cultural Trauma and Collective Identity*. Berkeley, CA: University of California Press.
Cohen, S. (1972) *Folk Devils and Moral Panics: The Creation of the Mods and Rockers*. London: MacGibbon & Kee.
Cohen, S. (2003) *Folk Devils and Moral Panics: The Creation of the Mods and Rockers*, 3rd ed. London: Routledge.
Critcher, C. (2003) *Moral Panics and the Media*. Milton Keynes: Open University Press.
Critcher, C. (2008) 'Moral Panics Analysis: Past, Present and Future', *Sociology Compass*, 2(10): 1127–44.
Ditton, J. (1979) *Contrology: Beyond the New Criminology*. London: Macmillan.
Durkheim, E. (1897) *Le Suicide*. Paris: Felix Alcan.
Erikson, K. (1966) *Wayward Puritans*. New York: John Wiley.
Garland, D. (2008) 'On the Concept of Moral Panic', *Crime Media Culture*, 4(1): 9–30.
Goode, E. and N. Ben Yehuda (1994) *Moral Panics: The Social Construction of Deviance*. Oxford, UK and Cambridge, MA: Blackwell.
Hall, S., C. Critcher, T. Jefferson, J. Clarke and B. Roberts (1978) *Policing the Crisis*. London: Macmillan.
Hier, S. P. (2002) 'Raves, Risks and the Ecstasy Panic: A Case Study in the Subversive Nature of Moral Regulation', *Canadian Journal of Sociology*, 27(1): 33–57.
Jenkins, P. (1992) *Intimate Enemies: Moral Panics in Contemporary Great Britain*. New York: Aldine and de Gruyter.
Lemert, E. (1967) *Human Deviance, Social Problems and Social Control*. Englewood Cliffs, NJ: Prentice Hall.
McRobbie, A. and S. L. Thornton (1995) 'Rethinking "Moral Panic" for MultiMediated Social Worlds', *British Journal of Sociology*, 46(4): 559–74.
Rothe, D. and S. L. Muzzatti (2004) 'Enemies from Everywhere: Terrorism, Moral Panic, and US Civil Society', *Critical Criminology*, 12: 327–50.
Thompson, K. (1980) 'The Organizational Society', in G. Salaman and K. Thompson (eds.), *Control and Ideology in Organizations*. Milton Keynes, UK: Open University Press, pp. 3–23.
Thompson, K. (1982) *Emile Durkheim*. London: Tavistock.
Thompson, K. (1997) 'Regulation, De-Regulation and Re-Regulation', in K. Thompson (ed.), *Media and Cultural Regulation*. London: Sage, pp. 9–52.
Thompson, K. (1998) *Moral Panics*. London: Routledge.
Tiryakian, E. (2005) 'Durkheim, Solidarity and September 11', in J. Alexander and P. Smith (eds.), *The Cambridge Companion to Durkheim*. Cambridge: Cambridge University Press, pp. 305–21.

Waddington, P. A. J. (1986) 'Mugging as a Moral Panic: A Question of Proportion', *British Journal of Sociology*, 37(2): 245–59.
Watney, S. (1987) *Policing Desire: Pornography, AIDS and the Media*. London: Methuen.
Wilkins, L. (1964) *Social Deviance, Social Policy, Action and Research*. London: Tavistock.
Young, J. (1971) 'The Role of the Police as Amplifiers of Deviancy', in S. Cohen (ed.) *Images of Deviance*. Harmondsworth: Penguin, pp. 27–61.

CONTRIBUTORS

Daniel Béland is Canada Research Chair in Public Policy and Professor at the Johnson-Shoyama School of Public Policy (University of Saskatchewan campus). As a sociologist studying politics and policymaking from a historical, political, and comparative perspective, he has published eight books and more than fifty articles in peer-reviewed journals. *www.danielbeland.org*

Nachman Ben-Yehuda is Professor of Sociology and Anthropology at The Hebrew University of Jerusalem; he has also taught at Stony Brook and the University of Toronto. Ben-Yehuda is the author of eight books, including *Deviance and Moral Boundaries* (University of Chicago Press), *Moral Panics* (Blackwell), and, most recently, *Theocratic Democracy* (Oxford University Press).

Joel Best research focuses on deviance and social problems. His current research concerns awards, prizes, and honors in American culture. He is a former President of the Midwest Sociological Society and the Society for the Study of Social Problems, and a former Editor of the journal *Social Problems*.

Chas Critcher is Visiting Professor in Media and Communications at Swansea University and Emeritus Professor of Communications at Sheffield Hallam University. He originally co-authored *Policing the Crisis* (Macmillan 1979), a study of social reaction to mugging. His most recent publications include *Moral Panics and the Media* (Open University Press 2003) and *Critical Readings in Moral Panics and the Media* (Open University Press, ed. 2006). His current research interests focus on exploring the relevance to moral panic analysis of the concept of moral regulation.

Mary deYoung PhD is Professor of Sociology at Grand Valley State University in Allendale, MI. She has presented papers at national and international conferences and published extensively on the nexus of trauma, memory, and culture. Her two most recent books are *Madness: An American History of Mental Illness and Its Treatment* (McFarland, 2010), and *The Day Care Ritual Abuse Moral Panic* (McFarland, 2004).

Frank Furedi is a Professor of Sociology at the University of Kent in Canterbury, England. During the past fifteen years, Furedi's studies have been devoted to an exploration of the cultural developments that influence the construction of contemporary risk consciousness. He has published widely about controversies relating to issues such as health, parenting children, food, and new technology. His *Invitation to Terror: Expanding the Empire of the Unknown* (Continuum 2007) explores the way in which the threat of terrorism has become amplified through the ascendancy of possibilistic thinking. At present he is engaged in a study of the changing cultural forms of authority.

Erich Goode is Sociology Professor Emeritus at Stony Brook University. He has taught at half a dozen universities, including New York University, the State University of New York at Stony Brook, and the University of North Carolina at Chapel Hill. Goode is the author of ten books—including one on moral panics—mainly on deviance and drug use, and is the editor of six anthologies. He is currently at work on a book on deviance in memoir and another on the domestication of drugs.

Sean P. Hier is Associate Professor and Chair of Sociology, University of Victoria, Canada. He has published several articles and book chapters on moral panic, surveillance, and social theory. He has also published six edited volumes. His recent book, *Panoptic Dreams: Streetscape Video Surveillance in Canada*, was published with the University of British Columbia Press (2010).

Alan Hunt is Chancellor's Professor at Carleton University. He is the author of *Governing Morals: A Social History of Moral Regulation* (Cambridge University Press 1999) and *Governance of the Consuming Passions* (Macmillan 1996). Previous books include *Foucault and Law* (with Gary Wickham, 1994), *Explorations in Law and Society* (1993), *Marx and Engels on Law* (with Maureen Cain, 1979), and *The Ociological Movement in Law* (1978).

Graham Knight is Professor and Chair of Communication Studies and Multimedia at McMaster University. His current research interests lie in the area of communication and public relations in regard to climate change. His recent work has appeared in *Communication and Critical/Cultural Studies*, *Social Movement Studies*, and the *International Journal of the History of Sport*.

Dan Lett is a PhD student at the University of Victoria, Canada. His recent publications appear in *Media, Culture and Society* (2007, with S. Hier, J. Greenberg, and K. Walby) and *Canadian Journal of Sociology* (with S. Hier and K. Walby). He is also co-editor of *Racism and Justice: Dialogue on the Politics of Identity, Inequality, and Change* (with S. Hier and S. Bolaria, 2009, Fernwood Press).

James Meades is a PhD candidate in the Department of Sociology at Carleton University. His research interests include: moral panic, critical realism, Marxism, public sector unions, and social movements.

Amanda Rohloff is a PhD Candidate at the Department of Sociology and Communications, Brunel University. Her PhD research is exploring the long-term development of climate change as a perceived social problem, drawing primarily from moral panic and Norbert Elias's theory of civilizing processes. She has published articles on moral panic in *Current Sociology* and *New Zealand Sociology*, and is currently working on several other publications on Elias, moral panic, climate change, and civilization.

Juliet Roper is Associate Dean, Sustainability, for the University of Waikato Management School, and Professor of Management Communication. She is also the President of the Asia Pacific Academy of Business in Society (APABIS), an organization dedicated to providing a platform for collaborative engagement and action amongst academic, business, NGO, and government sectors of the Asia Pacific region. Juliet is a current board member of the International Communication Association, and in 2006 she was a finalist for the Aspen Institute's Beyond Grey Pinstripes Faculty Pioneer award.

André Smith is Assistant Professor in the Sociology Department at the University of Victoria. His primary area of research concerns mental health and illness.

Dale Spencer research and teaching areas include sociology of the body, sociology of sport, organizational sociology, social problems, sociology of emotions, and criminology. He has published articles in *Criminology and Criminal Justice*, *Canadian Journal of Sociology*, *Canadian Review of Sociology*, *Punishment and Society*, and *Body and Society* and has forthcoming articles in *Journal of Youth Studies* and *Sociological Research Online*. Dale Spencer, Kevin Walby, and Alan Hunt are editors of a forthcoming collection entitled *Emotions Matter: For a Relational Approach to Emotions* (University of Toronto Press).

Kenneth Thompson is Emeritus Professor of Sociology, Open University. He is author of *Moral Panics* (Routledge 1998).

Sheldon Ungar is a Sociology Professor at the University of Toronto at Scarborough. He has researched real world events that have produced social scares, including the nuclear arms race, emerging diseases (Ebola), global climate change, and bird flu. His studies of climate change have resulted in regular invitations to research institutes in Germany. Beside his continued interest in the nuclear threat and climate change, his current work also focuses on an examination of knowledge and ignorance and seeks to identify how popular culture and new media affect 'cultural literacy'. As part of his study of the cultural production of ignorance, he has examined instances of the 'silencing of science.' Indeed, he has experienced 'silencing' himself, as papers he has done on climate skeptics have been rendered impossible to publish by reviewers who allow no sentence to pass unremarked. In the past few years, he has published papers on ignorance as a social problem (*British Journal of Sociology*), global coverage of bird flu (*Communicating Science*), total war, and faculty moral panics over students.

Kevin Walby is an SSHRC Postdoctoral Fellow at the Centre of Criminology, University of Toronto and Assistant Professor in the Department of Sociology, University of Victoria. He has a PhD in sociology from Carleton University. Peer reviewed articles include *International Sociology* (2011, with Sean Hier), *Qualitative Research* (2011), *Social Movement Studies* (2011, with Jeff Monaghan), the *British Journal of Criminology* (2011, with Justin Piché), *Punishment & Society* (2011, with Justin Piché), *Criminology and Criminal Justice* (2010, with Nicolas Carrier), *Social & Legal Studies* (2007), *Qualitative Inquiry* (2007), and *Critical Sociology* (2007). Walby is working on an edited volume entitled *Brokering Access: Power, Politics and Freedom of Information Process in Canada* with Mike Larsen, (University of British Columbia Press), and an edited volume entitled *Emotions Matter* with Alan Hunt and Dale Spencer (with University of Toronto Press). He is the prisoners' struggles editor for the *Journal of Prisoners on Prisons*.

1

INTRODUCTION

Bringing moral panic studies into focus[1]

Sean P. Hier

Moral panic studies traces back to Jock Young's (1971) analysis of the social meaning of drug taking and to Stanley Cohen's (1972) canonical investigation of the construction of the Mods and Rockers. Significant developments took place through the 1970s and 1980s, focusing primarily on the role that claims makers, moral guardians, and the media play in the construction, amplification, and exaggeration of deviance. Critical revisions invigorated moral panic studies in the 1990s, and some of the most recent contributions have widened the conventional focus of research by incorporating advances in risk communications, discourse studies, cultural sociology, and moral regulation.

Despite consistent interest in the concept of moral panic, debate about the purpose, application, and scope of moral panic studies persists. For instance, scholars within and beyond the panic literature commonly conceptualize moral panics as exceptional rather than ordinary phenomena to explain seemingly irrational reactions to putative threats. Conceived of in this way, critics charge that panic researchers deploy vague explanatory criteria to speculate disapprovingly about the underlying causes of random (even trivial) claims-making episodes. A small number of critical assessments of moral panic studies has started to demonstrate how moral panics are properly conceptualized as rational and routine forms of social action and how moral panic studies can contribute to and benefit from broader scholarship concerned with regulation, deviance, civilizing processes, and social control (e.g., Rohloff and Wright 2010; Hier 2008; Critcher 2009; Rohloff 2008; and see Goode and Ben-Yehuda 2009). Efforts to widen the conventional focus of research are gaining momentum, but moral panic studies remains divided among varying analytical orientations.

With some simplification, three analytical orientations characterize the moral panic literature: conventional, skeptical, and revisionist. Conventional analyses (the primary source of criticism for external observers) are based on selective readings of Cohen's original work and Goode and Ben-Yehuda's (1994, 2009) summary statement.

Regardless of the complexity of argumentation found in these studies (see below), the aim of empirically informed conventional analyses is to show how various social problems frames qualify as moral panics by applying Cohen's stages or testing Goode and Ben-Yehuda's five crucial indicators of panic (e.g., Rothe and Muzzatti 2004; Welch, Price, and Yankey 2002; Doyle and LaCombe 2000; Victor 1998).

By contrast, skeptical analyses tend to rely on selective readings of conventional models as a source of criticism to dismiss the explanatory power of moral panic. They do so by pointing to so-called amoral phenomena (e.g., assumed real-world, tangible threats) to qualify the explanatory power of moral panic or by arguing that specific responses to putative concerns are proportional and rational responses to empirically verifiable threats (e.g., Waiton 2008; Cornwell and Linders 2002; and see Ungar 2001 and Waddington 1986). Both skeptical and conventional orientations focus on a more or less agreed upon set of theoretical, methodological, and conceptual parameters that were institutionalized between 1972 and 1994; they rarely engage analytically with (or even acknowledge) studies that fall outside the conventional scope of analysis.

Revisionists approach moral panic studies in a different manner. Although revisionists recognize the continuing significance of conventional approaches (and endorse some of the insights offered by skeptics), they nevertheless seek to rethink (McRobbie and Thornton 1995; Hier 2003), reappraise (deYoung 1998; Thompson 1998; Critcher 2003), think beyond (Hier 2002a, 2002b, 2008), or widen the focus (Rohloff and Wright 2010; Critcher 2009) of conventional analyses. Revisionists simultaneously retain many of the defining components of conventional analyses and strive to link panic episodes to broader explanatory models in the sociologies of deviance, regulation, culture, and control. They do so to address persistent limitations with applications of conventional approaches and to enhance the analytical purchase of moral panic studies beyond a relatively narrow range of concerns in the sociology of culture. The project of revising moral panic studies by widening the focus of research traces to the 1980s (e.g., Ben-Yehuda 1986, 1985), yet what is unique about the resurgence of revisionist efforts is the cumulative and interactive debate that is starting to take hold.

As a contribution to the ongoing project of revising moral panic studies, the aim of this collection is twofold. The first aim is to critically assess theoretical, conceptual, and methodological debates among panic scholars, past and present, to bring the purpose and scope of moral panic studies into focus. Although revisionists are beginning to move beyond the limitations of conventional analyses, disagreement remains about the substantive scope and conceptual parameters of moral panic studies (see, for example, Rohloff and Wright 2010; Critcher 2009; Goode and Ben-Yehuda 2009; Rohloff 2008).

One reason why moral panic studies lacks clear focus concerns the popular use of the moral panic concept among journalists and politicians (Altheide 2008; McRobbie and Thornton 1995; Hunt 1997). Sociologists no longer enjoy exclusive control over how moral panic is applied and the concept is indiscriminately used for a broad range of purposes (far beyond social control processes). A second, related reason concerns expanding applications of moral panic to phenomena not traditionally associated with moral panic studies (Critcher 2009). As moral panic is applied to an expanding number of unfamiliar issues (inside and outside moral panic studies), problems with the analytical boundaries and political underpinnings of moral panic studies emerge. The chapters in the volume critically assess the strengths and limitations of conventional, skeptical, and revisionist approaches across a range of theoretical and empirical fields in a collective effort to bring the politics and analytical parameters of moral panic studies into focus.

An integral part of bringing moral panic studies into focus involves widening the focus by examining how moral panic contributes to and benefits from analytical advances in broader areas of inquiry – the second aim. Moral panics do not take place in a cultural vacuum. One of the main limitations of moral panic studies has been narrowing the focus of research to examine the short-term dynamics involved in episodes of 'deviance amplification.' This narrowing trend lends itself to conceptualization of moral panic as a heuristic device (Rohloff and Wright 2010) to rhetorically explain phenomena ranging from Satanism (Best 2003) and tabloid journalism (Eide and Knight 1999) to crime control (Innes 2004) and contemporary surveillance practices (Lyon 2003). The volume brings panic researchers into dialogue with scholars not commonly associated with moral panic studies to examine possibilities for how moral panic can benefit from and contribute to the sociologies of social problems, moral regulation, culture, and law, as well as the sociologies of emotion, health, fear, and environment.

The remainder of this chapter provides an overview of the shifting focus of moral panic studies. The purpose of the overview is to flesh out general trends in moral panic studies and to clarify the status of past and present research. I explain how the focus of moral panic studies increasingly narrowed between 1972 and 1994 and how recent efforts to widen the focus of research are simultaneously reconnecting with many of the original intentions of moral panic studies and drawing from broader trends in social and cultural theory.

The shifting focus of moral panic studies

Over the past 25 years, moral panic studies became institutionalized as an intellectual area of research. The positive benefits of institutionalizing moral panic studies flow from an expansive body of literature that enables us to explore the nuances and complexities of moralization. But institutionalization also has limitations. The growing number of books and articles that were published in the 1980s and 1990s increasingly focused on a narrow set of standard criteria to document the empirical features of short-term claims-making episodes. Such studies – whether supportive or critical of the explanatory purchase of moral panic – were often presented in the intellectual context of a set of exemplary studies and legitimized by an accompanying set of customary citations. Mostly forgotten (or at least taken for granted) in the process of institutionalization were the reasons why moral panic studies originally developed and the intellectual and political context it developed from (see Young 2009).

Moral panic studies arose from developments in 'the skeptical approach to deviance' (Cohen 2003: 3; Cohen 1971: 14). The skeptical approach to deviance was a deconstructionist reaction to traditional (British) criminologists (and, to an extent, conservative sociologists) who viewed deviance and social problems as a set of qualities inherent in a certain kind of person or behavior. The new radical criminologists took their lead from Becker (1967, 1964, 1963) and others (e.g., Lemert 1967; Erikson 1966, 1964; Schur 1965), who sought to reconnect deviance studies to mainstream concerns in sociology – especially the processes and dynamics involved in the social construction of normality and deviance. For radical criminologists inspired by labeling/transactional approaches to deviance and certain developments in subcultural theory, deviance and social problems, far from being fixed by a set of stable attributes, entailed a transaction of sorts between rule breakers and conformists.

More than this, radical criminologists were self-consciously political. In the few decades leading up to the 1950s, many traditional British criminologists, much like mainstream American sociologists, became apolitical, functionalist oriented, and/or administratively inclined. The epistemological force of Durkheim (1895) or Thomas (1928) – that is, studying deviance to learn about general social (and psychical) structures – was eclipsed by normative research pursuits influenced by government priorities. In aligning themselves with the critical constructionist orientation, radical criminologists adopted an explicit value orientation by denaturalizing deviance, defending subcultures, and challenging the appropriateness of reactions to putative problems.

The influence of radical deviancy theory on the rise of moral panic studies came to a head with Albert Cohen's (1965) attempt to formulate a general theory of deviant behavior. Cohen offered a corrective to anomie theory by linking the deviant act as a history of interaction processes to 'the normatively established division of labour' (p. 9) (i.e., the normative context that conditions the substance of claims-making and counter-claims-making activities). What was especially significant about Cohen's synthesis – at least for past and more recent developments in moral panic studies – was his brief commentary on moral indignation.

> The dedicated pursuit of culturally approved goals, the eschewing of interdicted but tantalizing goals, the adherence to normatively sanctioned means – these imply a certain self-constraint, effort, discipline, inhibition. What is the effect of the spectacle of others who, though their activities do not manifestly damage our own interests are morally undisciplined, who give themselves up to idleness, self-indulgence, or forbidden vices? What effect does the propinquity of the wicked have on the peace of mind of the virtuous? [...] In several ways, the virtuous can make capital out of this situation ... *building his self out of invidious comparisons to the morally weak.*
>
> (Cohen 1965: 6–7, original emphasis)

In other words, moral indignation signifies simultaneously a threat to one's own identity and a confirmation of it. Young (1971) picked up on the existential and phenomenological importance of moral indignation during the National Deviancy Symposia in the late 1960s, where he argued that social problems construction is motivated by not only conflicts of material interest and humanitarian concerns but also value conflicts. Indeed, as Young recently contends, 'if moral indignation depicts the chronic condition of moral disturbance, moral panic is its acute form' (2009: 7).

Although the language of moral indignation is not explicitly used in Stanley Cohen's first systematic statement on moral panic, it is part of the intellectual context that brought it to light. Cohen's (1972) assessment of the construction of the Mods and Rockers addresses the actions (i.e., youth subcultural behavior), reactions (i.e., societal reactions), and impacts (i.e., control cultures) of moral panic; it generalizes from case study to general sociological processes (i.e., subcultural formation, collective behavior, labeling); it criticizes the emergence of a control culture (i.e., moral panic as a fundamentally inappropriate response); and it theorizes moral indignation (i.e., perceived youth idleness and indulgence in the 1960s). In short, Cohen's analysis examines the empirical construction of the Mods and Rockers but it is as much about the self-fulfilling existential character of social control as it is about the phenomenology of deviance amplification.

Hence, the concept of moral panic grew out of radical deconstructionism in deviancy theory.[2] Moral panic was explained in terms of a broad set of sociological and criminological writings designed to denaturalize, contextualize, and criticize constructions of deviance but also to address a deeper source of moral indignation that links the identity of the regulator to that of the regulated (see Hier 2008, 2003, 2002a). Since Cohen's original assessment, the sociological emphases on the psycho- and socio-genesis of morality have become increasingly eclipsed by 'a rather listless depiction of mass media deception, of audience delusion, of simple mistakes in reason, the random displacement of grievances ... and on fleeting events, peripheral disturbances in an otherwise regulated universe' (Young 2009: 2; and see Garland 2008). Recent attempts to revise moral panic studies are more complex than Young's summary of contemporary panic scholarship suggests, but the literature as a whole has demonstrated a tendency towards narrowing the focus of analysis since the mid-1990s. Paradoxically, the narrowing focus contributed the marginalization of moral panic studies in the broader social scientific literature at the very moment that we entered the so-called age of moral panics (Thompson 1998).

Narrowing the focus

How did the focus of moral panic studies narrow? It is widely known that Cohen's (1972) study of the Mods and Rockers was quickly supplemented by Hall *et al.*'s (1978) Marxian-inspired investigation of how British elites exaggerated the threat of Black muggers to divert attention from rising inflation and a crisis in state economic policy. Both seminal contributions examine in detail how deviance/transgression is constructed and amplified, and both address the wider political and cultural environment that gives rise to deviance amplification. Whereas Cohen and his constructionist-oriented colleagues focus on relatively minor transgressions (e.g., youth deviance), however, Hall *et al.* explicitly address hardcore crime.

Hall *et al.*'s application of moral panic to harder forms of deviance had a twofold effect: first, it shifted the scope of panic analysis beyond radical currents in the sociology of deviance to the realm of criminality and law and order; simultaneously, second, it loosened the focus of analysis by extending the concept beyond its original parameters. Moral panic soon became a powerful 'debunking mechanism' (Garland 2008: 20) for criminologists beyond moral panic studies to dismiss official claims about rising crime rates – regardless of what the crime data actually suggested. The more frequent and flexible uses of moral panic not only contributed to divisions within liberal criminology (see Lea 1987; Kinsey, Lea, and Young 1986; Lea and Young 1984) but also obscured some of the original analytical intentions of moral panic scholarship.

The influences of Cohen's and Hall *et al.*'s studies are well known. Less recognized or acknowledged are developments in the 1980s that eventually informed the epistemological bases for Goode and Ben-Yehuda's (1994) benchmark contribution. At the same time that Marxian currents were gaining ground (and labeling studies were proliferating), Ben-Yehuda (1990, 1985, 1986) was trying to retain a focus on the sociological-phenomenological orientation found in Cohen, Becker, and especially Berger and Luckmann (1966). In his study of deviance and moral boundaries, for instance, Ben-Yehuda (1985) observes that the sociology of deviance is in theoretical chaos. The field lacks coherence, he maintains, and a set of small-scale studies about 'soft deviance' (p. 2) work against the interests of formulating a unified framework capable of explaining deviance in terms of total social structures (and see Liazos 1972). Ben-Yehuda therefore encourages sociologists to analyze the empirical relativity of deviance in the context of the boundary-maintaining and boundary-changing functions of total social systems to explain deviance as a sociological process without resort to any particular example.

This project is elaborated in *The Politics of Morality and Deviance: Moral Panics, Drug Abuse, Deviant Science, and Reversed Stigmatization* (Ben-Yehuda 1990). Here, Ben-Yehuda draws from neofunctionalism, symbolic interactionism, and non-Marxian conflict theory to develop an integrated analytical framework for the sociology of deviance – that is, to synthesize morality, activity/deviance, and power in a unified model. Ben-Yehuda argues that the legitimization of power is achieved through the struggles that ensue when symbolic-moral universes come into conflict (in wider structural context of diversification and social change) and that morality represents a system of value criteria that shape normative behavior and direct social actions toward specific goals (p. 50). Moral panic, therefore, represents a normative boundary-maintaining mechanism used by moral entrepreneurs to legitimize their moral and material interests.

Ben-Yehuda's efforts to link moral panic studies to the sociology of knowledge are admirable. Moral panics, far from irrational phenomena that emerge randomly from time to time, are conceptualized as central components of symbolic universe maintenance. As central components of social stability and change, Ben-Yehuda conceptualizes moral panics as rational structural phenomena that can be explained in terms of micro and macro power struggles involving various asymmetrical interests. In essence, Ben-Yehuda started to widen the analytical focus of moral panic studies by incorporating insights from the sociologies of knowledge, deviance, symbolic interactionism, and conflict theory.

Efforts to widen the focus of moral panic studies continued in Goode and Ben-Yehuda's (1994), *Moral Panics: The Social Construction of Deviance* – the first systematic statement on moral panic studies. Rather than widening the focus of moral panic studies and pushing it closer to the mainstream of sociology, however, *Moral Panics* was the main catalyst that narrowed the focus of research and debate (while no doubt simultaneously popularizing the concept). One reason why *Moral Panics* narrowed the focus concerns the way the book is framed. Following from Ben-Yehuda's earlier attempts to conceptualize moral panic in terms of general sociological processes, a central aim of the book is to situate moral panic studies in broader analytical currents in the sociology of social problems, deviance, collective behavior, and social movements. More implicitly, it also contributes to the sociology of knowledge (see Berger and Luckmann 1966). Yet *Moral Panics* lacks the analytical thrust or overt argumentation found in Ben-Yehuda's earlier books. Goode and Ben-Yehuda do not clearly illustrate moral panic's affinity with broader analytical currents. Nor do they attempt to explicate the existential underpinnings of the sociology of knowledge (i.e., Berger and Luckmann's [1966] 'metaphysical terrors' [p. 150, 98] and 'psychological economies' [p. 57]) as they pertain to moral panics or the material dimensions of symbolic universe maintenance (Berger and Luckmann 1966: 104–28). Instead, they provide a broad overview of moral panic studies, its general features, and its antecedents.

One consequence of the broad approach taken in *Moral Panics* is that subsequent writers have focused on the chapters examining indicators (especially disproportionality) and theories of moral panic, to the relative neglect of discussions about problems, movements, collective behavior, and deviance. Arnold Hunt's (1997) influential article on the changing uses of the moral panic concept illustrates this pattern well. Hunt uses Goode and Ben-Yehuda's three theories of moral panic – interest group, elite engineered, and grassroots – to trace problems associated with the changing, perhaps incompatible meanings of the concept. He argues that as applications of moral panic shifted from Durkheimian (Cohen 1972) and Marxian (Hall et al. 1978) concerns to grassroots foci on the continuous processes of moral discourse and practice (McRobbie and Thornton 1995; Lea and Young 1993), the status of the *panic* component of moral panic became unclear. Hunt is especially critical of Goode and Ben-Yehuda's attempts to conceptualize moral panic as an enduring feature of social structure (e.g., Hunt 1997: 630, 633–34, 644, 645), yet he demonstrates an understanding of neither the scope of *Moral Panics* (beyond the three theories) nor the wider neofunctionalist analytics that gave rise to it.

Hence, when *Moral Panics* appeared in 1994, moral panic studies had grown beyond the original concerns of the radical criminologists (a point recognized by Cohen 2003). Debates in social constructionism were well established by the early 1990s (see Miller and Holstein 1989; Best 1989; Woolgar and Pawluch 1985; Spector and Kitsuse 1977), allowing Goode and Ben-Yehuda to conceptualize moral panic studies as a form of contextual constructionism. As a form of contextual constructionism, moral panic studies involves examining claims-making activities without resort to some underlying material interest and measuring the validity of claims using a standard set of criteria – especially disproportional responses to putative threats. Panics emerge from several social locations, they maintain, and analysts need to link moral panic as a type of social problem to broader psycho-social explanatory frameworks concerned with collective behavior and social movements in order to understand the structural-institutional character of moral panic. *Moral Panics* was not received in this manner (in part because of the way the arguments are presented), and subsequent treatments of the book narrowed the focus of argument and debate – within and beyond moral panic studies.

Revising moral panic

At the same time that the focus of moral panic studies was narrowing, a set of influential studies designed to revise moral panic by calling into question many of the assumptions of conventional applications appeared in the literature. McRobbie and Thornton (1995) spearheaded the project of rethinking moral panic by assessing the conventional literature on three levels of analysis. They argue, first, that original models of moral panic (i.e., Cohen and Hall *et al.*) conceptualize society as monolithic and societal reactions to claims-making activities as inevitable. Related, second, they contend that, far from Cohen's Mods and Rockers and Hall *et al.*'s muggers, folk devils and their supporters sometimes fight back. Therefore, third, McRobbie and Thornton argue that moral panic research needs to better explain the diversity of media outlets in claims-making and counter-claims-making activities, as well as the diversity of claims making within the same media outlets.

McRobbie and Thornton's critique inspired several important studies in the moral panic and social problems literature. In her study of satanic daycare center panics, for example, deYoung (2004, 1998) argues that the daycare providers who became the focal point of satanic daycare panics throughout the 1980s were well integrated into their communities; they lacked the social marginality of conventional conceptions of folk devils (and see deYoung, Chapter 8 this volume). Thornton's (1995) investigation of British club cultures reveals that flyers, fanzines, pirate radio, telephone lines, web sites, and email distribution lists number among the plethora of media outlets regularly used to resist and subvert moralizing discourses in the mainstream media. Hier's (2002a) study of attempts to ban raves in the City of Toronto highlights the importance of diverse counter-claims and the heterogeneity of media outlets involved in the construction and contestation of moral panic. And Parnaby's (2003) analysis of the framing of squeegee kids demonstrates how many parties join forces to resist primary definitions. The general finding to emerge from these investigations is that the diversification of media outlets, the many voices now contributing to claims and counter-claims, and the social leverage exhibited by folk devils complicates continued explanatory reliance on conventional models.

Widening the focus

The project of rethinking the conventional parameters of moral panic studies inspired other panic scholars to widen the focus of analysis to account for and recapture the conceptual foundations of moral panic. Tracing in part to Thompson's (1998) argument that theoretical developments related to risk society and Foucauldian discourse theory need to be incorporated into moral panic research, efforts to connect moral panic to wider theoretical and methodological models are now underway (and see Critcher 2003, 2000).

Four main contributions compose the project of widening the focus of moral panic studies. The first influential (and paradoxically skeptical) contribution is Ungar's (2001) argument that the types of everyday, real-world issues associated with risk society theory complicate the explanatory purchase of anxieties associated with conventional moral panic analyses. For Ungar, we are witnessing a change in sites of social anxiety (from moral panic to risk society) which necessitates a rethinking of the theoretical, methodological, and conceptual assumptions related to claims making, social control, and perceptions of public safety. Ungar does not explicitly dismiss the potential for moral panic studies to explain risk society issues but rather problematizes the extent to which conventional analyses (especially Goode and Ben-Yehuda's five indicators of moral panic) can address real-world risk conditions.

Ungar's assessment of moral panic in the risk society led to a direct response from Hier (2003). Hier begins where Ungar ends, arguing that the logical conclusion of Ungar's argument is that it leads to a convergence, not a shift, in sites of social anxiety. Hier reasons that the pervasive and uncontrollable anxieties associated with risk society threats do not replace but rather conjoin with the existential anxieties that are endemic to (late) modern living. When sites of social anxiety converge, says Hier, they produce rather than extinguish moral panics as a form of social ordering practice.

Although Hier disputes Ungar's argument about changing sites of social anxiety, he agrees that the focus of conventional moral panic studies is too narrow to explain the complexity of relations that give rise to and constitute moral panic episodes. To widen the focus of moral panic studies, Hier (2008, 2002a, 2002b) conceptualizes moral panic as an acute expression or short-term manifestation of long-term moral regulation processes. Influential contributions to moral regulation studies maintain that, as a growing number of everyday activities become moralized in the form of dialectical judgments about what is right and wrong, moralization finds expression in the proxies of risk, harm, and personal responsibility (Hunt 1999). Although moralizing discourses do not remain stable over time, one common feature of neoliberal forms of moralization is that people are called upon to engage in responsible forms of individual risk management (e.g., exercise to avoid the risk of cardiovascular disease) and these forms of individual care of the self are discursively juxtaposed to collective representations of 'harmful others' (e.g., 'couch potatoes'). On a conceptual level, this implies that neoliberal forms of moralization are dialectical, situating individualizing discourses that call upon people to take personal responsibility to manage their own risk against collective or socializing discourses that represent the general dimensions of harm to be avoided.

For Hier (2002b, 2008), moralization is a rational sociological process involving various attempts to encourage perceived moral deviants (constructed as risky agents) to adopt a morally responsible ethos to refashion their personal or collective conduct (and see Hunt 1999). That is, moral regulation is a long-term, developmental process, whereby one group of people attempts to encourage certain forms of behavior and self-control in another (e.g., through no smoking and healthy eating campaigns). As volatile disturbances (i.e., perceived crises) in the long-term course of moral regulation, moral panics develop at the point when moral regulation is perceived to be in a state of calamitous failure – that is, when those who are the target of regulatory efforts fail to accept the call to act on their own behavior and are perceived as a threat to the moral or material well-being of moral entrepreneurs. During moral panic episodes, the moral dialectic that discursively juxtaposes individual risk-management strategies to collective dimensions of harm is inverted: moral panics discursively situate individualizing allocations of harm/blame against collective risk-management strategies. Moral panic is thus conceptualized as a volatile manifestation in the wider, long-term project of moral regulation.

The main point of Hier's framework is to conceptualize moral panic as a rational structural phenomenon whose effect is to affirm a sense of existential or phenomenal security – that is, to (re)affirm moral boundaries – in moments of perceived regulatory crisis. More than this, Hier attempts to move moral panic studies beyond continuing (and stagnating) debates about the problems associated with cognitive (i.e., disproportion), normative (i.e., irrationality), and behavioral (i.e., broad public concern) measures by addressing how morality claims (i.e., responsibility) conjoin with claims about rational action (i.e., risk management) under neoliberal governmental rationalities (i.e., politics). To establish a broader framework for analysis, then, Hier offers one set of explanations for how panics are empirically linked to, but analytically distinct from, moral regulation processes.

In a sympathetic yet critical rebuttal to Hier, Critcher (2009) offers the third contribution to the project of widening the focus. Critcher recognizes the need to connect moral panic studies with broader developments in social and cultural theory, but questions the extent to which Hier's framework is able to move moral panic studies forward. In Critcher's assessment, by linking moral panic to moral regulation, the range of issues that moral panic applies to is radically expanded. For Critcher, this poses analytical problems along three axes of analysis.

The first axis concerns moral order: the degree to which basic moral values are threatened. In conventional moral panic analyses, moral panic is applied to a set of normative issues that lend themselves to high levels of moralization (e.g., crime) – often using the unambiguous language of evil to denote the object of moral indignation. When less morally evocative issues, such as Internet pornography or sexually transmitted diseases, are incorporated into the scope of potential topics for moral panic analysis (via the link to moral regulation), the likelihood of panic is weakened. For Critcher, then, the point at which moral regulation transforms into moral panic is not clear, and the blurring of boundaries poses implications for the analytical precision – indeed the political thrust – of moral panic analyses.

The second axis concerns the extent to which morally contestable threats are constructed as amenable to resolution through social control processes (i.e., Hier's moments of crises). Following from his critique of moral order, Critcher explains that moral regulation discourses in their Foucauldian variant involve a series of attempts to entice others to act on their own conduct (e.g., drinking responsibly), thereby affirming the conduct and character of the reformers. As a more immediate form of intervention directed at the conduct of others, panics entail calls to act on the conduct of others rather than the self. The relationship between moral panic (as externally imposed social control) and moral regulation (as internally generated self-formation) requires further internal differentiation of the kinds of issues that lend themselves to social control processes.

The distinction between externally imposed moral regulation/social control and internally generated ethical self-formation leads to the third problematic axis: morals versus ethics. Critcher endorses Dean's (1994) distinction between codified systems of evaluation (morals) and the practical conduct of life (ethics) to conceptualize moral regulation as a form of activity and ethical character formation as a process of informal monitoring of the actions of the self. That is, morality represents a set of culturally inscribed codes that exist external to any single individual, but ethics represents an internal process of monitoring one's own thoughts and actions. Critcher argues that the distinction between morals and ethics cuts through the first axis of moral order because some moral regulation issues involve broad ethical self-formation (e.g., recreational drug use) but others (e.g., weapons offense) do not. Hence, because ethical self-formation dynamics are present in moral regulation processes only some of the time, we again need to clarify the relationship between moral panic and moral regulation if the former is conceptualized as a component of the latter.

Therefore, Critcher does not reject Hier's attempts to conceptualize moral panic as a form of moral regulation but rather presses Hier's arguments for greater conceptual and analytical clarity. By widening the focus of moral panic studies to incorporate the unfamiliar and epistemologically different terrain of moral regulation, great analytical clarity is needed on where panics start and regulatory processes stop.

The final (and most recent) contribution to widening the focus is Rohloff and Wright's (2010) conceptualization of moral panic as a component of the civilizing process (see, too, Rohloff 2008 and Chapter 5 this volume). In their attempt to go 'beyond the heuristic' (particularly associated with Cohen's original stages) and provide deeper insights into the historicity of moral panic, thereby addressing some of the continuing analytical problems, Rohloff and Wright explore the basic conceptual underpinnings of Norbert Elias's civilizing process.

In his writings on the civilizing process, Elias (2000) aims to show how the post-medieval social standard to which individuals were made to conform gradually replaced an external constraint with a self-constraint. He explains how social standards pertaining to speech, table manners, sexual behavior, and bodily functions were transformed by the social dynamism that advanced the threshold of embarrassment, shame, and repugnance but also how they were accompanied by changes to the psychological dynamics of individuals (feelings, emotions). Long-term trends in the character of individuals' emotional lives were influenced by increased interdependency and the demands of mutual identification in diversifying societies, and later the centralization of the state. For Elias, to understand the civilizing process as the formation of a European habitus is to interrogate it as a structural phenomenon.

Rohloff and Wright draw on Elias's general framework to conceptualize moral panics in terms of decivilizing processes/trends. Among the factors influencing civilizing processes are the state's monopoly over the means of violence, the technical calculation of danger, high levels of mutual identification, and culturally constituted standards of respect. When the state is perceived to be failing to reduce dangers and technical knowledge cannot calculate threat, levels of mutual identification weaken and decivilizing processes commence. As a component of nonlinear civilizing processes, decivilizing processes are perceived increases in the level of danger that do not reverse but rather influence the course of civilizing processes. By using Elias's historical theoretical method of examining long-term civilizing processes and short-term decivilizing trends, Rohloff and Wright contend that the problems associated with normativity, temporality, intentionality, and politics in conventional and revisionist moral panic analyses can be overcome.

Taken as a whole, the project of revising moral panic seeks to reframe or return to a conceptualization of moral panic studies in terms of social structure, history, and politics. Revisionists aim to simultaneously connect many of moral panic studies' original intentions with more recent developments in social and cultural theory (and see Cohen 2003). They are especially keen to conceptualize moral panic as a component of wider historical-structural processes involved in shaping the thoughts, feelings, emotions, and behaviors of one's self and others. The project of revising moral panic studies is only starting to take hold and statements about its impacts are premature. Revisionists, moreover, have undoubtedly provided imperfect conceptual and theoretical answers to the complex empirical and historical questions they pose. Still, what is emerging from revisionist efforts is a focused debate about the politics, parameters, and possible future directions of moral panic studies.

Moral panic studies: politics, parameters, and possibilities

In this chapter, I examined how moral panic studies initially developed out of analytical debates in the sociology of deviance. Original contributions to moral panic studies were aimed at examining the transactional character of deviance and critiquing apparatuses of social control. Despite its focused beginnings, the moral panic concept was quickly abstracted from its original context and applied liberally to a wider range of phenomena. Innovative attempts to widen the analytical focus by linking panics to total social structures appeared in the mid-1980s alongside certain prominent critiques of moral panic studies. The 1990s witnessed the publication of the standard text on moral panic studies that, although continuing with revisionist efforts, had the unintended side effect of narrowing the focus of research. A powerful set of critiques appeared at the same time that partially tilted the conventional focus from social control to the transactional negotiation of deviance (i.e., folk devils fight back), and since 1995 contributions to moral panic studies have cleaved in two general directions. The first direction – the conventional approach – draws on a standard set of criteria to demonstrate how various claims-making episodes qualify as a moral panic (sometimes acknowledging but rarely engaging analytically with the fragile dynamics of claims and counter-claims). The second direction – the revisionist approach – strives for analytical clarity by widening the parameters of moral panic research. Set in the broader context of uncritical popular and academic use of moral panic, and certain attempts to discredit the concept, the time has come to bring moral panic studies back into focus.

Although the debate that is beginning to develop among revisionists is designed to bring moral panic studies into focus by widening the scope of analysis and clarifying the purpose and application of research, there is a danger that revisions will reproduce rather than transcend the factionalism that characterizes moral panic studies (Rohloff and Wright 2010). To avoid this prospect, and to work towards a clearer, more comprehensive understanding of moral panic studies, I invited a group of scholars – some well known to moral panic scholars and others new or peripheral to the area – to critically reflect on conventional, skeptical, and revisionist perspectives. Although contributors to the volume come from different disciplinary backgrounds and draw from varying intellectual traditions, they share an enthusiastic interest in exploring the explanatory possibilities facing moral panic studies today.

The volume began from my own frustrations with the lack of cumulative, interactive development in moral panic studies and the broad, implicit assumptions that underscore (indeed, make possible) many contributions to the literature. For example, it is common to find references to emotion, fear, social problems, regulation, and social control in the literature, yet when this project was conceived it was not clear how developments in these wider areas of scholarly investigation contribute analytically to moral panic studies. Nor was it clear how researchers in related areas of investigations would respond when directly invited to reflect on moral panic studies. The chapters to follow address some of these issues, and together they bring greater focus to the problems and possibilities facing moral panic studies.

The book is presented in three sections. The first section, 'Conceptualizing moral panic studies', examines the scope of moral panic studies and how it relates to the sociologies of social problems and moral regulation. For decades, moral panic scholars have referred to moral panic as a type of social problem, yet the relationship between the sociology of social problems and moral panic studies has not been explicitly examined. Similar patterns are emerging with the sociology of moral regulation. The section is designed to identify central problems in moral panic studies and to think about possible resolutions by widening the focus of analysis to include insights from social problems and moral regulation research specifically, and the sociology of culture more generally.

The second section, 'Examining moral panic studies', addresses two taken-for-granted aspects of conventional and revisionist analyses of moral panic: emotions and folk devils. The moral panic literature is filled with reference to emotion (e.g., anxiety, outrage, fear, anger, hostility), but emotion is rarely granted analytical attention. The folk devil concept occupies a similar analytical status. Admittedly, there have been attempts to theorize folk devils as active agents in moral panic construction, yet in conventional and revisionist accounts folk devils remain under-analyzed. Collectively, the section is designed to explicate implicit assumptions pertaining to emotion and folk devils and to foreground these background assumptions in the literature.

The third section, 'Applying moral panic studies', presents a set of chapters that apply conventional, skeptical, and revisionist insights to specific empirical examples. The chapters investigate the relationship between long-term moralization and short-term panics, as well as matters pertaining to so-called good panics and to sites of moralization. The section is designed to apply developments in moral panic to a range of empirical domains to flesh out the appropriate theoretical, methodological, and conceptual focus of moral panic studies.

Notes

1 Thanks to Erich Goode, Chas Critcher, Amanda Rohloff, and Kevin Walby for reading, commenting on, and taming an early draft.
2 Tracing to its origins, moral panic studies is commonly located as a sub-disciplinary concentration in the sociology of deviance. This implies that, since the 1960s, moral panic studies has receded further into the sociology of deviance to the point of becoming an intellectual enclave. Yet contributions to moral panic studies after 1995 take little interest in engaging with the diversity of contributions and debates in the sociology of deviance (see Downes and Rock 1998). If moral panic studies were deeply rooted in the sociology of deviance, there would be little need to widen the focus of analysis or probe the politics and analytical parameters of moral panic studies. It is not that moral panic has receded into the sociology of deviance to the point of becoming an entrenched subdiscipline, but rather it has all but abandoned debates in deviance studies.

References

Altheide, D. (2008) 'Moral Panic: From Sociological Concept to Public Discourse', *Crime, Media, Culture*, 5(1): 79–99.
Becker, H. (1967) 'Whose Side Are We On?' *Social Problems*, 14(3): 239–47.
Becker, H. (1964) *The Other Side*. New York: The Free Press.
Becker, H. (1963) *Outsiders: Studies in the Sociology of Deviance*. New York: The Free Press.
Ben-Yehuda, N. (1990) *The Politics and Morality of Deviance: Moral Panics, Drug Abuse, Deviant Science, and Reversed Stigmatization*. New York: State University of New York Press.
Ben-Yehuda, N. (1986) 'The Sociology of Moral Panics: Toward a New Synthesis', *The Sociological Quarterly*, 27(4): 495–513.
Ben-Yehuda, N. (1985) *Deviance and Moral Boundaries*. Chicago: University of Chicago Press.
Berger, P. and T. Luckmann (1966) *The Social Construction of Reality*. New York: Anchor Books.
Best, J. (2003) 'But Seriously Folks: The Limitations of the Strict Constructionist Interpretation of Social Problems', in G. Miller and J. Holstein (eds.), *Constructionist Controversies: Issues in Social Problems Theory*. New Brunswick, USA: Transaction Books, pp. 109–30.
Best, J. (1989) *Images of Issues*. New York: Aldine de Gruyter.
Cohen, A. (1965) 'The Sociology of the Deviant Act: Anomie Theory and Beyond', *American Sociological Review*, 30(1): 5–14.
Cohen, S. (2003) *Folk Devils and Moral Panics: The Creation of the Mods and Rockers*, 3rd ed. London: Routledge.

Cohen, S. (1972) *Folk Devils and Moral Panics: The Creation of the Mods and Rockers*. London: MacGibbon & Kee.
Cohen, S., ed. (1971) *Images of Deviance*. Middlesex: Penguin Books.
Cornwell, B., and A. Linders. (2002) 'The Myth of "Moral Panic": An Alternative Account of LSD Prohibition', *Deviant Behavior*, 23(4): 307–30.
Critcher, C. (2009) 'Widening the Focus: Moral Panics as Moral Regulation', *British Journal of Criminology*, 49(1): 17–34.
Critcher, C. (2003) *Moral Panics and the Media*. Milton Keynes: Open University Press.
Critcher, C. (2002) 'Media, Government and Moral Panic: Paedophilia in the British Press 2000–1', *Journalism Studies*, 3(4): 521–35.
Dean, M. (1994) 'A Social Structure of Many Souls: Moral Regulation, Government, and Self-Formation', *Canadian Journal of Sociology*, 9(2):145–68.
deYoung, M. (2004) *The Day Care Ritual Abuse Moral Panic*. Jefferson: McFarland.
deYoung, M. (1998) 'Another look at moral panics,' *Deviant Behavior*, 19(3): 257–78.
Downes, D. and Rock, P. (1998) *Understanding Deviance: A Guide to the Sociology of Crime and Rule-breaking*. Oxford: Oxford University Press.
Doyle, K. and D. LaCombe (2000) 'Scapegoat in Risk Society: The Case of Pedophile/Child Pornographer Robin Sharpe', *Studies in Law, Politics, and Society*, 20: 183–206.
Durkheim, E. (1895) *Rules of Sociological Method*. New York: The Free Press.
Eide, M. and G. Knight (1999) 'Public/Private Service: Service Journalism and the Problems of Everyday Life', *European Journal of Communication*, 14(4): 525–47.
Elias, N. (2000) *The Civilizing Process: Sociogenetic and Psychogenetic Investigations*. Oxford: Blackwell.
Erikson, K. (1966) *Wayward Puritans*. New York: Wiley.
Erikson, K. (1964) 'Notes on the Sociology of Deviance', in Howard Becker (ed.), *The Other Side*. New York: The Free Press, pp. 9–22.
Garland, D. (2008) 'On the Concept of Moral Panic', *Crime Media Culture*, 4(1): 9–30.
Goode, E. and N. Ben-Yehuda (2009) *Moral Panics: The Social Construction of Deviance*, 2nd ed. Malden, MA and Oxford, UK: Wiley-Blackwell.
Goode, E. and N. Ben-Yehuda (1994) *Moral Panics: The Social Construction of Deviance*. Oxford, UK: Blackwell.
Hall, S., C. Critcher, T. Jefferson, J. Clarke, and B. Roberts (1978) *Policing the Crisis: Mugging, the State, and Law and Order*. London: Macmillan Press.
Hier, S. P. (2008) 'Thinking beyond Moral Panic: Risk, Responsibility, and the Politics of Moralization', *Theoretical Criminology*, 12(2): 173–90.
Hier, S. P. (2003) 'Risk and Panic in Late Modernity: Implications of the Converging Sites of Social Anxiety', *British Journal of Sociology*, 54(1): 3–20.
Hier, S. P. (2002a) 'Raves, Risks and the Ecstasy Panic: A Case Study in the Subversive Nature of Moral Regulation', *Canadian Journal of Sociology*, 27(1): 33–57.
Hier, S. P. (2002b) 'Conceptualizing Moral Panic through a Moral Economy of Harm', *Critical Sociology*, 28(3): 311–34.
Hunt, Alan (1999) *Governing Morals: A Social History of Moral Regulation*. Cambridge: Cambridge University Press.
Hunt, Arnold (1997) '"Moral Panic" and Moral Language in the Media', *British Journal of Sociology*, 48(4): 629–48.
Innes, Martin (2004) 'Signal Crimes and Signal Disorders: Notes on Deviance as Communicative Action', *British Journal of Sociology*, 55(3): 335–55.
Kinsey, R., J. Lea and J. Young (1986) *Losing the Fight Against Crime*. London: Blackwell.
Lea, J. (1987) 'Left Realism: A Defense', *Contemporary Crises*, 11: 357–70.
Lea, J. and J. Young (1993) *What Is to Be Done About Law and Order – Crisis in the Eighties*, 2nd ed. London: Pluto Press.
Lea, J. and J. Young (1984) *What Is to Be Done About Law and Order – Crisis in the Eighties*. Harmondsworth: Penguin.
Lemert, E. (1967) *Human Deviance, Social Problems, and Social Control*. Englewood Cliffs, NJ: Prentice Hall.

Liazos, A. (1972) 'The Poverty of the Sociology of Deviance: Nuts, Sluts, and Perverts', *Social Problems*, 20(1): 103–20.
Lyon, D. (2003) *Surveillance After September 11th*. London: Polity.
McRobbie, A. (1994) 'Folk Devils Fight Back', *New Left Review* (January/February): 107–16.
McRobbie, A. and S. L. Thornton (1995) 'Rethinking "Moral Panic" for MultiMediated Social Worlds', *British Journal of Sociology*, 46(4): 559–74.
Welch, M., E. A. Price and N. Yankey (2002) 'Moral Panic Over Youth Violence: Wilding and the Manufacture of Menace in the Media', *Youth and Society*, 34(1): 3–30.
Miller, G. and J. Holstein (1989) *Challenges and Choices: Constructionist Perspectives on Social Problems*. New York: Walter de Gruyter.
Parnaby, P. F. (2003) 'Disaster through Dirty Windshields: Law, Order, and Toronto's Squeegee Kids', *Canadian Journal of Sociology*, 28(3): 281–307.
Rohloff, A. (2008) 'Moral Panics as Decivilizing Processes: Towards an Eliasian Approach', *New Zealand Sociology*, 23(1): 66–76.
Rohloff, A. and S. Wright (2010) 'Moral Panic and Social Theory: Beyond the Heuristic', *Current Sociology*, 58(3): 403–19.
Rothe, D. and S. L. Muzzatti (2004) 'Enemies Everywhere: Terrorism, Moral Panic, and US Civil Society', *Critical Criminology*, 12(3): 327–50.
Schur, E. (1965) *Crimes without Victims: Deviant Behavior and Public Policy*. Englewood Cliffs, NJ: Prentice Hall.
Spector, M. and J. I. Kitsuse (1977) *Constructing Social Problems*. Menlo Park, CA: Cummings.
Thomas, W. I. (1928) *The Child in America*. New York: A. A. Knopf.
Thompson, K. (1998) *Moral Panics*. Routledge: London.
Thornton, S. (1995) *Club Cultures: Music, Media and Subcultural Capital*. Middletown, CT: Wesleyan University Press.
Ungar, S. (2001) 'Moral Panic versus the Risk Society: The Implications of the Changing Sites of Social Anxiety', *British Journal of Sociology*, 52(2): 271–91.
Victor, J. S. (1998) 'Moral Panics and the Social Construction of Deviant Behavior: A Theory and Application to the Case of Ritual Child Abuse', *Sociological Perspectives*, 41: 541–65.
Waddington, P. A. J. (1986) 'Mugging as a Moral Panic: A Question of Proportion', *British Journal of Sociology*, 37(2): 245–59.
Waiton, S. (2008) *The Politics of Antisocial Behaviour: Amoral Panics*. New York: Routledge.
Watney, S. (1987) *Policing Desire: Pornography, AIDS, and the Media*. London: Comedia.
Woolgar, S. and D. Pawluch (1985) 'Ontological Gerrymandering: The Anatomy of Social Problems Explanations', *Social Problems*, 32(3): 214–27.
Young, J. (2009) 'Moral Panic: Its Origins in Resistance, Ressentiment and the Translation of Fantasy into Reality', *British Journal of Criminology*, 49(1): 4–16.
Young, J. (1971) *The Drug Takers: The Social Meaning of Drug Use*. London: McGibbon and Paladin.

Part 1
Conceptualizing moral panic studies

This section presents four chapters addressing the scope of moral panic studies and how it relates to the sociologies of social problems and moral regulation. The moral panic literature is filled with references to social problems, and more recent contributions have begun conceptualizing moral panic as a component of moral regulation processes. Despite continuing reliance on the sociologies of social problems and moral regulation, however, these areas are, for the most part, absent presences in moral panic studies: relied upon, yet taken for granted explanatory frameworks for conducting moral panic analyses. The chapters in this section explicitly address the analytical complexity – and compatibility – among panics, problems, and regulatory processes.

Erich Goode and Nachman Ben-Yehuda introduce the section by grounding moral panic in contextual constructionism to better defend it against criticisms pertaining to exaggeration, disproportional representation, and amoral panics. They argue that, like contextual constructionist analyses of social problems, moral panic analyses entail examining definitions and conditions. But moral panic is conceptualized as a special kind of social problem, one that hinges on disproportionate reactions generated by putative threats to a moral universe. In Goode and Ben-Yehuda's assessment, then, the first purpose of moral panic analyses is to examine how putative threats are constructed (i.e., examining definitional processes) and to demonstrate how representations are out of proportion to actual threats (i.e., examining actual conditions).

However, Goode and Ben-Yehuda go further than this to conceptualize moral panics in terms of existential antagonisms that affirm the boundaries of moral orders. They do not privilege any single (vertical) moral order, but rather explain moral panic as a structural mechanism that functions to affirm a sense of existential security by playing on any number of moral antagonisms. For Goode and Ben-Yehuda, moral panics are by definition verifiably exaggerated responses to putative threats but the value of moral panic is not simply its 'debunking capacity.' Panics are empirical manifestations of deeper existential insecurities that play out in the moral domain.

In Chapter 3, Joel Best agrees that moral panic is a special kind of social problem. Yet unlike Goode and Ben-Yehuda, who aim to clarify how moral panic as an analytically autonomous concept fits the contextual constructionist framework, Best works through some conventional and revisionist limitations standing in the way of realizing moral panic's explanatory value as one among many dimensions of social problems construction.

For Best, the main difference between long-term social problems construction and short-term panics hinges on ownership. Social problems construction involves claims makers who take ownership of claims about *putative* conditions and deploy changing forms of rhetoric (a form of measurable activity) to mobilize audience members. Social problems ownership varies across social domains (e.g., congressional hearings, classrooms, research laboratories) and analysts need not concern themselves with 'the real' problem (because problems constructions are putative). Given the short-term duration of moral panics (appearing primarily in the traditional print media), they lack ownership. For Best, then, moral panics are one type of social problem that are short-lived, ownerless, media-centered claims about moral threats that signify some larger moral concern that might gain ownership in the social problems industry.

Alan Hunt's assessment of the relationship between moral regulation and moral panic (Chapter 4) reinforces many of the explanatory concerns raised by Best. Hunt begins by conceptualizing moral panic and moral regulation in terms of moral politics and the sociology of moralization. The field of moralization, says Hunt, involves popular actions on the part of activists who seek to mobilize concerns, worries, and anxieties related to moral and social values. But moral panic and moral regulation studies come from different places. Tracing to Cohen's (1972) study of the Mods and Rockers, panics have been conceptualized as short-term, undesirable, exaggerated, and disproportional responses to putative threats. Moral regulation studies, by contrast, maintain evaluative neutrality concerning claims-making activities, focusing on the long-term historical processes involved in how people are made into subjects by examining the deployment of discourses and practices that constitute self and other.

To demonstrate how moral panics are a special kind of moral regulation, Hunt turns to the concept of panic itself. Unlike Young (2009), who explains panic in terms of a strong, emotionally indignant ressentiment of undesirable others, Hunt argues that panics derive from dialectical hegemonic constructions pertaining to respectability. Respectability is a softer concept than ressentiment, says Hunt, allowing for analysis of the historicity of moral hegemony in terms of the respectable and the disrespectable. Empirically, respectability enables those who feel entitled to express indignation against others who do not directly affect their material wellbeing. Conceptually, emphasizing respect as the basis of moralization involves examining the construction of disrespectful others as well as respectable selves. Indeed, as Goode and Ben-Yehuda argue in Chapter 2, moralization often manifests as material threats (e.g., second-hand smoke) but it derives from a moral-existential antagonism involving constructions of respectable and disrespectable behavior.

Therefore, Best and Hunt agree that moral panic studies confronts a number of explanatory problems (e.g., normativity, disproportion, exaggeration), yet they also recognize the importance of moral panic as an explanatory concept in the long-term processes of problems construction and moral regulation. In the final chapter of this section, Rohloff addresses the long-term processes underscoring moral panics by reconceptualizing moral panic in terms of civilizing and decivilizing processes. She begins by explaining Norbert Elias's writings on the civilizing process. In a manner similar to Goode and Ben-Yehuda's argument that moral panics trace to conflicts among moral universes, Rohloff maintains that such conflicts are held in check when the state gains monopoly over the means of violence and taxation. One of Elias's main arguments was that processes of state formation and centralization stimulate changes in mutual identification and interdependence among members of the population. High levels of mutual identification (i.e., hegemonic moral universes) create predictable and stable social structures, thereby reducing fear associated with danger. Over time, moralized behaviors become increasingly associated with emotions that are internalized among members of the population and greater levels of self-restraint set in.

The civilizing process, however, is not linear. An actual or perceived weakening in either the state's control over individuals' behavior or the mechanisms of self-restraint can stimulate civilizing offences: attempts among self-perceived civilized people to act on the conduct of uncivilized others. Civilizing offences are components of the ongoing civilizing process that operate in a dialectical manner to constitute the conduct of self and other. Conceptualizing moral panics as civilizing offensives, says Rohloff, demands that panic researchers address the processual, relational, and developmental components of panics as civilizing processes. In other words, moral panics are a component of the long-term civilizing process and must be analysed as such. Not only will a fuller appreciation of moral panic as civilizing offensive address criticisms of temporality in moral panic studies, says Rohloff, but it can also help us to move beyond charges of normative biases.

Collectively, then, the chapters in this section locate moral panic studies in the context of long-term sociological processes related to state and extra-state agencies and actors. Moral panic studies continues to deal with conceptual challenges pertaining to normative biases and limited scope but the contributors to this section are clear that the focus of analysis can be broadened to more fully account for the developmental history of moral panics.

References

Cohen, S. (1972) *Folk Devils and Moral Panics: The Creation of the Mods and Rockers*. London: MacGibbon & Kee.

Young, Jock (2009) 'Moral Panic: Its Origins in Resistance, Ressentiment and the Translation of Fantasy into Reality', *British Journal of Criminology*, 49(1): 4–16.

2

GROUNDING AND DEFENDING THE SOCIOLOGY OF MORAL PANIC

Erich Goode and Nachman Ben-Yehuda

The moral panic concept is a whopping academic success. With each decade, the number of books, media stories, and academic journal articles on moral panic substantially increases. It is 'safe to say,' one observer declares, that moral panic 'has been far and away the most influential sociological concept to have been generated in the second half of the twentieth century' (Ditton 2007: 1). In fact, moral panic is so useful that if Stanley Cohen hadn't devised the term, 'it would have been necessary for someone else to invent it' (Garland 2008: 9).

Although the media and segments of the literate public find moral panic's rhetoric and irony deliciously alluring, the concept has stirred controversy among sociologists. Sociologists working outside the moral panic literature find the concept irksome when they try to situate it squarely in existing explanatory frameworks in the sociology of social problems, of deviance, and of collective behavior. Even among sociologists writing about moral panic, not all agree on appropriate analytical parameters. The uneasiness characterizing the application of moral panic consequently leads analysts to embrace only certain explanatory components in the existing literature or to dismiss it as a value-laden political attribute employed to denounce certain forms of social action.

In this chapter, we ground the sociology of moral panic in the broader literature on social problems. We argue that the conceptual terrain of moral panic is sufficiently open ended to encompass competing analytical approaches in the sociology of social problems; its utility as a key sociological concept is found in its flexible application. Moral panic represents a special kind of social problem that is empirically connected to but analytically distinct from processes of social problems construction. By grounding moral panic in the problems literature, we are able to better explain the foundations of moral panic and to defend the concept against criticism – both internal and external to the literature. We explain how panics are best situated in a contextual constructionist framework that enables us to simultaneously address conditions and definitions, and to empirically examine the criteria of disproportional and exaggerated representations to putative moral threats.

The chapter is presented in four parts. We begin by conceptualizing moral panic and by demarcating material from moral threats. We differentiate material (i.e., physical) from moral threats and, in the second section, conceptualize moral panic in terms of ongoing debates in the sociology of social problems. We do so to ground moral panic in a broader analytical field of research to show how moral panic analyses simultaneously entail examining definitions and conditions and to better position ourselves to respond to criticisms that flow from the problems literature. The third section addresses three central criticisms of moral panic, and the final section distinguishes between two analytical models of panic. We conclude by arguing that moral panics are rational, routine features of social order and that the flexibility of the moral panic concept enables a fuller explanation of volatile episodes of claims-making activity, where real threats are exaggerated in a disproportionate manner.

Conceptualizing moral panic

In light of the growing literature on moral panic (and the expanding uses of the concept), it is necessary to establish what we mean by moral panic. First, what is the 'moral' element in moral panic? In *Economy and Society*, Max Weber (1978) made the distinction between *Zweckrationalität*, or rationality based on the pragmatic, instrumental calculation of reaching a given goal, and *Wertrationalität*, or expressive/ moral rationality, which is based on the absolute valuation of a given goal or end. *Zweckrationalität* is amoral: the calculation of the most effective means of achieving a variety of goals, even murder, rape, and robbery. In contrast, *Wertrationalität* is based on the achievement of the end itself, regardless of the means chosen to achieve it. Hence, the 'moral' in a moral panic is the expression of outrage at the violation of a given absolute value, the undermining of something that a sector of the society regards as good in itself – that is, principles which embody decency, righteousness, and virtue. In the moral panic, hostility is expressed that an unacceptable behavior or condition subverts the enactment of good or acceptable behavior or conditions.

Generally, moral panic is *the outbreak of moral concern over a supposed threat from an agent of corruption that is out of proportion to its actual danger or potential harm*. The indictments that aggrieved parties lodge during the course of panic episodes are not always spurious – the threats named may be genuine – but such claims exaggerate the seriousness, extent, typicality, and/or inevitability of harm. Empirically assessed, the concern is *disproportionate* to the objective threat. For each episode, the society, or a sector of the society, *overreacts* to a perceived danger.

The principal 'actors' in moral panics are the media, which publish or broadcast stories about a supposed threat; the public at large, the members of which feel, verbalize, or act upon their concern; representatives of the law, including politicians, lawmakers, and police, who propose, enact, and enforce legislation; and social movement activists, who organize, recruit, proselytize, assemble, demonstrate, and lobby on behalf of their cause against the putative threat. Agents or actors in each sphere or 'station' of a moral panic manifest that a given threat *warrants* the expression of a certain level of concern, by feeling or acting out that sentiment. Actors express concern, whether in sentiment or actions, in these analytically *separate but mutually interpenetrating* realms.

Moral panic is always about *something*; it is neither irrational illusion nor misperception. That 'something' is the uproar and outrage generated by a putative threat to a moral universe and, concomitantly, the category of humans (usually) perceived as morally offensive.

> You cannot have a moral panic unless there is something morally to panic about, although it may not be the actual object of fear but the displacement of another fear, or, more frequently, a mystification of the true threat of the actual object of dismay. ... Further, in the most substantial cases, the objects of panic do represent a direct threat to the core values, the strategy of discipline, and the justification of rewards of those that panic. Only there is a direct threat in a moral and symbolic kind rather than in a material sense.
>
> *(Young 2007: 60)*

For instance, during the 1950s, social activists and the media claimed that a wave of sex crimes and violence against women and girls engulfed communities around the United States when no such increases had taken place. According to Chauncey (1993), these lurid tales circulated as much to keep women in the home and attending to their traditional female role as to physically protect women and girls from harm. In the 1980s, anti-pornography feminists did not stop at the charge that pornographic representations of women are ideologically and morally offensive – that, *in and of themselves*, such images *demean* and *debase* women; rather, they insisted that pornography causes men to inflict violence against women, especially rape (Lederer 1980). And in the early 2000s, communities and the media mounted strong opposition to the use of Ecstasy, particularly at raves, on the basis of a medical argument, namely that the youngsters who took the drug would collapse, pass out, and possibly die. This opposition, Hier (2002) maintains, represented an attempt at *moral regulation* – a hallmark of moral panics generally.

Hence, the *subtext* of the message of moral entrepreneurs is the moral antagonisms that derive from putative threats, even though the concern, fear, and hostility expressed is nearly always couched in material or physical terms (e.g., medical, risk, or criminal discourses). In other words, antagonisms among different social groups that are expressed through moralizing claims cannot be neatly conceptualized as ideological-discursive expressions of deeper, material threats. Rather, antagonistic moral struggles are commonly expressed as material/physical threats through the language and authority of risk. As Critcher explains, 'all moral panics are ultimately about reconfirming moral values' (2006: 9). The moral regulation function of the panic does not necessitate lockstep coordination or conspiracy among moral panic actors; often, independently, actors regard a given threat as entailing putative or actual subversion of the moral order, toward which an apt outrage or concern – albeit usually expressed in material terms – seems called for. Even if the putative condition has no real-world impact, its very existence is regarded as an existential *affront* to a given moral order and its supporters; it affirms the viability and validity of alternative orders.

Still, actors do not always have the same moral order in mind when they engage in claims-making activities. The very morality that one set of people attempts to support can be contested by another (McRobbie 1994; McRobbie and Thornton 1995). Moral panics have traditionally remonstrated against threats to the *dominant* moral order, but contemporary panics increasingly oppose threats to a *range* of moral orders – each of concern to particular audiences. This is not to suggest that panics with broad scope have disappeared; the society at large still regards street crime as threatening, and in many ways such concerns represent moral panics (Tonry 2004: 85–97). But the older models, based on the notion that the unit of analysis of moral regulation encompasses the society as a whole, has to be supplemented by an awareness that the regulatory ends to which panics are oriented include claims and counter claims in local settings as well.

Grounding moral panic in the sociology of social problems

Competing normative claims about material and moral threats that are found in moral panics mimic, to a certain extent, analytical claims in the social problems literature. The sociology of social problems is generally divided into two theoretical positions. The first, realist (objectivist) position holds that social problems research entails studying material conditions with more or less identifiable, verifiable properties. Objectivists study social problems as concretely real conditions that threaten or harm people by causing death, disease, or burdensome monetary cost on the society (Manis 1976; Best 1995: 3–7).

The second, definitional (constructionist) position entails investigating how real or perceived conditions are defined, framed, packaged, and explained. Constructionists strive to understand how the causes and solutions of putative problems are mediated through a variety of claims-making or definitional activities (Loseke 1999). Constructionists hold that a condition need not materially exist to be constructed as a social problem – witness the persecution of witches in Renaissance Europe (Ben-Yehuda 1985: 23–73). In other words, the materiality of problems is not the primary concern for constructionists.

However, constructionism comes in two varieties: radical or *strict* and moderate or *contextual* (Best 1995: 337–57). Strict constructionists assert that the material, objective dimension is simply one of many social constructs, incapable of being definitively verified or justified. One assertion about the seriousness of a condition is no more 'privileged' than any other, and assessments about the objective reality or seriousness of a given condition are outside the purview of constructionist research. In effect, it is not the mandate of the constructionist to assess competing claims about materially real social problems (Spector and Kitsuse 1977). The object of analysis is claims-making activities.

In contrast to strict constructionists, contextual constructionists argue that sociologists are not prohibited from assessing the materiality of competing claims about the nature and seriousness of harmful or threatening conditions. Indeed, they are required to evaluate the truth-value of empirical claims, making use of the same evidence and reasoning tools available to all observers. To both examine claims as social constructs and assess the validity of claims does not constitute a contradiction. Constructionist sociologists do *not* argue that mental disorder, deviance, and social problems are 'just' or *nothing but* constructions or labels; they do not argue that constructionism is the *only* permissible perspective through which to examine these phenomena. The real-world phenomena that a social construct points to – poverty, for instance – may have materially real causes and consequences, but its reality does not deny that it is *also* conceptualized, talked about, theorized, explained, legislated against, reported on, evaluated, and feared in certain historically and culturally specific ways (Best 2000).

How, then, does moral panic fit into the sociology of social problems? The objectivists have no use for moral panic; at least some of moral panic depends on misplaced fears, exaggerated concerns, and heightened hostilities (Johnson 1997) – all of which dwell more or less exclusively in the constructionists' realm. To the objectivist, the constructionist dimension is of interest only insofar as the scientist can reliably and definitively verify its reality, and 'concern' is far too vague, slippery, and amorphous a concept to satisfy this positivistic criterion (Cornwell and Linders 2002).

On the other side of the equation, the strict constructionists consider moral panic a contradiction in terms: it is dependent on the disproportion between a subjective phenomenon, concern, which is its domain, and an objective threat, the latter of which is outside the perspective's scope (Spector and Kitsuse 1977). The mixing of the objective and the subjective realms has been denounced as 'ontological gerrymandering' or violating conceptual purity (Woolgar and Pawluch 1985); that is, laying claim to the materiality of problems to test the validity or authenticity of claims-making activities.

Hence, moral panic could *only* have been developed by the contextual constructionist approach. Even without explicating the specific framework that guides investigation, *all* researchers of moral panic are contextual constructionists. This is important to recognize because it is not merely a question of epistemology. How researchers conceptualize their object of study poses implications for the kinds of methods they employ and the kinds of data they gather. When moral panic is conceived of in strict constructionist terms, analysts find themselves unable to differentiate a balanced and reasonable response to a real or putative condition from a disproportionate and exaggerated one. Similarly, when objectivists conceive of problems in purely materialist terms, they are unable to account for the gap between what people worry about and what objective data suggest they should worry about. Contextual constructionism offers grounds to negotiate these tensions and to better address certain key criticisms of moral panic.

Criticisms of moral panic

Grounding moral panic in the broader, more established literature on social problems helps to clarify some of the epistemological, theoretical, and methodological tensions arising from competing, if unacknowledged, perspectives and approaches impinging on moral panic analyses. The criticisms of moral panic persist, however, and in spite of the many criticisms that have been launched against it, moral panic 'just refuses to go away' (Jewkes 2004: 75).

In a review of the first edition of *Moral Panics* by Goode and Ben-Yehuda (1994), for example, Johnson (1997) argues that he is 'uncomfortable with the conceptualization of moral panics itself.' According to Johnson, 'the concept of the moral panic further muddles our catalogue of concepts to describe varieties of collective responses that appear irrational to the scholarly observer' (p. 1515). Researchers, he says, have devoted 'disproportional attention to the topic,' and the degree of panic that takes place in crisis situations has been 'wildly exaggerated' (p. 1515). This criticism sounds disturbingly similar to the declaration that if people are healthy most of the time, there's no point in studying illness.

What are some of the most significant arguments against moral panic? And to what extent have moral panic's advocates and defenders prevailed against them? In this section, we address three points of criticism that stand out in frequency and import. The first two center on the difficulty of establishing criteria to measure exaggeration and disproportional representation. The third concerns claims about amoral panics in the so-called risk society.

Exaggeration

In a symptomatic statement, Cornwell and Linders (2002) contend that the moral panic 'is so laden with ontological and methodological difficulties' that it is 'virtually useless as an analytic guiding light' (p. 314). Their most serious criticism is that society's concern about the use of LSD during the 1960s did *not* represent a moral panic, but rather a rational, reasonable response to the genuine threat it posed and the damage it caused. Hence, they reason, if the concern conveyed by the media, the public, and legislation at that time did not constitute a moral panic, this casts doubt on the very validity of the moral panic concept generally.

We disagree. In the case of LSD use in the 1960s, media representations that members of the public found credible, as well as legislation proposed and passed, brought to bear all of Cohen's original criteria for moral panic: *stereotyping, exaggeration, distortion,* and *sensitization* (Cohen 1972: 59–65). In 1966 the chair of the New Jersey Narcotic Drug Study Commission called LSD '*the greatest threat facing the country today*' (in Brecher *et al.* 1972: 369; our emphasis) – a verifiably false claim, the believability of which the hysteria of the era bolstered. LSD's threat was more panic-driven than materially real; many parties felt that the use of LSD posed a *distinctly deviant potential*. In the heat of the moment, members of the public often regard false, hyperbolic, and anomalistic stories as scarier, more interesting, and *truer* than empirically accurate and prototypical ones. The media reported LSD stories – irresponsibly, we now know, and should have known then – because these stories were newsworthy, both from journalists' professional judgment and from what they surmised the public's reaction would be. Under the influence, the press alleged, LSD users leapt off buildings, thinking they could fly; tried to stop speeding cars, thinking they were invulnerable; slashed their wrists in fields of lilies; and stared at the sun to the point of blindness. Reporters did not check their sources, assuming the claims were true because of the prevailing sentiment of the times. Media representatives should have been able to look around and see that such stories were bogus, unlikely, or wildly uncharacteristic. The implausible LSD stories they published were widely appealing and credible because they corresponded to notions of the sorts of things that new, and deviant, drugs are likely to do. And these scare stories took on energy not merely from their putative material threat but also from the fact that they introduced a *moral* dimension to their subjects and topics.

The claim that LSD damaged chromosomes (Cohen, Marinello, and Back 1967), which swept through the United States like a prairie fire, was based on research so shoddy (human blood cells placed in a culture containing LSD underwent chromosome breakage, and one mental patient who had been therapeutically treated with the drug had a higher-than-average level of chromosome damage) that a first-year biology major could have refuted its findings; a later study (Dishotsky *et al.* 1971) definitively established that LSD does not break or damage chromosomes.

Many commentators in the 1960s held that the use of LSD threatened the dominance of the middle-class work ethic, morality, and worldview. The very notion of otherworldliness that psychedelic propagandists were peddling, which very few users subscribed to, seemed acutely fearful. The claim that LSD transmogrified young people into hippies, psychedelic zombies, and psychotics with ravaged chromosomes was *credible* to the media, the public, and lawmakers; reading them, we know we are looking at a moral panic. Even though many actors in this drama *believed* LSD to be a genuine threat, the conviction took on credibility because these actors *already* regarded the drug as a morally tainted substance peddled or endorsed by morally suspect participants. Hence, Cornwell and Linders' argument that LSD use posed a genuine threat and hence could not have represented a moral panic — and thus, the moral panics concept itself lacks validity — is groundless. No one questions that LSD use is, and was, risky and potentially harmful. Nearly all contemporary researchers do, however, regard the portraits of the drug, its use, and its users that prevailed in the media and the public mind in the 1960s as substantially exaggerated and distorted, and would, in all likelihood, agree that moral panic actors then were *sensitized* to harm relative to the consumption of conventional substances.

Disproportion

Related to reactions to the criterion of exaggeration, some critics have challenged the moral panic concept by charging that the two elements or criteria comprising disproportion — concern and threat — are incommensurable. It is impossible, they allege, to verify the claim that a given level of concern is out of proportion to a given level of threat, since one cannot be measured or weighed against the other. *How much* concern is proportional to *how much* of a threat? These critics insist that, since concern and threat exist and operate on different planes or dimensions, observers have no means by which they can compare them with one another (Waddington 1986). However, the informed observer can produce an abundance of criteria of disproportion that demonstrate that this is an illegitimate argument. Below we address five ways this can be done.

Non-existent conditions or behaviors

Certain conditions or behaviors and threats are so implausible that any concerns they generate are *by definition* disproportionate to their supposed harm. For instance, anti-porn feminists claimed that women are murdered on camera to make 'snuff' films (MacKinnon and Dworkin 1997: 142, 384, 400) – disturbing if true, but nonetheless a claim demanding evidence that has never been produced. No search in the United States has turned up a verifiably genuine snuff movie (Donovan 2004: 27–60). Moreover, in the 1980s and 1990s, Christian activists and their allies claimed that tens of thousands of children were kidnapped and molested or murdered in the United States each year in horrific ritual ceremonies by a cabal of Satanists. All indications point to the fact that this claim was bogus, but at the time it was strongly believed in certain social circles (Victor 1998). Stories such as these illustrate that one criterion of disproportion between threat and concern is satisfied by the fact that some supposed threats are the basis of urban legends; they *simply don't exist*.

Implausible causal mechanisms

In the 1950s, many experts thought that comic books produce juvenile delinquency (Wertham 1954), and their concern generated a comic book scare or panic that touched off political oratory, congressional investigations, a flood of newspaper stories, and a radical transformation in the comic book industry itself (Hadju 2008). Also in the 1950s, many observers believed the few thousand communists in the United States were powerful enough to overthrow the American government. Subversion lurked everywhere, they charged, threatening to infect the society with the virus of Bolshevik political corruption, and popular culture voiced that concern in propaganda, news stories, magazine articles, comics, and films, and political witch hunts that rooted out leftists from positions in academia, the government, and the entertainment industry. Historians refer to this fear and concern as the 'Red Scare,' a moral panic about misplaced and exaggerated concern and fear of communist subversion (Barson and Heller 2001) – clearly, based on faulty cause-and-effect logic, one criterion of disproportion. During the first decade of the twenty-first century, spokespersons for interest groups claimed in the media that violent videogames caused a rash of school shootings. An empirical study of school violence found no such cause-and-effect link (Ferguson 2008), arguing that these claims represented a moral panic in action. All of these implausible but widely believed charges were based on the notion that people are motivated to act by mysterious and unrealistically powerful forces.

Exaggerated figures

If the figures cited to measure the scope of the threat are substantially larger than fearful and concerned claims assert, clearly, we satisfy the criterion of disproportion. In a moral panic, as Cohen says, 'the untypical is made typical' (2002: xix). In the early 1980s, a member of the Knesset (the Israeli Parliament), the police, and media representatives asserted that half of Israeli schoolchildren were smoking hashish; studies indicated that this figure was in the 3-to-5 percent range (Ben-Yehuda 1986) – an exaggeration of ten times. In a debate before the British House of Commons in 2007, a former minister of the Foreign Office claimed that 25,000 'sex slaves' worked in the United Kingdom; the *Daily Mirror*, a major newspaper, cited the same figure. A year later, the minister cited a figure of 18,000, which a police official endorsed. Researchers have presented data that indicate that these figures are both fabricated and hugely exaggerated, and that, in the western world at least, forced prostitution or 'trafficking' represents a small percentage of the sex-for-pay picture (Davies 2009). The exaggerated figures, seemingly precise, make the problem appear to be much larger than it actually is, and indicate that a moral panic very likely is at work here. The advocates of a given issue may believe these larger figures but, in presenting them, they make a tiny problem seem to be a huge one; and in so doing, they both communicate and foment a moral panic.

Conspiracy theories

Conspiracies exist, of course: the Bay of Pigs in 1961, the Cambodian invasion in 1970, the 'Iran-Contra' scandal in 1986. These were actual conspiracies because they entailed coordination between the American government and unofficial, off-the-record cadres, factions, and organizations, and they involved elaborate cover-ups and lies told by officials to the American people. But in comparison with these real-life conspiracies, conspiracy *theories* are more dramatic, more clear cut as to villains and victims, and typically crafted along the lines of a well-plotted thriller (Aaronovitch 2010).

Following the 2001 9/11 terrorist attack on the World Trade Center, dozens of conspiracies circulated, including the claim that planes did not hit the towers, which were brought down by 'controlled explosives' so that the U.S. military could justify invading Iraq and Afghanistan to seize their oil fields. None of the conspiracy theories about 9/11 can be documented, and strong evidence exists that refutes most of them. They offer a delusional interpretation of how the world works. Such theories instigate misplaced concern where none is necessary, and divert the focus away from spheres where concern is needed. Not all conspiracies are widely believed, but consider the fact that, after the attack, a poll indicated that 36 percent of the American public believed that the government promoted the 9/11 attacks or knew about them in advance and did nothing; 16 percent believed explosives brought down the towers; and 12 percent believed a cruise missile hit the Pentagon (Powell 2006). Conspiracy theories *nearly always* express misplaced concern, and hence, are a type of moral panic. Let's be clear on this point: the attack on the World Trade Towers constituted genuine harm, and it presaged a real and present ongoing danger to the United States, and so the concern it stirred up did *not* indicate a moral panic. The attack was real and the threat was real – but the conspiracy theories about the *nature* and *source* of the attack reflected a moral panic.

Changes over time

One clue to disproportion, and thus the moral panic, is a sharp increase in indicators of public concern, media attention, and political and legislative activity at a time when the condition or behavior remains stable or is declining. Between the 1990s and the first decade of the 2000s, the number of news stories on school shootings and school killings skyrocketed, at a time when the number of these incidents was plummeting (Cornell 2006). Each year, the Gallup Poll asks a sample of Americans whether there is more, or less, crime in the United States as compared with the year before. In 2008, the figure saying that there is more crime was 67 percent; in 2009, this figure had increased to 74 percent, substantially higher than in 2002, when it was 43 percent. Yet, between 1990 and 2009 the crime rate in the United States has been steadily declining, and even between 2008 and 2009, according to the FBI's *Crime in the United States*, it had decreased for all categories of crime, including a 10.0 percent decrease for murder and 18.7 for motor vehicle theft – both very reliable measures of the actual figures. Some commentators (Keohane 2010) argue that the public refuse to believe that crime is declining because they feel greater dissatisfaction with the way the country is going. Again, an *increase* in the perception of the seriousness of a problem at a time when its actual seriousness is *decreasing* provides one clue that a moral panic may be brewing.

Risk society and the amoral panic

The foundation for the moral panic framework has hitherto rested on *moralization* and folk devil construction. With the development of technological threats – nuclear, chemical, environmental, biological, and medical – our concerns no longer focus on the evil doings of an easily identifiable folk devil. Rather, today's enemy is unbounded, incalculable, faceless, and amoral (Beck 1992). Whereas in the past, traditional values made up the foundation stone of fear, hostility, concern, and threat, today, 'safety and protection of the victim' is the central feature of panics and scares. It seems 'to one degree or another we are all in a panic about something,' but the issue of morality is no longer relevant (Waiton 2008: 104).

This argument is predicated on the notion that if new medical and technological threats emerge, the older ones, based on morality, are no longer relevant. Though the recently emerged amoral 'risk society' threats have in fact emerged (along with the amoral natural threats, which have always been with us), the older moral threats still frequently erupt; they instill fear *in addition to*, rather than *instead of*, the classic scares that have always taken place. Harm from unfamiliar technological and medical sources is separate and independent of fears of subversion and threat from familiar immoral folk devils. The so-called amoral panic has not supplanted moral panic, but rather supplemented it (Hier 2003). The 'amoral panic' critique of the moral panic concept attempts to force an either–or dichotomy on a complex landscape that, with the arrival of the new technologies, has been rendered even more tumultuous – not less. Public concern is not a zero-sum game, as these risk society arguments imply.

Ungar advances a particularly muddled version of the risk society critique. His attempt to subsume moral panic under the rubric of the general category of 'social anxiety and fear' (2001: 271) is shaky, slipshod, and contradictory. He begins by finding the panic principally a form of risk (p. 272) and then reverses himself a dozen pages on (pp. 283–84) by knocking down the very 'straw-man' similarities he manufactures in the first place. Ungar argues that unnamed processes select folk devils following disasters (note the passive voice: 'fingers are pointed,' 'enmity was first directed,' 'cleanup efforts were discredited') through what he calls 'foraging' and 'roulette dynamics' (pp. 281–84) by scapegoating a vulnerable deviant. Yet Ungar argues against constructionism as an analytic strategy, a strategy he himself has already adopted. He accuses research on moral panic as 'generally' taking a top-down or elite approach to claims making, a decidedly false assertion; Goode and Ben-Yehuda devote an entire chapter to discussing the full range of explanations for the moral panic (1994: 124–43; 2009: 154–72). And he commits the same 'zero-sum' fallacy with which we charge Beck and Waiton. As Hier convincingly contends, Ungar offers 'a narrow conception of folk devils, claims making, and general perceptions of public safety,' and 'an over-socialized conception of individual choice.' Far 'from rendering moral panics obsolete … the emergence of the risk society presents fertile grounds for moral panics' (2003: 5).

Two models of moral panic

To this point, we have grounded moral panic in a contextual constructionist framework and responded to certain key points of criticisms launched from inside and outside the moral panic literature. In this section, we elaborate on moral panic research. Critcher (2008) notes that there are two models of the moral panic: the *processual* model devised by Cohen (1972, 2002) and the *attributional* model devised by Goode and Ben-Yehuda (1994, 2009). The processual model focuses mainly on the dynamics, development, and sequence of events of historical cases of claims about particular threats. It asks, 'What factors ignite panics at a particular time and place?' The attributional model also focuses on claims making in moral panics but provides a standard set of measurable attributes to apply to all moral panics. It asks, 'How does a given condition become defined as a threat? Who makes such claims and why? Do these claims resonate with what the media regard as a good story and what the public feels is threatening?'

We'd like to slice up the pie in a slightly different, yet overlapping fashion. We also find two models of the moral panic – rather, two poles at the ends of a continuum – but they vary slightly from Critcher's conception. On the one hand, the hierarchical or *vertical* model contends that moral panics erupt *on behalf of* the dominant moral order. On the other hand, the 'postmodern' or *horizontal* model argues for 'multi-mediation,' fragmentation, and a variety of audiences gripped by an array of moral panics. The distinction between these models is analytical; empirically, they shade into one another.

The vertical model is illustrated by Chambliss, who explained how, during the period from the 1960s to the 1990s, when the crime rate did not increase, a 'coalition of political, law enforcement, and mass media interests ... created a moral panic about crime.' This panic was created through 'the manipulation of public opinion,' he claims, to legitimate the passage of law-and-order legislation and the allocation of budgetary resources to crime control. The consequences of this panic were an over-policing of the poor and minority members, the creation of a hostile and divisive society, and a justification and institutional strengthening of racism (1995: 245, 249). According to Schissel (1997), the moral panic against youth is a 'social control strategy' instituted by a society stratified by race, class, and gender that 'creates the illusion' that the class located at the bottom of the social hierarchy is morally inferior, represents the dangerous class, and deserves poverty and punishment (1997: 181–82).

Arguments such as these are based on the vertical model: they allege that moral panics are engineered, usually by elites and agents, to serve the interests of preserving the status quo. Moral panics are 'about' power and social control. Consequently, the media are more likely to designate as folk devils excluded sectors of the society: the powerless, the poor, the marginal – such as the welfare 'scrounger,' the immigrant, the drug addict, and, after 9/11, the terrorist (Young 2007: 63). Schissel (1997: 51) identifies three different but equally marginalized media-identified folk devils: families living in poor communities, racially based gangs, and single mothers and mothers who work outside the home. The media are *not* diverse, and they are becoming increasingly centralized and oligopolized (Young 2007: 63); they orchestrate panics around sectors of society they can readily and plausibly cast into the role of the 'Other,' that is, folk devils. They do not 'Other' conventional, respectable categories of the population as targets of moral outrage. Hence, panics are *predictably structural*; that is, they do not explode here, there, and everywhere at random with respect to marginalization and exclusion.

The most fundamental feature characterizing whether we're looking at a vertical or horizontal model is the designated *audience*, actual or potential. The vertical model pictures *the society at large* as a moral panic's potential audience; only the folk devil stands outside this circle. For Cohen, the entire community of Clacton – and later, other beach communities, and still later, Britain as a whole – was the potential audience for the panic over the rowdy behavior of the unruly Mods and Rockers, delinquents, and later, unconventional youth; only transgressive and non-normative youth were, understandably, immune to the panic's siren song (although, significantly, Cohen emphasized that transgressive youth were not so much totally beyond the pale as distressingly *similar* in important ways to decent, middle-class folk). Similarly, in the 1970s, a panic about mugging – at a time when, the authors claimed, street crime was declining – gripped England; all decent Britishers should have joined in on the outrage, and only the street criminal stood outside the community of concerned citizens (Hall et al. 1978).

In the classic or conventional moral panic, the line-up was simple: *them* versus *us*, folk devils versus the rest of the society, the deviants versus the respectables. This vertical model envisions a single axis of moral panic focus and attention, regarding nearly all sectors of the society as potential audiences for a given moral panic. In a classic 'crime wave panic,' it's the criminals versus the law-abiding citizen; in the Satanic abuse panics, it's the presumed Satanists versus everyone else; in the many drug panics, it's the drug abusers versus reasonable, clean-living people who do not abuse drugs; in anti-immigrant panics, it's the immigrants versus citizens. Feminists who fought against what they saw as the corrosive and abusive impact of pornography regarded their potential audience as the society as a whole, or at least all women, or at least, all right-thinking, reasonable women; they did not see their argument as potentially appealing only to a tiny cadre of ideologically marginal feminists, and were caught off-guard when some of their harshest critics proved to be other feminists. The vertical model regards the society as a whole, or major swathes of it, as a real or potential audience for the moral panic.

In contrast, the postmodernists argue that we no longer live in a unified, monolithic, consensual society (if we ever did), one in which a given threat strikes fear into the hearts of all members. Instead, contemporary interpretations of reality and notions of truth are contradictory, diverse, and decentralized; no statement can be definitively verified and everyone is entitled to his or her own opinion. Today, the society is fragmented into diverse cliques, factions, niches, categories, sectors, strata, each with its own specialized issues, fears, concerns, claims, and problems. In contemporary society, moral panics rarely if ever grip − or are even *addressed* to − the full spectrum of the society, thus giving rise to a multiplicity of voices, a plurality of reactions, a multitude of panics. According to McRobbie (McRobbie 1994; McRobbie and Thornton 1995), this postmodern − what we refer to as *horizontal* − model is necessary to understand moral panics in our multi-mediated age. The horizontal model recognizes that, since audiences are fragmented, disparate, and morally and ideologically scattered, each is attuned only to its own specialized or focused issues of concern. Hence, moral panics burst forth over issues likely to enlist not the concerns of the society at large, but those of smaller, more specialized audiences. Society has hived into disparate cultural entities, each one of which generates its own moral panics.

In the horizontal model, micro-niches attend to micro-media that convey micro-claims about micro-issues. Far from being outsiders, parties previously marginalized and castigated by the mass media as folk devils are insiders, even heroes, within a given micro-public of concerned individuals. Unconventionality is not only an acceptable lifestyle, but in certain collectivities it is celebrated, and threats to it are met with relevant and appropriate cries of outrage. All society, it seems, has become divided into interest groups, each defending its right to be whatever its members choose to be. According to this model, we now see 'moral panics for every medium' (McRobbie and Thornton 1995: 567–70). Drug users denounce misrepresentations of their ilk in the media (p. 568). Homosexuals, once targets of moral panics, now vigorously give voice to outrage at challenges to their rights (p. 568). The very youth rebellions on which Cohen's analysis turned currently enjoy dozens of specialty magazines, not to mention, over the years, hundreds of television programs focusing on and endorsing their special concerns and point of view. In the horizontal model, society experiences many more but smaller, more limited moral panics than those conceptualized by the vertical model, taking into mind, of course, the qualification that, following Jenkins, *most* attempts at generating such stirs *fail to launch* (2009). But the ones that do burst forth will remain a source of fascination for as long as humans seek to decipher the paradoxes and conundrums of social life.

Both models of moral panic dovetail neatly with the contextual constructionist perspective. Just as constructionism is based on claims making about the reality of a given condition *by* particular groups or sectors of the society, likewise, the models of the moral panic see panics as 'tempests in teapots,' that is, as expressions of concern, hostility, and outrage about a supposed condition, again *by* certain groups or sectors of the society. The sociologist using each perspective does not, in some absolute sense, validate claims made by said sectors concerning problem-hood, nor the appropriateness of those outraged expressions that the good has been violated. *At the same time*, with the conceptual and theoretical tools at the sociologist's disposal, the contextual constructionist can assert that the social definitions of a given condition *as* a problem are disproportional, melodramatic, and inappropriate. The contextual constructionist *relativizes* and *particularizes* claims to problem-hood and the moral panic theorist looking out at the vista of contemporary society, likewise, sees particular expressions of concern and outrage that represent a disconnect on a number of fronts regarding the magnitude of those expressions and the objective danger, threat, or harm to the society.

Conclusion

Why has moral panic been so useful to social scientists, as well as to the media? And why has the public picked up and absorbed the concept into its everyday vocabulary? Why has it become such a powerful *successful* conceptual tool? We have two explanations for the success of moral panic.

The first answer is that, as with deviance, moral panic disrupts the routine operations of society, and it is when such disruptions take place that social structure and social dynamics are most clearly revealed. Far from representing exotic, marginal, atypical, uncharacteristic events, moral panic, much as the canary in the mine, indicates a dimension of social reality that would otherwise have remain concealed.

We also believe, second, that moral panic is an analytic category with widespread appeal and applicability that focuses attention on fundamental social process. Jewkes (2004: 75–83) complains that some of the central components of the moral panic – such as 'deviance,' 'morality,' and 'audiences' – are vague and imprecise, but that's precisely its appeal. The moral panic concept is not conceptually rigid or inflexible and hence does not produce a single explanation. Varying interpretations of the concept's key components can account for different panics. The moral panic is not a 'theory' but a concept; as Critcher says, it is best understood 'as an ideal type: a means of beginning an analysis, not the entire analysis in itself' (2009: 1138). The concept suggests a number of different theories, adaptable, as relevant, to uproars about a range of issues and supposed threats.

We agree with Cohen that the moral panic is appealing not just because studying it is 'fun,' or simply because its first step entails debunking the analyst's prime candidate for a misguided 'stink.' The concept's very adaptable, protean quality enables the analyst to read symbolic meaning into claims making, rhetoric, and discourse to understand complex cultural manifestations on an array of fronts. Deeper, unacknowledged reasons underlie the concern, fear, hostility, and outrage felt and ventilated about myriad issues and threats. Like any good detective investigating a murder mystery, the moral panic analyst searches out what's going on beneath the surface; sleuths conducting research on a multitude of scares have reaffirmed that the moral panic exemplifies what may be sociology's central maxim: 'Things are often not what they seem.'

References

Aaronovitch, D. (2010) *Voodoo Histories: The Role of the Conspiracy Theory in Shaping History*. New York: Riverhead Books.
Barson, M., and S. Heller (2001) *Red Scared! The Commie Menace in Propaganda and Popular Culture*. San Francisco: Chronicle Books.
Beck, U. (1992) *Risk Society: Towards a New Modernity* (trans. Mark Ritter). London: Sage.
Ben-Yehuda, N. (1985) *Deviance and Moral Boundaries*. Chicago: University of Chicago Press.
Ben-Yehuda, N. (1986) 'The Sociology of Moral Panics: Toward a New Synthesis', *The Sociological Quarterly*, 27(4): 495–513.
Best, J., ed. (1995) *Images of Issues: Typifying Contemporary Social Problems*. New York: Aldine de Gruyter.
Best, J. (2000) 'The Apparently Innocuous "Just", the Law of Levity, and the Social Problems of Social Construction', *Perspectives on Social Problems*, 12(1): 3–14.
Brecher, E. M., et al. (1972) *Licit and Illicit Drugs*. Boston: Little, Brown.
Chambliss, W. J. (1995) 'Crime Control and Ethnic Minorities: Legitimizing Racial Oppression by Creating Moral Panics.' In D. F. Hawkins, ed., *Ethnicity, Race, and Crime: Across Time and Place*. Albany: State University of New York Press.
Chauncey, G., Jr. (1993) 'The Postwar Sex Crime Panic.' In *True Stories from the American Past*, vol. II. New York: McGraw-Hill, pp. 160–78.
Cohen, M. M., M. J. Marinello, and N. Back (1967) 'Chromosomal Damage in Human Leukocytes Induced by Lysergic Acid Diethalymide', *Science*, 155: 1417–19.
Cohen, S. (1972) *Folk Devils and Moral Panics: The Creation of the Mods and Rockers*. London: MacGibbon & Kee.
Cohen, S. (2002) *Folk Devils and Moral Panics: The Creation of the Mods and Rockers*, 3rd ed. London: Routledge.
Cornell, D. G. (2006) *School Violence: Fears versus Facts*. Mahwah, NJ: Lawrence Erlbaum.
Cornwell, B., and A. Linders (2002) 'The Myth of "Moral Panic": An Alternative Account of LSD Prohibition', *Deviant Behavior*, 23(4): 307–30.
Critcher, C. (2006) *Critical Readings: Moral Panics and the Media*. Buckingham, UK: Open University Press.
Critcher, C. (2008) 'Moral Panic Analysis: Past, Present, and Future', *Sociological Compass*, 2(4): 1127–44.

Critcher, C. (2009) 'Widening the Focus: Moral Panic as Moral Regulation', *British Journal of Criminology*, 49(1): 17–34.
Davies, N. (2009) 'Prostitution and Trafficking – The Anatomy of a Moral Panic', *The Guardian*, 20 October. www.guardian.co.uk/uk/2009/oct/20/trafficking-numbers-women-exaggerated
Dishotsky, N. I., *et al.* (1971) 'LSD and Genetic Damage', *Science*, 172: 431–40.
Ditton, J. (2007) 'Folk Panics and Moral Devils'. Unpublished manuscript.
Donovan, P. (2004) *No Way of Knowing: Crime, Urban Legends, and the Internet*. New York and London: Routledge.
Ferguson, C. J. (2008) 'The School Shooting/Violent Video Game Link: Causal Link or Moral Panic?', *Journal of Investigative Psychology and Offender Profiling*, 5(1): 25–37.
Garland, D. (2008) 'On the Concept of Moral Panic', *Crime Media Culture*, 4(1): 9–30.
Goode, E., and N. Ben-Yehuda (1994) *Moral Panics: The Social Construction of Deviance*. Oxford, UK: Blackwell.
Goode, E., and N. Ben-Yehuda (2009) *Moral Panics: The Social Construction of Deviance*, 2nd ed. Malden, MA and Oxford, UK: Wiley-Blackwell.
Hadju, D. (2008) *The Ten-Cent Plague: The Great Comic-Books Scare and How It Changed America*. New York: Farrar, Straus & Giroux.
Hall, S., C. Critcher, T. Jefferson, J. Clarke, and B. Roberts (1978) *Policing the Crisis: Mugging, the State, and Law and Order*. London: Macmillan Press.
Hier, S. P. (2002) 'Raves, Risks and the Ecstasy Panic: A Case Study in the Subversive Nature of Moral Regulation', *Canadian Journal of Sociology*, 27(1): 33–57.
Hier, S. P. (2003) 'Risk and Panic in Late Modernity: Implications of the Converging Sites of Social Anxiety', *British Journal of Sociology*, 54(1): 3–20.
Jenkins, P. (2009) 'Failure to Launch: Why Do Some Social Issues Fail to Detonate Moral Panics?', *British Journal of Criminology*, 49(1): 35–47.
Jewkes, Y. (2004) *Media and Crime*. London: Sage.
Johnson, N. R. (1997) 'Review of Erich Goode and Nachman Ben-Yehuda, Moral Panics: The Social Construction of Deviance', Oxford, UK: Blackwell, *Social Forces*, 75: 1514–15.
Keohane, J. (2010) 'Imaginary Fiends', *The Boston Globe*, February 14. www.boston.com/bostonglobe/ideas/articles/2010/02/14/imaginary_fiends/
Lederer, L., ed. (1980) *Take Back the Night: Women on Pornography*. New York: William Morrow.
Loseke, D. R. (1999) *Thinking About Social Problems: An Introduction to Constructionist Perspectives*. New York: Aldine de Gruyter.
MacKinnon, C. A., and A. Dworkin, eds. (1997) *In Harm's Way: The Pornography Civil Rights Hearings*. Cambridge, MA: Harvard University Press.
McRobbie, A. (1994) 'Folk Devils Fight Back', *New Left Review* (January/February): 107–16.
McRobbie, A., and S. L. Thornton (1995) 'Rethinking "Moral Panic" for MultiMediated Social Worlds', *British Journal of Sociology*, 46(4): 559–74.
Manis, J. (1976) *Analyzing Social Problems*. New York: Praeger.
Pearson, G. (1983) *Hooligan: A History of Respectable Fears*. London: Macmillan Press.
Powell, M. (2006) '9/11 Conspiracy Theorists Multiply.' www.msnbc.msn.com/id/14723997/
Schissel, B. (1997) 'Youth Crime, Moral Panics, and the News: The Conspiracy Against the Marginalized in Canada', *Social Justice*, 24(2): 165–84.
Spector, M., and J. I. Kitsuse (1977) *Constructing Social Problems*. Menlo Park, CA: Cummings.
Tonry, M. (2004) *Thinking about Crime: Sense and Sensibility in American Penal Culture*. Oxford, UK and New York: Oxford University Press.
Ungar, S. (2001) 'Moral Panic versus the Risk Society: The Implications of the Changing Sites of Social Anxiety', *British Journal of Sociology*, 52(2): 271–91.
Victor, J. S. (1998) 'Moral Panics and the Social Construction of Deviant Behavior: A Theory and Application to the Case of Ritual Child Abuse', *Sociological Perspectives*, 41: 541–65.

Waddington, P. A. J. (1986) 'Mugging as a Moral Panic: A Question of Proportion', *British Journal of Sociology*, 37(2): 245–59.
Waiton, S. (2008) *The Politics of Antisocial Behavior: Amoral Panics*. New York and London: Routledge.
Weber, Max (1978) *Economy and Society*. California: University of California Press.
Wertham, F. (1954) *Seduction of the Innocent*. New York: Rinehart.
Woolgar, S., and D. Pawluch (1985) 'Ontological Gerrymandering: The Anatomy of Social Problems Explanations', *Social Problems*, 32(3): 214–27.
Young, J. (2007) 'Slipping Away – Moral Panics Each Side of "the Golden Age"'. In D. Downes, P. Rock, C. Chinkin, and C. Gearty, eds., *Crime, Social Control and Human Rights: From Moral Panics to States of Denial, Essays in Honor of Stanley Cohen*. Cullompton, UK: Willan Publishing, pp. 53–65.

3

LOCATING MORAL PANICS WITHIN THE SOCIOLOGY OF SOCIAL PROBLEMS

Joel Best

Moral panic studies and constructionist studies of social problems both have their roots in the labeling perspective on deviance. By the mid-1960s, labeling theorists had reconceptualized deviance in terms of societal reaction; in Howard Becker's phrase: 'deviant behavior is behavior that people so label' (1963: 9). This raised the question of the label's origins; Becker's answer was that labels are promoted by moral entrepreneurs who organize moral crusades to encourage people to define particular behaviors as deviant.

Labeling theory captured the imagination of a new generation of sociologists, not only in the U.S., but also in the U.K. British scholars began delivering papers inspired by the labeling approach at meetings of the National Deviancy Conference (NDC), and by the early 1970s some of this work was being published. Jock Young and Stanley Cohen were central figures in the NDC. Young (1971) was the first person to mention moral panics in print, although he used the term in passing. It was Cohen's *Folk Devils and Moral Panics* (2002) that developed and drew attention to the concept. Like moral entrepreneur and moral crusade, moral panic was intended to help conceptualize how concerns about deviance could be mobilized.

Cohen's book was built around the media reaction to a series of holiday-weekend seaside scuffles during 1964–65 between two stylistically distinct groups of working-class British youth: the Mods and the Rockers. The British press portrayed these minor disorderly incidents as emblematic of a crisis: out-of-control youth threatening the social order. And Cohen, in turn, named the exaggerated reaction a moral panic (Cohen 2002: 1).

Although neither moral crusade nor panic was defined precisely, Cohen's moral panics seemed different from Becker's moral crusades. The latter, typified by the Federal Bureau of Narcotics' campaign to criminalize marijuana, seemed more calculated: reformers or officials, motivated by moralistic concerns, designed a campaign to define some behavior as deviant; the outcome was often some enduring label. In contrast, moral panics, as exemplified by the concern over Mods and Rockers, seemed more spontaneous, more episodic, and shorter lived. As Cohen noted, anxiety about youth culture was 'one of the most recurrent types of moral panic in Britain' (Cohen 2002: 1). The focus on the Mods and Rockers was temporary; it was just one in a series of waves of anxiety about troubling youth, coming after worries about Teddy Boys and shortly before concern shifted to hippies.

By the mid-1970s, doubts about labeling theory had become widespread. In England, sociologists of deviance shifted to a more radical approach. The key statement of this position, *The New Criminology*, was written by three leading figures from the NDC – including Jock Young (Taylor, Walton, and Young 1973). In the U.S., labeling came under attack from several directions, including conflict theorists, feminists, and mainstream sociologists (Best 2004). In response, some sociologists of deviance moved to develop a constructionist theory of social problems.

Sociologists had long defined social problems as harmful social conditions, and they had long understood this was an unsatisfactory definition. The list of harmful conditions – everything from suicide to global overpopulation – was too diverse to support analysis. The solution was to define social problems as a process – the process by which people made claims that something ought to be considered troubling (Blumer 1971; Spector and Kitsuse, 1977; Best, 2008). The claims-making process was what everything on the list of social problems had in common.

Following Malcolm Spector and John I. Kitsuse's publication of *Constructing Social Problems* in 1977 (generally taken to be the key event in the emergence of the constructionist perspective), a substantial literature emerged to explore a range of claims-making trajectories: some claims originate with activists, but others start with victims, experts, journalists, or officials; some center around campaigns to attract public attention and arouse outrage, but others involve lobbying or other less visible activities; some become the focus for intense public debates over policy, but others fail to shape policy, and still others lead to policies without attracting much attention; some issues remain contentious and seem intractable, while others are resolved; and so on. From the view of sociologists of social problems, both moral crusades and moral panics are subtypes of the larger phenomenon of social problems construction.

In this chapter, I argue that analysts of moral panic have adopted excessively casual analytic standards, that they lack a clear, coherent definition of moral panic, and that the term has evolved to become a label of disapproval rather than a useful sociological concept. I begin by identifying some key characteristics of a 'classic' moral panic. I then argue that analysts have applied the term both expansively (in the sense that the list of items that has designated moral panics is quite diverse) and selectively (in the sense that moral panic is applied according to ideological rather than analytic rules). Finally, I argue that moral panic – defined more precisely – has the potential to be a far more useful concept, if it is located within the larger framework of social problems theory.

Elements of the classic moral panic

To appreciate causal nature of panic analysis and its relationship to social problems, consider British concerns about 'shag bands' (cheap plastic bracelets in various colors worn by school children). During the fall of 2009, the British press claimed that different colored bracelets stood for specific sexual acts that the wearer had to perform when a bracelet was broken.[1] This is an exemplary — what we might call a classic — moral panic in the Mods and Rockers tradition: a burst of attention in the British media, focused on an apparently minor phenomenon that could be interpreted as evidence of disturbing social trends (the sexualization of childhood, the commercialization of sexuality, and so on). It seems to be the most recent version of fears about cultural practices of randy youth — a successor to objects of concern stretching from petting parties[2] and spin the bottle to rainbow parties[3] and hooking up.

We can use the shag band story to clarify some key elements of the classic or conventional approach to moral panic.[4] Shag bands draw our attention to four key qualities of classic moral panics: they are short lived, irrational, media centered, and politically conservative.[5]

Duration

The classic moral panic doesn't last long — a few weeks, maybe a year or so. It is a sort of fad in public concern, a burst of attention that fades almost as quickly as it emerges (Best 2006). Criminologists have long recognized that crime waves are fluctuations not so much in the level of crime as in the level of media attention (Sacco 2005). Similarly, analysts of drug issues have documented the sequence of drug scares, in which first one drug and then another is portrayed as threatening the social order (Jenkins 1999; Reinarman 1994). In all of these cases, there are claims that there is some novel, newsworthy problem or pattern of behavior — shag bracelets, a new type of crime — that demands concern. However, in retrospect, analysts often conclude that there is little measurable evidence that the problem increased, although there was an evident surge in media coverage.

Why are classic panics short lived? In part, media coverage reflects issue-attention cycles: coverage rises when the media learn of some seemingly new, dramatic issue, but inevitably declines as the story becomes familiar and therefore less newsworthy (Downs 1972). This is particularly the case when the media play an active role in first bringing an issue to public attention. It is easy to see why newspapers wrote their initial stories exposing shag bracelets — linking sex to childhood always seems newsworthy — but harder to imagine the stories that might follow (particularly in the absence of documented cases of shag-band-induced sexual activity).

In contrast to panics, well-established social problems tend to have owners outside the media (often social movements that consider the issue central to their cause), and they have the resources to promote continued attention from the press, the public, and policy-makers (Gusfield, 1981). Thus, wilding and stalking both attracted considerable media attention when they emerged as new crime problems in the United States in 1989, but wilding soon faded from view, when no one made it their responsibility to maintain interest in the issue. But stalking was adopted by the existing movement against domestic violence; as the issue's owners, they pressed for new federal and state anti-stalking laws, and for research funding, so that stalking became a familiar topic, described in criminology textbooks and much studied by researchers (Best 1999). Almost by definition, classic moral panics fail to acquire such owners.

Irrationality

The very term moral *panic* suggests a second characteristic. These are understood as episodes that are, at least to a degree, irrational, in that people are panicked, and therefore not really in control of their fears or their behaviors. This is an invidious term, but it is not alone; analysts speak of the European witch *craze* (Goode and Ben-Yehuda 2009; Trevor-Roper 1969), drug *scares* (Reinarman 1994), health *scares* (Béland Chapter 14 this volume) and mass *hysteria* and collective *delusions* (Bartholomew 2001). Invoking such terms establishes the analyst as a judge of the research subjects' reactions, which are understood to be ill-founded fears.

Thus, in a classic moral panic, many people are supposed to be consumed by unwarranted fears. In identifying something as a moral panic, the analyst argues that lots of people are panicked. Typically, this level of panic is asserted rather than documented, and its manifestations are left to the imagination. What would constitute panic over shag bands? Shaking one's head in response to news reports? Repeating claims about the bracelets' sexual meanings? Forbidding one's child to wear the bands? A school banning the bracelets? Calls for someone to do something? The word 'panic' invokes images of a terrified crowd stampeding for the exits in a burning theater, but moral panics don't seem nearly that panicky (for that matter, neither do people trying to flee burning buildings – students of collective behavior argue that stereotypical panics are quite rare [Clarke 2002]).

In addition, the analyst of the classic moral panic argues that alleged anxieties are out of proportion to the actual menace posed. Indeed, Goode and Ben-Yehuda (2009, Chapter 2 this volume) identify 'disproportion' as one of the defining elements of moral panics. It is this disproportionate fear that makes the moral panic irrational; 'the analyst is pointing to not just an overreaction but to a form of neurotic behavior, a hysteria, a psychopathology and, by implication, to an underlying conflict that is producing the moral panic as its acting-out expression' (Garland 2008: 21). The problem here is not that the judgments about fears being excessive are necessarily misplaced – I too doubt that shag bands have had much effect on pre-teen sexual behavior. Rather, it is that people seeking to draw attention to some social problem find themselves competing with other claims; in order to get the public to focus on their problems, advocates routinely adopt rhetoric that emphasizes the size and severity of their issue (Best 2008). It is not clear that disproportionate concern distinguishes moral panics from other social problems; in fact, efforts to arouse disproportionate concern are arguably a characteristic of many, if not most, social problems claims.

Media's central role

Classic moral panics are manifested primarily through media coverage: 'mass media are typically the prime movers and the prime beneficiaries of these episodes' (Garland

2008: 15). Analysts point to increased media reports as evidence that there was a surge in concern. Typically, this has meant a surge in newspaper reports, because – at least until very recently – it has been easier for analysts to keep track of coverage in print than electronic media (Best 1999).[6] Implicit is the assumption that a wave of press coverage reflects a corresponding wave in public concern, but there is rarely any supporting evidence, such as public opinion polls, to document shifts in public opinion, let alone in the level of panicky behavior (Ungar 2001).

Here, it helps to recall that the concept of moral panic originated in British sociology, and to appreciate some differences between the U.S. and U.K. newspaper markets. For decades, most American cities have had a single daily newspaper. In contrast, England has several daily papers that effectively serve the entire country. One can go into a newsstand, convenience store, or supermarket and chose among half a dozen or more papers. While these papers vary in terms of political slant and seriousness, and although they are all affected by tighter budgets, they compete for readers' attention to a degree not seen in most American cities for decades (Jenkins 1992; Davies 2008). The resulting coverage strikes American readers as more sensationalistic than typical news in the United States. The basic formula for moral-panic coverage – a story that uses shocking language to warn about some alarming new phenomenon – occurs virtually every day, often in more than one story, in most British newspapers. Moreover, since there are fewer reporters, all of the papers share the sources for much of their news, so that there is a good chance that any story (e.g., shag bands) that finds its way into one paper will be picked up by several others – seeming proof of widespread concern. In other words, fairly routine newspaper coverage can seem to support analysts' claims about moral panics, particularly in the absence of opinion polls or other evidence that might be used to assess the overall level of public attention and concern. It is, then, easy to claim to have spotted a moral panic, and quite difficult to question such claims.

Conservatism

Finally, the classic moral panic – particularly in the U.K. – is understood to be an expression of politically and morally conservative values.[7] The Mods and the Rockers were viewed as out-of-control youth, threatening the established social order, while shag bands herald the spread of sexual immorality and promiscuity into childhood.

Here, it is important to appreciate that, especially during the final decades of the twentieth century, British sociology became more overtly political than its American counterpart. To be sure, the bulk of sociologists in both countries have long been more liberal than conservative, but British sociologists' analyses have been far more likely to link social processes to current events, to particular political episodes in the histories of Thatcherism, New Labour, and so on.

This has led to a difference in American and British sociologists' approaches to moral panics. American sociologists hear the term as moral *panic*; that is, they emphasize the disproportionate reactions to the alleged threat. In contrast, British scholars are more likely to think of these as *moral* panics, that is, concerns rooted in conventional morality. This explains Stuart Waiton's (2008) conceptual innovation: the *amoral* panic, which refers to fears, often promoted by authorities on the left, that are grounded in a rhetoric of science and risk, rather than moralism – the dangers posed by antisocial behavior, second-hand smoke, and so on. In Waiton's view, moralizing is the essence of the moral panic.

In sum, the classic conception of the moral panic was shaped by social conditions in the U.K. It was understood to refer to concerns – such as those over Mods and Rockers and shag bands – that were: (1) short-lived; (2) exaggerated, even irrational; (3) evidenced by heightened and sensationalistic media – and particularly newspaper – coverage; and (4) rooted in moral conservatism. Like crime wave or drug scare, the concept allowed analysts to locate particular concerns within a more general conceptual category.

The expansive use and questionable value of moral panic as a concept

Despite the conceptual trouble with moral panic, it has proved to be malleable. Sociologists have trouble defining concepts with precision, and it is common for an analyst to devise a new concept to characterize some particular phenomenon (often chosen because it is an extreme case that offers an especially clear illustration of the concept). If the concept catches on, other analysts often apply the term to an everwider range of phenomena. Of course, as a concept is applied to an ever broader range of phenomena, its meaning becomes less precise. In extreme cases, almost everything is understood to be within the term's meaning, and the concept loses whatever analytic usefulness it may have once had. Thus, once enthusiasts began insisting that almost all families are dysfunctional, then 'dysfunctional family' became little more than a synonym for 'family,' so that the utility of characterizing families as dysfunctional vanished.

The definition of moral panic offered by Cohen was vague. It could fit virtually any claim about a troubling condition – Mods and Rockers and shag bands to be sure, but also claims about rape, secondary smoke, or climate change. In practice, of course, sociologists are unlikely to speak of a moral panic about rape or climate change because most sociologists sympathize with these claims. Moral panic is an invidious label; to call something a moral panic is to diminish its legitimacy as an object of concern, to hint that such concern is irrational, or at least overblown. Thus, sociologists hesitate to use the term to describe causes they support: 'one reads of very few instances of moral panic analysis being applied to episodes where the underlying moral concern appears to be shared by the sociologists who invoked the term' (Garland 2008: 22). Thus, in the immediate aftermath of the September 11 terrorist attacks, sociologists were reluctant to term the reaction a moral panic (Walker 2002) but, as disenchantment with the War on Terror spread among liberals, concern about terrorism began to be designated a moral panic (Victor 2006). In other words, moral panic lacks a precise definition that allows analysts to identify and label specific phenomena as moral panics. There is a very loose definition which might be applied to all sorts of concerns, and an unspoken agreement to limit that application to claims with which the analyst – and the sociological audience – are unsympathetic.

The result is a term applied to a very wide range of cases. While the classic moral panic may be short lived, Goode and Ben-Yehuda's *Moral Panics* devotes a chapter to 'The Renaissance Witch Craze.' They call this 'a classic, historical instance of the moral panic,' although they concede it lasted 'an unusually long time for a moral panic' (Goode and Ben-Yehuda 2009: 169). Further, they acknowledge: 'It flared up at one time and place and subsided, burst forth later in another location and died down, and so on. A heated, continent-wide, panic-like craze spanning nearly three centuries is simply not sustainable' (Goode and Ben-Yehuda 2009: 42). It is not clear whether they envision this a single moral panic, or a series of localized panics.

In the classic moral panic, concern is irrational, or at least out of proportion, but this is a shifting standard; as we have seen, the decision to label concern as a moral panic seems to have more to do with the analysts' sympathies than some clear standard of proportionality. The classic moral panic is played out in the press, and analysts remain dependent on finding available sources, even though they fail to address how their own methods shape what does and does not become the subject of analysis. Also, the presumption that the classic moral panic is rooted in conservative moralizing is not addressed explicitly, although it remains apparent in the selective application of the term to concerns toward which sociologists feel little sympathy.

Some theorists have sought to move beyond the classic model of moral panic. For instance, there have been efforts to reconceptualize moral panics in term of moral regulation, governance, moralization, and risk (Critcher 2009; Hier 2008). Thus, Hier (2008) argues that moral panics reflect 'volatility of moralization' (i.e., campaigns to encourage citizens to both manage their own behavior so as to reduce risks, and insist upon responsible behavior from others). This approach argues that moral panics are revealed in policies such as sexual offender registration (whereby what are implicitly understood to be excessive fears are institutionalized). My own view is that these theoretically intricate discussions cannot successfully finesse the underlying problems with the notion of moral panic. They offer no clear definition distinguishing moral panics from other risk-centered concerns (e.g., second-hand smoke); the label continues to be applied both broadly (to encompass formal, institutionalized social control policies) and inconsistently (only to concerns that the analysts mean to question). The analysts' language may be more sophisticated, but the underlying problems with the concept remain.

In short, sociologists have used the concept of moral panic, but the concept's history follows the trajectory of other sociological concepts.[8] A vague definition has allowed analysts to apply the concepts to an ever broader range of examples ('Moral panics vary in intensity, duration, and social impact' [Garland 2008: 13]), until its meaning is both unclear (because the phenomena labeled moral panics are so diverse) and disingenuous (in that the use of the concept seems driven largely by unstated ideological assumptions). Like other sociological concepts, moral panic's meaning seems increasingly unclear. Some clarification is in order.

Moral panic as a type of social problem

One way to clarify – and specify – the nature of moral panic might be to locate the concept within the constructionist sociology of social problems. Constructionists intentionally define social problems broadly, as a general process; according to the best-known definition, social problems are 'the activities of individuals or groups making assertions of grievances and claims with respect to some putative conditions' (Spector and Kitsuse 1977: 75). It is important to appreciate that these are *putative* conditions, meaning that the analyst is focused on what is said about those conditions, rather than on the nature of those conditions. As the constructionist literature has evolved, analysts have come to appreciate that claims making is a multifaceted process, that while its domain certainly includes activists demonstrating to draw attention to troubling conditions, it also encompasses scientists and physicians making claims about such conditions, news and entertainment coverage of such claims and conditions, policy-makers seeking to devise formal methods of addressing such conditions, the various workers who must implement those policies, and all of those who evaluate or criticize policies in operation (Best 2008).

This is a large conceptual domain, and it certainly encompasses moral panics. Moral panics – like social problems, at least as they are understood by constructionists – involve a process, a form of societal reaction. The moral panic analyst's skepticism about the rationality of concern is consistent with the notion of a putative condition. However, even the concept's most enthusiastic proponents don't envision moral panics as broadly as constructionists think of social problems. Moral panics, then, are best seen as a type of social problem – but what, precisely, does this type involve? Here, it may help to consider some dimensions of social problems.

Duration

Social problems claims endure for various lengths of time. Some are short-lived campaigns that briefly attract attention before fading from view; others endure as concerns, sometimes for centuries. The former can originate with any willing claims maker who can assemble an audience. While short-lived claims can originate with social activists, many begin in the media (for example, crime waves often come to attention when news reports claim to identify some pattern in criminality) (e.g., Fishman 1978). The rise of the blogosphere has democratized this process; a blog gives an otherwise ordinary individual a media forum for making claims (Maratea 2008). In contrast, social problems constructions that endure usually involve ownership, people who take responsibility for continuing to press the issue. When a well-established social movement assumes ownership of an issue, this means not only continually calling for action, but also the movement gaining recognition as the authoritative voice for the cause, so that it is sought out for comment by the press and policy-makers whenever the topic attracts notice (Gusfield 1981). And, once a policy is in place, the agents responsible for implementing that policy also can assume ownership; they continue to justify their work as important and call for resources to continue their efforts.

The classic moral panic is, of course, a short-lived, episodic concern, and it makes more sense to restrict the use of the term moral panic to such short-lived social problems. Once a claim leads to some sort of institutional apparatus assuming ownership – an inquisition to ferret out witches, a presidential declaration of war on drugs or terror – the dynamics of making claims and maintaining concern are sufficiently different that the term moral panic no longer seems useful.

Rhetoric

All social problems claims are meant to persuade, to convince some audience to worry about or take action against some troubling condition. That means claims can be analyzed as rhetoric, dissected to determine which arguments are used to make the claim convincing. Claims-making rhetoric often changes over time; for instance, if claims makers discover that their initial arguments aren't effective, they may modify their claims in a search for language that will be persuasive. This means that the social problems process is interactive; claims makers must attend to their audiences' reactions, just as the audiences respond to claims.

Obviously, effective social problems rhetoric varies across time and space. In Puritan New England, for example, it was possible to construct witchcraft as a social problem: in that homogeneously religious world, people understood witchcraft as a real phenomenon and a plausible threat, and they had procedures for detecting witches. Today, when fewer people believe in witches – and even among believers there is probably less agreement about how witchcraft can be detected and addressed – it is far more difficult construct a witch problem. All claims reflect the culture and institutions within which they emerge.

Claims-making rhetoric can feature all manner of elements – disturbing examples, statistical evidence, appeals to values, and so on. For our purposes, we can ask how the rhetoric used to construct moral panics is likely to differ from the rhetoric found in other social problems claims. Several issues suggest themselves.

Substantive focus

One theme that runs through many contemporary social problems claims is inequality. Modern democratic societies are receptive to claims about discrimination based on race, ethnicity, religion, gender, and so on. There is an accepted principle that people have a right to equal treatment, and this principle is frequently extended, so that causes that might have once seemed unreasonable are increasingly seen as legitimate – the rights of homosexuals to marry or at least have legally protected unions, protecting the transgendered from workplace discrimination, and so on. This is a familiar way to construct a social problem: to argue that some group falls victim to some sort of discrimination.

There are of course other, analogous formulas: risk claims (essentially statistical arguments that something increases the likelihood of disease or some other bad outcome); ecological claims (arguments that something – pollution, resource depletion, overpopulation – jeopardizes the balance of nature); and so forth. Each of these formulas can be tied to forms of expertise (e.g., risk claims often come from public health authorities, and ecological claims often begin with environmentalists), to arenas within which the claims emerge, and to other social arrangements.

It helps to think about claims about equality, risk, and ecology because they seem divorced from the category of moral panic.[9] When someone calls for action to protect transgendered individuals from workplace discrimination, or for tougher standards to reduce second-hand smoke, sociologists are unlikely to speak of moral panics. What substantive focus, then, sets moral panics apart from other social problems claims?

Classic moral panics tend to be about *moral* threats, particularly to the *young*. They are framed not in terms of crime, or disease, or risk (all familiar frameworks for contemporary social problems claims), but in terms of morality. Once, morality was discussed in explicitly religious terms – as sin – but this language has fallen out of favor. In contemporary society, moral claims are likely to be articulated in more diffuse terms (e.g., 'That's not right'). And what's right is defined in fairly libertarian terms, so that individuals are presumed to have the right to behave as they wish – so long as they do not harm others. Thus, a broad range of sexual practices that once would have been judged immoral are now seen as matters of individual choice, or at least ignored, so long as the participants are consenting adults.

A principal exception is threats to children. Children are understood to be vulnerable, and in continual need of protection to keep others from taking advantage of them. Moral fears about young people take three basic forms. First, there is concern about adults directly exploiting children, as in the moral outrage directed at pedophiles and child pornographers. Second, there are fears that the larger culture – and particularly popular culture – threatens to corrupt children, as in the long history of fears about the damaging effects of each new form of pop culture directed at children (in which shag bands occupy a recent – if minor – place). And, third, there are worries that the young have been corrupted and are no longer behaving morally (this is perhaps the most common subject for moral panics – the Mod and Rockers threatening the social order, of course, but also all those shag-band-wearing schoolchildren who seem ready to descend into sexual immorality). In sum, the rhetoric of moral panics involves moral claims about threats to young people.[10]

In their defense of moral panic as a useful sociological concept, Goode and Ben-Yehuda (2009) argue that moral panics have a different substantive focus: the folk devil; that is, they argue that moral panics always involve a focus on some category of deviants who are the target of the concern. Other sorts of risks – such as diseases, environmental problems, or economic or political threats 'in the absence of folk devils or evildoers do not touch off *moral* panics' (Goode and Ben-Yehuda 2009: 42 – emphasis in original). This defense faces problems: many moral panics seem to revolve around the moral threats posed by cultural elements (such as shag bands). It seems more useful to focus on the threatened population, rather than the source of the threat.

Evidence

Another element in the rhetoric of social problems construction is evidence. Claims must be documented or supported in some way. Well-established social problems often can produce statistics that imply that experts or authorities support the claims (consider the importance such evidence plays in the construction of climate change as a social problem).

In contrast, moral panics – in part because they are short-lived concerns – rarely have time to develop much in the way of supporting evidence. Many moral panics are assembled from some newsworthy event that is constructed as a typifying example of a larger problem. No one argued that the seaside scuffles between Mods and Rockers were, in and of themselves, particularly momentous, but some people insisted that they were significant as *an instance* of a larger phenomenon (youth out of control), as a harbinger of larger troubles. This represents, in a way, a triumph of the sociological imagination. The news media no longer just report current events; rather, they imply that particular events are part of larger patterns or trends, perhaps not compelling when taken alone, but significant when understood to be exemplars of some bigger problem. Perhaps nothing bad happened to the child of a particular parent worried about shag bands, but who's to say how much hidden damage has been done by the sex-bracelet menace?

In sum, moral panics are not simply short-lived and largely ownerless claims, but they feature moral claims about threats to the vulnerable, supported by minimal evidence.

Claims makers and arenas

I have already noted that social problems claims require claims makers, someone to call attention to a troubling condition. Moreover, they may advance their claims in various arenas (Hilgartner and Bosk 1988). Some claims emerge within media coverage, and they are by definition visible. But claims making occurs in other venues – within particular institutions where the claims are often partially or even entirely obscured from public view (e.g., a congressional subcommittee holds a hearing, a religious denomination addresses church policy, lobbyists meet with officials). Since every arena has a carrying capacity – some finite number of claims that can receive attention at a given time – only a small proportion of social problems claims receive much media coverage. For instance, a newspaper has a finite amount of space – the so-called news hole – for each day's news stories, and editors must decide which of the many available stories deserve coverage, considerations that become more difficult as the number of reporters filing stories and of available column-inches falls (Davies 2008).

Cyber-boosters argue that shrinking newspapers are unimportant, that the Internet offers an infinite carrying capacity where all claims can be heard (Maratea 2008). But the Internet merely shows the logical extension of another trend: as media outlets proliferate, they focus on smaller, targeted audiences. The sizes of the audiences for the network news programs in the broadcast era, when most homes received signals from only a handful of channels, were far greater than any given news show can command in an era when cable and satellite signals deliver dozens, even hundreds of viewing choices. Similarly, there may be millions of blogs, but even the largest are seen by far fewer people than the traditional media reached.

These shifts in the organization of public arenas affect moral panics, because moral panics are understood to be topics of widespread public concern. No matter how panicky the rhetoric emanating from a particular blog or the host of a cable show, the audience attending to the messages is likely to be smaller, and demographically more homogeneous than those for traditional media. Their concerns don't seem to merit being labeled moral panic.

As a consequence, it seems most useful to think of moral panics as claims that originate in media coverage in traditional media, especially newspapers. The media have long been a source for original social problems claims during slow news cycles, but the media are innately fickle, always ready – even eager – to abandon one story in favor of fresher news. Thus, media-generated claims tend not to acquire owners dedicated to keeping the cause alive, and thus wind up being short lived, so that duration and venue tend to be linked.

Moral panic as a useful analytic category

In this chapter I have argued that the term moral panic lacks a precise definition. Theorists have developed the concept of moral panic using typifying case studies of classic moral panics, such as the Mods and Rockers, which were short lived, irrational, media centered, and conservative, the category's boundaries were fluid, and the term came to be applied to all sorts of other phenomena.

My goal has been to argue for a more restricted definition, one that locates moral panic firmly within the larger literature on social problems construction and that recognizes that moral panics are just one type of social problem. Specifically, moral panics are social problems claims that (1) are short lived (because they fail to acquire owners willing to devote resources to keeping an issue alive); (2) feature rhetoric that emphasizes moral threats to the young, and that relies heavily for its evidence on some glaring instance that is understood to stand for a larger, significant moral problem; and (3) are promoted primarily through traditional electronic – and particularly print – media. Our two examples of classic moral panics – the Mods and Rockers and shag bands – fit these criteria.

It may be argued that this characterization is flawed, that it is incomplete. To begin, this conceptualization of panics ignores two of the traditional elements associated with moral panics – irrationality, and conservatism. This is intentional. Both qualities invite the analyst to use moral panic as an invidious label to discount claims with which they feel little sympathy. This is dangerous, because it equates moral panic with exaggerated or distorted claims. The problem here is that – some cynical exceptions aside, most people who advance social problems claims seem to be more or less sincere, that is, they seem to believe that they are pointing to some troubling condition that deserves attention. Of course, not everyone finds these claims convincing. In extreme cases, skeptics may doubt the very existence of the troubling condition. There seem to be sincere people who believe in UFO abductions (even that they themselves have been abducted), or in a conspiratorial satanic blood-cult that conducts tens of thousands of human sacrifices annually, even though skeptics far outnumber believers, and the evidence for these claims is widely discounted. But a large share of social problems claims adopt rhetoric that is intended to make the most compelling case: they point to typifying examples that are, in fact, quite atypical; they promote statistics – numbers that often cannot bear critical scrutiny – that portray the problems as being very large; and so on. Often, they justify these exaggerations as necessary to arouse public concern for what is, they insist, a very serious problem, albeit perhaps not as large or dramatic as their claims make it seem. When analysts argue that claims about moral panics are exaggerated or disproportionate, they ignore the evidence that exaggeration is a fairly common element in all sorts of claims.

Similarly, because sociologists tend to have liberal/left sympathies, they have often been willing to use conservatism as a political litmus test for moral panics. Thus, claims by environmentalists, feminists, or animal rights advocates – regardless of how exaggerated or apocalyptic their rhetoric may be – are not classified as moral panics. Certainly analysts have a right to choose which arguments they wish to critique, but it is not clear that social scientific understanding can be advanced by highlighting questionable claims by one's opponents, while ignoring or excusing parallel errors by one's allies. In short, defining moral panics in terms of either irrationality or conservatism does not serve useful analytic ends.

A second sort of criticism of the conceptualization of moral panic that I've offered is that it is far too narrow, that, in particular, moral panics involve far more than threats to young people. For instance, in his introduction to the third edition of *Folk Devils and Moral Panics*, Cohen identifies seven subjects for moral panics, including anti-immigrant claims. Obviously, immigration can be constructed as a threat to a society's integrity; it is easy to construct claims that we are a people, and we should not be contaminated by outsiders, different from ourselves. In U.S. history, there are three great waves of opposition to immigration: the anti-Irish sentiment in the mid-nineteenth century; the campaign against the 'new immigration' from Southern and Eastern Europe; and the post-World War II concerns about undocumented immigration, particularly from Latin America and Asia. Similarly, we can point to contemporary concerns in European societies: German hostility to Turkish immigration; French concern about immigrants from North Africa; Japanese discomfort with Brazilian immigrant workers; and English worries about immigration from the Caribbean, Asia, and Eastern Europe.

The problem with viewing anti-immigration campaigns as moral panics is precisely that they are so well established. These are not short-lived issues; they are long-lasting disputes, they have owners (in the form of social movements, political parties, and so on), and they are rooted in economic interests (capital tends to favor immigration for the same reason labor often opposes it – immigration increases the labor supply and depresses wages). Often constructed as a social problem, immigration is a familiar issue. To be sure, there may be short-lived, moral-panic-like episodes in which attention focuses on some peculiar case (say, a homicide attributed to an undocumented immigrant), but overall concern with immigration does not seem to fit the pattern that I've suggested characterizes moral panic.

Parallel criticisms apply to labeling other sorts of social problems as moral panics. The concept's enthusiasts tend to promote moral panic as a general term, broadly applicable to all sorts of phenomena. I have argued that this is a mistake, that the further the term's definition is expanded, the less analytic value the concept has. Rather, I have argued that moral panics may be best understood within the broader framework of social problems theory, that a moral panic is a particular type of social problem construction – just as drug scares and crime waves are other types. If we restrict the use of moral panic to short-lived press coverage of moral threats to young people, we specify a pattern that may have its own dynamics, one that can help us better understand how issues emerge, evolve, and disperse.

Notes

1 See www.mirror.co.uk/news/top-stories/2009/09/25/band-them-115875-21698898/
2 See http://query.nytimes.com/gst/abstract.html?res=9F01EFD91E30EE3ABC4F52DFB4668389639EDE
3 See www.nytimes.com/2005/06/30/fashion/thursdaystyles/30rainbow.html
4 Actually, the truth is more complicated. Although the 2009 British press coverage treated shag bands as a new issue, versions of this story had circulated in the U.S., Canada, and Australia for more than five years [e.g., www.encyclopedia.com/doc/1P2–148312.html]. But, for our purposes, we will ignore that complexity.
5 I am not arguing that these four characteristics provide a complete definition of a moral panic, but rather that they are qualities found in classic moral panics. There is, however, some overlap with the five 'crucial elements' of moral panics identified by Goode and Ben-Yehuda (2009: 37–43): heightened concern, hostility toward specific figures, consensus, disproportion, and volatility.
6 The growth of the Internet and the availability of search engines has the potential to transform such research; however, as yet there are no generally accepted methodologies for measuring the spread of concern on the Web.
7 Although the concept's defenders deny that moral panic is an ideologically loaded term ('In the abstract, [moral panic] is politically neutral ... ' [Goode and Ben-Yehuda 2009: 47]), analysts concede that most claims labeled moral panics are grounded in conservatism (Garland 2008). In Altheide's analysis of journalists invoking the concept, 'we found only one instance in which a progressive movement/orientation was challenged as promoting a [moral panic]' (2009: 90–91).
8 The meaning of sociological concepts can be blurred further when usage spreads outside sociology, to other disciplines, and into the general culture. There is some evidence that this is happening with moral panic. One recent collection, *Moral Panics over Contemporary Children and Youth* (Krinsky 2008), features a dozen substantive chapters, only four of which are by sociologists. Of course the term has also made inroads into the popular press, particularly in the U.K., but elsewhere as well; Altheide (2008) surveys how media coverage uses the term.
9 Hier argues that the language of risk figures into contemporary moral panics and that, in particular, Toronto rave advocates managed to challenge claims about the risks of the drug Ecstasy (2002, see also 2008). To be sure, risk rhetoric has become commonplace, but social problems defined primarily in terms of risk are rarely understood as moral panics (while rave opponents may have adopted some risk rhetoric, their campaign also fits classic concerns about a new drug as a moral threat to the young).

10 In the not-so-distant past, moral panics also focused on threats to another vulnerable population: women (e.g., fears of white slavery [Connelly 1980]). The rise of feminism has redefined such protectiveness as a form of gender oppression. But this suggests that it is moral threats to those understood to be vulnerable that is the distinctive feature of moral panics.

References

Altheide, D. (2009) 'Moral Panic: From Sociological Concept to Public Discourse', *Crime, Media and Culture* 5(1): 79–99.
Bartholomew, R. E. (2001) *Little Green Men, Meowing Nuns and Head-Hunting Panics: A Study of Mass Psychogenic Illness and Social Delusion*. Jefferson, NC: McFarland.
Becker, H. S. (1963) *Outsiders: Studies in the Sociology of Deviance*. New York: Free Press.
Best, J. (1999) *Random Violence: How We Talk about New Crimes and New Victims*. Berkeley: University of California Press.
Best, J. (2004) *Deviance: Career of a Concept*. Belmont, CA: Wadsworth.
Best, J. (2006) *Flavor of the Month: Why Smart People Fall for Fads*. Berkeley: University of California Press.
Best, J. (2008) *Social Problems*. New York: Norton.
Blumer, H. (1971) 'Social Problems as Collective Behavior', *Social Problems* 18(3): 298–306.
Clarke, L. (2002) 'Panic – Myth or Reality?', *Contexts* 1 (Fall): 21–26.
Cohen, S. (2002) *Folk Devils and Moral Panics*, 3rd ed. London: Routledge.
Connelly, M. T. (1980) *The Response to Prostitution in the Progressive Era*. Chapel Hill, NC: University of North Carolina Press.
Crichter, C. (2009) 'Widening the Focus: Moral Panics as Moral Regulation', *British Journal of Criminology* 49(1): 17–34.
Davies, N. (2008) *Flat Earth News: An Award-Winning Reporter Exposes Falsehood, Distortion and Propaganda in the Global Media*. London: Vintage.
Downs, A. (1972) 'Up and Down with Ecology – The "Issue-Attention Cycle"', *Public Interest* 28(1): 38–50.
Fishman, M. (1978) 'Crime Waves as Ideology', *Social Problems* 25(5): 531–43.
Garland, D. (2008) 'On the Concept of Moral Panic', *Crime, Media, Culture* 4: 9–30.
Goode, E., and Ben-Yehuda, N. (2009) *Moral Panics: The Social Construction of Deviance*, 2nd ed. Malden, MA: Wiley-Blackwell.
Gusfield, J. R. (1981) *The Culture of Public Problems: Drinking-Driving and the Symbolic Order*. Chicago: University of Chicago Press.
Hier, S.P. (2002) 'Raves, Risks and the Ecstasy Panic: A Case Study in the Subversive Nature of Moral Regulation', *Canadian Journal of Sociology* 27(1): 33–57.
Hier, S. P. (2008) 'Thinking Beyond Moral Panic: Risk, Responsibility, and the Politics of Moralization', *Theoretical Criminology* 12(2): 173–90.
Hilgartner, S., and Bosk, C. L. (1988) 'The Rise and Fall of Social Problems', *American Journal of Sociology* 94(1): 53–78.
Jenkins, P. (1992) *Intimate Enemies: Moral Panics in Contemporary Great Britain*. Hawthorne, NY: Aldine de Gruyter.
Jenkins, P. (1999) *Synthetic Panics: The Symbolic Politics of Designer Drugs*. New York: New York University Press.
Krinsky, C. (ed.) (2008) *Moral Panics over Contemporary Children and Youth*. Burlington, VT: Ashgate.
Maratea, R. (2008) 'The e-Rise and Fall of Social Problems: The Blogosphere as a Public Arena', *Social Problems* 55(1): 139–59.
Reinarman, C. (1994) 'The Social Construction of Drug Scares', pp. 92–104 in P. A. Adler and P. Adler (eds.), *Constructions of Deviance*. Belmont, CA: Wadsworth.
Sacco, V. F. (2005) *When Crime Waves*. Thousand Oaks, CA: Sage.
Spector, M., and Kitsuse, J. I. (1977) *Constructing Social Problems*. Menlo Park, CA: Cummings.

Taylor, I., Walton, P., and Young, J. (1973) *The New Criminology: For a Social Theory of Deviance*. London: Routledge & Kegan Paul.

Trevor-Roper, H. (1969) *The European Witch-craze of the Sixteenth and Seventeenth Centuries and Other Essays*. New York: Harper.

Ungar, S. (2001) 'Moral Panic Versus Risk Society: The Implications of the Changing Sites of Social Anxiety,' *British Journal of Sociology* 52(2): 271–91.

Victor, J. S. (2006) 'Why the Terrorism Scare Is a Moral Panic', *Humanist* 66 (July–August): 9–13.

Waiton, S. (2008) *The Politics of Antisocial Behaviour: Amoral Panics*. New York: Routledge.

Walker, J. (2002) 'Panic Attacks: Drawing the Thin Line Between Caution and Hysteria after September 11', *Reason* 33 (March): 36–42.

Young, J. (1971) 'The Role of the Police as Amplifiers of Deviancy, Negotiators of Reality and Translators of Fantasy', pp. 27–61 in S. Cohen (ed.), *Images of Deviance*. Harmondsworth: Penguin.

4

FRACTIOUS RIVALS? MORAL PANICS AND MORAL REGULATION

Alan Hunt

Introduction

An extended field of inquiry in the sociology of moralization has taken as its starting point two discernible traditions: moral panics and moral regulation. The social construction and mediation of risk has more recently become an important supplement for understanding moralization projects (e.g., Moore and Valverde 2000). The field of moralization is one in which inquiry is directed at forms of popular action involving different kinds of activists who seek to mobilize the concerns, worries, and anxieties of citizens in pursuit of objectives that involve social or moral values. The field of moralization is of continuing importance because it involves controversial claims about the connection between alleged harms, proposed remedies, and the mobilization of anxieties, which raises normative disputes among observers of such projects.

The sociologies of moral panic and moral regulation grew up independently and took little interest in each other. Stanley Cohen's (1972) *Folk Devils and Moral Panics* initially conceptualized moral panic in terms of an episode whereby a condition, person, or group of persons is constructed and presented in a stylized and stereotypical fashion by the mass media, enacted as a threat to societal values and interests, and attended to by a social, legal, and/or political control culture. Following Cohen's original argument that moral panics represent fundamentally inappropriate societal reactions to relatively minor conditions, moral panic scholars have maintained that panics are typically undesirable responses to addressing social issues that involve some combination of exaggeration and disproportional representation between the harm claimed and the remedy pursued. Panic scholars, consequently, have overwhelmingly concerned themselves with counter-posing representations to actual conditions in an effort to identify real sources of anxiety.

The sociology of moral regulation has charted a different path. Rather than seeking to explicate the underlying reason for particular moral actions, moral regulation studies focus attention on the ways that discourses and practices are deployed to act on the conduct of self and other (with analysts trying to maintain evaluative neutrality about the contents of moralizing discourses). Moral regulation involves the deployment of distinctively moral discourses that construct a moralized subject and an object or target that is acted on by means of moralizing practices (Hunt 1999: 6–7). In any specific regulatory project, the weight of the controversy may be about the harm claimed, the remedy proposed, or the anxieties mobilized.

Identified in this way, it seems immediately apparent that the two main approaches to moralization (moral panic and moral regulation) are closely related. The perceived affinity between panics and regulatory processes raises the possibility that, rather than representing two somewhat fractious rivals, the approaches can be harmonized to make complementary contributions to the field of moral politics. Although this is the project explicitly pursued by Sean Hier (2002, 2008) and Chas Critcher (2009), their optimism needs to be tempered because each of the trajectories comes up against a considerable impediment in the form of their difficulty of dealing with the experiential intractability of anxiety.

I should make clear that I am not an innocent newcomer to this debate. I have contributed to and inspired a strand of investigation concerning moral regulation; in doing so, I have had some none-too-positive things to say about the sociology of moral panic. For instance, in *Governing Morals* I disapproved of moral panic because of 'its tendency to import negative normative judgment' (Hunt 1999:19). In this chapter, I will offer a more extended visit to the relationship between moral panic and moral regulation. I will argue that one of the disadvantages of the moral panic approach is that it imports an unwarranted preoccupation with the definition of moral panic. It is a feature of empiricist sociology that the definitional question occupies center stage by posing one or more definitions and then assessing the extent to which the case under discussion meets the definitional requirements. A significant feature of the moral panic literature is that it is preoccupied with debating either the general issue of the defining characteristics of a moral panic or whether or not the instance being examined qualifies as a moral panic. The definitional struggles, moreover, are usually framed in the broader context of explaining what the panic is really about (see, for example, Rothe and Muzzatti 2004). I do not wish to ignore the issue of definitions but, rather than pursuing the 'best' definition, I will argue that some of the problematic features of moral panic accounts are precisely located in definitional questions. I will argue that moral panics should be treated as a special but limited case of the moral regulation framework, and I will advance a case for a united approach that builds on the advantages of both and seeks to discard their weaknesses.

Assessing the two traditions

It is important to recognize that the sociologies of moral panic and moral regulation do not occupy the same terrain; they are not two different approaches to the same or similar phenomena. The moral panic approach starts from the identification of heightened concern about some social issue. It then sets out to explain the dynamic of how the action of social agents stimulates and amplifies a panic that is conceived in terms of some combination of exaggeration and disproportionality between the harm claimed and the remedy pursued. By contrast, the moral regulation approach focuses on a process in which moralizing discourses, techniques, and practices are brought to bear in order to regulate the social groups or practices deemed to be the potential cause of social harm. In other words, whereas panic scholars are preoccupied with tapping into the 'real' source of anxieties that motivate disproportional and exaggerated representations and responses, regulation scholars increasingly emphasize how subjectivities are enacted, promoted, institutionalized, internalized, and performed. Regulatory responses might take the form of a panic, but the latter is by no means typical of the cases to which the moral regulation approach is applied.

The moral panic concept has a somewhat narrower reach than the moral regulation concept. This can be illustrated by projects designed to regulate smoking. Nobody has suggested that anti-smoking campaigns are moral panics (that is, forms of exaggeration involving folk devil construction, blame allocation, and disproportional representation). This is because most of us (by now!) subscribe to the view that smoking is harmful. But a moral regulation line of inquiry into anti-smoking projects can contribute to an understanding of the trajectory of anti-smoking campaigns by drawing attention to the significant shift in the way in which smoking has been moralized. The shift from the earlier emphasis on the ethics of self-control (i.e., 'Just Quit') to one that gives prominence to 'second-hand smoke' has resulted in a move away from treating smoking as a matter of individual choice to the more politically powerful focus on 'harm to others'. The latter has stimulated the much more radical anti-smoking restrictions (bans on smoking in public transport, restaurants, etc.) that are the hallmark of the current phase of the campaign.

Sheldon Ungar's (2001) argument that medical issues such as AIDS and smoking cannot be treated as issues of moral panic or moral regulation because they involve some objective harm is another useful example. Ungar's argument is similar to Cohen's claim that issues like Bovine Spongiform Encephalopathy (BSE) do not fit the moral panic framework because the risk is primarily medical and technical rather than moral (Cohen 2002: xxvi). The weakness of this line of argument is that an increasing number of issues that stimulate some or all of the symptoms of moral panics contain a medical content and involve a moral valence. Ungar misses the important respect in which health issues can and do become both moral panics and objects of moral regulation (but see Hier 2003).

Thus moral panic analyses investigate temporally limited episodes (i.e., volatile eruptions) of claims-making activities, while moral regulation analyses are more conducive to extended time periods and chains of interaction. The strength of the moral panic approach is that it provides a neatly packaged way of engaging with the life histories of panic episodes – exemplified by Cohen's study of the Mods and Rockers. Cohen traced the events and the media coverage that set the panic in motion and followed it through several stages until concern subsided, leaving only Cohen's book as its memorable trace. It is significant that the focus was on the life history of the panic, without attempting to understand the ways that this specific manifestation of youth culture made possible the creation, amplification, and politicization of contending youth gangs as folk devils. Cohen was not concerned to explore the long-term moralizing processes that made possible the articulation of the Mods and Rockers, and his model laid the ground for a series of studies of other single panic incidents – especially those associated with youth culture.

Moral panics: a closer interrogation

To illustrate how the sociology of moral panic cannot be easily integrated into the sociology of moral regulation, I consider some of the deficient constituent elements of moral panic theory for explaining the complexity of moral politics. From a moral regulation perspective, the most troubling feature of the moral panic tradition is that it relies on the importation of negative normative judgments about the target of claims-making activities. Moral panic carries with it a tendency to commit analysts in advance to political disapproval or normative judgment about the issue under consideration. This tendency goes unnoticed because both the author and the reader are assumed to accept the same normative stance. When allegations of satanic ritual abuse or kidnapping of humans by aliens are under examination, it is all too easy to agree on the panic because author and reader agree that such allegations involve unacceptable negative stereotypes.

The moral panic concept is serviceable when the issue at hand is one that 'we' (i.e., liberal-left intellectuals) clearly disapprove of and where 'we' can feel indignant against objectionable moral entrepreneurs or amplified media claims about such issues as 'welfare scroungers' or 'illegal immigrants'. Such judgments are more troubling when the normative status of the folk devil is ambiguous or disputed. Genetically modified (GM) food is a good example. Although I have concerns about the political economy of genetic modification and its impact on third-world agriculture, I have not been convinced that there are any significant health risks associated with GM foodstuffs. Analysts might be inclined to inquire why there has been a moral panic over GM food, but to do so would offend those who sincerely hold the opposite view. What this instance discloses is that we are not going to be able to settle the matter by waiting until the evidence is unambiguous. The lesson is thus: at the outset analysts should avoid resting interpretation on the viewpoints of the left-liberal constituencies who have typically made use of moral panic analysis, and we should not feel obliged to abstain from interrogating controversial issues.

Cohen addresses the criticism that moral panic is a normative or value-laden concept applied by left-liberal positions against conservative projects as a way of condemning politically objectionable moral entrepreneurs. He advances an alternative use of moral panic that can be deployed in order to stimulate 'moral panics about mass atrocities and political suffering' in order to critique 'states of denial' by stimulating 'good' moral panics (2002: xxxiii). By this move Cohen provides a link between his early work on deviance and his later engagement with the sociology of atrocities and violation of human rights (Cohen 2001). In so doing, however, he unnecessarily introduces confusion by harnessing the analytic label of moral panic to the normative political project of challenging abuses and atrocities. To introduce a categorical distinction between 'good' and 'bad' moral panics only serves to amplify the criticism about the value-laden character of moral panic. By importing normative judgments at the start of the investigation, he restricts analyses to those situations where the investigator has already decided on the conclusion that will be reached (e.g., satanic daycare abuse). Beyond the easy cases that are characterized by widespread agreement about disproportional exaggeration, excluded are the more numerous and important instances where there is a legitimate field of contestation and where we do not know whether or not we approve of the positions taken up by the contesting parties (e.g., the 'terrorist' versus the 'freedom fighter'). If such judgments are to play any part in analyses, they should be part only of the conclusion and not be part of the definitional starting point. Moral panic approaches have partially attempted to deal with this problem by attending to the ways that folk devils fight back (McRobbie 1994). Even with this refinement, however, the scenario remains strongly normative.

A second defining characteristic of moral panic analyses is the definitional criterion of volatility (Hier 2008; Critcher 2009). The claim is that moral panics involve sensational, inflammatory, and spectacular discourse, and that they are eruptive, short lived, and quick to subside. This characteristic certainly works for some of the more classic moral panics such as Mods and Rockers (Cohen 1972), mugging (Hall *et al.* 1978), and satanic abuse (deYoung 1997). However, it is far from clear why a definitional fiat should exclude important, longer-running episodes such as those stimulated by paedophiles, pornography, and sex-violence in the media. While in some instances such cases do involve eruptive phases, by focusing only on these moments analysts take for granted, if not ignore, historical context. Many fields of moral politics are like smoldering fires that lie dormant for long periods only to erupt again not necessarily in the same form, but with changed configurations and points of rupture. They may also link up with some other field of moral politics, exemplified by the long-running moralization of alcohol that has recently been linked with youth, itself a persistent site of moral politics, in the preoccupation with binge drinking in the UK and drunk driving in North America. The failure to attend to the historical context of moral panics is illustrated in Hier's (2008) study that deals with one episode of anti-paedophile vigilantism in one English town in 2000.

Hier goes further in making the rather strange assertion that there has been an 'increasing volatility of moralization today' (2008: 183). Critcher makes a slightly more modest assertion that 'classic moral panics show no sign of abating' (Critcher 2003:148). Unfortunately, neither Hier nor Critcher provides evidence to support these claims, yet they are both confident that volatile moral panic episodes are 'alive and well'. Again, some of the classic moral panics do conform to this pattern, but this is a far from universal feature of the many and varied episodes that have been treated as moral panics in the literature.

There is an alternative to the volatility thesis: inquiry should focus on the historical location of each instance of an apparent moral panic. It is often the case that it is possible to detect a recurrence of related issues in which variant forms of problematizations appear in the historical record. Many dramatic incidents that occasion some of the features of volatility are instances of more deep-seated concerns that exhibit new forms or features. Concern over prostitution has a long history, but over the last decade the focus was first on juvenile prostitutes and then morphed into concerns about sexual trafficking; this shift exhibits a move towards presenting prostitution as a non-voluntary activity. In a similar pattern, we can witness a shift from a generalized concern with sexual representation; my favorite historical case is Anthony Comstock's agitation over lewd postcards purportedly handed out by 'Italians' outside New York schools (Beisel 1997). Protecting 'the young' has always figured prominently. It is not surprising that current anti-pornography movements have not only focused on the dangers of children encountering pornography over the Internet, but have also significantly shifted the focus to children as 'victims' in the new sense as the objects of pornographic representation.

It is evident that many of the specific features that excite panics have a long lineage, as is evident with the specific forms in which 'youth' have long been the target of campaigns of one form or another (Pearson 1983), as have 'gangs', homosexuals, and other assorted triggers of moral outrage. I do not wish to detract from the value of moral panic studies, but rather suggest that the most valuable are those that locate their study in a wider societal process. It is for this reason that *Policing the Crisis* (Hall *et al.* 1978) still stands out as the exemplary study of moral panics. It succeeded in locating a 'classic' moral panic instance of 'mugging' in England in 1971–72 against its political and cultural context, while at the same time projecting forward to predict the rise of the Thatcher law-and-order campaigns and the race politics of the late 1970s.

Perhaps the most important definitional component of the moral panic tradition is, third, Cohen's famous figure of the folk devil. There are innumerable exemplary cases in which the designation resonates with our immediate understanding of panic instances. Yet caution needs to be exercised because to focus the spot-light too sharply on readily identifiable 'folk devils' may prevent the recognition both of the representation of the wider targets of moral outrage and of the fact that even in some of the classic panics it is far from clear exactly who the folk devils are. Cohen's own study of the Mods and Rockers remains fascinating, but David Garland (2008) is correct to ask why it was that the 'Teddy Boys' who strode English streets only a few years earlier did not induce similar outrage. The moral panic framework has too often been used to take up instances where there is an evident folk devil, yet in the absence of inquiry into all the other significant instances of eruptions of moral politics that lack the visibility of folk devils.

One of the most striking cases of an ambiguous 'folk devil' is the 'Bulger case' in 1993, where a two-year-old toddler was abducted from a shopping mall and subsequently murdered by two 10-year-olds. As Hay demonstrates, the case served 'to "narrate" a great variety of morbid symptoms, while unambiguously attributing causality and responsibility to broken homes, irresponsible mothers, the breakdown of traditional morality, and so forth' (Hay 1995: 217). Despite the fact that Hay's analysis is subsumed within the moral panic literature, the example throws considerable doubt on whether or not a moralization of disturbing incidents that mobilizes dispersed social anxieties requires the presence of the hallmark criterion of the folk devil.

A similar, fourth reservation may be registered about that other well-known character in the moral panic drama: the 'moral entrepreneur'. This concept was introduced in Howard Becker's *Outsiders* (1963), after which it became widely adopted throughout deviancy theory and then in moral panic theory, such that little attention has been paid to it. It has served to mark both general disapproval and political critique of agents of moralization in that it implies a loose connection to some unspecified capitalist interest. In particular it has often been used as a stand-in for another favorite target of moral panic analysis: 'the mass media'. The moral entrepreneur concept does effective service where the primary agent of moralization is an active social movement (e.g., Mothers Against Drunk Drivers) or a state agency (e.g., police mobilization against biker gangs). Such cases are apposite, since the agent may benefit financially or from increased access to resources and thus can be plausibly thought of as an entrepreneur. However, the concept is much less serviceable when the active agents seek only to advance the cause they seek to promote (e.g., campaigns against genetically modified food, campaigns against peanuts in schools, etc.). It is preferable to make use of the much more neutral concept of 'agent' and from there to explore the characteristics of the various agents involved in projects of moralization and to examine the interests involved, the alliances formed, and the discourses deployed.

A fifth defining feature of the classical model has been the contention that moral panics are characterized by the disproportion of the reaction to the supposed harm posed by the problematized behavior. An extreme example of disproportional response was the Bush administration's reaction to the terrorist attacks of 9/11; homeland security legislation, the Guantanamo detention center, and rendition for torture overseas have widely been viewed as overreactions (Rothe and Muzzatti 2004). In contrast, Critcher (2003) argues that the response to AIDS did not constitute a moral panic, since the reaction in terms of health policy legislation was not 'disproportional', since the health threat was real. He goes further in arguing that scares over health epidemics or food contamination are not moral panics because they lack folk devils. Both of these strands need to be contested. First, the AIDS crisis did much to construct homosexuals as something very close to folk devils; it legitimized the preaching of an abstention doctrine in sex education and launched a backlash against sexual permissiveness by promoting an overreaction to the 'danger' of heterosexual transmission (Singer 1993). This point could be reinforced by reference to the long-running moralization of sexually transmitted diseases (e.g., in the form of the UK Contagious Diseases Acts in 1864, 1867, and 1869). The link between health scares and moralized reactions does much to underline the hesitation expressed above about whether moral panics 'need' folk devils.

Inspired by Waddington's (1986) critique of the disproportionality criterion, recent commentators (Garland 2008; Young 2009) have raised important empirical questions about how proportionality is to be measured or weighed against some objective measure of the extent of the problem and the harm occasioned. It is all too likely when sociologists disapprove of the reaction and do not wish to take seriously the normative viewpoint of those who are alarmed and anxious, that they will claim that the response is 'out of proportion'. Even if partisanship can be put aside, it will be difficult if not impossible to secure any agreed objective standard against which proportionality can be measured. There is a further problem associated with proportionality: Should the test be whether the proportionality is judged by the harm occasioned or by the level of anxiety experienced by those who press for action? Consider social reactions to the problem of missing children (Best 1990). It is known that a substantial proportion of 'missing' children are fleeing the conditions in their homes, but this in no way assuages the anxiety felt by many parents about the risk of child abduction by paedophiles; any consensus as to proportionality is unlikely. The same goes for contemporary concerns over sexual trafficking; should this be viewed as a moral panic stimulated by the latest form of anti-prostitution activism? It is unlikely that there will be any consensus as to the number trafficked as against those migrating into prostitution. Even if we now 'know' that the early twentieth-century 'white slavery' panic in the US that led to the Mann Act of 1910 relied on grossly inflated claims (Langum 1994; deYoung 1983), this is unlikely to facilitate consensus over current controversies around sexual trafficking.

I propose the radical solution that we should abandon the concern for proportionality, since this is nothing more than a different form of the problem of the normative evaluation of the project itself. If the researcher entirely or partially approves of the project, then there is a strong likelihood that this will result in a measure of approval of the means proposed to realize that goal; this is equivalent to the desired judgment of proportionality. Consideration of the proportionality of response, moreover, often gets linked to the question of whether moral panics are irrational – a final definitional characteristic. This happens particularly when there is an extreme lack of proportionality, as when allegations of satanic abuse of children in daycare facilities led to criminal prosecutions of daycare workers. It seems at first sight that extreme disproportionality is much the same thing as an irrational claim. There is, however, an important distinction. The argument that a project is irrational is about the claim advanced, while proportionality is about the remedy proposed. We can usefully separate out the small number of cases where the allegation is of irrationality (satanic abuse, alien abduction, and witchcraft). There is no reason to have an interest in issues of proportionality; rather, the focus of research attention is almost always likely to be the quite different question of trying to understand the causality of the irrational claim: Why do people believe in alien abduction? Why were claims of satanic abuse directed at daycare workers? The consideration of the two criteria of proportionality and irrationality can be summarized thus: irrationality is about the 'content' of a panic and 'proportionality' is about the response to the panic.

Ressentiment, respectability, and moral hegemony

Having considered some of the deficient constituent elements of conventional, skeptical and revisionist moral panic theory for explaining the complexity of moral politics, I now consider the concept of 'panic' itself. I do so in order to demonstrate how panics can be conceptualized as special kind of moral regulation, and that a broader engagement with the historical trajectory of moralizing projects is necessary for complete understanding. My interpretation of panic differs from Jock Young (2009), who lays the groundwork by introducing the key concepts of *ressentiment* and struggle for moral hegemony. I propose an amendment to Young's approach by suggesting that we need to supplement the strident concept *ressentiment* with the more mellow concept of respectability.

The concept of *ressentiment* has a long lineage that stretches from Nietzsche down through a number of persistent but subordinate strands in twentieth-century social thought (Nietzsche 1989; Scheler 1961; Ranulf 1964; Merton 1957). *Ressentiment* is manifest in diffuse feelings of dislike, hatred, envy, and impotent hostility directed against some social group or stratum. As Merton succinctly expressed it, *ressentiment* is a sour grapes response (Merton 1957:155): an intense emotion of disinterested indignation, in the sense that it does not require that the rejected 'other' actually impinge on the interests of those expressing the rejection. Respectable members of society, for example, need never have encountered drug users to express hostility. More importantly, there is no necessary interest that connects those exhibiting hostility to the disliked other. In one move, this sweeps aside the need for any inquiry about the proportionality or rationality of the response. But at the same time it helps to account for the mercurial eruption of hostility. In this vein, Young (2009: 8) advances the idea of 'triggers' that unleash sensitive feelings of indignation, unfairness, and anguish ('youth' is a persistent trigger; and there is much evidence that recently 'children', particularly 'innocent children' have become important triggers of moral politics).

The concept of *ressentiment* does not imply that all moral intervention emanates from the strongly negative associations of the Nietzschean version of the concept. We also need a somewhat softer conception of *ressentiment* that captures the strong sense of *disapproval* that underlies many moral panics and projects of moral regulation. Stronger sentiments of hatred and envy are mobilized in many classic instances of moral panic, but in other projects milder emotions are sufficient to unleash moral projects.

Of particular importance in promoting moral politics directed against 'lesser' wrongs are sentiments of *respectability* that allow those who feel entitled so to do to express disapproval of others.

A cult of respectability first came to the fore in Victorian society (Harrison 1982; Himmelfarb 1988; Laqueur 1976; Turner 1995). Gusfield presents the rise of temperance in America as a manifestation of 'the efforts of rural, native Americans to consolidate their middle class respectability' (Gusfield 1963: 36–37). Ranulf (1964) developed the thesis that it is this high self-restraint which the lower middle class imposes on itself that generates the envy that only in its sharpest forms manifests in *ressentiment*; crucially it is respectability that provides a self-assurance in the legitimacy of the cultural values of the respectable that distinguishes them from both the upper classes and the lower orders.

Jack Douglas (1970: 3) argues that individuals are concerned with their own moral worth relative to the moral worth of others. One can be moral or respectable only if others are considered immoral or disrespectable. Individuals construct these images of respectability and immorality; they then seek to stigmatize, degrade, and punish the immoral. A competitive struggle occurs to morally upgrade the respectable by morally downgrading others. It is the feelings of respectability and self-control of non-smokers, for example, that provides the justificatory discourse that sustains contemporary anti-smoking projects.

The significance of forms of moral politics that manifest the respectability of the active participants is not only that they construct their targets as 'others', but that they also assert their own hegemonic role. While the radical feminist anti-pornography movement of the 1980 was directed in the first instance at pornographers, the hegemonic project was directed against the eroticization of heterosexuality epitomized by the spread of pornography through popular culture (Dworkin 1981; MacKinnon 1987). This hegemonic role of moral politics is a further reason to resist the tendency of moral panic analysis to focus on singular moral targets. Today's moralization of alcohol and tobacco, for example, is never just about alcohol or tobacco; it is about the assertion of the virtues associated with the celebration of the self-control of the respectable classes. Risk and moralization.

In recent contributions to moralization, Hier (2008) and Critcher (2009) have suggested that it may be fruitful to explore the linkage between moral panics and risk theory. Hier advances the claim that there has been a proliferation of moral panics in risk society, since there are 'ubiquitous anxieties associated with late modern risks' (2008: 187). Some hesitation is needed before endorsing the claim that there has been a quantitative expansion of moral panics. This claim probably stems from an acceptance of Beck's risk society thesis that posits an expansion of the number of global risks (Beck 1992). While it may well be that the global risks arising from science and technology have increased, it is not self-evident that the risks of everyday life have undergone quantitative expansion. Lest we too summarily conclude that contemporary life is suffused with risk and insecurity, it should be remembered that many features of our lives have been rendered significantly more secure and predictable. Rather, we should recognize that there exists a complex dialectic of insecurity and security. It is far from self-evident that it is risks that have intensified; much more likely it is our perception of risk that has become magnified. While we should be cautious about accepting that there are a proliferation of moral panics in risk society, Hier might be correct in drawing attention to the proliferation of anxieties.

I will return to consider some of complex issues involved in the relationship between anxieties and moral politics; in the meantime there are some further issues about risk that require consideration. Ungar, following Beck, argues that the real-world fears and anxieties have expanded, rendering less significant the kinds of anxieties associated with classic moral panics (Ungar 2001). This is unconvincing because it assumes that 'classic' panics were necessarily over matters of major objective risks. This ignores what I take as the shared view of moral panic studies, that there is no necessary inherent importance in the issues which stimulate panic, but that the tradition is always concerned to attend to how it is that some specific stimulus generates a panic response. It may be that Ungar shares a common, but mistaken, view that risks are inherently 'real' or objective; as has been suggested above, this conflates 'risk' with the 'perception of risk'. An instance of this error is evident in David Garland's recent reflections on moral panics when he argues that there is a clear separation between moral panics and risks. Garland's focus is exclusively on Beck's global risks that involve risks to the health and welfare of whole populations (Garland 2008). His distinction is one of scale rather than substance or the type of harm envisioned. For example, the controversy over GM food, although wide ranging in its potential impact, is just as capable of exhibiting all the characteristics of a moral panic. The same is also true of the problems posed by major Beckian risks associated with invasive health epidemics such as avian and swine flu, SARS, and BSE (Lakoff and Collier 2008). While there are undoubtedly objective risks, they have also generated full-blown moral panics, not least because there is conflict between the experts as to how they should be handled. The often-invoked mass culling of domestic poultry or the slaughter of migratory birds can lead to panic symptoms such as attempts to hide life-supporting domestic poultry (Collier and Lakoff 2008).

The increasing prominence of risk analysis has generated an expansion and intensification of the moralization of everyday life. The recent escalation of risk discourses has produced an expansion of calculative approaches to uncertainty and has stimulated insurance and actuarial rationalities; there has also been a tendency for studies of risk to miss the moralization that frequently accompanies the way in which the invocation of risk intervenes in social life. But it is far from clear what kinds of quantification of risks are available. I am troubled by Hier's suggestion that legislation like Megan's and Sarah's laws mandating community notification of the location of sexual offenders serves to make the risk to the community 'collectively calculable' (Hier 2008: 138). I wonder what kinds of calculations he thinks communities make; his own evidence seems to suggest that the most extreme projections are made (if not by 'the community', at least by activists) that lead to vigilantism.

I have argued elsewhere that risk discourses and moral discourses are often found in close association, such that moral discourses function through proxies such that the moral dimension is not excluded, but rather becomes subsumed within discourses whose most evident features are ones that give them utilitarian or objectivist guises (Hunt 2003). This is most evident with respect to medical discourses which present self-evidently 'real' dangers while at the same time moralizing tendencies lurk beneath the surface; the classic instance has been those associated with AIDS which import the moralization of homosexuality and other forms of alleged deviant behavior such as needle sharing by intravenous drug users.

The outcome of this interconnection between moral discourse and risk discourse constitutes an instance of hybridity: the combination of two types of discourse in such a way as to merge their characteristics into a distinctively new form. The most striking feature of the hybridization of morals and risks is the creation of an apparently benign form of moralization in which the boundary between objective hazards and normative judgments becomes blurred. For example, the consumption of alcohol has long been a target of regulatory intervention; this used to be because drinking was deemed 'wrong' for religious or some other moral reason, but during the twentieth century the discourses underwent a fundamental transformation. There has been an increasingly utilitarian focus on 'harm to others', as in the material produced by Mothers Against Drunk Driving (MADD). Alternatively, harm is medicalized as a risk factor in discourses invoking the care of the self; thus the standard U.S. Surgeon General's warning on wine bottles reads: 'According to the Surgeon General women should not drink alcoholic beverages during pregnancy because of the risks of birth defects.' Individuals come to be assessed, or are invited to assess themselves, as being 'at risk'. A new expansionary cycle of responsibilization sets in. Responsibilization refers to a form of governing that discursively imposes specific responsibilities on individuals for their own conduct or for another for whom they are presented as being responsible. Much responsibilization is often entirely conventional; parents for their children, employers for the work of their employees. But the technique lends itself to expansion. Increasingly, pregnant women are responsibilized for the well-being of their fetus by abstaining from an expanding range of 'risky' behaviors.

No longer is it just a matter of taking responsibility for one's own drinking, but we are also called upon to care for the guests. Responsibilization is further compounded by what may be described as waves of expanding legal liability accompanied by prudential insurance and further litigation liability that seeks to protect against the consequences of the increasing risks that arise from the consumption of alcohol. In sum, we witness an expanded problematization of alcohol within which what may be characterized as a 'remoralization' occurs, in which conduct that had not previously been moralized becomes enmeshed in an expanding moralization; for example the responsible employer should no longer serve alcohol at office parties. Alcohol has increasingly been remoralized to such an extent that we probably have entered a 'new temperance' phase.

Risk analysis or assessment has been projected as a technical procedure, but the technical dimensions of risk do not eliminate moral and normative judgments. It is a key component of my argument that risk practices are deeply moralized. As Mary Douglas argues, risk, danger, and sin have been reconnected in contemporary discourses (Douglas 1992: 26). By moralization I mean that social practices are subjected to scrutiny in moral terms requiring judgments about whether practices are 'right' or 'wrong'; this involves appeal to some set of criteria that work through a continuum of evaluation that moves from conduct that is morally neutral, to varying degrees of wrongness or immorality of the practice. This moralization process is a social process in that it is always located within social contexts and relations. It is significant that, despite the scientization of risk assessment, explanations of risks are still frequently grounded in moral discourses that call into play issues of ethnicity, sexuality, and other social stereotypes; the classic exemplar in the case of HIV/AIDS that was moralized as the 'gay disease' of homosexuality and also by overemphasizing the risk of heterosexual transmission.

There is something additional that risk discourses bring forth: they transpose anxieties into an objectivist problematic. The subjectivism inherent in discourses of anxiety is displaced and each anxiety becomes conceived as a 'risk' that is 'real' and is thereby provided with a rational form of legitimization that opens up the possibility of adopting practices of risk avoidance and risk management. In contrast, anxieties alone tend to give voice to the concern that 'something ought to be done', without necessarily specifying any concrete course of action.

Yet there is no guarantee that risk analysis yields reliable quantification; it holds out just such a promise, but all too often it functions as a form of normative judgment. Most significantly, risk serves to objectify anxiety. The Supreme Court of Canada in R. V. Butler (1992) ruled that pornography constitutes a 'significant risk of harm' to women. This formulation provides a more pragmatic justification for censorship than the traditional assertion that pornography is obscene. Yet the court's formulation ensures that it is not necessary to be able to demonstrate that any identifiable harm is caused, merely that there is a risk of such harm. Thus, 'risk' serves merely to widen the catchment of censorship and to weaken the prosecution's burden of proof. This formulation exemplifies the conflation of 'risk' and 'harm' which is a widespread feature of contemporary risk discourses

The particular significance of risks posed as 'moral questions' is that they act as a mechanism of closure by excluding or refusing other forms of discursive interrogation. The first-stage moralizing discourses homogenize a variety of different issues. For example, in recent child pornography debates, the moralizing response has insisted that any photograph of a naked child is pornographic, such that parents are now careful that their children are clothed before taking holiday snapshots at the beach. The second step is the act of closure; the assertion that the issue is a 'moral question' excludes considerations other than issues of moral judgments. Thus, if child pornography is defined as inherently evil, then there can be no space to consider such matters as artistic merit or speech rights. Perhaps the clearest instance is provided by the slogan 'abortion is a moral issue'; this formulation acts as a closure that disallows consideration of any other dimension such as entitlement to exercise self-control over fertility.

In an epoch in which overt moralization runs the risk of being greeted with suspicion, risks are frequently posed in such a way as to downplay a moral dimension by highlighting medical discourses. This has produced a powerful new force, that of medico-moralization. One of the more significant manifestations of such medico-moralization was provided by the 'discovery' of secondary or passive smoking, such that smoking is no longer a choice about personal health, but rather a form of harm imposed on others.

What is the impact of this shift from 'dangerousness' to 'risk' upon the forms and practices of moral regulation? The provisional answer is that the techniques of moral regulation remain much the same as they were in the classical period of moral regulation strategies at the end of the nineteenth century. In so far as there is a difference between these historical forms of moralization it is that contemporary moralization appears superficially more benign, less overtly moralizing. Thus the conjunction of risk discourse with long-standing strategies of moral regulation serves only to change its surface. A society of risk discourses (as distinct from a 'risk society') is far less 'new' than the more extravagant claims of 'risk society' theory.

The proliferation of risks and their concomitant responsibilities produces an opposite response that can involve either a refusal of responsibility or, more significantly, a denial of responsibility that is affected by the transfer of responsibility to others. This alternative reaction I term *deresponsibilization*, which flags those responses to risk in which individuals refuse to accept responsibility for risks resulting from their own choices and instead transfer responsibility and blame onto others. Perhaps the classic instance of deresponsibilization is witnessed among individual smokers who sue tobacco companies, seeking compensation for smoking-related ill-health. We need have little sympathy for the tobacco companies in order to note the significance of the denial of personal responsibility for lifestyle choices such as smoking, which has long been recognized as a significant health risk and which, perhaps more significantly, has been the target of long and sustained campaigns of self-responsibilization. It is, I conclude, evident that moral regulation, as a broader or more inclusive framework than moral panic, is best able to handle the difficult and complex entanglements associated with the problematization of risks and harms. In addition, a moral regulation approach avoids being required to commit to a normative judgment about the phenomenon under investigation.

The concept of moral regulation is not, however, without its own problems. The link between morality and regulation requires attention. In its most positive sense, it draws attention to the association between moral judgment and the social action that results. But to think of the resulting social response in terms of 'regulation' has its problems. It is most appropriate in cases where a social movement seeks to promote legislative intervention as a response to the social problem identified, as when the moralization of drug users stimulates projects for the criminalization of drug use and drug users or, alternatively, the adoption of harm-reduction practices. But since 'regulation' tends to suggest a somewhat formal or at least rule-based mode of intervention, the concept 'moral regulation' is less convincing when applied to informal processes of moralization such as the respectability reaction against smoking and, even more so, to the mechanism of self-control or ethical self-formation, such as those that characterize healthy lifestyle projects. Critcher suggests that the concept 'moral order' may be more helpful to differentiate moral projects (Critcher 2009). He argues that 'binge drinking' cannot be posed as a serious threat to moral order in the way that paedophiles and illegal immigrants can be regarded as more serious. However, this seems to import an ad hoc ranking of moral problems. This is evident if we consider his contention that sexually transmitted diseases are necessarily 'low-ranking' as threats to moral order, but he seems to have forgotten the AIDS panic of the late 1980s! Similarly he insists that while child abuse is 'evil', 'obesity' never will be. Is he so sure? Obesity is fast climbing the slopes of moral condemnation. The idea of a fixed moral league table strikes me as inherently problematic.

Rather than 'moral regulation' or 'moral order,' attention should most fruitfully be focused on the process of moralization itself. Moralization needs to be grounded in Foucault's concept of problematization.

> What I tried to do from the beginning was to analyze the process of 'problematization' – which means: how and why certain things (behavior, phenomena, processes) became a *problem*.
>
> *(Foucault 1988: 17)*

This is precisely what both moral panic and moral regulation studies have all along been addressing. How do social practices come to be brought under scrutiny, moralized, and then acted upon? And to borrow one other element from Foucault, to stress that this action on moralized 'problems' can and does involve projects both of governing others and of self-governance or of ethical self-formation.

Conclusion: the problems with anxiety

Lurking in every discussion of moralization – whether framed by a panic or regulation framework – is the troubling concept of anxiety. In its simplest form, accounts of moral politics always seem to depend on the explanatory power of motivational anxieties. In his reflections on methodological problems associated with moral panic, for instance, Cohen stresses that successful moral panics owe their appeal to their ability to 'find points of resonance with wider anxieties' (2002: xxx). But such 'background anxieties' are not always discernable, and Garland notes the epistemological problem that we rarely have an objective measure of the anxieties mobilized (Garland 2008: 14). Not only is it difficult to provide substantive evidence of the link between background anxieties and any specific target, but in connection with moral panics about drugs, it is likely that the anxiety is not about drugs as such, but about various aspects of the lifestyle attributed to drug users, who are viewed as hedonistic and rejecting of approved social values of work and discipline. All too often the very fact of a social reaction is presumed to 'prove' the presence of anxiety and this compounds the difficulty of proving the existence of such an anxiety (Critcher 2003: 147).

These are important issues but they may not necessitate discarding attention to the link between anxiety and moral politics. In the first instance, it is crucial that attention be focused on 'social anxiety'. This is not the social anxiety addressed by social psychologists focusing on the problems experienced by individuals in sustaining social relationship arising, for example, from shyness. In the present context, social anxiety is taken as referring to anxieties shared by a significant number of people. Thus, while many individuals may be anxious about flying, this is not a 'shared' anxiety and does not generate any call for action; while anxiety about street prostitution in a neighborhood or the location of a needle exchange facility are 'social anxieties'. Beck suggests that it is this 'commonality of anxiety' that generates a 'solidarity from anxiety' that becomes a political force (1992: 49).

It is true that the extent of a social anxiety account cannot be measured in any satisfactory quantitative manner; surveys that report that people are more worried about paedophiles than in the previous year tell us little or nothing. However, such anxieties can be demonstrated to exist, especially where evidence from a variety of different sources is available; for example, complaints recorded by police, letters to newspapers, speeches by politicians, blog sites, etc. provide cumulative evidence of the existence of an anxiety. It is possible to make quasi-quantitative judgments about greater or lesser anxieties. Whether or not such judgments are useful is controversial, but may not be required. My suggestion is that we do not need to attempt to measure a connection between the degree of anxiety and the social reaction that is elicited. Rather, it is sufficient that the presence of a social anxiety acts as a trigger or spark sufficient to ignite a societal reaction. But what remains a problem is that not every social anxiety ignites a reaction. As I have suggested above, caution is needed in pursuing the attempt to link a specific anxiety to some determinate social response. It may be more productive to explore the way in which a social anxiety exhibits a condensation of different discourses that come together to frame a specific target. A good illustration is provided by Lynda Nead's exploration of how the mid-Victorian crisis of empire manifested in the Indian Mutiny of 1857 was linked to a profound concern with domestic immorality signified by prostitution. She justifies her linkage between 'prostitution' and 'empire' by pointing to parallelism of the discourses of moral and dynastic degeneration and the imagery of decline and fall; thus explaining how the two anxieties sustained both a moral and an imperial narrative (Nead 1988: 94).

This approach suggests the potential of invoking the concept of symbolism as employed by Gusfield in his account of the rise of the temperance movement in the US; alcohol was absent from the culture of rural Protestantism but symbolized the lifestyles of the cities, immigrants from Southern Europe, and Catholicism and was thus an entirely appropriate target of moral regulation. Similarly, Stuart Hall's study of 'mugging' explores the phenomenon as a symbolism that incorporates the elements of race, of youth, of violence and of the inner city that 'works' powerfully in a way that provides a convincing link to the wider socio-political currents in British society in the early 1970s. One of the impressive features of *Policing the Crisis*, rare in moral panic studies, is that it pays attention to the aftermath of the mugging epidemic. The study notes that by the end of 1973 the term 'mugging' in its classic form of street robbery by black teens on elderly citizens disappears from the news media, only to return again in 1974, but now in a different form as a synonym for 'hooliganism' and stripped of its racial angle, only to return a few months later as the synonym for black youth crime and flare into a full-blown outbreak of racial confrontation.

What remains as an open and unresolved issue is a satisfactory account of why it is that some episodes of social anxiety unleash eruptions of moral politics while others may continue to simmer, but yield no immediate social action. This chapter suggests that the best we can hope for is that evidence of the aggregation or condensation of social anxieties, moralizing discourses, and potential social forces may provide, if not proof, then at least strong evidence for persuasive accounts of the eruption of episodes of moral panics and moral regulation.

References

Beck, U. (1992) *Risk Society: Towards a New Modernity* [1986] (trans. Mark Titter) London: Sage.
Becker, H. S. (1963) *Outsiders*. New York: Free Press.
Beisel, N. K. (1997) *Imperiled Innocents: Anthony Comstock and Family Reproduction in Victorian America*. New Jersey: Princeton University Press.
Best, J. (1990) *Threatened Children: Rhetoric and Concern with Child-Victims*. Chicago: University of Chicago Press.

Butler, R. V. (1992) 1 S.C.R. 452. Supreme Court of Canada. February 27.
Cohen, S. (1972) *Folk Devils and Moral Panics: The Creation of the Mods and Rockers*. London: MacGibbon & Kee.
Cohen, S. (2001) *States of Denial: Knowing about Atrocities and Suffering*. Cambridge: Polity Press.
Cohen, S. (2002) *Folk Devils and Moral Panics: The Creation of the Mods and Rockers* (3rd ed.). London: Routledge.
Collier, S. J. and A. Lakoff (2008) 'The Problem of Securing Health.' In A. Lakoff and S. J. Collier (eds.), *Biosecurity Interventions: Global Health and Security in Question*. New York: Columbia University Press, pp.173–94.
Critcher, C. (2003) *Moral Panic and the Media*. Buckingham: Open University Press.
Critcher, C. (2008) 'Moral Panic Analysis: Past, Present, and Future', *Sociological Compass*, 2 (4): 1127–44.
Critcher, C. (2009) 'Widening the Focus: Moral Panic as Moral Regulation', *British Journal of Criminology*, 49(1): 17–34.
deYoung, M. (1983) 'Help, I'm Being Held Captive! The White Slave Fairy Tale of the Progressive Era', *Journal of American Culture*, 6(1): 96–99.
deYoung, M. (1997) 'The Devil Goes to Day Care: McMartin and the Making of a Moral Panic', *Journal of American Culture*, 20(1): 19–26.
Douglas, J. D. (1970) 'Deviance and Respectability: Social Construction of Moral Meanings.' In Jack D. Douglas (ed.), *Deviance and Respectability: Social Construction of Moral Meanings*. New York: Basic Books, pp. 3–30.
Douglas, M. (1992) *Risk and Blame: Essays in Cultural Theory*. London: Verso.
Dworkin, A. (1981) *Pornography: Men Possessing Women*. New York: Basic Books.
Foucault, M. (1988) 'On Problematization', *History of the Present*, 4(1): 16–17.
Garland, D. (2008) 'On the Concept of Moral Panic', *Crime, Media, Culture*, 4(1): 9–30.
Gusfield, J. R. (1963) *Symbolic Crusade: Status Politics and the American Temperance Movement*. University of Illinois Press: Urbana.
Hall, S., C. Critcher, T. Jefferson, J. Clarke and B. Roberts (1978) *Policing the Crisis: Mugging, the State, and Law and Order*. London: Macmillan.
Harrison, B. (1982) *Peaceable Kingdom: Stability and Change in Modern Britain*. Oxford: Clarendon Press.
Hay, C. (1995) 'Mobilization Through Interpellation: James Bulger, Juvenile Crime and the Construction of a Moral Panic', *Social and Legal Studies*, 4(2): 197–223.
Hier, S. P. (2002) 'Conceptualizing Moral Panic through a Moral Economy of Harm', *Critical Sociology*, 28(3): 311–34.
Hier, S. P. (2003) 'Risk and Panic in Late Modernity: Implications of the Converging Sites of Social Anxiety', *British Journal of Sociology*, 54(1): 3–20.
Hier, S. P. (2008) 'Thinking Beyond Moral Panic: Risk, Responsibility, and the Politics of Moralization', *Theoretical Criminology*, 12(2): 173–90.
Himmelfarb, G. (1988) 'Manners into Morals: What the Victorians Knew', *The American Scholar*, 57(3): 223–32.
Hunt, A. (1999) *Governing Morals: A Social History of Moral Regulation*. Cambridge: Cambridge University Press.
Hunt, A. (2003) 'Risk and Moralization in Everyday Life.' In Richard Ericson and A. Doyle (eds.), *Morality and Risk*. Toronto: University of Toronto Press, pp. 165–92.
Lakoff, A. and S. J. Collier (eds.) (2008) *Biosecurity Interventions: Global Health and Security in Question*. New York: Columbia University Press.
Langum, D. J. (1994) *Crossing Over the Line: Legislative Morality and the Mann Act*. Chicago: University of Chicago Press.
Laqueur, T. W. (1976) *Religion and Respectability: Sunday Schools and Working Class Culture 1750–1850*. New Haven: Yale University Press.
MacKinnon, C. A. (1987) *Feminism Unmodified: Discourses on Life and Law*. Cambridge, Mass: Harvard University Press.

McRobbie, A. (1994) 'Folk Devils Fight Back', *New Left Review*, 203: 107–16.
Merton, R. K. (1957) 'Social Structure and Anomie.' In *Social Theory and Social Structure*. Glencoe, Ill: Free Press, pp. 131–60.
Moore, D. and M. Valverde (2000) 'Maidens at Risk: Date Rape Drugs and the Formation of Hybrid Risk Knowledge Formats', *Economy and Society*, 29(4): 514–31.
Nead, L. (1988) *Myths of Sexuality: Representations of Women in Victorian Britain*. Oxford: Blackwell.
Nietzsche, F. (1989) *On the Genealogy of Morals* (ed. Richard Schacht). Cambridge: Cambridge University Press.
Pearson, G. (1983) *Hooligan: A History of Respectable Fears*. London: Macmillan.
Ranulf, S. (1964) *Moral Indignation and Middle Class Psychology: A Sociological Study* [1938]. New York: Schocken Books.
Rothe, D. and S. L. Muzzatti (2004) 'Enemies Everywhere: Terrorism, Moral Panic, and US Civil Society', *Critical Criminology*, 12(4): 327–50.
Scheler, M. (1961) *Ressentiment* [1912] (ed. Lewis Coser). Glencoe: Free Press.
Singer, L. (1993) *Erotic Welfare: Sexual Theory and Politics in the Age of Epidemics*. New York: Routledge.
Thompson, K. (1998) *Moral Panics*. London: Routledge.
Turner, M. J. (1995) *Reform and Respectability: The Making of the Middle-Class Liberalism in Early Nineteenth-Century Manchester*. Manchester: Carnegie.
Ungar, S. (2001) 'Moral Panic versus the Risk Society: The Implications of the Changing Sites of Social Anxiety', *British Journal of Sociology*, 52(2): 271–91.
Waddington, P. A. J. (1986) 'Mugging as a Moral Panic: A Question of Proportion', *British Journal of Sociology*, 37(2): 245–59.
Young, J. (2009) 'Moral Panic: Its Origins in Resistance, Ressentiment and the Translation of Fantasy into Reality', *British Journal of Criminology* 49(1): 4–16.

5

SHIFTING THE FOCUS?

Moral panics as civilizing and decivilizing processes

Amanda Rohloff

Introduction

Drawing from the work of Norbert Elias and the figurational approach to research, this chapter builds on the original concept of moral panic and on the contributions of Alan Hunt (2003, 1999, Chapter 4 this volume), Sean Hier (2002a, 2008) and Chas Critcher (2009). My aim is to assess some of the main assumptions of moral panic research and, specifically, to elaborate on the *developmental* research of Hunt, Hier and Critcher, all of whom conceptualize volatile panic episodes *in relation to* long-term, wider social processes.

I will argue that conceptualizing moral panics as short-term episodes that emerge from long-term moralization processes can be enhanced by shifting the focus of moral panic research towards the work of Norbert Elias. I do not argue that we should develop a strictly 'Eliasian' approach to moral panic at the expense of all the other very important work that has been undertaken in this field (most recently, focusing on the work of Foucault, governmentality and moral regulation). Rather, I highlight how Elias's work is of great value to emerging and more traditional moral panic research.

It is surprising that the work of Norbert Elias has been little mentioned in the same context as moral panic; the 'figurational approach' of Elias and, in particular, the concepts of *civilizing processes*, *decivilizing processes* and *civilizing offensives* have much in common with moral panic analyses, albeit there are fundamental differences. The first effort to link Elias and moral panic traces to the 1980s with Eric Dunning *et al.*'s work on football hooliganism.[1] However, this early work did not attempt to develop a synthesis of Elias and moral panic; rather, these figurational studies on football hooliganism merely mentioned moral panic in passing, referring to the media's amplification of incidences of football hooliganism and the perceived inappropriate reaction by policy-makers.

We can find shadows of Elias in recent work on moral panic which draws upon Alan Hunt's work on moral regulation (Hunt 1999). While largely rejecting the concept of moral panic, Hunt uses both Elias and Foucault to explore historical projects of moral regulation (campaigns that others might classify as moral panics). In his analysis, Hunt explores how moral regulatory projects work to govern both others and the self. Sean Hier has since taken up Hunt's analysis and applied it to moral panics, arguing that moral panics are volatile episodes that emerge from everyday regulatory projects, where the focus shifts from ethical self-governance to the governance of 'dangerous' others (Hier 2002a, 2002b, 2003, 2008). Chas Critcher (2008, 2009) has also joined the debate, albeit with some disagreement as to the extent to which we can apply the concept of moral regulation to moral panic.

The chapter focuses on using Elias's concepts of civilizing processes, decivilizing processes and civilizing offensives, in combination with the figurational approach to research, to facilitate several shifts in the focus for moral panic research. Elias's approach to research, along with the concepts he developed, enables us to explore panics in relation to long-term and short-term processes and to explore the contradictory, countervailing processes that occur before, during and after panics. This is important because previous moral panic studies, bar a few exceptions, have tended to focus on what happens *during* a panic, and the *impact* a panic may have, while neglecting the *antecedents* to the panic (see Critcher 2003: 26; Rohloff and Wright 2010).

I begin by providing a brief overview of Elias's theory of civilizing and decivilizing processes, before critically discussing the possibility of conceptualizing moral panics as decivilizing processes. In response to the limitations of a narrow conceptualization of moral panics as decivilizing processes (which, I argue, can be applied only to *some* 'classical' moral panic cases), I discuss a dialectical understanding of (de)civilization. Here, I introduce the concept of civilizing offensive, which may involve a fusion of both civilizing and decivilizing trends, as a useful conceptual tool to move beyond a normative dichotomy of 'good' and 'bad' moral panic, and instead to further explore the complex, paradoxical, ambivalent processes that may occur before, during and after moral panics. I then compare Elias's 'figurational approach' to moral panic research, not only fleshing out some of the commonalities between the areas of research, but also highlighting what a figurational approach can add to moral panic research. Specifically, I argue that the concept of 'involvement-detachment' and of 'secondary involvement' facilitate establishing a mode of research that does not entail a normative, debunking presupposition that the reaction (or panic) is inappropriate (although research can still be informative in this regard, as will be discussed later). Elias's approach to research focuses on historical and comparative research; applying his ideas to moral panic research encourages us to comparatively explore empirical examples that do not fit the 'classic' model of a moral panic, which forces us to question many of the assumptions about moral panic, including the normative presupposition. I conclude by using the example of climate change to illustrate several points made throughout the chapter, including how moral panics can be conceived as both civilizing and decivilizing processes (considering both long-term and short-term processes), and how moral panics can be conceived as civilizing offensives – attempts to 'civilize' the 'self' and/or the 'other' – in a time of perceived crisis.

Civilizing processes

In *The Civilizing Process* (2000), Elias explored 'civilization' in two very different ways. First, he explored the development of the *normative* concept of 'civilization': the process whereby one group of people come to see themselves as more 'civilized' than another group of people, thereby enabling these self-identified 'civilized' people to commit acts that at other times would be seen as 'uncivilized' (indeed, the first part of his book is devoted to the 'sociogenesis', or development, of the normative concepts of 'civilization' and 'culture' in everyday language). While Elias did not want to use the term 'civilizing process' to refer to *progress*, he did seek to understand how the concept of 'civilization' in its everyday usage had attained these connotations of 'progress' and 'self-betterment' (as opposed to the 'uncivilized', and the 'barbaric').[2]

In contrast to the normative, everyday understanding of 'civilization', Elias sought to develop a second, more technical and sociological understanding of 'civilization'. In his examination of Western Europe from the Middle Ages, Elias developed his 'central theory' (Quilley and Loyal 2005) of civilizing processes by empirically exploring the interrelationship between long-term changes in standards of behaviour and long-term changes in state-formation and other wider processes.

Following on from the first part of *The Civilizing Process*, 'On the sociogenesis of the concepts of "civilization" and "culture",' Elias explored how the development of the concept of 'civility' played out in notions of what constituted 'civilized' behaviour. He explored these changes in standards of behaviour by analysing etiquette books and other documents, beginning with Erasmus's 1530 publication, 'On Civility in Boys'. Throughout his analysis of these etiquette books, Elias traced an overall pattern of gradual changes in standards of behaviour relating to everyday interactions (e.g., behaviour at the table, blowing one's nose, toileting practices). These books illustrated, for Elias, behaviour that was deemed to be acceptable, or 'civilized', as well as behaviour that was seen as unacceptable, or 'uncivilized'. Elias observed that, over time, certain behaviours that were seen to be more 'animalistic' (such as bodily functions) came to be associated with shame and disgust and were increasingly 'shifted behind the scenes'. At the same time, the regulation of these and other behaviours came increasingly to be regulated by self-control rather than external force. This is what Elias calls the social constraint towards self-constraint.

In relation to state-formation and other wider social processes, Elias traces how competition between various groups of people, with associated conflict between these groups, culminated in the establishment of a monopoly of one group and the eventual formation of a state. This process of state-formation brought with it changes in the way people were connected with one another, leading eventually to greater integration and greater interdependence between people, which brings with it changes in relations between them. As Elias puts it, as people become more reliant upon one another via increasing differentiation and increasing interdependence,

> ... more and more people must attune their conduct to that of others, the web of actions must be organized more and more strictly and accurately, if

each individual action is to fulfill its social functions. Individuals are compelled to regulate their conduct in an increasingly differentiated, more even and more stable manner.

(Elias 2000: 367)

This process, Elias argued, is in part dependent upon a gradual stabilization of a central state authority, with an associated state monopolization over the forces of violence and taxation. These processes, Elias argued, contribute towards a notion of stability, where dangers come to be perceived as fewer and, when they occur, as more predictable (that is, where dangers are known, and so life becomes less uncertain). Elias offers the example of 'When a monopoly of force is formed, pacified social spaces are created which are normally free from violence' (Elias 2000: 369). When violence does occur, it is often either hidden 'behind the scenes' or legitimated in some way by the state.

To summarize, Elias's theory of civilizing processes holds that, as a central state authority grows and gains increasing monopolization over the control of violence and taxation, people come to be increasingly integrated and interdependent with one another. These changes in wider social processes exert pressures towards changes in behaviour, compelling people towards increasing foresight, mutual identification and increased self-restraint, thus contributing to more even, stable behaviours and relations between people. In later works, Elias examined how these changes were intertwined with gradual changes in modes of knowledge, from 'magico-mythical' knowledge towards increasingly 'reality-congruent' knowledge[3] (Elias 2007).

Decivilizing processes

It is important to note that Elias did not regard his theory of civilizing processes as unilinear or inevitable; it was neither a theory of 'progress' nor a proclamation of the superiority of Western 'civilization' (Kilminster and Mennell 2008). Indeed, Elias observed that the process of civilization is 'in a continuous conflict with countervailing decivilising processes. There is no basis for assuming that it must remain dominant' (Elias 2008: 4).

Building on Elias's work, Stephen Mennell has developed some 'possible symptoms of decivilizing'. Put simply, '*De*civilizing processes are what happens when civilizing processes go into reverse' (Mennell 1990: 205) (see also Fletcher 1997). One of the potential 'reversals' that Mennell elaborates on is 'a rise in the level of danger and a fall in its calculability' (Mennell 1990: 215). As Elias argued,

The armour of civilized conduct would crumble very rapidly if, through a change in society, the degree of insecurity that existed earlier were to break in upon us again, and if danger became as incalculable as it once was. Corresponding fears would soon burst the limits set to them today.

(Elias 2000: 532)

In other words, as danger becomes increasingly incalculable, so too people's behaviour changes accordingly – it is perhaps more conducive for your survival if, where there is a great deal of uncertainty surrounding potential danger, you tend to err on the side of caution in relations with the 'social' and the 'natural' world (for example, the 'fight or flight' response).

Stephen Mennell observes that the perception often exists today that we are living in a more violent world. He refers to Geoffrey Pearson's historical study that illustrates the periodic commonality of such 'fears of escalating violence, moral decline, and the destruction of "the British way of life"' (Mennell 1990: 214). Here, Mennell critiques the idea that this qualifies as a decivilizing process, stressing that an *actual* increase in violence may not necessarily be occurring (aside from periodic short-term increases). But perhaps merely the *perception* of an increase in violence may affect the development of other decivilizing trends, as may be the case with some moral panics.

Another possible symptom of decivilizing processes that Mennell suggests relates to 'changes in modes of knowledge':

> During times of social crisis – military defeats, political revolutions, rampant inflation, soaring unemployment, separately or in combination – fears rise because control of social events has declined. Rising fears make it still more difficult to control events. That makes people still more susceptible to wish fantasies about means of alleviating the situation.
>
> *(Mennell 1990: 216)*

In other words, there occurs a shift back from 'reality-congruent' to increasingly 'magico-mythical' knowledge.

These changes may then potentially coincide with changes in behaviour, where certain acts that were formerly seen as 'uncivilized' or 'barbaric' become increasingly more acceptable, where there may occur a shift away from violence 'behind the scenes', back to the re-emergence of violence in the public sphere, where mutual identification between people (or particular groups of people) decreases (Mennell 1990). A classic example of this is Elias's own study of Nazi Germany (Elias 1996). Although, as Mennell observes, these decivilizing trends were only partial reversals: the extermination of the Jews still had to be kept 'behind the scenes' to a certain extent, suggesting that there was still a degree of mutual identification with the Jews (Mennell 1990).

Moral panics as decivilizing processes?

As already mentioned, decivilizing processes may occur where there is a weakening of the state, for example, in the aftermath of social or natural crises. However, with moral panics, there need not be an *actual* weakening, only a *perceived* weakening. This could include the perception that governmental regulations, and the enforcement of those regulations, are failing to control a particular perceived problem; or, conversely, that individuals are failing to regulate their own behaviour and therefore there is a need for a stronger external force (from either within or outside 'the state'[4]) to 'control' these 'uncontrollable' deviants.

A further indicator of decivilizing processes is the increase in the level of danger posed, as well as an increasing incalculability of danger; that is, where danger becomes more prominent and increasingly difficult to predict. In the case of moral panics, it could be argued that the 'exaggeration and distortion' of reporting on phenomena (reporting of both past events and potential future risks) have contributed to a sense that we now live in an increasingly dangerous society, where the occurrence of dangers is perceived to be difficult to predict.

In addition to Mennell's symptoms of decivilizing, Jonathan Fletcher (1997: 83) has proposed three main criteria for decivilizing processes: (1) a shift from self-restraint to social constraint (i.e. governance of the other, rather than self-governance); (2) a shift towards 'less even', 'less stable' patterns of behaviour (i.e. where people's behaviour fluctuates in different situations and with different people, to the point where people's behaviour, and responses to others, become increasingly unpredictable); and (3) 'a contraction in the scope of mutual identification', where people come to identify and empathize with an increasingly smaller group of people. Fletcher goes on to say that these three main criteria 'would be likely to occur in societies in which there was a decrease in the (state) control of the monopoly of violence, a fragmentation of social ties and a shortening of chains of commercial, emotional and cognitive interdependence' (Fletcher 1997: 84). He further adds that these societies would likely be characteristic of Mennell's symptoms of decivilizing (as outlined above).

Rather than regarding moral panics as a *complete* decivilizing process, we can see how perceived increase in danger, and/or perceived failure of central state authority to protect citizens from perceived dangers, may be enough to bring about *partial* decivilizing processes, similar to those outlined above. If a particular issue (danger or threat) becomes highlighted and mass communicated (for example, via the media), fears may increase and danger may come to be perceived as increasingly incalculable with regard to the given issue. In turn, 'folk devils' may be created. During this process, folk devils may come to be increasingly dehumanized and come to be seen as the dangerous 'uncivilized' other, thereby enabling the use of more 'cruel' measures that would, under other conditions, be deemed 'uncivilized'. In the haste to address the given issue, solutions may be proposed that are not necessarily well informed, and may not function adequately to address the given issue; indeed, they may have the unintended consequence of contributing to the problem. In addition, in attempts to alleviate the perceived problem, the state, or even citizens themselves, may draw upon more violent, 'uncivilized' measures in an attempt to try to contain the problem; for example, the development of new laws that may override certain civil liberties, or the development of vigilantism (Rohloff 2008).

However, while the above may apply to *some* cases that have been classified as moral panics, I wish to argue that it is not simply the case that all moral panics are merely decivilizing processes. Indeed, as Elias himself would no doubt have argued, civilizing and decivilizing processes (and thereby, moral panics) are much more complex than this. Potentially, civilizing processes may contribute to the emergence of moral panics, and moral panics may, in turn, feed back into civilizing processes. It is here that we need a shift in the focus of moral panic research in order to attend to the complexity of moral panics.

Civilizing offensives: towards a dialectical understanding of (de)civilization

In his discussion of the complexity of civilizing and decivilizing processes, Robert van Krieken (1998, 1999) draws upon the concept of 'civilizing offensives' (a concept derived from the work of Elias; see Mitzman 1987). Civilizing offensives have been defined as 'deliberate (but not necessarily successful) attempts by people who consider themselves to be "civilized" to "improve" the manners and morals of people whom they considered to be "less civilized" or "barbaric"' (Dunning and Sheard 2005: 280). In this way, 'civilizing offensives' bear a strong resemblance to those moral regulation campaigns that are analyzed by Alan Hunt in *Governing Morals* (Hunt 1999), which, in turn, bear some resemblances to what others have termed 'moral panics' (as well as processes that Howard Becker (1991) earlier termed 'moral crusades' by 'moral entrepreneurs').

Robert van Krieken argues 'for a more *dialectical* understanding of social relations and historical development, one which grasps the often contradictory character of social life' (van Krieken 1998: 132). Here, van Krieken is arguing that processes of civilization can themselves give rise to decivilizing trends in the form of 'civilized barbarism'. To illustrate this point, he draws upon the example of the 'stolen generations' in Australia. In their project to 'civilize' indigenous Australian children, Europeans forcibly removed the aboriginal children from their homes and families in an attempt to make the aboriginal children more like European children (i.e., to 'civilize' them). This project took the form of a 'civilizing offensive', and was carried out in the name of civilization. Civilizing processes were present, with the exception that mutual identification was limited between Europeans and the indigenous population. However, there was still a degree of mutual identification; the 'stolen generations' were integrated amongst the Europeans, rather than obliterated (although other aborigines were killed), and it is important to highlight that this civilizing offensive was carried out, in philanthropic terms, as an attempt to *improve* (as they saw it) the lives of the aboriginals (van Krieken 1999).

Therefore, while 'civilizing offensives' can be compared with projects of moral regulation (and, by extension, episodes of moral panic), they may involve within them a *fusion* of civilizing and decivilizing trends. If we combine this idea of a civilizing offensive involving a fusion of civilizing and decivilizing trends, and then apply it to the concept of moral panic, we can use this to develop a more encompassing concept of moral panic, one that takes account of the complex (civilizing and decivilizing) processes that intertwine before, during and after a moral panic, thereby overcoming the dichotomous, normative conceptualization of moral panics as being *either* 'bad' *or* 'good' panics.[5] One potential way to overcome this normative dichotomy is by integrating some of the aspects of figurational research with moral panic research.

Moral panic and figurational research

A figurational (or process) approach to research is derived from Elias's own approach to research, most explicitly outlined in *What is Sociology?* (Elias 1978), as well as in numerous articles and other publications (for example, see Elias 1956, 1987). Rather than giving an exposition about a figurational approach,[6] I flesh out some of the core assumptions of the approach by comparing figurational research with moral panic research.

Commonalities

There are already many commonalities between figurational research and the concept of moral panic. Both moral panic and figurational research are *processual*, in that they both seek to ask questions about the processes by which something has come to pass. For example, Elias explored how some people came to see themselves as more 'civilized' than others (Elias 2000). With moral panic research, a 'processual model' (Critcher 2003) is used to explore how a particular reaction to a perceived social problem has developed.

The figurational approach and moral panic research also focus on *relations*. The foundations of moral panic within symbolic interactionism and labeling theory have ingrained the concept with a focus on relations between people, including *changing* power relations between the 'control culture' and the 'folk devils' (Ben-Yehuda 2009). Epistemologically, moral panic research sees 'social reality' as constantly in flux — continually contested and forever changing as relations between people change. This is similar to how Elias conceptualizes 'social reality'. Elias was very critical of the notion that one could discover eternal laws about social relations — static laws that are similar to those in the physical sciences. Thinking in terms of *processes*, *relations* and *development*, Elias did not regard the 'nature' of 'social reality' as static and unchanging; rather, he saw it as a continual process of development, resultant from the complex interactions between interdependent players (be they humans, other animals, etc.) (for example, see Elias 1978).

As we have already seen, via the concepts of civilizing processes, decivilizing processes and civilizing offensives, moral panic and figurational research also share an interest in exploring changes in the regulation of behaviour — both regulation of the self and regulation of the other. However, there are several existing points of departure. Rather than viewing these differences in research approaches as problems, I now wish to discuss how these points of departure can be used to further develop moral panic research and to attend to some of the recent criticisms and debates surrounding moral panic.

Points of departure: involvement, detachment and the 'political project'

An important inclusion that figurational research can bring to moral panic research is via the concept of 'involvement-detachment'. Recent debates in the moral panic literature have discussed normativity and the 'political project' of moral panic research. On the one hand, the concept of moral panic, as first developed by Stan Cohen, Jock Young and others, entailed within in it several assumptions about the purpose and focus of moral panic research.[7] As Cohen himself observes:

> It is obviously true that the uses of the [moral panic] concept to expose disproportionality and exaggeration have come from within a left liberal consensus. The empirical project is concentrated on (if not reserved for) cases where the moral outrage appears driven by conservative or reactionary forces ... the point [of moral panic research] was to expose social reaction not just as over-reaction in some quantitative sense, but first, as *tendentious* (that is, slanted in a particular ideological direction) and second, as *misplaced* or *displaced* (that is, aimed – whether deliberately or thoughtlessly – at a target which was not the 'real' problem).
>
> (Cohen 2002: xxxi)

There thus exists an assumption (or presupposition) that, with moral panic research, the reaction to a perceived social problem under investigation is somehow inappropriate and, therefore, wrong. To be sure, some moral panic studies have consisted of analyses of reactions to *imagined* social problems (for example, 'satanic ritual abuse'). However, to have a concept, and a mode of research, that carries with it a debunking presupposition is limited in what it may achieve.

In response to the problem of normativity, as well as other problems, several authors have either rejected the concept altogether or have begun to develop a reconceptualization that attempts to overcome this normative assumption (and other limitations) (Hier 2008). However, the attempt to remove the 'political' aspect of moral panic, informed in part by Foucault, has come with some criticism from others (see Critcher 2008, 2009). It seems that there exists a tension between those who want the concept to retain its political project and those who want to develop a more detached approach to moral panic research.

One way to overcome this apparent divide is through the application of the figurational concept of 'involvement-detachment' (Elias 2007). Elias was very critical of the intrusion of 'heteronomous valuations' into research, and endeavoured to develop sociology into a relatively autonomous 'science' (Elias 1978). Normative ideological intrusions, such as those outlined earlier, could be construed as a type of heteronomous valuation where the researcher's identification with a particular group (in this case, the 'deviants'), combined with a political project to 'liberate' the particular group, may influence the degree to which the researcher can step back and see the development of, in this case, a 'moral panic', as being more than a short-term irrational aberration.

This does not mean that Elias advocated a 'value neutral' sociology, which he would have regarded as an impossible and undesirable task. One can never be completely involved or completely detached. Sociology consists of the study of relations between interdependent people, and a degree of involvement was desirable in order to aid our understanding of human relations. While an initial 'involvement' in something may spark interest to investigate that particular topic, Elias argued that this initial involvement should be accompanied by an attempt at 'stepping back' through a 'detour via detachment'. The idea being that one can contribute to a more 'reality-congruent' knowledge if one is not too constrained by the short-term aim of achieving some political goal (Elias 1978, 2007). If we then apply this to moral panic research, it would mean that when undertaking a 'moral panic study', we would endeavour not to have a prior judgment about what we might find (in terms of the 'appropriateness' of reactions to perceived social problems), nor would it involve any overtly political aim; if a 'political project' were to occur, it would come *after* the research, with the intention of lessening the intrusion of one's own biases upon the research (Rohloff and Wright 2010). In this way, the concept of 'involvement-detachment', while at first glance appearing to be incompatible with moral panic research, may indeed be one way to further develop the concept of moral panic and overcome the normative divide.

The problem of a normative presupposition

While there is nothing wrong with some moral panic research leading to the debunking of claims, it should not be imbued within the concept as a fixed criterion. Otherwise, one runs the risk of having the concept of moral panic determine what the researcher will find. The concept then becomes useless, as it can then be applied only *following* research, rather than used as a guiding principle; it also limits the applicability of the concept. As an illustrative example of this normative presupposition, I recently received reviewers' comments on a manuscript that I had under consideration. The article was on climate change, moral panic and civilization. Despite the fact that I clearly outlined in my paper that I was reconceptualizing moral panic, and was not using it in a debunking capacity, the normative debunking connotations associated with 'moral panic' were ever present in the reviewers' minds, leading them to call me a 'climate change skeptic' and calling my paper a piece of 'climate change denial'. While some may disagree with my application of moral panic to climate change (for various reasons), these comments served to illustrate for me that the concept of moral panic is highly imbued with connotations of irrationality and debunking *at the outset*. Therefore, this reaffirms the necessity for a shift of focus in moral panic research towards an approach that does not entail such a normative presupposition (while still retaining the potential for a 'critical', informative reflection post-analysis), including examination of issues that do not fit the 'classic' moral panic model.

Dichotomous thinking

An additional way in which figurational research differs from much moral panic research is in its attempts to move beyond dichotomous thinking. Another recent debate within moral panic literature has been concerned with the issue of moral panic versus risk society, or moralized social problems versus concerns over 'natural' issues (such as health, the environment). Some authors have argued that 'moral' is somehow seen as a separate sphere. For example, Kenneth Thompson argues, 'Sometimes panics about food (e.g., the BSE scare about infected beef) or health have been confused with panics that relate directly to morals' (Thompson 1998: vii). Such arguments seem to suggest that 'panics about food' cannot contain a moral element (a view echoed by Cohen and Critcher); it is a question of moral panics *versus* risk panics (Ungar 2001). However, others, such as Hunt and Hier, disagree, arguing that risks can be *moralized* and that moral panics themselves involve risk discourses. A question for exploration could be: Why are some moral panic researchers so intent on limiting the applicability of the concept? Can this perhaps tell us something about the *function* of the concept for sociologists, and the *motivations* behind (some) moral panic research? Perhaps a further shift in focus could be on the sociology of the sociology of moral panic?

Short-term campaigns and long-term processes

One way that moral panic research and figurational research can further develop one another is via a fusion of the two. As it currently stands, moral panic research tends to focus on short-term processes, to the relative neglect of how long-term processes relate to short-term episodes of moral panics (Rohloff and Wright 2010).[8] When the time-frame for research is extended, it is often on the *aftermath* of the panic, not on the antecedents that fed into the panic (Critcher 2003). A focus on the short-term also implies a sort of 'epistemic rupture' that constitutes a revolutionary change in the way (some) people may perceive a particular social problem. In some instances, this short-term focus has also placed greater emphasis on the intentional actions of crusading reformers, to the relative neglect of more long-term unplanned developments that may influence the development of a moral panic.

Conversely, figurational research has been criticized for its relative neglect of deliberate intentional campaigns, such as civilizing offensives. Such a criticisim may perhaps be unjust, for Elias conceptualized social development as being a *combination* of intended and unintended developments:

> ... the interweaving of the planned acts of many people results in the development of the social units which they form with each other, unplanned by any of the people who brought them about. But the people who are thus bonded to each other constantly act intentionally, and purposefully from within the course of developments which they have not planned, and with results that feed back into the unplanned course of development. ... a dialectical movement between intentional and unintentional social changes.
>
> *(Elias 1998: 204)*

Nevertheless, the concept of civilizing offensives has received comparatively less attention than that of more long-term unplanned developments associated with civilizing (and decivilizing) processes (Dunning and Sheard 2005: 280). Yet, within a figurational approach, conceptually there exists the possibility to explore the relation between short-term intentional campaigns and more long-term wider social processes – moral panic research may be one way to pursue such an exploration.

Moral panics as civilizing and decivilizing processes: beyond the normative divide

What, then, would a figurational approach to moral panic research look like? And how can moral panics be conceptualized as *both* civilizing *and* decivilizing processes and what would such a conceptualization mean?

A figurational approach to moral panic research might involve exploring the interplay between long-term regulatory processes (moral regulation, or civilizing and decivilizing processes) and short-term campaigns (moral panics). This could involve the study of how various processes have been gradually developing in the long-term, including changes in standards of behaviour, changes in the communication of knowledge, changes in state-formation, changes in social and self-regulation, changing power relations between people. This could then be combined with an exploration of various short-term campaigns (instances of moral panics), and how these short-term campaigns relate to the more gradual wider social processes. Such a focus on long-term developmental research could then provide us with a greater insight into the complex, dialectical processes that develop in relation to moral panics.

As an example, consider the topic of climate change. There has already been some figurational research that has argued that the development of ecological sensibilities could be seen as a type of civilizing process (Quilley 2009; Schmidt 1993). Moral panic research has also been undertaken on the topic of global warming where it is argued that global warming campaigns constitute 'social scares' (a concept derived from moral panics) (Ungar 1992, 1995). One could also argue, perhaps, that certain outcomes of processes of civilization have given rise to decivilizing consequences, in the form of *excess* capitalism and *over*consumption, to the relative detriment of the environment and social life as a whole (see also Ampudia de Haro 2008). Potentially, campaigns surrounding climate change could be used as civilizing offensives, or moral panics, to bring about a civilizing 'spurt'. However, these campaigns could also, potentially, bring with them decivilizing disintegrative processes; for example, via the development of 'good' and 'bad' behaviours into 'good' and 'bad' people (this is already happening, to a certain extent, with some animal rights and environmental activists who prioritize animal/environmental rights over the rights of 'other un-eco-friendly' people, where increasing mutual identification with other animals and the environment goes hand-in-hand with decreasing mutual identification with other people) (for example, see Quilley 2009: 133). So, potentially, moral panics over climate change could be regarded as both civilizing and decivilizing processes.

Moral panics are highly complex processes. To further tap into the complexity of moral panics, it is necessary to abandon some of the former dichotomous thinking regarding moral panics, as it limits our perception about what moral panics might be and what they might entail. Such dichotomies include: moral/risk, rational/irrational, 'good'/'bad', and civilizing/decivilizing. Through collapsing these dichotomies, and expanding the scope of moral panic research to other types of examples, as well as longer time-frames of analysis, we can gain a greater insight into how moral panics develop and how they relate to more long-term processes.

Notes

1 For example, see: Dunning, Murphy and Williams (1986, 1988); Dunning and Sheard (2005); Murphy, Dunning and Williams (1988); Murphy, Williams and Dunning (1990).
2 For introductions to Elias's work, see: Dunning and Hughes (forthcoming); Fletcher (1997); Hughes (2008); Kilminster (2007); Mennell (1998); van Krieken (1998, 2003).
3 It is important to highlight that this shift from 'magico-mythical' to 'reality-congruent' knowledge, like other processual shifts that Elias traces, is never absolute.
4 This could either come from 'official' authorities, such as those of 'the state', or non-state groups, such as social movement or reform groups, vigilante groups, 'terrorist' groups, etc.
5 On the idea of 'good' and 'bad' panics, see Cohen (2002, pp. xxxi–xxxv).
6 For introductions to a figurational approach, see: Bloyce (2004); Maguire (1988); Murphy, Sheard and Waddington (2000). On discussions of method and 'methodology' in Elias's work, see Dunning and Hughes (forthcoming).
7 For further discussion of the sociology of moral panic, see Garland (2008) and Rohloff and Wright (2010).
8 Although some authors, such as Hunt, Hier, and now Critcher, are beginning to address this neglect of the relationship between short-term campaigns and long-term processes via a fusion, of sorts, of moral panic with moral regulation; exploring the relationship between short-term regulatory episodes (i.e., panics) and more long-term projects of moral regulation.

References

Ampudia de Haro, F. (2008). *Discussing Decivilisation: Some Theoretical Remarks*. Paper presented at the First ISA Forum of Sociology: Sociological Research and Public Debate.
Becker, H. S. (1991). *Outsiders: Studies in the sociology of deviance*. New York: Free Press.
Ben-Yehuda, N. (2009). 'Foreword: Moral panics – 36 years on', *British Journal of Criminology*, 49(1), 1–3.
Bloyce, D. (2004). 'Research is a messy process: A case study of a figurational sociology approach to conventional issues in social science research methods', *Graduate Journal of Social Science*, 1(1), 144–66.
Cohen, S. (2002). *Folk devils and moral panics: The creation of the Mods and Rockers* (3rd ed.). London: Routledge.
Critcher, C. (2003). *Moral panics and the media*. Buckingham: Open University Press.
Critcher, C. (2008). 'Moral panic analysis: Past, present and future', *Sociology Compass*, 2(4): 1127–44.
Critcher, C. (2009). 'Widening the focus: Moral panics as moral regulation', *British Journal of Criminology*, 49(1): 17–34.
Dunning, E., and Hughes, J. (forthcoming). *Norbert Elias, sociology and the human crisis: Interdependence, power, process*. Cambridge: Polity Press.
Dunning, E., and Sheard, K. (2005). *Barbarians, gentlemen and players: A sociological study of the development of rugby football* (2nd ed.). London: Routledge.
Dunning, E., Murphy, P., and Williams, J. (1986). 'Spectator violence at football matches: Towards a sociological explanation.' *British Journal of Sociology*, 37(2): 221–44.

Dunning, E., Murphy, P., and Williams, J. (1988). *The roots of football hooliganism: An historical and sociological study*. London: Routledge.
Elias, N. (1956) 'Problems of involvement and detachment', *British Journal of Sociology*, 7(3): 226–52.
Elias, N. (1978). *What is sociology?* New York: Columbia University Press.
Elias, N. (1987). 'The retreat of sociologists into the present', *Theory, Culture & Society*, 4(2): 223–47.
Elias, N. (1996). *The Germans*. Cambridge: Polity Press.
Elias, N. (1998). 'The civilizing of parents.' In J. Goudsblom and S. Mennell (Eds.), *The Norbert Elias reader* (pp. 189–211). Oxford: Blackwell.
Elias, N. (2000). *The civilizing process: Sociogenetic and psychogenetic investigations* (Revised ed.). Oxford: Blackwell.
Elias, N. (2007). *Involvement and detachment (The Collected Works of Norbert Elias, Vol. 8)*. Dublin: University College Dublin Press.
Elias, N. (2008). 'Civilisation.' In R. Kilminster and S. Mennell (Eds.), *Essays II: On civilising processes, state formation and national identity (The Collected Works of Norbert Elias, Vol. 15)* (pp. 3–7). Dublin: University College Dublin Press.
Fletcher, J. (1997). *Violence and civilization: An introduction to the work of Norbert Elias*. Cambridge: Polity Press.
Garland, D. (2008). 'On the concept of moral panic', *Crime Media Culture*, 4(1): 9–30.
Hier, S. P. (2002a). 'Conceptualizing moral panic through a moral economy of harm', *Critical Sociology*, 28(3): 311–34.
Hier, S. P. (2002b). 'Raves, risks and the ecstasy panic: A case study in the subversive nature of moral regulation', *Canadian Journal of Sociology / Cahiers canadiens de sociologie*, 27(1): 33–57.
Hier, S. P. (2003). 'Risk and panic in late modernity: Implications of the converging sites of social anxiety', *British Journal of Sociology*, 54(1): 3–20.
Hier, S. P. (2008). 'Thinking beyond moral panic: Risk, responsibility, and the politics of moralization', *Theoretical Criminology*, 12(2): 173–90.
Hughes, J. (2008). Norbert Elias. In R. Stones (Ed.), *Key sociological thinkers* (2nd ed., pp. 168–83). Houndmills, Basingstoke, Hampshire: Palgrave Macmillan.
Hunt, A. (1999). *Governing morals: A social history of moral regulation*. Cambridge: Cambridge University Press.
Hunt, A. (2003) 'Risk and Moralization in Everyday Life.' In R. Ericson and A. Doyle (Eds.), *Morality and Risk* (pp.165–92). Toronto: University of Toronto Press.
Kilminster, R. (2007). *Norbert Elias: Post-philosophical sociology*. London: Routledge.
Kilminster, R., and Mennell, S. (2008). 'Note on the text.' In R. Kilminster and S. Mennell (Eds.), *Essays II: On civilising processes, state formation and national identity (The Collected Works of Norbert Elias, Vol. 15)* (pp. xi–xxii). Dublin: University College Dublin Press.
Maguire, J. (1988). 'Doing figurational sociology: Some preliminary observations on methodological issues and sensitizing concepts', *Leisure Studies*, 7(2): 187–93.
Mennell, S. (1990). 'Decivilising processes: Theoretical significance and some lines of research', *International Sociology*, 5(2), 205–23.
Mennell, S. (1998). *Norbert Elias: An introduction* (rev. ed.). Dublin: University College Dublin Press. [First published as *Norbert Elias: Civilization and the human self-image*. Oxford: Blackwell, 1989].
Mitzman, A. (1987). 'The civilizing offensive: Mentalities, high culture and individual Psyches', *Journal of Social History*, 20(4): 663–87.
Murphy, P., Dunning, E., and Williams, J. (1988). 'Soccer crowd disorder and the press: Processes of amplification and de-amplification in historical perspective', *Theory, Culture & Society*, 5(3): 645–73.
Murphy, P., Sheard, K., and Waddington, I. (2000). 'Figurational sociology and its application to sport.' In J. Coakley and E. Dunning (Eds.), *Handbook of sports studies* (pp. 92–105). London: Sage.

Murphy, P., Williams, J., and Dunning, E. (1990). *Football on trial: Spectator violence and development in the football world*. London: Routledge.

Quilley, S. (2009). 'The land ethic as an ecological civilizing process: Aldo Leopold, Norbert Elias, and environmental philosophy', *Environmental Ethics, 31*(2), 115–34.

Quilley, S., and Loyal, S. (2005). 'Eliasian sociology as a "central theory" for the human sciences', *Current Sociology, 53*(5): 807–28.

Rohloff, A. (2008). 'Moral panics as decivilising processes: Towards an Eliasian approach', *New Zealand Sociology, 23*(1): 66–76.

Rohloff, A., and Wright, S. (2010). 'Moral panic and social theory: Beyond the heuristic', *Current Sociology, 58*(3): 403–19.

Schmidt, C. (1993). 'On economization and ecologization as civilizing processes', *Environmental Values, 2*(1): 33–46.

Thompson, K. (1998). *Moral panics*. London: Routledge.

Ungar, S. (1992). 'The rise and (relative) decline of global warming as a social problem', *Sociological Quarterly, 33*(4): 483–501.

Ungar, S. (1995). 'Social scares and global warming: Beyond the Rio Convention', *Society and Natural Resources, 8*(4): 443–56.

Ungar, S. (2001). 'Moral panic versus the risk society: The implications of the changing sites of social anxiety', *British Journal of Sociology, 52*(2): 271–91.

van Krieken, R. (1998). *Norbert Elias*. London: Routledge.

van Krieken, R. (1999). 'The barbarism of civilization: Cultural genocide and the "stolen generations"', *British Journal of Sociology, 50*(2): 297–315.

van Krieken, R. (2003). 'Norbert Elias and process sociology.' In G. Ritzer and B. Smart (Eds.), *Handbook of social theory* (pp. 353–67). London: Sage.

Part 2
Examining moral panic studies

Each chapter appearing in Part 2 strives to explicate what is implicit in moral panic studies (i.e., existential antagonisms, social problems constructions, the dynamics of moral regulation, civilizing processes). The chapters flesh out the conceptual foundations of moral panic studies and in doing so develop fuller explanations for panic episodes. Yet each chapter also operates with its own taken-for-granted assumptions concerning the dynamics of moral panics. In the first two chapters of this section, the significance of emotion for moral panic studies is addressed. In the following two chapters, the status of folk devils is interrogated.

Frank Furedi introduces the section by examining the relationship between fearing and morality by building on Rohloff's (Chapter 5) general arguments about perceived threats as decivilizing processes, with their attendant decreases in common or shared meaning, and on Hunt's (Chapter 4) general arguments about the proxies through which moralizing is transmitted. Furedi argues that fear is a cultural idiom for interpreting life. Contemporary discourses of fear have assumed an objective character, largely facilitated by the language and rationality of risk. The objectification of fear has contributed to the decoupling of fear-risk discourses from the grammar of morality and so-called objective risk factors are experienced individually. The privatization of fear through the mediation of risk not only reduces the shared experience of fear but also lends itself to what Goode and Ben-Yehuda conceptualize as horizontal moral panics (see Chapter 2). In this way, Furedi connects the sociology of fear with Hier's (2008) arguments about the importance of moralization in everyday life and with Rohloff's arguments about mutual identification as a mitigating force against moral contestation.

Whereas Furedi focuses on the moral component of moral panic to address some of the extra-discursive emotional dynamics contributing to moral panics, Kevin Walby and Dale Spencer emphasize the panic component. They argue that moral panic researchers neglect the analytical significance of emotion. Moral panic scholars rely on various emotions – fear, hostility, anger – to develop arguments, yet they rarely theorize how emotion works in interaction.

Walby and Spencer begin by addressing problems associated with theorizing emotion in relation to media reporting, disproportionality, and consensus. They argue that we too readily use media as a measure of public concern. What we need to do, they contend, is connect media reporting to a broader set of interactions among court officials, claims makers, folk devils, etc. to avoid monolithic anxiety accounts. Similarly, moral panic analysts' continued reliance on disproportionality creates problems when emotion is taken for granted. Claims about disproportionality obviously rely on emotions such as anger and fear but the analytical place of emotion is assumed in moral panic studies.

To get beyond these problems, Walby and Spencer invoke Young's distinction between short-term volatile surface emotions (resentment) and more deep-seated, longer-term emotions (ressentiment). They maintain that the distinction starts to get us past ongoing problems with the criterion of disproportionality because, as Young says, disproportionality applies to the actual event but not the anxiety/emotion (the latter needs to be somewhat proportional for a panic). The trouble with Young's understanding of emotion, however, is that emotions are taken-for-granted as an a priori, replete with a deterministic character. In other words, emotions do not simply flow from ressentiment; they emerge as actants with their own causal powers and influences (and see Meades, Chapter 9 this volume).

In the next two chapters, the status of folk devils is addressed. In Chapter 8, Mary deYoung reconsiders the status of folk devils in moral panic studies in light of conventional and modern folk devil constructions. Tracing to Cohen and Hall *et al.*, she argues that folk devils have been composed of socially marginal groups that, to some extent, enables their symbolic expurgation in panic episodes. That is, folk devils are composed of groups that were marginalized before their nomination as folk devils. The process of symbolic expurgation based on a clearly defined, vertical moral order is, therefore, relatively straightforward.

Folk devil construction in plural societies complicates conventional explanations. Reminiscent of McRobbie and Thornton's (1995) arguments, deYoung contends that modern folk devil construction entails folk devils who fight back, who are heterogeneous, and whose actions have lasting effects. Beyond McRobbie and Thornton's arguments, however, deYoung argues that the blurring of moral regulation and panic via risk poses broader implications for moral panic theory. If panics are conceptualized as rare and extreme risk discourses within a process of moral regulation, as Critcher (2003) suggests, they have embodied folk devils whose already-existing marginality threatens the moral order and gives rise to social control processes. For deYoung, such conceptualization contributes to the under-theorization of folk devils. But if panics are conceptualized as routine features of moralization in everyday life (Hier 2008), then folk devils need to be reconsidered in light of the conventional criterion of marginality and embodiment. Modern folk devils need not be embodied persons; they can take the form of conditions and issues as well as 'proxies, patsies, or pawns' (to use deYoung's phrase). The challenge for modern analysts, then, is not only to reconceptualize folk devils as active participants in moral panics but also to reconsider and examine the wider politics of risk and moralization.

In the final chapter of the section, James Meades extends deYoung's examination of folk devil, and in doing so begins to address the conceptual core of moral panic studies. Tracing to Cohen's original writings, says Meades, folk devils exist in a dual nature. On the one hand, folk devils are conceptualized as symbolic or discursive representations of harm (phenomenal forms). On the other hand, folk devil representations trace back to real people who exist in material relations with others (essential relations). Meades seeks to reunite the estranged, yet necessary components of folk devil analyses by applying the theoretical method of critical realism.

References

Critcher, C. (2003) *Moral Panics and the Media*. Milton Keynes: Open University Press.

Hier, S. P. (2008) 'Thinking Beyond Moral Panic: Risk, Responsibility, and the Politics of Moralization', *Theoretical Criminology*, 12(2): 173–90.

McRobbie, A., and S. L. Thornton. (1995) 'Rethinking "Moral Panic" for Multi-Mediated Social Worlds', *British Journal of Sociology*, 46(4): 559–74.

6

THE OBJECTIFICATION OF FEAR AND THE GRAMMAR OF MORALITY

Frank Furedi

Introduction

Discourses of fear are pervasive in contemporary western cultures. Fear is frequently represented as a defining cultural mood; a set of popular catch phrases – e.g., politics of fear, fear of crime, fear of the future, fear factor – attests the significance of fear as a cultural idiom for interpreting life. The institutionalisation of discourses of fear through media alerts about health warnings or terrorist threats should not be interpreted as proof that the quantity of fears has increased, however. The perceived tangible reality of a culture of fear merely indicates that fear functions as a historically specific metaphor for making sense of and interpreting a range of experiences.

The normalisation of fear narratives has important implications for students of moral panics. Fear serves as a cultural metaphor to express claims, concerns, values, moral outrage, and condemnation. Yet in the twenty-first century, the authority to allocate responsibility for fear is contested; it is now common for people to blame politicians, institutions, advocacy organisations, and businesses for 'playing the fear card' or for practising the 'politics of fear'. The allocation of blame pertaining to the promotion of fear parallels the tendency to condemn people and institutions for participating in the construction and dissemination of moral panics (see Hunt 1997). In this regard, contemporary representations of fear are closely linked to representations of panics.

The aim of this chapter is to examine the distinct quality of twenty-first-century representations of fear and to explore the relationship between fear and moral panic. I argue that contemporary cultures of fear have three important dimensions. First, in recent decades fearing has become increasingly privatised. Despite a common cultural idiom characterised by the mediation of fear, responses to perceived threats often assume a privatised, individuated character. Discourses of fear, in this regard, are dialectical: they situate individual risk management strategies against collective dimensions of harm. The absence of a shared experience of fearing both exposes and reinforces the relative weakness of a common web of meaning through which western societies make sense of the threats they face. This expresses a tendency towards the disassociation of fearing from the grammar morality – a second important dimension of contemporary fear cultures. The decoupling of fear claims from the language of morality endows fearing with an objective character, and this third dimension of contemporary fear culture has important implications for moral panic theory.

Fear and meaning

The conception of fear employed by social scientists frequently draws on the distinction between fear and anxiety elaborated by Freud in *Beyond the Pleasure Principle*. From Freud's perspective, '*anxiety* relates to the condition and ignores the object, whereas in the word *Fear* attention is focused on the object' (Freud 1952: 103). For example, some studies of the fear of crime have sought to draw a distinction between 'concrete fear, or fear about specific crimes' and 'formless fear that is a general feeling of being unsafe due to crime and disorder in the immediate environment' (Silverman and Della-Giustina 2001: 947). Indeed, social scientists' tendency to represent the state of anxiety rather than the state of fear as the main threat to collective and individual well-being is echoed by Giddens: 'anxiety also differs from fear in so far as it concerns (unconsciously) perceived threats to the integrity of the security system of the individual' (Giddens 1991: 44, 45). Anxiety is conceptualised as a far more destructive condition than fear because it directly touches upon existential security.[1]

The distinction between fear and anxiety has some conceptual utility, particularly in relation to interpreting the response of individuals. However, as Hunt (2003; and see Hunt, Chapter 4 this volume) implies, this distinction is less useful when it comes to analysing wider socio-cultural processes. At the level of social interaction, a response to specific threat interacts with a more diffuse cultural mood. How society fears and the signals it transmits about how people should feel and respond to events is not reducible to the threats it faces. Society-wide sentiments such as the fear of the unknown or of uncertainty or anxiety of the future are processed through the prevailing system of meaning. The conversion of a fear response into a specific event is mediated through cultural norms that inform people about what is expected of them when confronted with a threat and how they should respond and feel (Furedi 2007a).

Yet, all too often, fear is represented as a natural, stand-alone emotion. This naturalistic orientation was systematically presented in the works of Charles Darwin in his 1872 classic, *The Expression of Emotions in Man and Animals*. Darwin concluded, 'fear was expressed from an extremely remote period in almost the same manner as it now is by man' and that this emotional response is 'part of our evolutionary heritage' (Darwin 1998: 308, 362). Naturalistic and ahistorical perceptions of the problem are reinforced by the tendency of every era to interpret its anxieties and fears in taken-for-granted terms. 'Anxiety is part of the human condition because the set of things we love is small compared to the list of things we fear' (Dozier 1998: 139). However, the framing of fear and anxiety in such general terms fails to capture the way they interact with social experience. As Holloway and Jefferson argue, 'the universal condition of anxiety' manifests itself 'differently in particular historical periods and places' (Holloway and Jefferson 1997: 262).

Fearing has its own history. Bourke (2005: 27, 34, 75) reminds us that in the eighteenth century it was death that the English feared the most, but at the end of the nineteenth century the 'dread of being buried alive' haunted people; by the 1950s, the 'fear of pain loomed larger than the fear of the hereafter'. But fear does not always convey negative connotations. The sixteenth-century English philosopher Thomas Hobbes regarded fear as essential for the realisation of the individual and of a civilised society (Robin 2004). For Hobbes, fear constituted a dimension of a reasonable response to new events. Moreover, as late as the nineteenth century, the sentiment of fear was frequently associated with an expression of 'respect' and 'reverence' or 'veneration' (Parkin 1986). From this standpoint, the act of 'fearing the Lord' could have connotations that were culturally valued and affirmed.

Matters are complicated by the fact that the words and expressions used to describe fear are culturally and historically specific. The language we use today represents fear through idioms that are unspecific, diffuse, and therapeutic. Bourke points to the importance of the 'conversion of fear into anxiety through the therapeutic revolution' (Bourke 2005: 191). Anxieties about being 'at risk' or feeling 'stressed', 'traumatised', or 'vulnerable' indicate that an individualised therapeutic vocabulary influences our sensibility of fear. These idioms of individual vulnerability point towards the privatised character of the fear experience.

Yet despite privatising trends, fear is both mediated and regulated through moral norms. High levels of anxiety and the imperative of moral regulation are often associated with one another. The current volatility and proliferation of moralising discourses discussed by Hier (2008: 174) can be understood as symptomatic of a degree of cultural confusion about the assumptions, conventions, and values through which society gains meaning about uncertainty and threat. One important reason for the volatility of moralising and of fearing, says Parkin, is a shift in attitude from a concept of fear that 'encompassed that of respect' to what he calls 'raw fear'. Whereas the former is described as 'institutionally controlled fear', 'raw fear' has more of a free-floating and unpredictable character (Parkin 1986: 158, 159). It is a form of fear that is relatively uncontained by taken-for-granted moral conventions and practices.

Raw fear is bound up with circumstances where cultural authority is weak, diffuse, or contested. In such conditions, 'not knowing' how to respond becomes the norm. The difficulty that society has in bringing meaning to uncertainty is what gives contemporary fear its raw character. The distinction that Parkin made between the predictability of respectful fear and the uncontained trajectory of raw fear can be understood as an expression of the growing tendency to contest the meaning of a threat. Increasingly, the questions of what we should fear and who to blame have become subjects of acrimonious debate. Lack of consensus over the meaning of misfortune bequeaths fearing a private, individuated, and even arbitrary character.

The privatisation of fear

In an important discussion on how culture is used, Ann Swidler observes that people vary greatly in how much culture they apply to their lives (Swidler 2001: 46). But in the very act of using culture, people 'learn how to be, or become, particular kinds of persons'. Swidler claims that such 'self-forming' continually uses the symbolic resources provided by the wider culture. 'Through experience with symbols, people learn desires, moods, habits of thought and feeling that no one could invent on her own' (Swidler 2001: 75). These habits of thought and feeling influence the way individuals make sense of their experience, how they perceive threats, and how they respond to them. Threats are mediated through cultural norms that instruct us how to respond.

Arguably, the mediation of culture is more significant today than in previous times. Individual fears are cultivated through the media and are less and less an outcome of direct experience (Grupp 2003). 'Fear is decreasingly experienced first-hand and increasingly experienced on a discursive and abstract level', Grupp concludes (p. 43), and suggestively notes that 'there has been a general shift from a fearsome life towards a life with fearsome media' (Grupp 2003: 43). This point is echoed by Altheide, who claims that 'popular culture has been the key element in promoting the discourse of fear' (Altheide 2002: 177).

The influence of the discourse of fear is not a direct outcome of the power of the media, however. The cultural dynamics of individuation have encouraged fear to be experienced in a fragmented and atomised form. That is why fear is rarely experienced as a form of collective insecurity in the ways that previous generations experienced fear. Today, conversely, fear is internalised in an isolated form – what Hubbard (2003) characterises as 'ambient fear'. Hubbard notes that this is 'fear that requires us to vigilantly monitor every banal minutia of our lives', since 'even mundane acts are now viewed as inherently risky and dangerous' (Hubbard 2003: 72). Outwardly, it is the flourishing of low-grade fears and risks that captures the imagination. But the real significance of this development is the highly personalised, even arbitrary manner in which fear is experienced.

Bauman argues that postmodernity has privatised the fears of modernity: 'With fears privatized ... there is no hope left that human reason, and its earthly agents, will make the race a guided tour, certain to end up in a secure and agreeable shelter' (Bauman 1992 : xviii). The privatisation of fear encourages an inward orientation towards the self. People interviewed about the personal risks they faced tended to represent 'crisis, fears and anxieties as self-produced and individual problems, the products of "personal biography"' (Tulloch and Lupton 2003: 38).

In the absence of a master-narrative that endows misfortune with shared meaning, people's response to threats has acquired an increasingly subjective and personalised character. A diminished capacity to share meaning endows the act of fearing with an atomised character. The absence of consensus about interpreting adversity encourages competitive claims making about the problems facing society. The consequence of such claims-making activity is to convert underlying uncertainties and anxieties into more tangible fears. It also provides a medium through which claims for resources can be made.

Claims making involves making statements about problems that deserve or ought to deserve the attention of society. A claim constitutes a warrant for recognition or some form of entitlement. Claims demanding that a newly discovered object of fear be taken seriously draw on prevailing assumptions about being at risk. As Joel Best reports, 'how advocates describe a new social problem very much depends on how (they and their audiences – the public, the press, and policy-makers) are used to talking about, already familiar problems' (Best 1999: 164). The narrative of fear provides the idiom for many claims-making activities. There is nothing peculiarly novel about claim-making activities based on fear. Throughout history claim makers have sought to focus people's anxiety towards what they perceived to be the problem. However, the activities of moral entrepreneurs today do not represent simply a quantitative increase over the past. In the absence of a consensus over meaning, competitive claims making is both extensive and intrudes into all aspects of life.

Competitive claims making about the object of fear is intensified by the perpetual contestation of moral norms and values. At a time when competing lifestyles and attitudes towards personal behaviour are subject of acrimonious debate, it is rare for different sections of society to unite against traditional folk devils. In the UK, traditional folk devils (e.g., the paedophile and the anti-social youth) still excite the public imagination, but the pluralisation of competing lifestyle-based moral identities has tended to endow fearing with a more privatised and arguably more volatile character. This development has important implications for the working of moral panics. As McRobbie and Thornton (1995: 573) argue, 'moral panics are now continually contested'. Moral crusaders frequently compete with each other and call into question each other's moralising initiatives. As Hier (2008: 181) suggests, moralization as a project is volatile and not always 'coherently formulated'.

The objectivation of fear

One of the distinguishing features of contemporary fearing is that it appears to have an independent existence. Hunt has noted that, 'risk discourse transposes anxieties into an objectivist problematic' (Hunt 2003: 174). Fear is also increasingly perceived as an autonomous problem. It is frequently cited as a problem that exists in its own right, disassociated from any specific object. Classically, societies associate fear with a clearly formulated threat (e.g., the fear of death or hunger). In such formulations, the threat was defined as the object of such fears. Today, however, we frequently represent the act of fearing as a threat itself.

A striking illustration of this development is the fear of crime. Fear of crime is conceptualised as a serious problem that is to some extent distinct from the problem of crime. As Garland (2001) observes, 'fear of crime has come to be regarded as a problem in and of itself, quite distinct from actual crime and victimization, and distinctive policies have been developed that aim to reduce fear levels, rather than reduce crime' (Garland 2001: 10). Indeed it seems that the fear of crime is 'now recognized as a more widespread problem than crime itself'. (Bannister and Fyfe

2001: 808). A similar point can be made in relation to the fear of terrorism, which often appears to acquire a life of its own (Furedi 2007a).

With the objectification and autonomisation of fear, the task of analysis is to reveal not simply the causes of fearing but also the potential negative consequences of this emotion. This perspective often encourages the strategy of managing feelings of fear rather than sources of the problem. If people feel that their health is at risk, then this fear is often seen as a risk to their well-being (Furedi 2004: 137). Some public health officials depict fear as an independent, quantifiable source of ill-health. According to one account,

> 'the effects of fear are harmful to health, no less than the physical harm from some toxic agent or pollutant, and these can and should be measured and economically quantified to help identify the most efficient approaches to improving public health'.
>
> *(Ropeik 2004: 59)*

The report 'Facing the Fear' (2009), developed by the UK-based charity Mental Health Foundation, is paradigmatic in this respect. It claimed that its poll of 2,000 adults showed that 77 per cent of the respondents found the world more frightening than in 1999. The Chief Executive of this charity concluded that, since 'fear is having a serious negative impact on the mental and physical health of the nation', a 'mental health promotion campaign would be of immense public benefit' (O'Hara 2009: online). In this case warnings about the threat of fear turn fearing itself into a threat, which becomes a problem in its own right.

The objectification of fear is systematically accomplished through the discourse of risk. According to one account, 'fear itself is a risk and must be part of risk-management policy making' (Gray and Ropeik 2002: 106). The legal system in the US and the UK has also internalised this trend and there is a discernible tendency on the part of courts to compensate fear, even in the absence of a perceptible physical threat. As Guzelian noted, in the past 'fright' (i.e., a reaction to an actual event) was compensated, whereas now the fear that something negative would happen is also seen as grounds for making a claim (Guzelian 2004).

The phenomenon widely described as the *politics of fear* can be understood as symptomatic of the autonomisation of fear. It has little to do with any specific object of fear, such as terrorism or unemployment. 'The politics of fear does not imply that citizens are constantly afraid of, say a certain enemy, day in and day out', writes Altheide, who concludes that the 'object of fear might change, but fear of threats to one's security is fairly constant' (Altheide 2006: 20). The autonomisation of fear represents a challenge to the analysis of moral panic. The objectification of fear appears to diminish the role of moral enterprise in its construction. In such circumstances the moral dimension of the response to a fear appeal becomes more difficult to discern.

The disassociation of fearing from the grammar of morality

The estrangement of contemporary western culture from a grammar of morality means that threats and dangers are unlikely to be conveyed in an explicit moral form.

Moral regulation has an amorphous form and is often promoted indirectly through the language of health, science, and risk. Consequently, fear appeals frequently appear as a response to non-moral and scientifically affirmed objective imperatives.[2] The objectification of fear is paralleled by a consciousness that frequently perceives contemporary moral anxieties through the idiom of risk. From this standpoint, the moral dimension of panicking becomes more difficult to discern. Unlike conventional forms of moral panic, which were directed against clearly recognisable folk devils, twenty-first-century anxieties are frequently focused on phenomena that are less tangible and less familiar but whose impact is seen to have catastrophic consequences. The current catastrophic imagination is also drawn towards a growing range of potential 'conditions' that threaten human extinction. Outwardly at least, fear appeals about the dangers of global terrorism, superbugs, or global warming appear to be very different to the traditional targets of moral panics (e.g., juvenile delinquents, drug addicts, single mothers).

Indicative of this trend is Ungar, who writes that whereas 'moral panic is constituted by a relatively small pool of mostly familiar threats', the 'risk society is constituted by a vast number of relatively unfamiliar threats, with new threats always lurking in the background' (Ungar 2001: 276). From this perspective, there is a qualitative distinction between the objective character of the old and new threats. Ungar insists that 'the impact of manufactured accidents' tends 'to be more severe and chronic than those associated with moral panics' (Ungar 2001: 284). He claims that risk society threats appear as far more real than the ones which initiate traditional moral panics. Ungar draws the conclusion that since risk society threats are objective, they should not be conceptualised as the outcome of social construction. 'With risk society accidents being highly unpredictable and uncontrollable, the social constructionist concern with exaggeration is largely undermined as an analytic strategy' (Ungar 2001: 276). Through representing claims about risk society threats as objective ones, Ungar calls into question the moralising imperative element of fear appeals and implicitly endorses the legitimacy of the contemporary culture of fear.

It is ironic that so many serious attempts to engage with the concept of moral panic tend to underestimate or overlook the moral dimension of this experience of fearing. Yet fearing and panicking are highly moral activities. These responses to perceived threats are underwritten by beliefs about values and uncertainties concerning the boundary that separates morality from immorality. How threats are represented and perceived is inextricably linked to the web of meaning through which people make sense of their everyday life. Research carried out on disasters indicates that fear and the intensity with which it is felt are not directly proportional to the physical impact of a specific threat (Furedi 2007b). Fearing is not directly proportional to the intensity of a threat to personal security.

The threats that characterise the so-called risk society often acquire a catastrophic and disorienting dimension precisely because the prevailing systems of meaning find it difficult to make sense of them. Theories of risk society often give expression to this moral confusion and inadvertently affirm the fear culture that dominates our times.

Ulrich Beck, the leading proponent of the risk society thesis, has internalised a narrative of incomprehension towards global threat. In his discussion of global terrorism, Beck argues that we lack a language for making sense of events like 9/11, which in his words symbolises the 'silence of language'. According to Beck, '11th September stands for the complete collapse of language' and 'ever since that moment we've been living and thinking and acting using concepts that are incapable of grasping what happened then' (Beck 2003: 25; Beck 2002: 39). If indeed we lack a language to interpret contemporary reality, it has consequences that go way beyond linguistic difficulties. Language is the most important source of symbolic meaning in everyday life. If we are genuinely lost for words, it has serious implications for our ability to interpret the threats confronting society.

In contrast to risk society theorists, who emphasise the change in the objective status of global threats, Laidi (1998) links the silence of language to what he calls the 'world crisis of meaning'. His observation that the 'need to project ourselves into the future has never been so strong, while we have never been so poorly armed on the conceptual front to conceive this future' provides the context for language of incomprehension with which global threats are addressed (Laidi 1998: 1). The perception that language has collapsed serves as a metaphor for communicating confusions about how to endow experience with meaning. Beck actually goes so far as to argue that 'through our past decisions about atomic energy and our present decisions about the use of genetic technology, human genetics, nanotechnology and computer science, we unleash unforeseeable, uncontrollable, indeed even *incommunicable* consequences that threaten life on earth' (Beck 2003: 257). The formulation 'incommunicable consequences' is used to highlight the claim that society lacks the intellectual resources with which to interpret future trends. Terms like 'incommunicable' compete with words like 'incalculable' and 'unpredictable' to draw attention to the difficulty of giving meaning to contemporary threats.

One of the defining features of our times is that anxiety about the unknown appears to have a greater significance than the fear of known threats. Often politicians and campaigners darkly hint about the grave challenge posed by threats that are perilous precisely because they are unknown. These are threats to which as yet we can give no name and whose trajectory can not be calculated. Zygmunt Bauman gives voice to this vision of unnamed threats when he states that 'by far the most awesome and fearsome dangers are precisely those that are *impossible* or excruciatingly *difficult* to anticipate, the *un*predicted, and in all likelihood *unpredictable* ones' (Bauman 2006: 11). Although this vision is generally communicated through the language of risks, Bauman understands that this sensibility towards unknown dangers is dominated by the idea of evil. 'We resort to the idea of "evil" when we cannot point to what rule has been broken or bypassed for the occurrence of the act for which we seek a proper name' (Bauman 2006: 54; and see Critcher 2009). However, contemporary society rarely engages with moral categories like evil in an explicit form and opts for the apparently more value-neutral and objectified language of science. The idea of transgression is often communicated through an apparently morally neutral language of science.

Risk society theories reflect the objectification of the catastrophic imagination transmitted through popular culture. It appears that it is not moral entrepreneurs but scientists who are responsible for providing the script for our culture of fear. From this objectivist perspective, 'factual' claims trump 'moral' ones and the role of social construction is called into question (Ungar 2001: 277). For example, some sociologists believe that the objective threat to the environment is so serious that constructionist arguments are ethically dubious. As Burningham and Cooper note, social constructionist critiques of risk society panics are attacked for 'denying independent agency to the natural world' and also for holding a position that is 'dangerous and morally wrong' (Burningham and Cooper 1999: 299–300). Yet as Hannigan noted, 'environmental problems do not materialise by themselves: rather, they must be "constructed" by individuals or organisations who define pollution or some other objective conditions as worrisome and seek to do something about it' (Hannigan 1995: 2). The moral condemnation of those who question risk society panics illustrates the trend towards a competitive trajectory. One person's moral panic is for another an example of ethical behaviour.

The tendency to objectify risk society threats encourages the normalisation fears. Indeed some advocates of this approach portray fear promotion as an ethically legitimate and responsible enterprise. Consequently, the risk society thesis also conveys the implication of a warning. 'Paradoxically, scaremongering may be necessary to reduce risks we face' (Giddens 1999). The promotion of fear alerts about scientifically warranted objective risk often serves as conduits for the promotion of moral regulation.

Advocates of the objectifying of risk society threats are inconsistent in their decoupling of moralising from fearing. They regard some forms of the politics of fear as legitimate and indeed indispensable for moral renewal. The belief that social solidarity is far more likely to be forged around a reaction against the bad than the aspiration for the good exercises a strong influence over politicians, opinion-makers and academics. Instead of being concerned about the destructive consequences of the mood of anxiety and fear that afflicts the public, some social theorists regard them as sentiments that can be harnessed for the purpose of forging social cohesion. Beck believes that the threat of global terrorism has this potential. He argues that 'in an age where trust and faith in God, class, nation and progress have largely disappeared humanity's common fear has proved the last – ambivalent – resource for making new bonds' (Beck 2002: 46). This attempt to turn fear into a positive asset has the effect of validating it.

In the UK, Beck's approach is forcefully advocated by Giddens, who self-consciously attempts to reframe people's fear into a resource for moral renewal. He is distinctly upbeat about his project. He claims that 'this is probably the first time in history that we can speak of the emergence of universal values'. Why? Because these values are now driven by the 'heuristic of fear' as we confront the 'threats which humanity has created for itself' (Giddens 1994: 20). From this perspective, scaring the public is represented as an act of civic responsibility. For example, the American political scientist George Marcus asserts that anxiety assists individuals to be more informed citizens. 'Most Americans do not know very much about politics in general or where candidates for office stand on the sundry issues of the day,' he argues. But 'anxious citizens are well informed because the emotional incentives have caused them to grasp the importance of issues in uncertain times', he adds (Marcus 2002: 103–4).

No doubt advocates of campaigns designed to 'raise awareness' of catastrophic risks confronting humanity perceive themselves as implacable foes of the politics of fear promoted by the Bush administration. But those who played the terrorism card and insisted that the risk of catastrophic terrorism required fundamental changes to people's lives do not have a monopoly on the politics of fear. Once fear has become objectified and normalised it serves as a cultural resource for competing claim makers. In a world where 'we raise awareness' but they 'play the fear card', terms like moral panics and the politics of fear need to be handled with care. When fearing is celebrated as a form of civic awareness there is a danger that its connection to moral regulation is overlooked. It may also lead to a selective interpretation of which forms of fearing constitute the foundation for a moral panic.

Discussion

The disassociation of fearing from the grammar of morality does not mean that fearing is absent from moralization. What it signifies is that the contemporary culture of fear finds it difficult to draw on the authority of an uncontested moral code. There are issues – e.g., paedophilia, violent crime – which provoke an explicitly formulated moral outrage. But fear promotion tends to avoid the grammar of morality and communicates its warning through focusing on risks to health, personal well-being, and the environment. Nevertheless, these risk society fear appeals are oriented towards regulating personal behaviour and are no less prescriptive than traditional moral crusades. Indeed, fear entrepreneurs often self-consciously assert the moral authority of their enterprise.

The example of public health campaigns against obesity provides a useful illustration of how a moral crusade turns a physical condition into a moral threat. This is a moral crusade that openly boasts of its mission to alter people's personal behaviour. Public health professionals have no inhibitions about turning a health issue into a moral one, since 'the social stigma attached to obesity is one of the few forces slowing the epidemic' (Roberts 2007). One environmental researcher claims that, 'given the crushing burden of obesity on individuals and society, all potential sources of motivation need to be stressed' (Higgins 2005: 201).

In previous times, religious leaders denounced sinners for being responsible for the misfortune afflicting their community. The twenty-first century has rediscovered the old sin of gluttony, rebranding it in terms of risk. Obesity is a case in point. This is a lifestyle that is deemed inherently morally repugnant and one that possesses grave consequences for humanity. One public health advocate, Ian Roberts, indicts the very pathway to obesity as the beginning of an immoral journey to global destruction. It all starts when someone 'decides to drive rather than walk the half mile to the office, just to get there a few minutes earlier'. Yet this seemingly innocuous small gesture contains the potential for truly dreadful outcomes. Now in full flow, Roberts points out that such a indolent individual might have 'gained a kilogram of fat, and as the weight continues to pile on he eventually finds it harder to move around and is loath to walk or cycle anywhere' (Roberts 2007: online). Slothful fat people waddling around, gasping for air soon become afflicted with 'back pain, arthritis and shortness of breath, or worse', claims the public health professional turned preacher. By now Roberts can not resist really raising the stakes. He warns that obesity 'increases the risk of heart disease, stroke, diabetes, osteoarthritis, infertility, gallstones, and several types of cancer'. What's worse is that obesity also leads to low self-esteem 'which leads to comfort eating and perhaps heavier drinking too'. This descent into existential hell is bad enough, but worse still are the consequences for the environment – 'his greater bulk and higher metabolic rate will cause him to feel the heat more in the globally warmed summers, and he will be the first to turn on the energy-intensive air conditioning' (Roberts 2007: online).

The message of eat less and thereby save yourself and the planet is endorsed by moral entrepreneurs on both sides of the Atlantic. American public health experts and environmentalists frequently join up the two panics. The merging of the two scares is regarded as an effective way of reinforcing the message and thereby strengthening a crusade that is self-consciously targeting people's lifestyles. 'This may present the greatest public health opportunity that we've had in a century,' enthused Jonathan Paz, a health science professor at the University of Wisconsin and president of the International Association for Ecology and Health. According to Paz, obesity is the 'number one epidemic' blighting the US. He claims that the leading causes of death are 'related to either sedentary lifestyle, air pollution or motor vehicle accidents and if we could begin to confront climate change and have greener cities and more walkability and bikeability, we would have increased level of fitness, reduced air pollution, and reduced greenhouse gases'. In recent years the promotion of the obesity–climate change nexus has gained the backing of public health officials.

According to Howard Frumkin, director of the U.S. Center for Disease Control's National Center for Environmental Health/Agency for Toxic Substances and Disease Registry, his organization is evaluating the promotion of the 'co-benefits' of tackling global warming and obesity-related illnesses through encouraging daily exercise like walking to school or work. Frumkin argues that 'a simple intervention like walking to school is a climate change intervention, an obesity intervention, a diabetes intervention, a safety intervention' (cited in Borenstein 2007). In the same vein, one researcher boasts that he can demonstrate that

> 'adopting previously recommended levels of daily exercise by substituting the distances covered during one hour of walking or cycling for car travel could help alleviate three of the most pressing problems that all countries face: oil dependence, climate change and health care'.

(Borenstein 2007)

In his classic study on moral enterprise, Howard Becker concluded that the 'final outcome of the moral crusade is a police force' (Becker 1963: 156). Moral crusaders do not simply argue, they are in the business of promoting the policing of everyday life. Although not yet criminalised, parents of children deemed to be obese face official sanction in the UK. In early November 2008 a six-year-old boy from Derby was taken into care by social workers for being overweight. This was the first time that obesity had been listed by social workers as one of the reasons for taking a child away from its family (BBC 2008: online). But behind the scenes, more and more families are targeted by social services. In October 2008 it was reported that seven obese children had been put into care and that obesity was a factor in at least 20 child protection cases during the previous years (Irvine 2008: online).

Public officials and child protection experts have taken it upon themselves to police the weight of youngsters. Many of them take the view that parents who allow their children to become overweight or obese are actually guilty of child abuse. Back in February 2007, when two men in Cambridgeshire were convicted of causing unnecessary suffering by allowing their dog to become obese, child protection entrepreneurs responded by inviting the state to react the same way to abusive parents. 'We wouldn't treat a dog this way,' argued Tam Fry of the Child Growth Foundation, before stating that since child obesity is a form of abuse, parents should be held to account. Dr Tom Solomon, a doctor at Royal Liverpool University Hospital, pointed out that that since the state punishes parents who do not send their children to school, why not penalize them for making their kids fat? The crusade to expand the meaning of child abuse to encompass obesity has gained significant momentum. Only a few months previously, David Rogers, the public health spokesman for the Local Government Association, announced that 'parents who allow their children to eat too much could be as guilty of neglect as those who did not feed their children at all' (Templeton 2007: online).

The threat of obesity is represented not just as a physical hazard but as a danger to the natural order of things. Public health messages about obesity mutate into a moralising narrative that legitimises new forms of moral regulation. This moral crusade communicates its claims through an alarmist discourse that encourages fearing and panic. For example, the World Health Organization insists that obesity is a 'chronic disease' which has spread like a 'global epidemic'. The crusade against obesity may lack a coherent moral language. But through assigning responsibility and blame in the objective language of science and medicine it accomplishes the mission of moral regulation. In all but name obesity has been recycled as an evil that is used to morally distance us from those who are inferior to us. All that's required is the recruitment of a few more folk devils.

Notes

1 In one of the first explicit studies of fear published in a sociological journal, Riezler drew attention to a 'kind of fear that is not fear of something definite for something definite'. He adds that 'it can be described as fear of everything for everything or of nothing' and

warned that in 'extreme cases this indefinite fear can be more "total" and worse than the fear of death' (Riezler 1944: 490, 491).
2 Fear appeals directed against smoking are paradigmatic in this respect. See Thompson, Barnett and Pearce (2009).

References

Altheide, D.L. (2002) *Creating Fear; News and the Construction of Crisis*. New York: Aldine De Gruyter.
Altheide, D.L. (2006) *Terrorism and the Politics of Fear*. Lanham: AltaMira Press.
Bannister, J. and Fyfe, N. (2001) 'Introduction: Fear and the City', *Urban Studies*, 38(5–6): 807–13.
Bauman, Z. (1992) *Intimations of Post-Modernity*. London: Routledge.
Bauman, Z. (2006) *Liquid Fear*. Cambridge: Polity Press.
BBC (2008) 'Weight Worry Sees Child in Care.' 3 November. http://news.bbc.co.uk/2/hi/uk_news/england/derbyshire/7707165.stm
Beck, U. (2002) 'The Terrorist Threat: World Risk Society Revisited', *Theory and Culture*, 19(4): 39–55.
Beck, U. (2003) 'The Silence of Words: On Terror and War', *Security Dialogue*, 34(3): 255–67.
Becker, H.S. (1963) *Outsiders: Studies in the Sociology of Deviance*. New York: The Free Press.
Best, J. (1999) *Random Violence: How we Talk About New Crimes and New Victims*. Berkeley: University of California Press.
Borenstein, S. (2007) 'Scientiest Suggest Cutting Calories and Carbon Dioxide Could Help Save Lives and Place.' 12 November. http://news.google.com/newspapers?nid=2202&dat=20071119&id=GYYlAAAAIBAJ&sjid=pPQFAAAAIBAJ&pg=4531,1929919
Bourke, J. (2005) *Fear: a Cultural History*. London: Virago.
Burningham, K. and Cooper, G. (1999) 'Being Constructive: Social Constructionism and the Environment', *Sociology*, 33(2): 297–316.
Critcher, C. (2009) 'Widening the Focus; Moral Panics as Moral Regulation', *British Journal of Criminology*, 49(1): 17–34.
Darwin, C. (1998) *The Expression of Emotions in Man and Animals*. Oxford: Oxford University Press.
Dozier, R.W. (1998) *Fear Itself: The Origin and Nature of the Powerful Emotion That Shapes Our Lives and Our World*. New York: Thomas Dune Books.
Freud, S. (1952) *A General Introduction To Psychoanalysis*. New York: Garden City.
Furedi, F. (2004) *Therapy Culture; Cultivating Vulnerability In An Uncertain Age*. London: Routledge.
Furedi, F. (2007a) *Invitation to Terror: The Expanding Empire of the Unknown*. London: Continuum Press.
Furedi, F. (2007b) 'The Changing Meaning of Disaster', *Area; Journal of the Royal Geographic Society*, 39(4): 482–89.
Garland, D. (2001) *The Culture of Control; Crime and Social Order in Contemporary Society*. Oxford: Oxford University Press.
Giddens, A. (1991) *Modernity and Self-Identity: Self and Society in the Late Modern Age*. Cambridge: Polity Press.
Giddens, A. (1994) *Beyond Left and Right*. Cambridge: Polity Press.
Giddens, A. (1999) 'Reith Lecture – Runaway World.' www.fortunecity.com/emachines/e11/86/reith992.html
Gray, M.G. and Ropeik, D.P. (2002) 'Dealing with the Dangers of Fear: The Role of Risk Communication', *Health Affairs*, 21(6): 106–16.
Grupp, S. (2003) 'Political Implications of a Discourse of Fear; The Mass Mediated Discourse of Fear in the Aftermath of 9/11', (unpublished paper: Berlin).
Guzelian, C.P. (2004) 'Liability and Fear', *Ohio State Law Journal*, 65(4), http://papers.ssrn.com/sol3/papers.cfm?abstract_id=526182.

Hannigan, John (1995) *Environmental Sociology: A Social Constructionist Perspective*. London: Routledge.

Higgins, P. (2005) 'Exercise-based Transportation Reduces Obesity, Oil-dependence, and Carbon Emissions', *Environmental Conservation*, 32(3): 197–202.

Hier, S. (2008) 'Thinking beyond Moral Panic: Risk Responsibility, and the Politics of Moralization', *Theoretical Criminology*, 12(2): 173–90.

Holloway, W. and Jefferson, T. (1997) 'The Risk Society in an Age of Anxiety: Situating Fear of Crime', *British Journal of Sociology*, 48(2): 255–66.

Hubbard, P. (2003) 'Fear and Loathing at the Multiplex: Everyday Anxiety in the Post-industrial City', *Capital & Class*, 80: 1–12.

Hunt, A. (1997) '"Moral panic" and moral language in the media', *British Journal of Sociology*, 48(4): 629–48.

Hunt, A. (2003) 'Risk and Moralization in Everyday Life', in R.V. Ericson and A. Doyle, (eds), *Risk and Morality*. Toronto: University of Toronto Press.

Irvine, Chris (2008) 'Seven Obese Children Placed in Canada.' *Daily Telegraph*. 29 October. www.telegraph.co.uk/health/3277298/Seven-obese-children-placed-in-care.html

Laidi, Z. (1998) *A World Without Meaning: The Crisis of Meaning in International Politics*. London: Routledge.

McRobbie, A. and Thornton, S. (1995) 'Rethinking "Moral Panic" for Multi-mediated Social Worlds', *British Journal of Sociology*, 46(4): 559–74.

Marcus, G. (2002) *The Sentimental Citizen; Emotion in Democratic Politics*. University Park, Penn.: Pennsylvania State University Press.

Mental Health Foundation (2009) *Facing Fear*. http://docs.google.com/

O'Hara, M. (2009) 'Nation's Growing Unease "Hindering Recovery".' *Guardian*. 14 April. www.guardian.co.uk/society/2009/apr/14/mental-health-study-fear

Parkin, D. (1986) 'Toward an Apprehension of Fear' in D.L. Scruton (ed.), *Sociophobics: The Anthropology of Fear*. Boulder: Westview Press.

Riezler, K. (1944) 'The Social Psychology of Fear', *The American Journal of Sociology*, 49(6): 489–98.

Roberts, Ian (2007), 'How the Obesity Epidemic is Aggravating Global Warming.' *New Scientist*. 27 June. www.newscientist.com/article/mg19426105.600-how-the-obesity-epidemic-is-aggravating-global-warming.html

Robin, C. (2004) *Fear: The History of a Political Idea*. New York: Oxford University Press.

Ropeik, D. (2004) 'The Consequences of Fear' *EMBO Reports*, vol. 5, special issue.

Silverman, E.B. and Della-Giustina, J.A. (2001) 'Urban Policing and the Fear of Crime', *Urban Studies*, 38(5/6): 941–57.

Swidler, A. (2001) *Talk of Love: How Culture Matters*. Chicago: University of Chicago Press.

Templeton, S.-K. (2007) 'The Thin Line between Poor Diet and Child Abuse.' *The Times*. 25 February. www.timesonline.co.uk/tol/news/uk/health/article1434671.ece

Thompson, L.E., Barnett, J.R. and Pearce, J.R. (2009) 'Scared Straight? Fear Appeal Anti-smoking Campaigns, Risk, Self Efficacy and Addiction', *Health, Risk and Society*, 11(2): 181–96.

Tulloch, J. and Lupton, D. (2003) *Risk and Everyday Life*. London: Sage Publications.

Ungar, S (2001) 'Moral Panic versus the Risk Society: The Implications of the Changing Sites of Social Anxiety', *British Journal of Sociology*, 52(2): 271–92.

7

HOW EMOTIONS MATTER TO MORAL PANICS[1]

Kevin Walby and Dale Spencer

Introduction

The conception of 'panic' that is integral to the moral panic literature has been highly productive for discussing the intensity of public responses to contentious events. Yet, whereas some moral panic analysts argue that the idea of 'panic' should be understood as a metaphor or heuristic (e.g., Young 2009; Critcher 2009), others argue that the panic concept should be abandoned because of various analytical problems (e.g., Hunt 1999). In this chapter, we draw from the sociology of emotions to assess whether 'panic' is the most appropriate object of analysis for scholars interested in volatile public reactions to ostensible crime and deviance.

The chapter contributes to ongoing discussions about how moral panic studies should advance by connecting moral panic scholarship to the sociology of emotions. Moral panic scholars often skip a step or two in their claims about how emotions matter to moral panic analyses. Emotion is not well defined in the moral panic literature, and panic scholars drift from discussing emotion at the individual level, to the collective level, without attention to issues of scale. Several questions remain unanswered: How are emotions generated at the individual level? How are emotions experienced and shaped at the collective level? And how do emotions contribute to action (e.g., violence) as well as a sense of community?

In what follows, we argue that emotions are best conceptualized as neither cause nor effect, but rather immanent to a set of embodied symbolic interactions *in situ*. We explain how moral panic scholars would be better off empirically investigating what emotions do, how emotions align certain communities against others, and how emotions move people towards certain (sometimes violent) actions against others whose actions pose alleged harms. To understand how emotions work, moral panic scholars need to develop methodological strategies (some of which are available in the sociology of emotions) to comprehend interactions. Indeed, a criticism of current moral panic scholarship is an over-reliance on media analysis, which does not allow for the kinds of research required to understand emotions in action during moral panics.

The chapter is presented in three parts. We begin by briefly discussing some of the limitations of the moral panic literature. Next, we discuss emotions in relation to media communication, to the idea of 'disproportionality,' and to crowds as per previous claims by moral panic scholars. We then offer an exegesis of three prominent theorists in the sociology of emotions: Randall Collins' concept of interaction ritual chain, Jack Katz's work on how emotions are shaped and experienced in interaction, and Sara Ahmed's arguments about how emotions circulate in an affective economy.

Moral panic and emotion

Moral panic scholars rightly indicate that emotions are integrally involved in public reactions to particular cases of so-called deviance, but they provide neither analytical nor methodological resources to explain how emotions actually work. Irvine (2007) suggests that it is important to focus on how the emotions of a moral panic emerge in a particular space and time. Discussing panics that emerge concerning sexuality, she argues that the moral panic concept is stronger when attending 'to how emotion weaves through structural, cultural, and political processes, as well as to how public settings produce collective feelings' (p. 4). There needs to be some kind of focused action (e.g., a crowd gathering, a public march) for analysis of emotions at the group level (the level of politics) to be valuable.

In a related vein, Critcher (2003: 143) argues that a 'peculative notion of social anxiety' is found throughout moral panic scholarship. One example is Cohen's (2002: xxix) argument that 'discrete and volatile moral panics might indeed once have existed but they have now been replaced by a generalized moral stance, a permanent moral panic resting on a seamless web of social anxieties.' A second example is Thompson's (1998) argument that we are seeing a more rapid succession of moral panics. These assertions mirror broader claims concerning a supposed culture of fear that has gripped Western societies on a grand scale (Furedi 2002, this volume Chapter 6; Glassner 2000). How can we accept these claims if the connection between emotions and panic is so underdeveloped?

Emotions are invoked in the moral panic literature as a way to connect concerns sparked by media reporting with the hostility oriented towards folk devils and the consensus somehow generated in a unified public response. Emotions are also invoked in the idea of 'volatility' (the crescendo of moral panics), and the eruption of hostility that can result in outrage and confrontation (Hier 2008; Goode and Ben-Yehuda 2009). But to adequately incorporate the sociology of emotions into moral panic scholarship, researchers must be concerned with how panic happens in a corporeal manner and what emotions *do* during the process. The workings of emotion must be mapped if we are to comprehend the nature of moral panics in their full depths occurring over time. We need to ask: How do emotions work in the interactions between those involved in any moral panic and how do these emotions align some participants together and against others?

Emotions and the media

Moral panic research relies heavily on media accounts as a primary form of data, but rarely demonstrates how emotion is generated out of media reporting in a way that would satisfy sociologists of emotions or audience reception scholars. The mass media, so the argument goes, take the stories that interest groups tell and spin them as cold, hard fact (see Jenkins 1992). The claim concerning media and emotions hinges on the idea of consensus amongst segments of the public. But who is the 'public segment' of moral panics? How is the 'public' of any panic constituted if not by emotions? Consensus is said to be orchestrated by highly emotive claims and fear-based appeals, yet rarely do moral panic scholars conduct empirical research regarding how emotions work at any level of analysis in establishing consensus (see deYoung 1998). Hostility is not demonstrated empirically in claims about media messaging. Moreover, it is assumed that consensus is achieved in lieu of examining the emotional dimensions through which consensus might be formed but then might also fail (see Hier *et al.* 2007). Moral panic scholars evince the volatility of panics as a kind of rise and fall movement without demonstrating how volatility translates into some transcendent action by the subject or by a group of subjects.

'Panic' may be a trope of mass media reporting, but, if experienced at all, panic is likely to involve many other emotions besides fear and anxiety (the two emotions most commonly emphasized). As Altheide (2009) recently observed, the mass media play an important role in amplifying deviance and orienting hostility towards particular targets. Altheide argues that this is achieved through a 'fear narrative' underscoring the plot of media reporting. For Altheide, such a fear narrative figures centrally in moral panics:

> The major impact of the discourse of fear is to promote a sense of disorder and a belief that 'things are out of control.' Fear, crime, and victimization, and more recently, terrorism, are experienced and known vicariously through the mass media by audience members. The discourse of fear has been constructed through news and popular culture accounts.
>
> *(p. 95)*

Altheide (1997) further argues that journalists must accentuate these fear narratives to keep their jobs. Furedi (2002) has made similar comments about discourses of fear. The resulting claim is that fear is transmitted to the public and acted upon – a passive model of communication. It is not clear how this claim about fear narratives could be substantiated without audience research. Nor is it obvious to what extent a fear narrative differs from more classical narrative tropes used to frame story telling (e.g., tragedy). This is the monolithic notion of societal reactions that McRobbie and Thornton (1995) urged moral panic scholars to move away from. Instead of assuming what the media effects of sensationalist reports are, it is important to consider how emotions mediate interpretation of news reporting.

Would communication studies scholars be content to make claims about public responses informed by television programming without conducting audience research? The answer, we hope all social scientists would agree, is no. We are, then, left wondering why moral panic scholars are content to make claims about public responses to people and events constructed as so-called deviant without investigating the emotional and interactional dimensions. Even when people have the same feeling they do not share the same relationship to a feeling (Ahmed 2004a), which means it is problematic to claim that viewers 'catch something' (or the same thing) from watching television or reading the newspaper. An exception here is Cottle's (2005) analysis of the mediatized public crisis following the killing of Stephen Lawrence in 1993. Cottle does not limit his analysis to identification of a particular narrative but examines the interactions among court processes, media reporting and public support campaigns that led to change at the institutional level. The testimony and the investigation itself were mediatized in a way that enacted new political forms and successfully worked upon the shame of British citizenry. Part of our argument is that moral panic scholars have spent so much time applying the moral panic label to social processes that they have failed to investigate what 'panic' could possibly mean and what the relationship is between emotions and panic.

Emotions and 'disproportionality'

The analytical link between mass media and emotions in moral panics relates to a second difficulty: the 'disproportionality' problem. Disproportionality assumes that public response to the folk devil is excessive and amplified. Claims about disproportionality are often invoked with reference to emotions, and specifically the measurement of emotion strength or weakness. Goode and Ben-Yehuda (2009, Chapter 2 this volume), for instance, claim that we should measure the proportionality and disproportionality of anxiety as a criterion for designating whether some public response is a moral panic or not. Public response can be considered moral panic only when the response is out of proportion to the putative harm generated by the folk devil.

To address the disproportionality problem, Young (2009) offers an account of moral panic that attempts to theorize the role of emotions. He differentiates between volatile emotions in the short term and more deep-seated emotions that are the basis for the antagonism. Young argues that moral indignation and righteous anger permeate the present of panics, while feelings of *ressentiment* span in between. The French term *ressentiment*, meaning vengeful desire not readily consummated because of group power differentials, is related to social structural forces, whereas the English equivalent, 'resentment,' refers to shorter-term, individual reactions (Meltzer and Musolf 2002). Resentment is more likely to become *ressentiment* if it is directed against an enduring target that generates unease. The scapegoat is said to be the source of the volatile, present emotions, although 'the anger is not a misapprehension' (Young 2009: 14). The anger is underscored by more long-standing differences between groups. Moral panic is thus recast as an age-old class battle. Young tries to settle the problematic argument about 'disproportionality' by pointing to these apparent long-standing differences:

> ... the notion of disproportionality is something of a paradox. For the response to the event is somewhat proportional to the anxiety, otherwise it would simply not be a fully fledged moral panic. What is disproportionate is the reaction to its immediate manifestation. It is proportional to the anxiety, not to the actual event. It is, on the surface of things, a mistake in reason, but it is not, on a more in-depth level, a mistake in emotion. Now, as a matter of fact, one might well disagree with this emotion – it is, after all, too frequently a feature of ressentiment, a creature of reaction, an obstacle to progress.
>
> (p. 14)

Past emotions are important in the present and for creating desired futures – this is what Young argues. In this sense, 'we use emotional pasts as foundations for situated actions' (Mattley 2002: 364). Past emotions influence how we make sense of the emotional present. But Young's discussion of resentment and *ressentiment* tries to settle the 'disproportionality' problem as an a priori, in a way that is methodologically neither visible nor verifiable. Young tries to address the 'disproportionality' problem transcendentally instead of looking at how situated and context-specific emotion reconstitutes the boundaries between social groups in the 'here and now' by circulating between bodies (also see Ahmed 2004b).

Disproportionality is not a problem worth solving; it is a badly formed problem, which presupposes some sort of stable relationship between the contentious event and the emotions at play without investigating the relationship. Focus on 'disproportionality' also displaces a consideration of the emotional dynamics concerning how moral panics start. Disproportionality is a question of measurement (Garland 2008). It is difficult to study subjectively experienced and shared emotion, the area with which the sociology of emotion is most concerned, but measurement might not help us very much in achieving a greater understanding of how emotions work. As we discuss more below, emotions can be studied well by drawing from phenomenology and symbolic interactionism.

Emotions and the spectral crowd

Moral panic scholars make claims about emotions with a sort of spectral crowd in mind. Claims are made about emotions and public responses to signal crimes as if the body of a crowd has built up a consensus about the moral wrongdoing of some folk devil and is waiting, in response, to exact some publicity of disgrace upon the target. The idea of 'consensus' upon which claims regarding moral panic are based assumes a mass of people moving upon the folk devil almost instinctively. This is a Le Bonian vision of the crowd in public. Le Bon (1968) argued that crowds form a mental unity, just like cells make up the body in a biological unity. The crowd is easily swayed by suggestion to become intolerant and impulsive. The crowd, Le Bon argues, removes undesirable elements of the social body. Panic runs through the crowd like a contagion. Panic is conceptualized as contagious and communication is theorized as suggestibility.

Yet the bodies of these crowds are rarely present in moral panic analysis. There are no bodies amassed waiting with a vengeance. Instead, there is only the spectrality of the crowd, this Le Bonian vision of the public as irrational and vengeful. An exception in this regard is Critcher's (2002) brief comments concerning vigilantism and the dynamics of a crowd outside a known pedophile's house. Yet the account is based on newspaper articles, not observation or interviews thereafter. *An in situ analysis of emotions in moral panic crowds needs to account for the interactions between crowd members, between the folk devil and the crowd members, moral entrepreneurs and the crowd, the police and crowd members.* What is more, the claim about spectral crowds is that emotion pervades them as a kind of *contagion*. Even when there is some demonstrable crowd, the actions and emotions of the crowd cannot be explained as a type of contagion. The contagion theory of crowds assumes that emotions operate from the outside in during public gatherings, in ways that herd people towards certain actions and broader sentiments. The contagion theory of crowds and emotions has fallen out of fashion because it is mechanistic and deterministic. We cannot assume a connection between the interactional level and the collective of emotions in advance, because this can be demonstrated only by careful analysis of sequences of group interactions.

How emotions matter to moral panics

We have problematized a few claims made by moral panic scholars regarding emotions. Some scholars have already tried to resolve these difficulties. For example, Critcher (2003) argues we need to make significant changes to the moral panic research agenda. In advocating a move from the attributional to the processual model of moral panic, however, Critcher (2003) misses a golden opportunity to reorient moral panic studies away from discourse analysis and towards the sociology of emotions. The weaknesses in current moral panic scholarship as it concerns emotions, and where the sociology of emotions can help, are represented in Figure 7.1. Emotions will matter in other relationships represented in this rudimentary figure, for instance with moral entrepreneurs as the face of victimization that they often bring to the process of moral panic (see Hier *et al.* 2007). However, in this chapter we focus only on the three areas delineated by dashed lines. Beginning from the left side of Figure 7.1, the sociology of emotions requires that the path from the media to public emotion not be inferred but

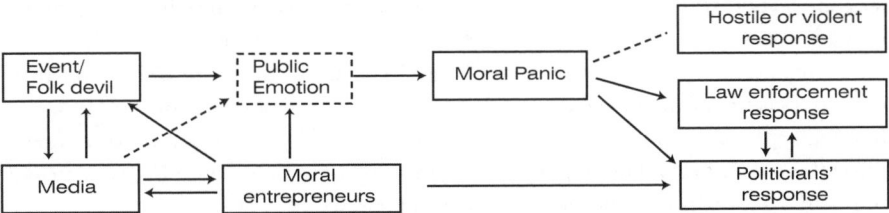

Figure 7.1 Emotion and moral panic.

instead be studied using an appropriate methodology (e.g., ethnography, audience research). The moral panic literature treats emotion as a black box, but does not develop an empirical understanding of how emotion is experienced and shared. The sociology of emotions can contribute here through its emphasis on how emotion should be understood and studied *in situ* (see Katz 1999).

Nor is it clear what constitutes 'public emotion,' insofar as moral panic scholars have focused heavily on responses to contentious events as 'disproportional' instead of offering a phenomenological or symbolic interactionist account that prefaces how emotions work as a form of sociality. The sociology of emotions can contribute here through its emphasis on how emotions align some bodies and some communities together and against others (see Ahmed 2004a). Finally, there has been little empirical research on how, once in process, moral panics engender hostility or violent action. As discussed above, current moral panic scholarship operates with a spectral crowd model. The sociology of emotions can contribute to moral panic scholarship by emphasizing how emotions work in micro-settings of violence and conflict (see Collins 2008).

Having problematized some claims made by moral panic scholars as regards emotions, we now comment on how the sociology of emotions could supplement the moral panic framework.

Randall Collins, interaction rituals, and forward panics

The model of emotions that Collins (2005) provides is located firmly in the sort of ritual analysis Erving Goffman described. There are several necessary ritual elements according to this approach. First, group assembly brings bodies together. Second, there is a mutual focus amongst participants, which may involve some bodily interaction. Third, this shared attention creates a shared mood. Fourth, the shared mood 'posits an emotional contagion among the person present' (p. 107). This is what Collins refers to as emotional entrainment: the building up of confidence and solidarity in one another through some ritual doing. Fifth, the shared mood demarcates the group and prevents outsiders from entering. The bridge between these elements and the outcomes of the interaction is collective Effervesce: the emotional energy of people acting together. Group solidarity is one possible long-term outcome. What Collins calls emotional charging of the individual is another possible outcome of the interaction ritual.

Righteous anger is an emotion that Collins (2005) focuses on in relation to scapegoats. The interaction ritual model assumes that the scapegoat has a symbolic relevance, the group is constituted prior to the scapegoat being designated as heretic, and that group binary maintenance takes on an eschatological character. Group security is thrust to the fore because of the generation of righteous anger through processes of 'deviance-hunting' (p. 128). Emotions such as anger need to be empirically corroborated through observation of bodily postures and movements, ethnomethodological analysis of bodily coordination in groups, as well as interviews.

Collins' (2005) model of emotions and interaction ritual chains demands that researchers investigate ongoing and actually occurring interactions in order to make claims about emotions and what they do. However, Collins follows a contagion model of emotion as it circulates in groups. He argues that people in groups are 'swept into a common mood' (p. 111). The contagion model of emotions fails to account for breakages from the interaction ritual chain. The idea of emotional contagion, which asserts that emotion leaps from body to body, pushes a metaphor too far, discounts contingent phenomenological differences in terms of experiencing emotions, and is contrary to symbolic interactionist understandings of communication generally. The contagion theory of emotions is also evident in some moral panic scholarship, for instance when Goode and Ben-Yehuda (2009: 52) discuss the power of moral panics to 'seize' members of a society. Although Collins offers a corrective to the ontology of emotions that moral panic theorists operate with, since he does not assume disproportionality and provides an embodied account of the crowd, he falls back to a contagion model of emotions at the group level, so his model also needs to be supplemented.

Emotions are also crucial to violence. Collins (2008) argues that violence is rare, compared to the potential for it, since most interaction is governed by a confrontational tension that stalls actual violence. Violence is not based on a background characteristic of any individual or some variable related to childhood socialization. Instead, Collins argues that the resources we need to explain instantiations of violence and the actual rarity of violence stem from *situational* interactions themselves. Collins (2008: 83–133) has introduced the concept of *forward panic* to describe moments of physical violence that overcome confrontational tension. Forward panic begins with a build-up of confrontational tension that is released into a frenzied attack when the situation makes it easy to do so. Forward panics are typified primarily by being patently unfair, where crowds converge on an individual or tiny group. As Collins (2008: 128) states, the 'size of the group present – the sheer number of bodies at the scene – increases the tendency for forward panic.' The composite mood of a forward panic is derived from the transformation of tension/fear into aggressive frenzy, usually centered on rage. Forward panics are characterized by a climax of noise and violence. The emotion of a forward panic, whatever its composition, has two prime attributes. First, it is a 'hot emotion,' a situation of being highly aroused, steamed up. It comes on in a rush, explosively, and it takes time to calm down. Second, it is an emotion that is rhythmic and strongly entraining. People in the throes of a forward panic keep repeating their aggressive actions (e.g., continuous kicking and punching of a victim). The emotionality of the situation involves group entrainment, where aggressive actions in some promote aggressive actions in others.

What can the concept of forward panic contribute to the analysis of moral panics? With the frequent spectrality of the crowd in the moral panic literature, forward panic can give the crowd an embodied form. Drawing from the analytical intricacies of a forward panic, we come to understand the ways in which crowds not only form but are sustained through emotions. In this sense, we come to understand the nature of crowds that search out and confront an enemy (like the folk devil). This is commonplace in responses to sex offenders in communities where crowds, shouting various protestations regarding the presence of the sex offender, seek to expel the sex offender through violent means (see Spencer 2009). In a phenomenological sense, Collins' model can be used as a framework for comprehending the emotion work of moral panic crowds and what propels them to resort to violence. In addition, the concept of forward panic gives us a sense of how moral panic crowds, in terms of their actions, appear as a coherent mob descending to depths of violence that they would not as individuals engage in. But if this contagion theory of the crowd evident in Collins' work assumes how emotion generates action in a rather linear way, what other understandings of emotions can we turn to for a supplemental discussion?

Jack Katz's ontology of emotion

Scholars often end up analyzing talk about emotions rather than emotions as they are experienced. Katz (1999) argues that emotions are not forms of talk and not even forms of conscious expression. Katz's whole project is to move social science towards study of emotions as they are actually experienced in sequences of interaction, rather than focusing in on representations of emotions found in talk. Emotions are experienced 'here and now' and contribute to how people orient themselves towards a situation and move out of the situation into a future sequence of events. Katz's approach builds on the contributions of phenomenology insofar as he is attentive to the way emotions require a presence of the subject:

> ... emotions emerge in our experience as previously tacit ways of embodying experience edge into our awareness. Emotions do not typically burst into our awareness as thoughts, which 'self-reflection' may commonly imply. Emotions emerge in experience as a bodily awareness, an internal tension, a sensual self-reflection; they arise in various corporeal, aesthetic forms ...
> (Katz, 2002a: 375)

People may shape their emotional conduct to fit the obligations of a situation, yet people may experience emotions when not in the co-presence of others. In experiencing and shaping emotions, people draw upon their body as a store of communicative and agentic potentials. Emotions are not simply a matter of transcending situations and moving from sequence to sequence of interaction. Emotions also involve a metamorphosis of self and one's orientation towards the events and people around them. The self can be engulfed by emotion in a situation and become unable to transcend the event taking place, leading to breakages in the seamless functioning of any interactional sequence.

As Katz (2002b: 260) puts it, 'the extraordinary modesty of a theory of social ontology, as an effort simply to describe, takes on a radical potential because of the limitations that define substantive theories ... .' This kind of fundamental ontology of emotions that Katz posits has methodological implications. The first is a commitment to naturalistic observation of actually occurring conduct and experience in face-to-face situations. This requires ethnography, participant observation, perhaps use of videos and pictures – any techniques for getting at emotional life as it happens. Such a methodological commitment does not preclude use of interview data, but interview data as an account of those present at some event can be only secondary to strategies of naturalistic observation and should be supplemented with accounts of the perceptions of others present at the event. Katz (1999: 11) is skeptical about generalizations and contends that 'analytic induction' is the only useful logic for analyzing and writing about emotions. Such an approach seeks to explain how a phenomenon develops sequentially and leads to metamorphoses in lives of those who experience emotions. Katz is critical of theorists who begin with abstractions when discussing emotions.

A secondary component of Katz's ontology of emotions is that emotions are situated in relation to narrative projects. Katz thinks of narrative projects as meanings that arch across interactional sequences that provide some resources for making sense of the actions of others as well as ourselves. People make sense of these narratives artfully, so the narratives do not simply provide a script that is robotically followed. The work to be done by the social scientist, however, is not to point out the existence of such narratives. The task of the social scientist is to try to get at how the narrative is made sense of in sequential interaction.

Katz's (1988) phenomenological writings regarding the sensual attractions of doing a stick-up have relevance beyond discussions of emotions and the doing of crime. The ontology of emotions he provides might be more useful to us for understanding the micro-sociological fundaments of public reactions to deviance. How would Katz's ontology of emotions matter for discussing particular emotions that are relevant to moral panics, rage for instance? According to Katz, we should not attempt to look outside the phenomenon for an external explanatory element, nor should we focus simply on the psychological as explanatory. Katz has a tripartite model. First, Katz considers the symbolic interactions of participants *in situ*. Second, he considers the embodied elements of the experience for participants. Third, he considers the elements of transcendence that relate to defining the situation anew or create an ending to the strip of interaction as it is occurring. The task is not simply to point out the existence of a fear narrative, but (*pace* the moral panic literature) to see how emotion manifests during *in situ* interaction, embodied action and the movement of people through the moments of their lives.

Katz's model calls for careful long-term ethnographies that, in the case of moral panics, would involve the compiling of empirically rich data sets documenting the manifestation of emotions within interactions of various individuals and groups. It also calls on researchers to analyze the metamorphosis of individuals (e.g., particular moral entrepreneurs) central to moral panics and their orientation towards the events and people around them. Newspaper presentations of a particular event would serve as only a signal to the instantiation of a moral panic. Therein the job of moral panic researcher qua ethnographer begins; documentation predicated on embodied immersion and engagement with the key event(s) and key players commences. Katz's model accounts for non-linear moments of emotional emergence that lead to future action, but beyond narrative how can we account for emotional histories and group boundaries that divide some emotional subjects from others?

Sara Ahmed and affective economies

Emotions are socially shared in particular contexts, since they cannot be restricted to any particular individual (Ahmed 2004a). But, *pace* Collins, emotions are not shared according to a contagion model. Ahmed is critical of both inside-out and outside-in models of emotions. The inside-out model of emotions assumes emotion begins inside the individual and is something one can express to others. The outside-in model of emotions assumes emotions begin outside the individual in a crowd or social body, and then shape the movement of the mass. The inside-out model of emotions is problematic, since it precludes discussion of shared emotion. The outside-in model of emotion is problematic, since it precludes the crowd feeling different emotion, multiple emotions, or otherwise being highly differentiated. Ahmed's argument is that emotions circulate in an affective economy and it is through emotions that boundaries between the 'I,' the 'we' and the 'other' are formed. Through the circulation of emotions, there is what she terms 'intensification' insofar as bodies and worlds materialize and take shape, or the effect of boundary, surface and fixity are produced (Ahmed 2004b: 24). There is no 'we' or 'other' in a particular context before emotions do something, align some with others or against other others. The question of what emotions 'are' is displaced to focus on what emotions 'do' and how people talk about emotions (Ahmed 2004b). According to Ahmed, 'emotions *do things*, and they align individuals with communities … ' (p. 119).

Not only does Ahmed provide more analytical precision concerning how the 'we' and the 'other' are constituted in any context, she does so with an attunement to the emotions said to be prominent in moral panics. Hate, for instance, is an emotion that generates its object as a defense against perceived injury. The proximity of the object threatens to take away something from the subject, and hate therein moves communities to align themselves against the object. Not only is an us-versus-them binary formed, but a spatial organization of bodies, a moving away from the object of hate, and also a volatile lashing out onto the body of the hated. Social space is reformed through the circulation of hate in a way that is observable in sequential vignettes. Disgust also marks bodies is sensory ways. Disgust is experienced on the surface of the skin as a pressing near of others. Whereas hate can be experienced at a distance, disgust requires perilously close contact. Contact between the self and the other generates a recoiling and an expulsion of the other's body. Yet emotion can stick: the disgust does not dissipate with the recoiling of bodies, but is a bodily reminder of the distance to be maintained. In this sense, Ahmed's discussion of affective economies could be helpful to scholars attempting to materialize their claims concerning 'us' and 'them' as the symbolic basis of hostility and volatility during moral panics.

Whereas hate marks some bodies as 'others' in a very sensory way, fear works towards a containment of those other bodies. As Ahmed (2004b: 69) puts it, 'fear works to restrict some bodies through the movement or expansion of others.' Fear does something: it re-territorializes assumed distances between bodies. As she puts it, 'through fear not only is the very border between self and other affected, but the relation between the objects feared … is shaped by histories that "stick," by making some objects more than others seem fearsome' (Ahmed 2004a: 127). Fear works to contain the bodies of others and enhance the mobility of the fear subject. Detainment or restraint of hated bodies is the result of the affective politics of fear. More powerful than fear in marking and containing the other, however, is love. Love is for the idealized community. Love is the result of fearing others, it is a love for the self against others. Emotions, therefore, are not origins but effects. Emotions result from movement and the contact of bodies over time. 'Emotions are the very "flesh" of time,' writes Ahmed (2004b: 202), insofar as past encounters live on the surfaces of our bodies as antagonisms that separate communities.

In relation to moral panics, the utility of Ahmed's model is the way emotions not only effectively constitute the objects of hate, fear and disgust, in the case of folk devils, but also constitute those demonizing the folk devils or objects the folk devils supposedly pose a threat to. While child killers, sex offenders and drug users are viewed as threats to the family and, hence, constituted as objects of fear, the family is (re)constituted as an object of happiness that must be protected from harm or intrusion (see Ahmed 2008).

Emotions and moral panics revisited

Moral panic literature flattens out any sense of emotions by failing to adequately characterize the interactional context through which emotions emerge and facilitate differences at the group level. We have argued that the sociology of emotions can provide numerous conceptual tools to help moral panic scholars adequately conceive of how emotions are generated at the individual level, as well as how they contribute to action and a sense of community.

With his focus on interaction rituals, the discussion that Collins offers specifies an interactionist level of analysis that is necessary if we are to investigate how emotions matter to the kind of public reaction that moral panics scholars discuss. But the contagion theory of crowds and emotions is limited by its inability to account for different bodies within the crowd and the diversity of emotions ongoing within those sequences of crowd movement. With a focus on confrontational tension that builds up over the course of interactions, his model allows for an understanding of how crowds associated with moral panic may resort to violence based on processes associated with forward panic. Katz's ontology of emotions demonstrates that in experiencing emotions there is a phenomenological transcendence, a break from the previous strip of interaction that leads to a further action. It is on this basis, we claim, that emotions do something, they move us towards certain actions and not others. Yet Katz's model is not structured specifically to investigate the ways that this transcendence of the situation leads to affective politics – it does not purposely problematize difference and group boundaries. Ahmed's contribution is to discuss how emotions align, hive off, contain, and secure various bodies. Accounting for difference, Ahmed's arguments have serious implications for theorizing the relationship between racialized bodies and public responses to contentious events. However, Ahmed does not often provide empirical evidence that emotions are being experienced in the way she describes at the group level. Where Katz and Collins can supplement Ahmed is in their call for claims about emotion to be backed by scrupulous ethnographic and participant observation research.

For all the weight put on emotion by moral panic scholars, the theorization of emotion has been rather thin. We have argued that moral panic scholarship needs to become closer to its symbolic interactionist roots vis-à-vis investigation of how emotions matter to these processes of public response. We have argued that it is not enough simply to name some emotions that are hypothetically the outcome of media reporting. Moral panic scholars must consider bodily practices and *in situ* interaction if they want to understand how emotions align communities against one another.

Ontological and epistemological claims translate into methodological practices. If we attempt to think through emotions anew in moral panic scholarship it is ultimately the methodological side of moral panic studies that we would expect to see change most drastically, with more attention being paid to ethnography and participant observation as data collection methods. There is consensus amongst sociologists that emotions must be studied *in situ* and with a mind towards bodies as they interact. This does not mean that emotions have some transcendental or universal value – it means that local constructions of emotions articulate themselves through the body, through touching, through sensing. Taking emotions seriously in moral panic scholarship will ultimately require ethnographic research practices and less reliance on newspaper analysis.

Note

1 Thanks to Sean P. Hier, Carolyn Côté-Lussier, and Chris Hurl for their helpful comments.

References

Ahmed, S. (2008) 'Sociable Happiness', *Emotion, Space and Society*, 1(1): 10–13.
Ahmed, S. (2004a) 'Affective Economies', *Social Text*, 22(2): 117–39.
Ahmed, S. (2004b) *The Cultural Politics of Emotion*. New York: Routledge.
Altheide, D. (2009) 'Moral Panic: from Sociological Concept to Public Discourse', *Crime, Media, Culture*, 5(1): 79–99.
Altheide, D. (1997) 'The News Media, the Problem Frame, and the Production of Fear', *The Sociological Quarterly*, 38(4): 647–68.
Cohen, S. (2002) *Folk Devils and Moral Panics: The Creation of the Mods and Rockers*, 3rd edition. London: Routledge.
Collins, R. (2008) *Violence: A Microsociological Theory*. Princeton: Princeton University Press.
Collins, R. (2005) *Interaction Ritual Chains*. Princeton: Princeton University Press.
Cottle, S. (2005) 'Mediatized Public Crisis and Civil Society Renewal: the Racist Murder of Stephen Lawrence', *Crime, Media, Culture*, 1(1): 49–71.
Critcher, C. (2009) 'Widening the Focus: Moral Panic as Moral Regulation', *British Journal of Criminology*, 49(1): 17–34.
Critcher, C. (2003) *Moral Panics and the Media*. Buckingham: Open University Press.
Critcher, C. (2002) 'Media, Government and Moral Panic: the Politics of Paedophilia in Britain 2000–2001', *Journalism Studies*, 3(4): 521–35.
deYoung, M. (1998) 'Another Look at Moral Panics: the Case of Satanic Day Care Centers', *Deviant Behavior*, 19(3): 257–78.

Furedi, F. (2002) *Culture of Fear: Risk-taking and the Morality of Low Expectation*. London: Continuum.
Garland, D. (2008) 'On the Concept of Moral Panic', *Crime, Media, Culture*, 4(1): 9–30.
Glassner, B. (2000) *The Culture of Fear: Why Americans are Afraid of the Wrong Things*. New York: Basic Books.
Goode, E. and N. Ben-Yehuda (2009) *Moral Panics: The Social Construction of Deviance*. Cambridge, Massachusetts: Blackwell Publishers.
Hier, S. (2008) 'Thinking beyond Moral Panic: Risk, Responsibility and the Politics of Moralization', *Theoretical Criminology*, 12(2): 173–90.
Hier, S., J. Greenberg, K. Walby, and D. Lett (2007) 'Beyond Responsibilization and Social Ordering: Media, Communication, and the Establishment of Public Video Surveillance Programs', *Media, Culture, and Society*, 29(5): 727–51.
Hunt, A. (1999) *Governing Morals: A Social History of Moral Regulation*. Cambridge: Cambridge University Press.
Irvine, J. (2007) 'Transient Feelings: Sex Panics and the Politics of Emotions', *GLQ*, 14(1): 1–40.
Jenkins, P. (1992) *Intimate Enemies: Moral Panics in Contemporary Great Britain*. New York: Aldine de Gruyter.
Katz, J. (2002a) 'Response to Commentators', *Theoretical Criminology*, 6(3): 375–80.
Katz, J. (2002b) 'Start Here: Social Ontology and Research Strategy', *Theoretical Criminology*, 6(3): 255–78.
Katz, J. (1999) *How Emotions Work*. Chicago: University of Chicago Press.
Katz, J. (1988) *Seductions of Crime*. New York: Basic Books.
Le Bon, G. (1968) *The Crowd: A Study of the Popular Mind*. Dunwoody: Berg Publisher.
McRobbie, A. and S. Thornton (1995) 'Rethinking "Moral Panic" for a Multimediated Social World', *British Journal of Sociology*, 46(4): 559–74.
Mattley, C. (2002) 'The Temporality of Emotion: Constructing Past Emotions', *Symbolic Interaction*, 25(3): 363–78.
Meltzer, B. and G. Musolf (2002) 'Resentment and Ressentiment', *Sociological Inquiry*, 72(2): 240–55.
Spencer, D. (2009) 'Sex Offender as Homo Sacer', *Punishment and Society*, 11(2): 219–40.
Thompson, K. (1998) *Moral Panics*. London and New York: Routledge.
Young, J. (2009) 'Moral Panic: its Origins in Resistance, Ressentiment and the Translation of Fantasy into Reality', *British Journal of Criminology*, 49(1): 4–16.

8
FOLK DEVILS RECONSIDERED

Mary deYoung

For nearly four decades, sociological and criminological scholarship on moral panics has paid homage to the groundbreaking works of Stanley Cohen (1972) and Stuart Hall *et al.* (1978). Their classic investigations into the excessive reactions of moral entrepreneurs, the media, and control culture to particular moral transgressions not only inaugurated moral panic studies, but also insisted that folk devils are key elements of it.

The folk devils of Cohen's analysis were, of course, the eponymous Mods and Rockers: the factions of two youth subcultures in Great Britain in the 1960s. The former were middle class and *sang-froid*; the latter, *lumpen* and politically reactionary. The differences between them – from attitude and aspiration, to preferred music and mode of transportation – were stark as far as the factions' insiders were concerned, of no great interest at first to outsiders, and ignored completely when they were discursively transformed into folk devils after their altercation on the streets of the English seaside resort of Clacton-on-Sea over the rainy Easter weekend of 1964.

Their clash may have resulted in more than £500 in property damage and 100 arrests, but for Cohen it was their discursive makeover that was of more interest. They were stereotypically represented as youth hooligans by the media and by what he refers to as the 'right-thinking' people who publicly and politically reacted to their altercation, and made the subject of jeremiads by those same moral entrepreneurs who warned of the threats posed to the moral and social order by such dissolute youth; a 'full scale demonology and hagiology' was constructed (Cohen 1972: 44). The Mods and the Rockers thus achieved a certain pride of place in the 'gallery of contemporary folk devils' (p. 44).

Muggers were added to that gallery by Hall *et al.* in their analysis of another British moral panic over violent street criminals. Focusing on the media's role in constructing folk devils, they lay out the complex process of news making. They argue that the media are dependent upon, rather than independent from, what they refer to as the 'primary definers,' that is, those individuals and groups with the authority and/or expertise to set out the terms of the debate over a social issue. In this moral panic, the primary definers were representatives of the state, the police, and politicians whose warnings about street crime were then translated by the media into a 'public idiom' that gave a discursive reality to the inchoate fears of the public. In a discursive loop, the public's reactions to the reporting were then fed back to the primary definers as indicators of public opinion, thus stoking the intensity of their rhetoric and repressive reactions.

Central to all of this is the 'signification spiral.' Hall *et al.* coined the term to describe the process by which a specific social anxiety is mapped onto a matrix of other social anxieties by media reportage and the rhetoric of representatives of the state. As these disparate anxieties converge, the 'threat-potential' amplifies and the need to contain it becomes urgent. It is here that the folk devil is constructed out of the strands of converging social anxieties to stand in proxy for the threat potential. Thus the folk devils of this moral panic were not muggers left lurking in the dark shadows of imagination; rather, they were embodied in the persons of young, urban, black males – symbols of the converging social anxieties of the era about alienated youth, urban decay, and strained race relations. Projected across 'thresholds' of social tolerance by sensationalist reportage, they were depicted not just as threats, but as violent threats, thus legitimating coercive state intervention.

Hall *et al.* do not so much recapitulate Cohen's model of moral panics as renovate it. While the theoretical and analytical differences between the two models have been sharply dissected by others (Critcher 2003; Jones 1997; Thompson 1998), what is of concern here is the pre-eminent role of the folk devil in these pioneering works. In both, they had a certain liminal status before they were nominated as folk devils of the moral panics. Cohen's Mods and Rockers, relatively affluent, mobile, insouciant, were 'imposters, reading the lines which everyone knew belonged to some other groups' (Cohen 1972: 195). Not securely located within the in-group, or as Cohen remarks, 'not quite in their places' (p. 195), they threatened prevailing norms and blurred the moral boundary between conventional and deviant society. The muggers of Hall *et al.* were inarguably deviant and had been the targets of criminal justice intervention well before they were nominated as the folk devils of the moral panic. While this closer look at the folk devils reveals a fundamental difference between the two pioneering works – for Cohen, deviant action was followed by social reaction, yet for Hall *et al.* intervention revealed the deviant action which set off social reaction – the critical point is that the folk devils of each were socially marginalized before they ever were crafted into folk devils.

Indeed, there is a morally sinister air about the folk devils of subsequent moral panic analyses influenced by Cohen and Hall *et al.* There are the coarse women of the witch-hunts (Ben-Yehuda 1980); the indolent dole scroungers and feckless single mothers of the Welfare State panics (Ortiz and Briggs 2003; Shepard 2007); the rebellious recreational users, 'heroin chic' popular culture icons, antisocial addicts, and pushers of the drug crusades (Armstrong 2007; Denham 2008; Goode 1990; Hier 2002a); the dangerous working class and the alienated middle-class males of the crime and bullying scares (Hay 1995; Hoeri 2002; Schinkel 2008); the sleazy pornographers, child molesters, and cyber-predators of the stranger-danger alarms (Critcher 2002; Ost 2002; Sandywell 2006); and the shadowy foreigners of the asylum-seeking, illegal immigration, and terrorism scares (Altheide, 2006; Rothe and Muzzatti, 2004). All folk devils, to one degree or another, were marginalized, gendered, stigmatized, racialized, and/or criminalized as cultural strangers well before they even were nominated and then constructed into the moral panics' folk devils.

The very notion of socially marginalized folk devils, powerless victims of the bloated rhetoric of moral entrepreneurs and the stereotypical representations of the media, is so securely ensconced in moral panic analyses inspired by Cohen and Hall *et al.* that it has had all of the tranquility of an axiom. But for some quite recent scholars, the axiom is far from tranquil.

Why is this so? The general answer can be contextualized within the discussion that has been ongoing for some time, over re-theorizing the concept of moral panic by linking it to moral regulation and risk theory, two salient themes in contemporary sociological, criminological, and cultural theory. While there is disagreement about how those linkages should be forged, and quite frankly whether they should be at all, the very prospect of doing so is intriguing for the purposes of this chapter because it problematizes folk devils.

It does so in the following ways. If, on the one hand, moral panics are considered extreme and rare instances of 'risk discourse within a process of moral regulation' (Critcher 2009: 17), then they invariably will have embodied folk devils, most likely already socially marginalized, whose putative threat to the moral order requires immediate social control. This reconceptualization retains not only much of the classic notion of moral panics à la Cohen and Hall *et al.*, but also much of the temptation to continue to under-theorize folk devils as social actors. If, on the other hand, moral panics are considered much more common instances of volatile eruptions of the moralization in everyday life, 'transmitted through configurations of grievance and risk' (Hier 2008: 171), then these folk devils really do become problematical. They may have to be 'foraged for,' as Ungar (2001: 281) so nicely puts it, and if found they may be not socially marginalized, and far from powerless. And they may not exist at all, at least not in an embodied form, replaced, instead, by issues such as health concerns that not only have apologists and adversaries, but that also pose no tangible threat to the moral order, and require more self-regulation than social control (Critcher 2009).

Regardless of the reconceptualization, and whether outside the social margins or within, embodied or not, folk devils are being problematized by recent efforts to revise moral panics. In this chapter, I reconsider folk devils in light of revisionist efforts. For the purposes of clarity, not to mention symmetry, I will use the terms 'conventional' and 'modern' to tag the two opposing re-conceptualizations previously discussed; the folk devils of each will be tagged that way as well. My analysis uses social marginality as the primary variable, and searches for the ways and means not only by which 'conventional' and 'modern' folk devils are constructed, but also by which they might be theorized as social actors who use what variously may be referred to as their personal power, agency, social capital, or resource mobilization capacity to influence the claims, course, and consequences of moral panics.

This analysis takes to heart Young's (2007) reminder that moral panics always are collective processes, and should be analyzed in such a way that a 'sense of energy and intensity of this happening and that' (p. 56) is captured. To that end, I will rely on a variety of moral panic case studies to advance my own analysis.

'Conventional' folk devils

If moral panics are re-conceptualized as extreme and rare instances of risk discourse within a process of moral regulation, and therefore as conceptually distinct from it, they still require folk devils. As embodiments of the constructed threat to the moral order, folk devils can be identified, acted against, and socially controlled. I propose that most, but not all, of those nominated as folk devils in conventional moral panic analyses will have been socially marginalized *before* their nomination, that their social marginality, in fact, raises their profile as potential threats to the moral order and facilitates their discursive construction into folk devils.

To begin, social marginality can be thought of as being outside the mainstream of productive activity and/or social reproductive activity (Leonard 1984). While it may be said that some individuals and groups voluntarily seek and maintain that social location – as examples one might think about artists working outside of traditional artistic spaces (Lazarides 2008), or perhaps nativist extremist groups (Mulloy 2004) – the fact remains that most do not. Their social marginality is involuntary and often, although certainly not always, spatially designated. Thus they are not only frequently excluded from privileged social spaces, but relegated to the marginal regions of desolate areas, inner cities, enclaves, ghettoes, housing projects, foreign lands, or even on the ethereal fringes of cyberspace (Ferguson *et al.* 1992; Wacquant 2007).

Social marginality may be its own affront; however, it also renders those who experience it vulnerable to political, economic, psychosocial, and ideological threats. Among those threats is the arrogation of their identity by the dominant groups of society. Thus, those on the social margins are characterized and represented not only as 'different' but potentially, if not actually, as threateningly different. What they are imagined as threatening might be generically referred as 'order,' but this, when unpacked, reveals itself as the *moral* order: an elusive concept, it is true, but one that is 'perceived as a necessary condition for social order' (Hunt 1999: 215). Sociological scholarship, in fact, provides a number of templates for imagining and thinking about such morally threatening difference, from Bauman's (2001, 2006) 'the Other' to Schmitt's (1996) 'enemy,' Foucault's (2003) 'monster, and Agamben's (1998) *Homo Sacer*, or 'bare life.'

All of this is by way of emphasizing the fact that, as 'atypical actors against a background that is overtypical' (Cohen 1972: 45), the folk devils of conventional moral panic analyses are already perceived as threats to the moral order. Thus, upon nominating them as folk devils, the discourse of moral entrepreneurs and media representations only has to amplify their deviance and threat in order to transform them into 'personifications of evil ... stripped of all positive characteristics and endowed with pejorative evaluations' (Hier 2002a: 313).

I suggest that this is an, if not an effortless, then at least relatively uncomplicated process. A couple of insights from conventional moral panic analyses provide the justification for this suggestion. First, because they are located on the social margins, 'atypical actors' already have been the subjects of occasional moral discourse and attempts at moral regulation as well as social control. Practiced in that discourse, moral entrepreneurs and the media have only to amplify their deviance and their threat; already primed to that discourse, social audiences are unlikely to be critical of the amplification. This reflects, although it does not restate, Cohen's (1972) notion of 'sensitization': the transformation of atypicality into potent threat, and of atypical actors into folk devils.

Hall et al.'s (1978) notion of signification spirals provides the second justification. They posit that there are thresholds of tolerance that symbolically mark the perceived threat to the social and moral order; these they label in sequence as permissiveness, legality, and violence. When moral entrepreneurs and the media engage in convergence, that is, the linking of 'deviant' activities from different sources and the linking of atypical actors, such as single mothers, to juvenile delinquents, dole scroungers, and drug abusers, they create a signification spiral that not only amplifies the threat, but also propels it and those who embody it across the thresholds of tolerance in order to legitimate social control. This is a more onerous task when all three thresholds have to be crossed, as I will discuss later, and a slightly less onerous task when only two thresholds have to be crossed. But for atypical actors, already represented and perceived as being on or near the last threshold of violence, the onerousness of the task diminishes considerably.

What might be considered evidence of this? The folk devils of conventional moral panic analyses tend to be tightly constructed, that is, they are quite easily identifiable, whether by appearance, behavior, or social location. This tight construction is both the effect and the cause of coherent discourses and representations that amplify their putative threat to the moral and social order. The word 'coherent,' of course, is not tantamount to 'consistent' – there is an opportunity here, although only infrequently taken, to search for competing discourses and representations, including those that may be attributed to the folk devils themselves. All of this, in turn, may account for the volatility of the moral panics, as well as what often is their serial nature, in which one moral panic serves as a resource, of sorts, for subsequent and rapidly cycling moral panics (Goode and Ben-Yehuda 1994).

In conventional analyses of moral panics, that is, those in which the socially marginalized are targeted as folk devils, there is little room to consider the reactions of folk devils to the discourses and representations that demonize them. As a result, their 'Otherness' is reified, their reactions and resistances to their demonization are under-theorized, and their impact on the claims, courses, and consequences of moral panics are under-analyzed (deYoung 1998; McRobbie and Thornton 1995; Miller and Kitzinger 1998).

I propose that, while there may be little room, there is a lot of reason to consider folk devils as social actors. There is a respectable body of sociological and criminological scholarship on stigma contests, deviance neutralization, and the politics of deviance that can serve as exemplars for such inquiries (*cf.* Cohen 2004; Goffman 1963; Lauderdale 2004; Schur 1980; Simi and Futrell 2009). Interestingly, these approaches do not just pass over social marginality without comment, as conventional moral panic analyses too often do, but interrogate it as a variable that is linked to shifting moral boundaries and stratification, status hierarchies, social identity, and social mobility.

Reason also can be found in criticisms of the conventional moral panic model by those who agree that is 'deeply in need of revisiting and revamping' (McRobbie 1994a: 198) if it is to retain its explanatory power in late-modern society. The criticisms are several-fold (see Critcher 2003: 143–54 for a summary), but two will be focused on here. Although neither is completely redressed by considering folk devils as social actors, both are at least partially redressed by doing so. One criticism is aimed at the consensual notion of society in the conventional moral panic model, a notion that eliding the 'distinctions between the media and the state, the media and public belief, and between the state and other social institutions and groups' (Miller and Kitzinger 1998: 216), certainly underestimates the pluralism of late-modern society. It is that pluralism that opens up avenues for even already socially marginalized folk devils to find allies and advocates, build constituencies, and exercise agency.

A separate but related criticism is broadly aimed at the determinism, perhaps even the *over* determinism of the conventional model that maps out the trajectories of moral panics often without considering the fact that the very act of doing so imposes a temporal and logical order that most moral panics never really have. Most moral panics ricochet about, progressing in fits and starts, losing and gaining moral entrepreneurs, achieving some social control ends and failing, often miserably, to achieve others (deYoung 2004). And while much of that erratic trajectory is due to the very features of late-modern society, the classic model under-analyzes – the conflicting interests, the inconsistent claims, the contradictory media representations, the plurality of social reactions – some of it very well may be due to the counterclaims and resistance strategies of the moral panics' folk devils.

Still, the fact remains that the opportunity to consider folk devils as social actors has not often been taken. There are some interesting exceptions (*cf.* St Cyr 2003; Griffiths 2010; McRobbie 1994b), one of which will be reviewed in detail here. Lumsden (2009) examines a localized moral panic in Aberdeen, Scotland over 'boy-racers,' young men already socially marginalized as dissolute youth with too much time on their hands and too much money spent unwisely, who cruised and sometimes raced down a beachfront boulevard in modified cars with loud exhausts and even louder stereo systems. Their antics were uneasily tolerated until redevelopment brought business and middle-class residents to the boulevard, transforming it into a contested space. What followed was consistent with all of the conventions of a classic moral panic: the boy-racers were demonized in discourse and representation as antisocial and dangerous, their putative threat to the moral and social order was exaggerated, and there were both calls and efforts to control and punish them.

What was unconventional about this analysis was that Lumsden, in the role of participant observer, interacted with the folk devils the boy-racers had become, and did so with the specific intent of examining how their reactions to their demonization impacted on the moral panic. What she discovered was that the boy-racers engaged in in-group identity politics in an effort to negotiate their demonization. Those who raced or engaged in dangerous driving only infrequently distanced themselves from those who regularly did so. Representing themselves as 'respectable' members of an otherwise stigmatized subculture, they allied with the moral entrepreneurs and the media against the 'disreputable' members, using niche media to make their cases, and even turned in the names of egregious offenders to the police. In the end, Lumsden concludes, none of these strategies for negotiating a spoiled identity had any appreciable impact on the course, claims, and consequences of the moral panic which, far from being volatile, surged and ebbed for years. Her analysis, however, reveals that, far from being helpless dupes, even socially marginalized folk devils are social actors and should be appreciated as such in moral panic analyses.

Lumsden's analysis raises interesting questions, though. If the nominated folk devils of a moral panic did *not* represent an already socially marginalized group, might their attempts to influence the claims, course, and consequences of the moral panic be any different – that is, would they have access to, and use of, different resources? And, in the end, might they be more likely to be successful?

In the case of the ritual abuse moral panic that ricocheted across the United States for a decade beginning in the early 1980s, the answer is 'yes' to both questions (deYoung 2004). The unlikely folk devils were day care providers, most of them middle-aged, middle-class, and otherwise socially conforming women engaged in what traditionally and even nostalgically is referred to as 'women's work': the low-status, low-paid, but socially valuable work of caring for young and vulnerable children. Over the course of that decade, scores of them were accused of sexually abusing, terrorizing, and torturing their young charges in bizarre satanic rituals. The accusations provoked unrelenting media scrutiny, public opprobrium, and in many cases resulted in criminal prosecution and, for those found guilty, draconian prison sentences.

The ritual abuse moral panic is a pristine example of a moral panic, if only because the putative threat to young children was wholly illusory and had to be discursively constructed out of strands of fundamentalist religious exhortations, popular culture representations, and therapeutic pseudoscience. Moral entrepreneurs and the media not only had to weave these strands into a convincing master narrative, but simultaneously had to demonize the otherwise ordinary day care providers into the quintessence of evil. As it turned out, and compared to most other moral panics, this was not an effortless task.

Briefly, I propose four imbricating reasons why that was so. First, far from being cultural strangers, the day care providers were familiar and trusted members of their respective communities. Each was recognized in the community, to one extent or another, not just for her performance in the role of day care provider, but for other role performances (e.g., neighbor, church member) as well as for idiosyncratic characteristics (e.g., kindness, sense of humor). Their social integration, in other words, not only problematized attempts to transform them from typical to atypical actors, and from ordinary to evil, but protected them from facile expressions of outgroup homogeneity bias (Quattrone and Jones 1980), that is, discourse that aims to persuade that all of them were alike not only in character but in threat to the moral order. Second, the proliferation of mass, micro, and niche media, the Internet, and the conflation of news with entertainment, produced many different and contradictory discourses about the day care providers. The wide variety of audiences to which these media played assured a vigorous debate not only over their guilt or innocence, but about the honesty and accuracy of the claims being made against them. Third, moral entrepreneurs and the media were not practiced in moral discourse aimed at socially integrated individuals. They often had difficulty in convincingly converging the alleged deviance of the day care providers with other deviant acts or actors, and often chose, instead, to link them with inchoate fears about other imaginary threats to the moral order, such as devil worship, mind control, and end times eschatology. While these convergences produced morally fueled signification spirals that propelled the day care providers as folk devils across the thresholds of social tolerance, they also were loosely, sometimes even sloppily, and certainly inconsistently and contradictorily, constructed, thus leaving more than a little space for contestation and resistance.

Finally, these otherwise socially integrated folk devils fought back. Whether their resistance is labeled as the exercise of personal power or agency, the expenditure of social capital, or the mobilization of resources, the fact remains that they used the media to proclaim their innocence and to reclaim their biographies from the hysterically pitched discourse of the moral entrepreneurs; built constituencies of loyal supports who used their own personal power to put counter-discourses into circulation; and even defended their integrity and reputations by bringing civil suits against their accusers and detractors.

In the short term, the resistance of day care providers to their demonization had diverse but largely localized impacts on the ritual abuse moral panic. A couple of examples will have to suffice. The women's resistance often forced a change in the discursive strategy of moral entrepreneurs and the media, who, their demonizing discourse challenged and ridiculed, opted for pathologizing the day care providers, producing what Watney (1987) refers to as 'monstrous representations' whose sickness, rather than evil, is disguised by a thin veneer of sociability. This type of discourse, interestingly, was easier for the day care providers to contest and harder for community members familiar with them to accept, thus raising the volume of the public debate over the accusations. The stigma contests in which the day care providers engaged also created highly politicized rifts in local communities that called into question the legitimacy not only of the agents but of the systems of social control, such as the legal system, that had institutionalized the moral panic's ideology.

It has been more than a decade since the ritual abuse moral panic ended, but the effects of the day care providers' resistance continue to reverberate. With only a few exceptions, those who were imprisoned have had their convictions overturned, and while some now live quiet lives of ignominy, others have transformed themselves, or *have been* transformed from folk devils into folk heroes. Called upon to be arbiters by the very media that had once demonized and pathologized them, they use their newly accrued moral capital as folk heroes to comment on contemporary moral panics involving sexual threats to children, whether by pedophiles, priests, or Internet predators.

By way of summary, if moral panics are re-conceptualized as rare and extreme instances of risk discourse in the process of moralization, and therefore conceptually distinct from moralization, they still require embodied folk devils that can be identified and acted against. With exceptions, these folk devils are most likely to already be socially marginalized, that liminal status vesting them with an aura of threat to the moral order that has only to be amplified and converged with other threatening acts and actors. So, the challenge for this conventional re-conceputalization of moral panics is twofold: first, to consider the differences in folk devil construction and demonization when the nominated folk devils are not already socially marginalized; and second, to theorize folk devils as social actors by examining how they use what personal power and resources they have access to resist their demonization and how that resistance, in turn, impacts on the claims, course, and consequences of moral panics.

'Modern' folk devils

If moral panics are re-conceptualized as quite commonly occurring eruptions of the moral regulation of everyday life, constructed through discourses of grievance and risk, then these modern folk devils are not likely to resemble those of conventional analyses. If embodied, they may be situated well within the margins of society and have personal power, institutional resources, and corporate embeddedness; they may be proxies; they may be rendered ambiguous or indefinite by their conflation with conditions, issues, or acts; or, as I will begin this discussion, they may not exist at all, at least in embodied form.

Cohen (1972), himself, suggests that a 'condition' or an 'episode' can be defined as a threat to societal values and interests, and although the bulk of analyses inspired by his and later Hall *et al.*'s (1978) work has given that suggestion short shrift, he invites considerations of moral panics *sans* embodied folk devils. What makes the invitation more enticing now is that this modern re-conceputalization blurs or, some may argue, erases, the boundary between moral regulation and moral panic; thus many conditions that are the subject of the former – such as health or personal safety matters – can be volatilized into the folk devils of the latter.

Bearfield (2008) offers an example. Although he theorizes no linkages to risk theory or moral regulation, choosing instead to substitute a condition for a folk devil and then to conduct a classically inspired analysis of a moral panic, the linkages can be read between the lines. In the immediate wake of the September 11, 2001 terrorist attacks in the United States, pointed questions were being asked about how the terrorists were able to breach airport security and hijack four commercial airliners. Because two of those airliners, both of which were crashed into the twin towers of the World Trade Center, originated in Logan Airport in Boston, Massachusetts, attention turned to that airport's security record. The *Boston Globe*, a top-tier daily newspaper, uncovered nearly 200 reported breaches of security at the airport over the previous three years. Reading between the lines now, it is clear that the airport, as a modern, high-technology institution that has as one of its functions the monitoring of, and the protection from, risk for the flying public, was alarmingly failing to do so.

In the burgeoning moral panic over public safety, Bearfield continues, the *Boston Globe*, rival media, moral entrepreneurs, and a host of both credentialed and newly minted experts searched for folk devils. While it could be convincingly argued that the managers of the airport and the directors of security were available for demonization, attention turned instead to the patronage system that had put them into their positions of authority in the first place. As a result, Bearfield concludes, the historically vilified, only weakly morally/ethically regulated condition of patronage, that is, the political appointment of cronies, in this case with no credentials or experience in either aviation or security, was nominated as the folk devil of the moral panic.

In his conventional approach to moral panic analysis, Bearfield does not consider the fact that conditions such as patronage have constituencies and stakeholders who, like folk devils as social actors, exert influence on the discourse, course, and even the consequences of a moral panic. That said, I suppose it is likely that the patronage system that had persisted for so long *sub silentio* and was so morally/ethically compromised had no public defenders, thus there were limited opportunities, if any at all, for stigma contests.

Perhaps there is a parallel here to the embodied folk devils of classic moral panic analyses. The more socially marginalized the condition, the more rooted in historical moral/ethical anxiety, the easier it is for moral entrepreneurs and the media to converge it with risk. And, it might be argued, the greater the severity and scope of the constructed risk, the fewer defenders will publicly engage in the politics of deviance over an already stigmatized condition. Judging patronage against pedophiles, in the end, may do little more than recall Shakespeare's observation that 'comparisons are odorous,' but for the purposes of conventional versus modern moral panic analyses they also may be worthy of consideration.

There are other comparisons also worthy of consideration. Levi's (2009) analysis of white-collar crime moral panics and their links to moral regulation and risk provides ingress for this discussion. Predicating his analysis on the assumption that the actions of corporate fraudsters only occasionally are interpreted as something more risky than the routine functioning of capitalism, he considers why some white-collar crimes, such as investment fraud, identity theft, selling toxic debts, and product contamination become the folk devils of moral panics while others do not. He then goes on to consider how some actions-as-folk-devils are neutralized, while others are not.

Levi concludes that structural arrangements, status considerations, and victim ideology all are at work in the folk-devilling process. Specifically, when moral entrepreneurs are politically powerful, media are unrestricted and uncensored, criminal or regulatory actions are discrete, subterranean values (e.g., 'greed is good') surface for debate, victims increase in number and are portrayed as having behaved with adequate due diligence before the transaction, and the white-collar crime is perceived both as a risk to the economic order and a threat to the moral order, the criminal act will become the folk devil of a moral panic, but the criminal actor most likely will not (p. 62). There are two particularly intriguing propositions here: first, white-collar crime moral panics are more likely to occur if the risk is perceived as *both* economic and moral; second, the anonymizing corporate environment renders the task of identifying embodied folk devils and 'damn[ing] them without ambiguity' (p. 62) all the more difficult, if not impossible.

If indeed a white-collar crime does becomes the folk devil of a moral panic, as was the case with the importation, sale, and recall of lead-painted toys in the United States in 2007, risk can be transformed or even neutralized with a discursive sleight-of-hand. It was the health risks to young children that provided the emotive fuel for the moral panic, but when the Mattel Corporation found an ally in American trade unions committed to finding and retaining jobs, the risk was transformed into an economic one that had to do with the dangers of out-sourcing and sub-contracting, particularly with a country whose ideologies and political system stood in stark contrast to those of the United States. The case study is instructive not only for the revealing the ways in which the corporation environment can 'hide' what could, and probably should, be the embodied folk devils of a moral panic, but how the absence of a 'social vocabulary of corporate crime' (McMullan 2006) mutes the reactions of the media, moral entrepreneurs and the public, stifles their attempts at convergence and deviance amplification, and may significantly shorten the course of the moral panic and lessen its control consequences, as it did in this case.

All of this discussion about what I am referring to as 'modern' moral panics has to do with risk. Risk is a tricky concept. By definition, it is a calculable danger, but it often is not so much the calculable that intensifies the sense of threat and insecurity in late modern society. Rather, it the unexpected and the invisible, that is, the risks to health, safety, stability, and well-being brought on by rapid social and economic changes, the collapse of traditional authority, the shifting sources of identity, the introduction of new methods of production, the forces of globalization, and the advancements in nuclear, chemical, biological, and environmental technologies (Beck 1992; Giddens 1991; Holloway and Jefferson 1997). It is these that create what Bauman (2006) refers to as the 'liquid fears' of modernity.

That risk is pervasive in today's society, and that the consciousness of it has engendered a particular way of 'understanding the self and world that differs dramatically from different eras' (Lupton 1999: 11) is axiomatic among sociologists. But whether *all* discourses about, and reactions to, the constant stream of emergencies, scandals, epidemics, and disasters produced by risk constitute moral panics is not (Miller 2006; Miller 2007; Ungar 2001). Arguably, then, late-modern society quite recently has experienced moral panics over designer drugs (Jenkins 1999), AIDS (Watney 1987), obesity (Campos *et al.* 2006), global warming (Ungar 1992), and genetically modified 'Frankenfood' (Frewer, Miles, and Marsh 2002), among others.

But who are the folk devils of these risk-related moral panics? Because most risk-related incidents that set the liquid fear flowing often expose complex institutional and political relations, and complicated human decision making, responsibility, representation, and blame are likely to be diffused. This necessitates foraging for folk devils (Ungar 2001), grabbing what is more likely than not to be a pawn, patsy, or proxy – a 'bureaucratic stranger' as Beck (1998) might say – who very well may have resources, constituencies, and institutional affiliations – to be the folk devils of the brewing moral panic.

Consider, in a brief example, what happened with the British bovine spongiform encephalopathy (BSE) moral panic. Jasanoff's (1997) incisive analysis reveals that ignorance, indifference, and incompetence about the risks of BSE were widely spread among public officials and throughout government ministries and private agencies. The moral panic filled the vacuum created by what she refers to as the 'civil dislocation' that occurred when there was a mismatch between expectations about what government is supposed to do to reduce and remedy risk incurred by the people, and what it actually does. The civil dislocation brought about a precipitous decline in trust in government and caused the public to look to other institutions, the media, and each other for support, thus perpetuating the moral panic. Bluntly stated, there was more than a little blame to go around, in the sixteen-volume report on the investigation of the moral panic offered several Tory ministers and their advisors as proxy folk devils, stating that they were responsible for playing down the health risks of BSE and failing to coordinate an effective government response. The government, of course, was caught in a dilemma: it had to put forth folk devils to satiate the public, but it also had to reassure the untrusting public that their incompetence was not a reflection of the government, itself. Thus the report was carefully worded, stating that there was no deliberate intent on the part of the proxy folk devils to protect farming interests at the expense of public health; the proxy folk devils therefore were relieved of any imputation of moral failure, but placed in the rather humiliating position of admitting to managerial inefficiency.

With the diffusion of responsibility, the discursive sleights-of-hand, the corporate or bureaucratic protection that are de rigueur in modern moral panics that have conditions, issues, and acts or, for that matter, proxies, as folk devils, the nature of stigma contests changes from what Schur (1980) once called the 'micropolitics' of deviance to the 'institutional' politics of deviance (p. 27). The latter is in many ways more complicated, since it is likely to involve a variety of differently situated parties and groups with a range of often competing interests, varying degrees of allegiance, commitment and obligation, and a range of resources ready to be mobilized. The challenge for modern moral panic analyses, then, is to enter the arenas where these stigma contests are occurring and to evaluate their influences on the claims, courses, and consequences of moral panics.

Hier (2002b) provides an interesting example of doing just that, but in doing so also demonstrates the changing nature of the folk devil in modern moral panic analyses. In this examination of the rave moral panic in Toronto, Canada, the folk devil was as much the rave dance parties and the illicit drug ecstasy, as it was the embodied ravers or the few among them who actually used ecstasy. And, if that were not indeterminate enough, the resistance to the demonization of all of these versions of the folk devil primarily came from rave promoters and various groups with institutional interests in the rave parties, rather than political interest in drug use, or personal interest in the ravers.

The moral panic burgeoned when three young participants in raves – dance parties held in locations such as abandoned warehouses and open fields – died from taking the drug ecstasy. Analyzing the content of mainstream newspapers, Hier reveals the discourse and representations that converged concerns about raves with even more alarmist concerns about the dangers and risks of ecstasy use, with the result that raves, which in fact had been city sanctioned, immediately were banned from city property and spaces by local officials.

Using the Foucauldian (1997) concept of the 'microphysics of power,' Hier examines three strategies used by the advocates of rave parties to subvert the risk discourse of moral entrepreneurs and the media, and manipulate it to their own ends. Keeping in mind that the advocates were differently situated and interested, and that they had to coalesce in order to be effective, they took to the media with the counterclaim that there actually was more risk in driving raves into unsafe and unhygienic venues than in holding them in city-sanctioned spaces; they filed a report contesting pending legislation to regulate raves; and they staged a protest outside of City Hall. These exercises in discursive subpolitics, as Hier terms them, not only successfully challenged the risk discourse of moral entrepreneurs and the media, but redefined the nature and the context of the risks associated with raves, thus redistributing blame to city representatives who were intent upon banning raves from city property and driving them underground.

Hier finds reasons to be cautious about generalizing his findings to other moral panics. Advocates of the folk devils in this moral panic were well-heeled promoters and corporate representatives with various interests and stakes in the outcome, and the embodied folk devils, themselves, were white, middle class, and otherwise socially integrated. His analysis, however, not only exemplifies the nature of modern moral panics, with their emphasis on risk rather than moral threat, but also demonstrates that even somewhat ambiguously constructed folk devils 'can and do fight back' (p. 52).

Conclusion

My brief in this chapter was to reconsider folk devils. If my epistemic gaze was sharpened at all, it was in response to the clarion call of this volume to expand the scope of moral panics by linking them to moral regulation and risk theory. There is no question that moral panic analyses would benefit from those linkages, although there are questions about how they should be forged.

This chapter leaves those questions unaddressed to consider how folk devils would fare if moral panics were reconceptualized. To facilitate the analysis, I differentiated between 'conventional' and 'modern' moral panics, the former describing rare and extreme instances of 'risk discourse within a process of moral regulation' (Critcher 2009: 17), and the latter describing much more common instances of volatile eruptions of the moralization in everyday life, 'transmitted through configurations of grievance and risk' (Hier 2008: 171). Each problematizes folk devils, but in different ways.

The folk devils of classic moral panic analyses invariably are embodied, already socially marginalized, and, quite frankly, rather easy to demonize. The problem here is not so much about re-analyzing the demonization process as it is about re-theorizing folk devils as social actors who use what personal power, agency, social capital, or capacity for resource mobilization they have to resist their demonization. The challenge then arises to examine and evaluate the influence of their resistance on the claims, courses, and consequences of moral panics. In contrast, the folk devils of modern moral panic analyses are considerably more difficult to pin down: they may be conditions, issues, or acts, rather than actors, and if they are embodied actors, they may be socially integrated, powerful, or protected, or they may be proxies, patsies, or pawns. The problem here, then, is not only to re-conceptualize the folk devil, but also to conceptualize the politics of risk, the arenas in which it is played out, as well as the strategies folk devils, however they are constructed, use to fight back, and with what, if any, results.

The future of moral panic analyses has never looked brighter. The discussion and debate over widening the scope of moral panic analyses, the linkages to moral regulation and risk theory are invigorating, but no matter how that debate is decided, if indeed it ever definitively is, the fact remains that folk devils – in some form or other – will always play a pivotal role in moral panics, both as those acted upon and as actors.

References

Agamben, G. (1998) *Homo Sacer*. Stanford: Stanford University Press.
Altheide, D.L. (2006) *Terrorism and the Politics of Fear*. Lanham: AltaMira Press.
Armstrong, E.G. (2007) 'Moral panic over meth', *Contemporary Justice Review*, 10: 427–42.
Bauman, Z. (2006) *Liquid Fear*. Cambridge: Polity Press.
Bauman, Z. (2001) *Community: Seeking Safety in an Insecure World*. Cambridge: Polity Press.
Bearfield, D.A. (2008) 'The demonization of patronage: Folk devils, moral panics and the *Boston Globe's* coverage of the terrorist attacks of 9–11', *International Journal of Public Administration*, 31(5): 515–34.
Beck, U. (1998) 'How neighbours become Jews: The political construction of the stranger in the age of reflexive modernity', in U. Beck, *Democracy Without Enemies*. Cambridge: Polity Press.
Beck, U. (1992) *Risk Society: Towards a New Modernity*. [M. Ritter, trans.]. London: Sage.
Ben-Yehuda, N. (1980) 'The European witch craze of the 14th and 17th centuries: A sociological perspective', *American Journal of Sociology*, 86(1); 1–31.
Campos, P., Saguy, A., Ernsberger, P., Oliver, E., and Gaesser, G. (2006) 'The epidemiology of overweight and obesity: Public health crisis or moral panic?', *International Journal of Epidemiology*, 35(1): 55–60.
Cohen, C. (2004) 'Deviance as resistance', *Du Bois Review*, 1: 27–45.
Cohen, S. (1972) *Folk Devils and Moral Panics: The Creation of the Mods and Rockers*. London: MacGibbon & Kee.
Critcher, C. (2009) 'Widening the focus: Moral panics as moral regulation', *British Journal of Criminology*, 49(1): 17–34.
Critcher, C. (2003) *Moral Panics and the Media*. Buckingham: Open University Press.

Critcher, C. (2002) 'Media, government and moral panic: The politics of paedophilia in Britain 2000–2001', *Journalism Studies*, 3(4): 521–35.
Denham, B. (2008) 'Folk devils, news icons, and the construction of moral panics', *Journalism Studies*, 9(6): 945–61.
deYoung, M. (2004), *The Day Care Ritual Abuse Moral Panic*, Jefferson: McFarland.
deYoung, M. (1998), 'Another look at moral panics', *Deviant Behavior*, 19(3): 257–78.
Ferguson, R., Gever, M., Trinh, T.M., and West, C. (1992) *Out There: Marginalization and Culture*. Cambridge, MA: MIT Press.
Foucault, M. (2003) *Abnormal: Lectures at the College de France 1974–1975*. London: Verso.
Foucault, M. (1997) 'Technologies of the self', in P. Rabinow (ed.), *Ethics: Subjectivity and Truth*, New York: New Press.
Frewer, L.J., Miles, S., and Marsh, R. (2002) 'The media and genetically modified foods: Evidence in support of social amplification of risk', *Risk Analysis*, 22: 701–11.
Giddens, A. (1991) *Modernity and Identity: Self and Society in the Late Modern Age*. Cambridge: Polity Press.
Goffman, E. (1963) *Stigma: Notes on the Management of Spoiled Identity*. Englewood Cliffs: Prentice Hall.
Goode, E. (1990) 'The American drug panic of the 1980s: Social construction or objective threat?', *International Journal of the Addictions*, 25(9): 1083–98.
Goode, E., and Ben-Yehuda, N. (1994) *Moral Panics: The Social Construction of Deviance*. Oxford: Blackwell.
Griffiths, R. (2010) 'The gothic folk devils strike back', *Journal of Youth Studies*, 13(3): 403–22.
Hall, S., Critcher, C., Jefferson, T., Clarke, J., and Robertson, B. (1978) *Policing the Crisis: Mugging, the State and Law and Order*. London: Macmillan.
Hay, C. (1995) 'Mobilisation through interpellation: James Bulger, juvenile crime and the construction of a moral panic', *Social and Legal Studies*, 4(2): 197–223.
Hier, S.P. (2008) 'Thinking beyond moral panic: Risk, responsibility, and the politics of moralization,' *Theoretical Criminology*, 12(2): 173–90.
Hier, S.P. (2002a) 'Raves, risks and the ecstasy panic: A case study in the subversive nature of moral regulation', *Canadian Journal of Sociology*, 27(1): 33–57.
Hier, S. (2002b) 'Conceptualizing moral panic through a moral economy of harm', *Critical Sociology*, 28(3): 311–34.
Hoeri, K. (2002) 'Monstrous youth in suburbia', *Southern Communication Journal*, 67(3): 259–75.
Holloway, W. and Jefferson, T. (1997) 'The risk society in the age of anxiety', *British Journal of Sociology*, 48(3): 255–66.
Hunt, A. (1999) *Governing Morals: A Social History of Moral Regulation*. Cambridge: Cambridge University Press.
Jasanoff, S. (1997) 'Civilization and madness: The great BSE scare of 1996', *Public Understanding of Science*, 6(3): 221–32.
Jenkins, P. (1999) *Synthetic Panic: The Symbolic Politics of Designer Drugs*. New York: New York University Press.
Jones, P. (1997) 'Moral panic: The legacy of Stan Cohen and Stuart Hall', *Media International Australia*, 85(1): 6–16.
Lauderdale, P. (ed.), (2004) *A Political Analysis of Deviance*. Ontario: de Sitter.
Lazarides, S. (2008) *Outsiders: Art by People*. London: Random House.
Leonard, P. (1984) *Personality and Ideology: Towards a Materialist Understanding of the Individual*. London: Macmillan.
Levi, M. (2009) 'Suite revenge? The shaping of folk devils and moral panics about white collar crime', *British Journal of Criminology*, 49(1): 48–67.
Lumsden, K. (2009) '"Do we look like boy-racers?" The role of folk devils in contemporary moral panics', *Sociological Research Online*, 14. www.socresonline.org.uk/14/1/2.html
Lupton, D. (1999) *Risk*. London: Routledge.
McMullan, J.L. (2006) 'News, truth, and the recognition of corporate crime', *Canadian Journal of Criminology and Criminal Justice*, 48(6): 905–39.

McRobbie, A. (1994a) *Postmodernism and Popular Culture*. London: Routledge.
McRobbie, A. (1994b) 'Folk devils fight back', *New Left Review*, 203: 107–16.
McRobbie, A. and Thornton, S.L. (1995) 'Re-thinking moral panic for multi-mediated social worlds', *British Journal of Sociology*, 46(4): 559–74.
Miller, D. and Kitzinger, J. (1998), 'AIDS, the policy process and moral panics', in D. Miller, J. Kitzinger, K. Williamson, and P. Beharrell (eds), *The Circuit of Mass Communication: Media Strategies, Representation and Audience Reception in the AIDS Crisis*. London: Sage.
Miller, P.G. (2007) 'Media reports of heroin overdose spates: Public health messages, moral panics, or risk advertisements?', *Critical Public Health*, 17(2): 113–21.
Miller, T. (2006), 'A risk society of moral panic', *Cultural Politics*, 2(3): 299–318.
Mulloy, D. (2004) *American Extremism*. New York: Routledge.
Ortiz, A.T., and Briggs, L. (2003) 'The culture of poverty, crack babies, and welfare cheats: The making of the healthy white baby crisis', *Social Text*, 21(1): 39–57.
Ost, S. (2002) 'Children at risk: Legal and social perceptions of the potential threat that possession of child pornography poses to society', *Journal of Law and Society*, 29: 436–60.
Quattrone, G.A. and Jones, E.E. (1980) 'The perception of variability within in-groups and out-groups: Implications for the law of small numbers', *Journal of Personality and Social Psychology*, 38, 141–52.
Rothe, D., and Muzzatti, S.L. (2004) 'Enemies, everywhere: Terrorism, moral panics and US civil society', *Critical Criminology*, 12(3): 327–50.
Sandywell, B. (2006) 'Monsters in cyberspace, cyberphobia and cultural panic in the information age', *Information, Communication and Society*, 9(1): 39–61.
Schinkel, W. (2008) 'Contexts of anxiety: The moral panic over "senseless violence" in the Netherlands', *Current Sociology*, 56(5): 735–56.
Schmitt, C. (1996) *The Concept of the Political*. Chicago: University of Chicago Press.
Schur, E. (1980) *The Politics of Deviance: Stigma Contests and the Uses of Power*. Englewood Cliffs: Prentice Hall.
Shepard, B. (2007) 'Sex panic and the welfare state', *Journal of Sociology and Social Welfare*, 34(2): 155–71.
Simi, P. and Futrell, R. (2009) 'Negotiating white power activist stigma', *Social Problems*, 56: 89–110.
St Cyr, J. (2003) 'The folk devil reacts', *Criminal Justice Review*, 28(1): 26–46.
Thompson, K. (1998) *Moral Panics*. London: Routledge.
Ungar, S. (2001) 'Moral panic versus risk society: The implications of the changing sites of social anxiety,' *British Journal of Sociology*, 52(2): 271–91.
Ungar, S. (1992) 'The rise and (relative) decline of global warming as a social problem', *Sociological Quarterly*, 33(4): 483–501.
Wacquant, L. (2007) *Urban Outcasts: A Comparative Study of Urban Marginality*. Cambridge: Polity Press.
Watney, S. (1987) *Policing Desire: Pornography, AIDS, and the Media*. London: Metheun.
Young, J. (2007) 'Slipping away – Moral panics each side of the "Golden Age"', in D. Downes, P. Rock, C. Chinkin, and C. Gearty (eds), *Crime, Social Control and Human Rights*. Devon: Willan Publishing.

9
THE DUALITY OF THE DEVIL
Realism, relationalism and representation

James Meades

While the concept of moral panic remains on the fringes of mainstream sociology (Ungar 2001), it is ready for a substantial and sustained breakthrough. A recent surge of articles on moral panic (Doran 2008; Garland 2008; Hier 2008; Critcher 2009; Jenkins 2009) indicates that it is time to 'rethink' (McRobbie and Thornton 1995), 'think beyond' (Hier 2008) and 'widen the focus' (Critcher 2009) of moral panic analysis. To this end, I interrogate a central, yet taken-for-granted component of moral panic analysis: folk devils.

The folk devil concept exists in a dual nature. On the one hand, it is a stylistic representation or abstracted social construct of some condition, episode, person or group of people. That is, folk devils exist as ideological representations of harm. On the other hand, representations of folk devils emerge from and depend upon essential actions of real people who exist relationally to others, both directly and indirectly. Cohen recognized the dual nature of folk devils when he wrote,

> [I]n the first part, the Mods and Rockers are hardly going to appear as 'real, live people' at all. They will be seen through the eyes of the societal reaction and in this reaction they tend to appear as disembodied objects, Rorshach blots on to which reactions are projected. In using this type of presentation, I do not want to imply that these reactions – although they do involve elements of fantasy and selective misperception – are irrational nor that the Mods and Rockers were not real people, with particular structural origins, values, aims and interests. Neither were they creatures pushed and pulled by the forces of the societal reaction without being able to react back. I am presenting the argument in this way for effect, only allowing the Mods and Rockers to come to life when their supposed identities had been presented for public consumption.
>
> *(Cohen 2002: 15)*

Cohen understood the relational nature of folk devils in terms of representation and social relation, yet he emphasized the representational elements 'for effect', thus bracketing off the real people and essential relations behind the representational idiom. As a result, the discursive construction of folk devils has become a primary focus of moral panic analysis, to the neglect of folk devil agency (deYoung 2007; also see deYoung, Chapter 8 this volume).[1]

In this chapter, I reunite the dual nature of folk devils as essential and representational phenomena using the theoretical and conceptual tools offered by critical realism.[2] I explore how the critical realist conceptualizations of stratification and emergence can methodologically advance moral panic studies by articulating a critical and holistic understanding of folk devils. I begin by briefly exploring the role of the mass media in moral panic and how the concept of ideology aids the analysis of media discourse. From this, I incorporate Roy Bhaskar's criteria for critiquing ideology to examine the representational domain of folk devils – what I call the phenomenal form. Next, I draw on Sean Creaven's conceptualization of emergentialist material dialectics, Roy Bhaskar's Transformational Model of Social Action and Margaret Archer's stratification of the person to offer a set of analytical tools to address folk devils as real people. In this way, I explain how critical realism offers a comprehensive way to understand the complexity of the dual nature of folk devils in terms of essential and phenomenal relations. In other words, I explain how critical realism can perform the necessary 'methodological underlabouring' for future studies of moral panic to better examine the explanatory gulf between representation and reality.

Media and the phenomenal form

Mass media play a prominent, if not causal, role in all instances of moral panic. Indeed, Critcher argues that 'modern moral panics are unthinkable without the media' (2003: 131). Critcher makes this argument because information about what constitutes criminal, sick or otherwise-deviant behaviour is often received second hand through the media. Cohen notes that 'a considerable portion of what we call "news" is devoted to reports about deviant behaviour and its consequences' (2002: 8), which in turn helps to formulate the normative boundaries for acceptable social action. More importantly, Cohen contends that 'the media have long operated as agents of moral indignation in their own right: even if they are not self-consciously engaged in crusading or muck-racking, their very reporting of certain "facts" can be sufficient to generate concern, anxiety, indignation or panic' (ibid).

Analyses of the role of the media during episodes of moral panic are confronted with several empirical and theoretical problems. At root, the tension lies in the relation between representation and reality. Before examining the tension between representation and reality, two initial considerations must be explored. First, it is important to avoid reducing the occurrence of moral panic to the volatility of media discourse. For some scholars (e.g., Welch, Price and Yankey 2002), the way in which the media focus intensely on a particular moral offence and its danger for a short duration of time constitutes the empirical boundaries of moral panic. During this time, the potential harm is extrapolated and exaggerated to signify a more widespread societal problem that requires an immediate solution (deYoung, Chapter 8 this volume). Without warning or inherent reason, news coverage of the apparent threat then declines, signaling that the moral panic has passed.

Given that moral panic is volatile by definition, using media discourse as an empirical boundary of moral panic may appear heuristically attractive, but it ultimately proves methodologically unsound. Equating moral panic with its volatile manifestation in the media poses at least two problems: first, media discourse of a particular event or phenomenon serves as a poor measure of social anxiety (Goode and Ben-Yehuda 1994; Hier 2002a; Hier 2002b; Walby and Spencer, Chapter 7 this volume); second, this equation unnecessarily limits the possible scope of scholarly analysis of moral panic to media discourse, ignoring the complex web of social relations involved in longer-term processes of moralization (Hier 2002b, 2008) and social problems construction (Best, Chapter 3 this volume).

The second consideration pertains to the nature and shape of media in contemporary society. On the one hand, McRobbie and Thornton (1995) point out that while the media appear as a monolithic entity in Cohen's study, developments in telecommunications have diversified media sources and altered the ways in which folk devils are constructed. They contend that these developments have fuelled a rise of niche and micro media sources (e.g., flyers, zines, web pages etc.), concomitantly offering new discursive spaces for folk devils to construct counter-narratives against their demonization. On the other hand, new discursive media spaces have largely occurred on the fringe of media operations, as mainstream media have become increasingly conglomerized into fewer and fewer corporations (McChesney 1997; Cottle 2003; Flew 2007). In this regard, mass media comes 'to speak in one voice',[3] albeit a contradictory one. Contemporary folk devils often find their interests defended in the same mass media sources responsible for amplifying claims against them. With 'a flare for the sensational' (Hier 2002b: 315), the issue of moral panic is no longer strictly a question of social control, but rather can be seen as an integral component to the way mass media attempts to sell the news.

Discourse, ideology and the phenomenal form of folk devil

How does the concept of ideology aid analyses of media discourse? At a theoretical level, the concept of ideology presents an innovative, yet under-appreciated, avenue for the analysis of media discourse during episodes of moral panic. However, before moving on to examine the innovative approach ideology provides for theorizing moral panic, it is worthwhile to clarify the conceptual distinction between discourse and ideology. Broadly speaking, discourse refers to the more semiotic or linguistic features, as opposed to the tangible and physical aspects, of social life. More specifically, 'discourse allows certain things to be said and impedes or prevents other things from being said' (Purvis and Hunt 1993: 485), thereby constructing parameters through which the communication of ideas/events takes place. Conversely, ideology, at least in the sense used here, refers to a false belief or a set of false beliefs (more on this below).⁴ In maintaining this distinction we see that discursive formations contribute to ideological positions and that ideological positions are embodied in, and gain articulation through, discursive forms. With this distinction in mind, there are two somewhat different uses of ideology as an explanatory concept within the moral panic literature.

The first is offered by Stuart Hall *et al.*, wherein moral panic serves an ideological function to provoke and legitimate, 'a coercive reaction by both the public and the state' (1978: 225) to deal with the purported problem in question. However, the real issue for Hall *et al.* is not the ideological but, rather, hegemonic function of moral panic. That is, Hall *et al.* are primarily concerned with how moral panic can create the 'exceptional' moment to orchestrate public consent for coercive measures. In this way, the ideological aspect of moral panic functions as a distraction from the structural problems of capitalism (unemployment, inflation, etc.). For Hall *et al.*, ideology mystifies real relations and casts representation on the purported harm posed by 'muggers', while at the same time the state strengthens its coercive power (i.e., toughing sentencing for petty crime, more governmental funding for police, military etc.).

The second use of ideology as an explanatory concept emerges from the work of Hier (2002b). While there are several evident similarities between Hall *et al.* and Hier, the distinction lies in how Hier emphasizes the more subjective rather than structural features of ideology. In other words, Hier attempts to develop a conceptualization of ideology that addresses the complex relation between media messages and media audiences, without lapsing into an ideological determinism that views social actors as mystified dupes of media messages. He argues that

> there is an important analytic distinction to be maintained between what people think and what they do, and an even greater level of analytic care to be exercised concerning what appears in the media and what people accept as factual.
>
> *(2002b: 313; cf. Ungar 2001)*

For Hier, it is theoretically necessary 'to discriminate analytically between the production, reproduction and transmission of cultural meanings on the one hand, and the functions to which those meanings and representations extend on the other' (Hier 2002b: 316). Integrating the concept of ideology, argues Hier, provides the grounds to make this analytical distinction, with two additional benefits: one, it allows for an examination of how dominant and subordinate subject relations are reproduced at the level of social action (Hier 2002b); two, it allows for the conceptual inclusion of *directionality*: the processes by which ideology functions to serve the interests of one group while neglecting or marginalizing the interests of another (Purvis and Hunt 1993; Hier 2002b). Methodologically, these two benefits constitute the conceptual frame to characterize the demonization of folk devils as a function of ideology, which places the folk devil into a subordinate subject position. Evidently, for Hier, the emphasis is on the function and the effect of ideology, on how we come to identify ideological systems only when they manifest objectively in discourse. In other words, Hier comes close to conflating ideology with discourse, even though he explicitly states the importance of maintaining their separation. Fortunately, it is easy to uphold the distinction between discourse and ideology, without sacrificing the conceptual advances made by Hier.

It is true that the ideas possessed by social actors impact on their actions, including but not limited to the ways in which they relate to others, but it is insufficient to move forward only when using the concept of ideology analytically. In fact, the concept of ideology has less to do with the effect of a false set of beliefs and far more to do with explaining how a false set of beliefs is necessitated in the first place. In other words, ideology moves backwards from false beliefs to investigate how the false beliefs arise (i.e., social relations), rather than forward to how those false beliefs are received. The shift here is towards critiquing the structures that are necessitated and sustained by ideology, rather than the effect of ideology that manifests objectively in discourse. Stated differently, through this conception of ideology it is possible to integrate the contributions of both Hall *et al.* and Hier into a singular mode of investigation. The advantage in making this shift for analysis of moral panic is the opportunity to move from description and analysis to critique. That is, it allows me to extend the theoretical value of the concept of ideology one step further by integrating the logical system for critiquing ideological positions from the work of Bhaskar (1998), while still situating the role of a causal explanation at the forefront.

Bhaskar and the critique of ideology

In approaching Bhaskar's argument for critiquing ideology, we must begin by clarifying a pressing theoretical problem. Namely – emerging from the Humean tradition – the contention that the 'transition from "ought" to "is", value to factual statements, although frequently made, is logically inadmissible' (1998: 54). According to Bhaskar, this contention hinges on two corollary propositions that he calls Hume's Law. First, that any factual conclusion is dependent on at least one factual proposition; second, that any value conclusion is dependent on at least one value judgment. For Bhaskar, however, not only is the transition from 'is' to 'ought', from factual to value statements, logically acceptable, it is also mandatory for any emancipatory science, provided a minimum set of criteria are met to characterize a belief(s) as ideological (these criteria are addressed below).

Before moving on to the criteria necessary for characterizing a belief as ideological, it is imperative to understand how the transition from value to factual statements is made. In doing so, it is crucial to bear in mind that 'to criticize a belief as false is *ipso facto* not only to criticize any action or practice informed or sustained by that belief, but also anything that necessitates it' (Bhaskar 1998: 63). Thus, for Bhaskar, if one possesses a theory that explains why a false belief is necessary, then one can make a negative assessment of the conditions, relations, structure etc. that necessitate the false belief in question without recourse to additional value judgments. Further, Bhaskar anticipates the objection 'that the fact/value distinction only breaks down in this way because one is committed to the prior valuation that truth is good' (ibid.). However, he contends that a positive valuation of truth is a condition for both moral and factual discourse and thus 'cannot be seized upon as a concealed (value) premise to rescue the autonomy of values from factual discourse, without destroying the distinction between the two, the distinction that it is the point of the objection to uphold' (ibid.).

At this point, we can shift our attention to the three types of criteria Bhaskar provides for characterizing a belief, or a set of beliefs, as ideological: critical, explanatory and categorical.

Bhaskar's three types of criteria

To consider the *critical* criteria first, in order to designate I as 'ideological' one must be in possession of a theory (or a consistent set of theories) T which can do the following:

1) Explain most, or most significant, phenomena, under its own descriptions, explained by I (under I's descriptions, where these are 'incommensurable with those of T).
2) Explain in addition a significant set of phenomena not explained by I.

To satisfy the *explanatory* criteria for the designation of I as 'ideological', T must be able to do the following:

3) Explain the reproduction of I (that is, roughly the conditions for its continued acceptance by agents) and if possible, specify the limits of I and the (endogenous) conditions for its transformation (if any), specifically:
3a) In terms of a real stratification or connection (that is, a level of structure or set of relations) described in T but altogether absent from or obscured in I.
4) Explain, or at least situate, itself within itself.

Finally, to satisfy the *categorical* criteria for the designation of I as 'ideological', I must be *unable* to satisfy either of the following:

5) A criterion of scientificity, specifying the minimum necessary conditions for the characterization of a production as scientific; or
6) A criterion of domain-adequacy, specifying the minimum necessary conditions for a theory to sustain the historical or social nature of its subject-matter.

And T must be able to satisfy both.

(Bhaskar 1998: 67–68)

In examining Bhaskar's criteria, we can see that both (1) and (2) refer to ways in which T must contain a higher degree of cognitive appeal in relation to I; that is, there are reasonable grounds for accepting T over I. In addition, (3a) specifies a particular type of cognitive appeal necessitated by a depth ontology lacking in I because of its false, phenomenal form. What (3) does is distinguish our social and natural scientific explanations necessitated by the internal relation of social theories to their subject matter. Thus, social scientific explanations must consider both the beliefs about a certain phenomenon as well as the phenomenon in and of itself. In turn, given the internality of social theories to their subject matter, we can see that (4) indicates a necessary criterion of reflexivity. Lastly, (5) and (6) stipulate that T must specify the necessary conditions for forming social scientific explanations – that is, a critical realist philosophy of science (see Bhaskar 1998, 2008; Sayer 2000).

Taken together, these criteria provide the logical basis for engaging in a critique of ideology. For Bhaskar, the concept of ideology 'reveals not only a gap between how an object is and how it appears to be, but a contradiction … between the way it presents itself in experience and the way it really is' (1998: 70). Furthermore, since phenomenal forms are a requisite for engaging in (making meaningful) social activity, Bhaskar contends that they are 'internally related to (that is, constitute necessary conditions for) the essential structures that generate them' (ibid). Lastly, 'it is important to stress that such contradictions, which involve merely the necessary co-existence in social reality of an object and a categorically false presentation of it, can be *consistently described*' (ibid.; italics in original) and therefore, altered.

In terms of moral panic, Bhaskar's conceptualization of ideology, alongside his criteria for critiquing ideological positions being endorsed here, can supplement moral panic studies in several crucial respects. First, explicating the phenomenal form of folk devil through Bhaskar's conceptualization of ideology shows, at least on one level, how folk devils can exist in a dual nature as categorically false representations and as real people. Inherent to this duality is a contradiction between the way in which folk devils are experienced, largely through the media, and the way they really are. Stated differently, the folk devil is the experience but the possibility for this experience to emerge depends on actions and relations of real people. Moreover, this contradiction is itself internally related to, and emergent from, the constitutive relation between folk devils and claims makers (henceforth FD/CM). Yet, despite being emergent from the FD/CM relation, the phenomenal form of folk devil cannot be reduced to this initial relation. Instead, the phenomenal form of folk devil, as an objective social fact, possesses its own causal powers, capable of influencing the course of the FD/CM relation as well as how the general public perceives the threat folk devils represent.

Second, this conceptualization of ideology provides the logical connection, as well as the political impetus, to maintain an emphasis on the existent social relation between folk devils and claims makers. If we are to advance our understanding of moral panic by addressing the dual nature of the folk devil, its emergence from and effects on existent social relations must be maintained. Further, the emphasis on the existent FD/CM relation presents the theoretical opportunity to deconstruct the real people from which folk devils emerge. In this regard, Bhaskar offers the grounds to explore how Archer's stratification of the person can contribute to a more nuanced understanding of folk devil agency and the social processes involved when 'folk devils fight back'.

Third, and most importantly, Bhaskar's argument sets out the theoretical grounds for critiquing the misrepresentation of folk devils, in addition to the generative structures and antecedent conditions necessitated by instances of moral panic. Since the phenomenal form of folk devil can be consistently described, it is possible to engage in a critique that can aid in altering the conditions that produce moral panic. This mode of critique, I argue, is the best suited to answer McRobbie and Thornton's call to re-examine, 'the labyrinthine web of determining relations which now exist between social groups and the media, "reality" and representation' (1995: 560) because the emphasis is placed not merely at the ideological representation but more importantly at the antecedent conditions and resulting actions that emerge from the false belief in question. However, to fully answer the challenge posed by McRobbie and Thornton requires examining the reality behind the representation, to which I can now turn my attention.

The agency of folk devils

Having established the theoretical grounds for critiquing the representation of folk devils through the concept of ideology, I now to turn to the question of folk devil agency. To do so requires a brief exploration into the FD/CM relation as the basis from which the agency of folk devils can be grasped. First, I review how the three primary explanatory models for moral panic identified by Goode and Ben-Yehuda (2009) prove problematic for conceptualizing the FD/CM relation. Second, I draw on the critical realist concept of emergence to reposition the FD/CM relation as both internally and dialectically related. Third, I argue that this conceptualization is better equipped to incorporate a notion of change required to grasp the internal dynamics of the FD/CM relation. It is only here, I maintain, that folk devil agency can be adequately addressed.

Explanatory models of moral panic

The three explanatory models identified by Goode and Ben-Yehuda (2009) prove problematic for analyzing the FD/CM relation. Succinctly, both the interest group and the elite-engineered model conceive of the FD/CM relation as one dimensional. For the interest group model, claims are transmitted from a distinctive body within civil society outwards to state officials and the general public. For the elite-engineered model, claims-making activities are transmitted from political and economic elites to civil society in a top-down manner. Since both the interest group and elite-engineered models conceptualize moral panic as a process, and a linear process at that, there is little room to incorporate a non-linear internal dynamic to the FD/CM relation.

By contrast, in the grassroots model, moral panic is not characterized by its process but, rather, by its attributes. Thus, claims-making activities are reduced to the 'more or less spontaneous' (Goode and Ben-Yehuda 1994: 127) outbreak of an already existing feeling of widespread fear and concern within the social body. However, Goode and Ben-Yehuda limit their own conceptualization by admitting that this constant (though latent) state of fear 'sometimes requires being assisted, guided, triggered or catalyzed' (ibid.) by interest groups, social movements or political elite before becoming a moral panic. While the grass-roots approach does gain some ground on the interest group and elite-engineered models by opening the analysis to a wider array of possible causal mechanisms, it simply replaces a one-dimensional FD/CM relation with a spontaneous and indeterminate eruption of social anxiety. Evidently, such a conceptualization cannot address the internal dynamic of the FD/CM relation because there is nothing internal that can be properly related. Instead, the result of the grass-roots approach is an ontological flatness that favours description over causal analysis.

The critical realist conceptions of causality and emergence can restore the internal dynamic of the FD/CM relation. In brief, critical realism holds that the way phenomena enter the empirical (i.e., observable) domain is premised upon the notion that causal powers exist regardless of whether they are active, being counter-acted or are altogether dormant in *any* one event. As a result, emergence is conceptualized as the interaction and counter-action of different mechanisms to produce phenomena, further entailing that phenomena 'have properties which are irreducible to those of their constituents [causal powers], even though the latter are necessary for their existence' (Sayer 2000: 12). In other words, the emergence of phenomena rests contingently upon the inter- and counter-action of mechanisms, which in turn constitute the necessary conditions for its emergence; yet, phenomena are irreducible to their specifically necessary, though contingently produced, conditions.

With these concepts in mind, the FD/CM relation reveals itself to be both a distinct emergent phenomenon and a necessary internal relation. While Cohen recognized the folk devil as an emergent phenomenon from the social definitions of claims makers, I argue that this phenomenon results from a far more differentiated and antagonistic social process. The first step to uncover this process is to explicitly position folk devils and claims makers as necessarily constituting an internal relation. I take this move to be uncontroversial, since many of our social roles and identities exist as internal relations (Sayer 2000). For example, to understand the role of a landlord requires understanding the role of a tenant – the two roles necessarily form an internal relation. The importance of characterizing the FD/CM relation as internal results from the fact that 'individuals obtain novel characteristics by virtue of their insertion within *specific kinds* of social relations, not simply by pooling their individual capacities or powers' (Creaven 2002: 137). Two propositions can be made concerning folk devils and their relation to claims makers. First, the conditions for folk devil emergence depend upon the contingent interaction of causal powers through which one social group attempts to demonize the behaviour or conduct of another group. Second, this process creates an internal relation in which both folk devils and claims makers obtain novel characteristics, but it is crucial to note that these characteristics are irreducible to this relation.

The second step is to explain how the relation between FD/CM functions. Given the methodological difficulty of explaining an interaction between abstract social roles, I will move forward by conceiving the folk devil/claims maker relation dialectically. In this regard, Hier's (2002b) work provides an initial point of departure. Hier argues that moral panic operates as a political technology, 'through a dialectical process of signification (discursively articulated in terms of "us"/"them")' (2002b: 329). For Hier, the dialectic depends on the discursive construction of a harmful 'other' that poses a threat to 'us' all. Yet, through critical realism this dialectic can be extended beyond the discursive to examine how FD/CM constitute a material (that is, extra-discursive) social relation.

Moral panic and material dialectics

To conceptualize this process, I draw on the work of Sean Creaven (2002), whose synthesis of critical realism and dialectical materialism proves invaluable for understanding how we can view the folk devil/claims maker dialectic as a social relation and not solely a discursive configuration. The shift from discursive to material dialectic requires addressing how we form concepts and decipher dialectics. First,

> Concepts are the product of real conditions, shaped by existential contradictions, even if they have to be abstracted from their objects, and subjected to rational procedures of scientific testing, then reapplied to their objects in the form of more sophisticated concepts, if they are to apprehend the nature of real world processes and structures.
>
> *(Creaven 2002: 140)*

Dialectics, conversely, are not the *products* of real conditions, but rather the internal dynamics of the conditions themselves. Creaven argues that dialectics cannot be constructed by the active will of a researcher, but only identified through empirical investigation. In his own words, he contends that 'dialectics is no ready-made formula into which the real world has to be fitted, but must instead be discovered by means of empirical-scientific investigation into the different facets of the world' (2002: 148). In both cases, the emphasis remains on the empirical to form concepts and identify dialectics. However, the assumption of ontological stratification – that is, the founding assumption of critical realism, that reality exists below the surface of things – requires viewing empirical phenomena as emergent from the events of the Actual and the mechanisms of the Real. In this ontological model, the Real comprises mechanism, events and phenomena, the Actual comprises events and phenomena, while the Empirical comprises only phenomena (Bhaskar 2008). As a result of this ontological framework, Creaven argues that the merger of critical realism and dialectical materialism offers the conceptual grounding to develop an 'emergentialist material dialectic'.

Immediately, Creaven foresees the possible objection, 'that dialectical materialism is not an emergentialist ontology at all' (2002: 144), thus making it unnecessary and unrewarding for critical realism to engage, conceptually or otherwise, with dialectic materialism. While there is no need to rehearse the entirety of Creaven's response to this hypothetical objection, the three arguments he posits in defense deserve brief mention because they demonstrate why I have chosen to formulate the FD/CM relation as an emergent material dialectic. First, Creaven argues that 'dialectical concepts are in fact explicit *descriptions* of the reality of stratification and emergence' (2002: 144). Second, 'such concepts are as reasonable a way as any of capturing in the most general terms the reality of the world as a "differentiated unity"' (2002: 145). And third,

> dialectical concepts are *successful* in historicizing stratification and emergence. That is, they allow us to grasp the dynamics or processes through which higher-order levels of the material world develop out of lower-order levels, not as 'radical contingency' but as integral aspects of a continually evolving totality of interrelated systems.
>
> *(2002: 146)*

In the context of moral panic, these three responses establish the necessary theoretical foundation for grasping the internally dynamic relation between FD/CM. Further, premising the analysis of this relation on conditions of emergence opens considerable theoretical space for a more complex conceptualization of the extra-discursive elements intrinsic to how claims-making processes create folk devils.

Conceptualizing the FD/CM relation as an emergent material dialectic allows for an important theoretical advance concerning the issue of change. As Bhaskar and Norrie argue, the addition of dialects to critical realism involves treating dialectics 'ontologically, as the dynamic of conflict and the mechanism of change' (1998: 562; *cf.* Creaven 2002: 151). This, however, does not mean treating processes of change as historically teleological or epistemologically tautological. Instead, Creaven argues that

> Change is now grasped as the collision of social or physical oppositions, without the certainty that a specific resultant or fixed end-state must follow from initial causes or conditions, in advance of the development process itself, as would the conclusion of a problem in logic from its initial premises.
>
> *(2002: 140)*

This approach to change can avoid the tendency in studies of moral panic to either a) present their analysis ahistorically or b) view the dialectic of FD/CM as a reductive social construction (i.e., moral panic is constructed by claims makers) or as a structural determination (i.e., structural forces create folk devils, and thus moral panic)'.

Integrating this notion of change serves a larger purpose than simply conceptualizing the FD/CM dialectic as internally dynamic. Rather, it opens the theoretical space for posing serious questions regarding agency, especially the agency of folk devils. In freeing the folk devil from a purely phenomenal form of discursive representation, emergent dialectical materialism presents the opportunity to explore the emergent properties and causal mechanisms specific to active human agents. In critical realist terms, the shift from the discursive to the material reveals the symbiotic relation between the intransitive and transitive dimensions of knowledge. In other words, the discursive representation of a folk devil (transitive) emerges from, but is irreducible to, the real referent, the actual people (intransitive), who are characterized as folk devils. This distinction requires bringing the real referent of the folk devil into the transitive dimension of knowledge if either our concepts or explanations are to have methodological merit at both the ontological and epistemological levels.

On agency and moral panic

The question of agency has yet to be thoroughly incorporated into conceptualizations of moral panic. On the one hand, the agency of claims makers has been taken for granted, since to make a claim is to act. On the other hand, the agency of folk devils has been marginalized, resulting from the problematic way in which scholars fail to treat folk devils as real people with structural origins, values and interests. In the final section of this chapter, I argue that the concept of agency needs to be at the forefront in analysis of moral panic. First, I examine how the works of McRobbie (1994), Hier (2002a) and deYoung (2007, Chapter 8 this volume) have begun to address the question of folk devil agency. Second, I argue that, through Bhaskar's Transformational Model of Structure and Agency and Archer's stratification of the person, the question of folk devil and claims maker agency can be resolved. In addition, Archer's stratification of the person provides the context to establish the conceptual connection between folk devils as real people, as well as (mis)-representations of some future harm to come.

McRobbie (1994) provides the first notable attempt to examine the agency of folk devils. However, her emphasis is not the agency of folk devils, per se; instead, she sets out to examine how the folk devil label can be seized, contested and overcome by various organizations in civil society. Specifically, McRobbie argues that 'new centres of conviction politics', such as 'social movements, pressure groups and other voluntary organizations' (1994: 114) have arisen to defend contemporary folk devils by providing 'oppositional views and alternative information and analysis' (1994: 115). From this, she argues that '[o]ne of their most important functions lies not just in challenging the discrimination against folk devils but also in actively redefining the [political] agenda' (ibid.). She continues by highlighting that 'folk devils can also fight back by producing their own media, given the relative cheapness and availability of new technology' (1994: 114; also see McRobbie and Thornton 1995). The crucial point to note here is how McRobbie's argument reveals the transformative potential involved in counter-claims processes when folk devils, or their defenders, fight back.

To better illustrate McRobbie's argument of how folk devils can fight back, Hier's (2002a) analysis of the 'rave and ecstasy panic' proves instructive. In Toronto, Ontario during the summer of 2000, a moral panic developed over the consumption of the designer drug ecstasy at raves. While raves are often characterized as secretive, underground dance parties held in abandoned warehouses, factories or open fields, Hier notes that 'on 15 December 1999 Toronto city council voted unanimously to regulate raves held in the city under the auspices of The Protocol for the Operation of Safe Dance Events/Raving' (2002a: 38). This Protocol set out guidelines for rave venues concerning security, ventilation and other health and safety precautions.

However, following the deaths of three teenagers, the issues of ecstasy use and raves took a more politicized and more prominent place in the media, causing the city to retract its support for holding raves on city property. Yet, supporters of the rave community quickly undertook to subvert their demonization in the media, seeking to characterize 'Toronto's rave communities as being "at risk" … by amplifying and accentuating the risks associated with forcing raves into locations containing substandard facilities' (Hier 2003: 10). This case study, as Hier correctly argues, emphasizes 'social actors as dynamic agents capable of penetrating and contesting moralized political projects' (2002a: 35), providing one of the clearest examples of how folk devils can, and do, fight back.

The second, and most explicit, attempt to address the agency of folk devils comes from Mary deYoung. She argues that the agency of folk devils, 'their reactions and resistances to their demonization and social control, as well as the effects these have on the courses and outcomes of moral panics' (2007: 4) remain under-theorized in studies of moral panic. In her paper, deYoung identifies three ways that scholars can begin to recognize and assess folk devils as active agents.

First, deYoung suggests that scholars must avoid the tendency of reifying 'Otherness' (ibid.) by treating folk devils as 'objects' instead of as 'subjects' in their analysis. Avoiding a reified conception of the 'other', deYoung argues, opens up space for considering that contemporary folk devils may not be the 'cultural strangers' or the atypical actors characteristic of traditional moral panic studies (deYoung, Chapter 8 this volume). Instead, as subjects, folk devils can be viewed as 'typical actors against a background that is atypical' (deYoung 2007: 6), possessing the resources and social standing to resist and challenge attempts to demonize their behaviours.

Second, deYoung suggests that scholars reconsider how media representations and societal reactions operate in late-modern society. There are two related issues at work: first, the proliferation of media sources that allow for folk devils to launch counter-claims; second, the transmission of news/entertainment across national boundaries, leading to the internationalization of particular moral panics. Since I briefly dealt with the first issue above, I will focus solely on the second issue here. Citing Critcher (2006: 14), deYoung argues that developments in media communications facilitate the internationalization of moral panic as operative beyond discrete national spheres. By implication, she contends that while mass media outlets can spread the information of a moral panic across national boundaries, they can also 'serve as conduits for differently situated folk devils to share strategies of resistance and challenge, and to recruit international constituencies' (deYoung 2007: 7). Evident in deYoung's argument is that the rise of international news media creates a unique method for folk devils to exercise their agency and unite to fight back.

Third, deYoung argues that conceptualizations of folk devil agency could be improved by integrating notions of risk. While recognizing that risk is 'a tricky concept' (2007: 7), deYoung contends that risk society issues are presenting new conditions for moral panic, and thus, for creating new types of folk devils. Since risk issues generally involve more complex institutional relations, deYoung notes that 'responsibility, representation and blame are likely to be more diffused' (2007: 9) than in conditions of traditional moral panic. In turn, the integration of risk into moral panic can necessitate 'foraging for folk devils' (Ungar 2001: 283) because clear demarcations between 'us and them' are not readily apparent. However, as we saw in Jasanoff's (1997) analysis of the BSE panic in Britain, identifiable folk devils can emerge from risk-related incidents. The implication, for deYoung, is that these new folk devils often emerge already possessing 'resources, constituencies and institutional affiliations' (2007: 9), granting them greater autonomy in contesting their folk devil status (deYoung, Chapter 8 this volume).

While deYoung does provide some ground to open more theoretical space for considering the agency of folk devils, her analysis leaves several important issues unresolved. In particular, her emphasis on the agency of folk devils marginalizes the personalizing effects of social structures on individual human conduct. That is, she marginalizes the powerful effect that structural forces as well as their enforcers (i.e., the legal structure and the police) have on governing individual behaviour. Second, though deYoung correctly identifies the problem of the subject/object analytical duality, her argument to avoid reifying Otherness is insufficient from a methodological point of view. Third, deYoung's analysis remains tied to the empirical, leaving no room for a concept of stratification or the theorization of underlying causal mechanisms. However, I argue that these issues can be overcome with the insights provided by critical realism.

A realist account of agency

The first step to providing a realist account of agency is to develop the conceptual framework provided by Bhaskar's Transformational Model of Structure/Agency (TMSA). Concisely, the TMSA views structure and agency as distinct yet interrelated phenomena. In this conceptualization, social structures constitute both the product of, and necessary conditions for, human agency that in turn are capable of transforming or reproducing social structures. Bhaskar's model proves invaluable because 'its emphasis on material continuity can sustain a genuine concept of *change*, and hence, of *history*' (1998: 37; italics in original). Further, since the potential for change is a requisite for transformative action, the TMSA constitutes the only acceptable conceptualization of structure and agency. However, for my purpose here, the role of social structures is secondary. Since moral panic will affect particular communities at particular moments in time, the identification of particular structural influences will involve intensive empirical investigation. The important point to bear in mind here is how social structures play a distinct role in enabling or constraining human agency. Specifically, it is crucial to note that, while structural causal powers will vary in any one particular instance of moral panic, depending, of course, on whether they are active, being counter-acted or dominant, this can provide only the pre-conditions, and not the determinate outcome, of human action. Thus, while it is uncontroversial to acknowledge social structures as a causal power in producing moral panic, the lack of contention solely depends upon developing the conceptual pre-conditions of change detailed above.

Moving forward from the TMSA, I can now examine the issue of folk devil and claims maker agency and, by conceptual extension, develop a stratified conceptualization of the folk devil and the claims maker. In dealing with the emergence of folk devils through dialectical materialism, I hinted towards how a stratification of a folk devil is not only possible but also necessary for theorizing agency. There, I offered an initial stratification of the folk devil as possessing a phenomenal form and a real referent. The phenomenal form, I argued, consists of the stylized and exaggerated representation of folk devils in the media. In other words, it refers to the way in which the representation of the folk devil develops a set of false beliefs (i.e., ideology) regarding the potential social harm. The real referent, by contrast, consists of the actual people labeled or characterized as folk devils. Recalling that concepts emerge from the process of engaging in material activity, the folk devil, even as an ideal type, requires that particular social actors engage in particular social actions for an instance of moral panic to emerge. As a result, I would like to extend the conceptualization of the real referents (that is, the actual people) of the folk devil also in terms of stratification.

To develop a stratified conception of people, Archer (2003) makes the initial analytical distinction between agents and actors. For Archer, '"agents" are defined as *collectivities* sharing the same *life-chances*' (2003: 118) and can be dealt with only in the plural. From this, two related propositions can be extracted: one, all people are necessarily agents because of their position in the social distribution of resources; however, two, simply being a part of a collectivity of people via resource distribution is not sufficient for a strict social identity (ibid.). Actors, on the other hand, are properly singular and possess the criteria for acquiring a unique social identity based upon a definite number of social roles available to them at particular times. Thus, people become agents as an involuntary product of birth, while to become an actor requires a deeper sociality within the field of social relations. That is, it requires agents to assume particular social identities (parent, teacher, etc.) and to engage in the internal and external relations inherent to social life.

Further, Archer provides an analytical distinction between Primary Agents and Corporate Agents that bears particular relevance for conceptualizing folk devils as well as claims makers. On the one hand, primary agents are simply agents as defined above. Corporate agents, on the other hand, are those collectivities that 'have articulated their aims and developed some form of organization for their pursuit' (Archer 2003: 133*n*). Stated differently, the movement from primary to corporate involves examining 'our social contexts, asking and answering ourselves (fallibly) about how we can best realise the concerns, which we determine ourselves, in circumstances that were not of our choosing' (Archer 2003: 133). It is precisely this shift that deYoung alluded to when discussing how media proliferation has opened space for 'folk devils to share strategies of resistance and challenge, and to recruit international constituencies' (2007: 7). The methodological value deriving from Archer's distinction lies in the ability to conceptualize how different agents respond to folk devil status and how folk devils can exist in a dual nature as both real people and false phenomenal representations.

Moreover, the stratified conception of people also provides an insight into the emergence of claims makers. To become a claims maker in an instance of moral panic requires that agents move from a primary to a corporate form. By collecting their shared feelings, anxieties and concerns, primary agents shift to corporate agents, and only in becoming corporate agents can the social role of a claims maker be satisfied. As I argued in the first section of this chapter, the act of making claims is not particular to instances of moral panic, but rather, is a routine feature of social life. What gives claims-making activities their special character in moral panic depends upon how successful claims-makers are in taking on this corporate form and in articulating the diverse interests of individual actors as a common interest. As Goode and Ben-Yehuda argue,

> Professional associations, police departments, the media, religious groups, may have an *independent* stake in bringing an issue to the fore ... altering legislators, demanding stricter law enforcement, instituting new educational curricula, and so on.
> *(1994: 139; emphasis in original)*

Yet, in order to succeed, this independent stake must come to be viewed as beneficial to other interest groups, social movement and agents. In other words, the special quality of claims-making activities in moral panic emerges from the successful transition from primary to corporate agents. When examined together, the TMSA and the stratification of people offer a fresh perspective for understanding the complex social roles and social relations involved in instances of moral panic.

Conclusion

In this chapter I have sought to reunite the dual nature of the folk devil into a holistic mode of analysis. Using the conceptual and theoretical tools offered by critical realism, I have developed an analytically and methodologically nuanced mode of inquiry that does not depend on either reification or reduction when attempting to address the folk devil of moral panic. Through the concept of ideology as well as Bhaskar's criteria for critiquing ideological positions, the first section explored not only how future research into moral panic can deal with the complexity of news representations but also how the concept of ideology opens the possibilities for altering the disproportional characterization of harm posed by folk devils. The second section then sought to develop the material basis for changing and challenging the conditions that produce instances of moral panic. Using Creaven's emergentialist material dialectics, Bhaskar's TMSA and Archer's stratification of the person, I argue, affords a richer avenue for addressing the lingering questions regarding the agency of folk devils. When they are taken together, the dual nature of the folk devil ceases to be theoretically or methodologically problematic.

More importantly, the political impetus inherent to critical realism as a philosophy of science committed to the production of emancipatory knowledge strikes at the heart of what moral panic, as an empirical phenomenon and not solely as an academic concept, is really all about. Moral panic does not merely demonstrate the complex relations between political bodies, interest groups, the media and the general public, nor does it simply illuminate sites of social anxiety, but it does both simultaneously. In the process, instances of moral panic force academics and non-academics alike to face some serious and difficult questions about current modes of social organization. In critical realist terms, an instance of moral panic, as a set of false beliefs, necessitates questioning the antecedent conditions that led to its emergence as well as the practices informed and/or sustained by its emergence. On the academic side, this means that moral panic analysis is going to get a whole lot messier. However, this is precisely why the concept of moral panic is so ripe for revival. For, echoing Critcher, 'if there is a better guide than the moral panic concept ... then it has yet to be discovered' (2006: 3).

Notes

1 Mary deYoung presented this paper at the American Sociological Association's Annual General Meeting in 2007. The page numbers cited in my discussion of deYoung's work are based on the original Word document of the paper.
2 As a comprehensive philosophy of science, it is impossible for me to provide a complete inventory of critical realism's essential features. Andrew Sayer's *Realism and Social Science* (2000) provides a thorough account of critical realism for further consultation.
3 Viewers of *The Daily Show with Jon Stewart* will be familiar with the montages depicting various guests and pundits from the major news networks (Fox, MSNBC, CNN, etc.) repeating the same hackneyed phrases and clichés on the issue of the day.
4 As Eagleton (1991) notes, the concept of ideology possesses an array of possible definitions. I have elected to follow Bhaskar (1998) and take a firm stance on what ideology 'is' by confining ideology specifically to false beliefs.

References

Archer, Margaret. (2003) Structure, Agency and the Internal Conversation. Cambridge: Cambridge University Press.Bhaskar, Roy. (1998) The Possibility of Naturalism: A Philosophical Critique of the Contemporary Human Sciences. 3rd ed. London: Routledge.
Bhaskar, Roy. (2008) A Realist Theory of Science. 3rd ed. London: Verso Publishing.
Bhaskar, Roy and Alan Norrie. (1998). Introduction: Dialectic and Dialectical Critical Realism. In Margaret Archer, Roy.
Bhaskar, Andrew Collier, Tony Lawson and Alan Norrie (editors). Critical Realism: Essential Readings. New York: Routledge.
Cohen, Stanley. (2002) Folk Devils and Moral Panics: The Creation of the Mods and Rockers. Third Edition. London: Routledge.
Cottle, Simon. (2003) Media Organization and Production. London and Thousand Oaks: Sage.
Creaven, Sean. (2002) Materialism, Realism and Dialectics. In A. Brown, S. Fleetwood and J.M. Roberts (editors). Critical Realism and Marxism. London: Routledge.
Critcher, Chas. (2002) Media, Government and Moral Panic: The Politics of Paedophilia in Britain 2000–2001, Journalism Studies, 3(4): 521–35.
Critcher, Chas. (2003) Moral Panics and the Media. Milton Keynes: Open University Press.
Critcher, Chas, ed. (2006) Critical Readings: Moral Panics and the Media. Buckingham: Open University Press.
Critcher, Chas. (2009) Widening the Focus: Moral Panics as Moral Regulation, British Journal of Criminology, 49(1): 17–34.
deYoung, Mary (2007) Considering the Agency of Folk Devils. Presented at the American Sociological Association's Annual General Meeting.

Doran, Nob. (2008) Decoding encoding: Moral Panics, Media Practices and Marxist Presuppositions, Theoretical Criminology, 12(2): 191–221.
Eagleton, Terry. (1991) Ideology: An Introduction. London: Verso.
Flew, Terry. (2007) Understanding Global Media. New York: Palgrave Macmillan.
Garland, David. (2008) On the concept of moral panic , Crime, Media, Culture, 4(1): 9–30.
Goode, Erich and Nachman Ben-Yehuda. (1994) Moral Panics: The Social Construction of Deviance. London: Blackwell.
Goode, Erich and Nachman Ben-Yehuda. (2009) Moral Panics: The Social Construction of Deviance, 2nd ed. Malden, MA and Oxford, UK: Wiley-Blackwell
Hall, Stuart, Chas Critcher, Tony Jefferson, John Clarke and Brian Roberts. (1978) Policing the Crisis: Mugging, the State, and Law and Order. London: MacMillan Press Ltd.
Hier, Sean. (2002a) Raves, Risks and the Ecstasy Panic: A Case Study in the Subversive Nature of Moral Regulation , Canadian Journal of Sociology, 27(1): 33–57.
Hier, Sean. (2002b). Conceptualizing Moral Panic through a Moral Economy of Harm , Critical Sociology, 28(3): 311–34.
Hier, Sean. (2003) Risk and Panic in Late Modernity: Implications of the Converging Sites of Social Anxiety, British Journal of Sociology, 54(1): 3–20.
Hier, Sean. (2008) Thinking Beyond Moral Panic: Risk, Responsibility, and the Politics of Moralization, Theoretical Criminology, 12(2): 171–88.
Jasanoff, Sheila. (1997) Civilization and Madness: The Great BSE Scare of 1996 , Public Understanding of Science, 6(3): 221–32.
Jenkins, P. (2009) Failure to Launch: Why Do Some Social Issues Fail to Detonate Moral Panics?, British Journal of Criminology, 49(1): 35–47.
McChesney, Robert. (1997) Corporate Media and the Threat to Democracy. New York: Seven Stories Press.
McRobbie, Angela. (1994) Folk Devils Fight Back , New Left Review. I/203.
McRobbie, Angela and Sarah L. Thornton. (1995) Rethinking Moral Panic for Multi-mediated Social Worlds, British Journal of Sociology, 46(4): 559–74.
Purvis, Trevor and Alan Hunt. (1993) Discourse, Ideology, Discourse, Ideology, Discourse, Ideology{...}, British Journal of Sociology, 44(3): 473–99.
Sayer, Andrew. (2000) Realism and Social Science. London: Sage Publications Inc.
Ungar, Sheldon. (2001) Moral Panic versus the Risk Society: The Implications of the Changing Sites of Social Anxiety , British Journal of Sociology, 52(2): 271–91.
Welch, Michael, Eric A. Price and Nana Yankey. (2002) Moral Panic Over Youth Violence: Wilding and the Manufacture of Menace in the Media , Youth and Society, 34(1): 3–30.

Part 3
Applying moral panic studies

This section presents five chapters designed to examine revisions to moral panic studies by applying them to empirical cases. The first two papers directly address the relationship between moral panic and moral regulation. Lett, Hier, Walby, and Smith introduce the section by examining a moral panic over hooded tops in Britain. In 2005, hooded tops were banned from a shopping mall in Kent. Soon, a panic broke out over hooded tops in public places that reached beyond the shopping mall. Through an examination of governmental and extra-governmental claims-making activities, Lett, Hier, Walby, and Smith illustrate how the volatile panic over hooded tops was tied to the British government's long-term law and order agenda. In doing so, they show how the moralization of reform and respect can fuel moral panic in moments of perceived crisis or breakdown.

In Chapter 10, Chas Critcher continues examining the relationship between moral regulation and moral panic by assessing the political economy of the moral regulation of pleasure. Previously, Critcher made two important contributions to the panic literature. First, he pushed moral panic studies closer to adopting a comparative framework (Critcher 2003). Second, he critically examined the relationship between moral panic and moral regulation (Critcher 2009). In this chapter, he brings these contributions together to compare reactions to twenty-first-century binge drinking to the eighteenth-century gin craze. His aim is to glean insights into the relationship between moral panic and moral regulation.

The next two chapters expand the application of moral panic to environment and scandal by addressing what Cohen (2003) conceptualizes as 'good' moral panics. Sheldon Ungar begins by offering a revision to moral panic studies by using debates about climate change to expose problems with conventional models. Climate change has been on the global agenda for 20 years. Unlike conventional emphases on conservative claims making that culminates in 'bad' moral panics, however, climate change claims making involves left-liberal climate advocates who contribute to 'good' low-grade and volatile moralization. What is interesting about climate change as an empirical anomaly for moral panic studies, says Ungar, is that it began as an elite engineered panic orchestrated by scientists but spread among interest groups who possess limited understandings of science. Differences in expertise among claims makers not only lead to different kinds of disproportional claims making that are conditioned by different kinds of rationality. They also pose difficulties for the kinds of moral claims that can be made about folk devils and morally culpable agents. For Ungar, then, climate advocates conceal the disproportional character of their claims by artfully orchestrating low-grade anxieties and situational-specific volatile episodes through a forging for viable folk devils.

Graham Knight and Juliet Roper continue to examine 'good' moral panics in the following chapter. Knight and Roper use the example of a death that occurred following residential electricity suspension to critically reflect on the relationship between scandals and panics. Both scandals and panics entail the mediation of harm and the allocation of blame. Where they differ is in terms of the kinds of emotions they induce; the proximity of folk devils, claims makers, and victims; and the direction of claims. The scandal they analyze – based on a state-owned electricity company that disconnected electricity to a house where a mother of four relied on an oxygen machine – illustrates the unfolding of a good moral panic conceptualized as scandal, whereby the actions of the powerful were subjected to critical public scrutiny and blame allocation. For Knight and Roper, studying good moral panics requires moving beyond the realm of conventional claims making to address the institutional and communicational dynamics involved in managing allocations of harm among society's more powerful agents.

In the final chapter of the section, Béland continues to investigate the complexity of claims making beyond conventional concerns by focusing on the mediation of health scares. Health scares, he explains, are similar to moral panics: they erupt suddenly, situate collective risk management strategies against individual sources of harm, and subside rather quickly. Yet some health scares last longer than others and only some develop into moral panics. To broaden debate about risk and moralization by gleaning insights into health scares and moral panics, he compares BSE to SARS. Béland concludes that the 2003 SARS scare qualifies as moral panic but the 1996 BSE scare does not fit a moral panic framework.

References

Cohen, S. (2003) *Folk Devils and Moral Panics: The Creation of the Mods and Rockers*, 3rd ed. London: MacGibbon & Kee.
Critcher, C. (2003) *Moral Panics and the Media*. Milton Keynes: Open University Press.
Critcher, C. (2009) 'Widening the Focus: Moral Panics as Moral Regulation', *British Journal of Criminology*, 49(1): 17–34.

10
PANIC, REGULATION, AND THE MORALIZATION OF BRITISH LAW AND ORDER POLITICS*

Dan Lett, Sean P. Hier, Kevin Walby, and André Smith

Introduction

Our aim in this chapter is to contribute to ongoing debates about widening the focus of moral panic studies by examining the relationship between moral panic and moral regulation. We argue that moral panic scholars have correctly emphasized tendencies for folk devils to resist both typification and regulation (McRobbie 1994; McRobbie and Thornton 1995; Hier 2002a), and that moral panics derive from, or represent volatile manifestations of, periodic crises in long-term moral regulation projects (Hier 2002b). We argue, however, that processes of moralization – that is, dialectical normative judgments about right and wrong, good and bad, safety and danger – are more complex than recent (progressive) commentary suggests, and we demonstrate that, although folk devils can and do fight back, resistance efforts can also be met with the state's ongoing regulatory force. In other words, whereas the moral panic literature has hitherto been concerned to show how resistance to primary definitions and dominant claims making is possible, we demonstrate how resistance efforts can also be resisted.

To substantiate some of the theoretical claims, and to contribute to the emerging project of widening the focus of moral panic studies, we examine the emergence of 'hoodies' as an assumed indicator of moral decline among youth in contemporary Britain.

On 11 May 2005, the Bluewater Shopping Centre in Kent, England implemented a code of conduct forbidding attire that conceals customers' facial features from the gaze of nearly 400 video surveillance cameras distributed throughout the complex. The ban prevented anyone wearing a hooded top (a.k.a. 'a hoodie') from entering the mall. The garment is a favored mode of attire for British youth and the ban functioned to exclude groups of young people from gathering in the mall. National newspaper and television media granted extensive coverage to the Bluewater ban in the months to follow, keeping pace with contemporary media discourses that address perceptions of youth as a source of risk (Thompson 1998; Critcher 2003). A hoodies discourse developed in media reports and public policy debate to mark what was represented as a pattern of moral decline among British youth, and the hoodie began to infer inherent delinquency.

Although moral regulation vis-à-vis the signification of hoodies garnered momentum from a cultural impulse to moralize the activities of youth (Cohen 1972; Thornton 1994; Coleman 2005), discourses opposing the ban appeared in the mass and alternative media. British government officials invoked the hoodies signifier to address assumed youth tendencies towards anti-social behavior and to justify legislative attempts to impose regulatory measures on British youth. However, folk devils and their supporters 'fought back' against the problematization of hoodies in mainstream and alternative media counter-claims. The struggle to define the problem of hoodies occurred in the context of an established debate concerning the British government's Anti-Social Behaviour Act of 2003. These processes were indicative of what Hall et al. (1978) conceptualized as a signification spiral: a mode of signifying events by the convergence of a newly identified concern with other social problems, escalating the perceived threat of the emergent events beyond the thresholds of societal tolerance.

In what follows, we neither quantify the regularity of 'Anti-Social Behaviour Order' deployment by authorities nor account for the legal technicalities of ASBOs; a burgeoning literature on youth and crime in the UK has already made these contributions (see Crawford 2009, 2007, 2006; Millie, 2008; Pearson 2006; Simester and von Hirsch 2006). Rather, our aim is to conceptualize the debate about hoodies using recent developments in the sociologies of moral regulation and moral panic and to show how volatile panics emerge from and are tied to long-term regulatory processes – in this case, the moralization of British law and order politics. Whereas the moral panic literature has hitherto been concerned to show how contestation of primary definitions and dominant claims making is possible, we demonstrate how these claims can be countered with reference to New Labour's 'Reform and Respect Agenda'. The analysis is particularly important in the context of Waiton's (2008) argument that the contemporary politics of antisocial behavior has ushered in the era of amoral panics.

Moral regulation and the volatility of panics

Although efforts to 'rethink' moral panic theory have called into question the assumptions of conventional theories of moral panic, they have led to the deconstruction of conventional models without a reconstruction of alternative modes of explanation (Hier 2008). In most moral panic research, there is an assumption that the harm believed to be posed by folk devils is disproportional to the harm that actually exists. This speaks to a tendency in moral panic studies to impose a negative normative judgment on explanations of volatile moralizing discourses as 'irrational' evaluations of the threat(s) posed (see Hier 2008). Even though revisionist efforts have problematized the empirical bases through which these analytic judgments are rendered, they are forced to rely on normative value judgments to render assessments pertaining to the 'irrationality' of public beliefs.

To remedy these theoretical difficulties, Hier (2008) draws from the sociology of governance studies to conceptualize 'moralization' (i.e., moral regulation) in terms of dialectical constructions of self and other that are transmitted through everyday discourses of risk management and harm avoidance. As everyday activities become moralized in the form of judgments pertaining to what is right and wrong, moralization finds expression through the proxies of risk, harm, and personal responsibility. One common feature of moralization in everyday life is that people are called upon to engage in responsible forms of individual risk management that exist in tension with collective subject positions of 'harmful others' (also see Hunt 2003).

The volatility of moralization brings into play a different nexus of values and emotions (Hier 2008). Through the deployment of a set of sensational discourses that erupt suddenly, and subside quickly, the moral dialectic that situates individualized risk management against a collective dimension of harm is inverted. Discourses that call upon individuals to engage in responsible forms of self-conduct to manage risk are transposed into collectivizing discourses of risk management. The latter take the form of defensive group reactions against what is represented as an immediate dimension of harm posed by 'irresponsible' others: those who fail to engage in individual risk management. As a volatile disturbance in the course of moral governance, 'moral panics' are short-lived disturbances focused on limiting the agency of 'folk devils'.

The regulation of British youth

Moral regulation projects in Britain are attendant to the activities of a wide range of people, yet 'no age group is more associated with risk in the public imagination than that of "youth"' (Thompson 1998: 43; also see Fionda 2006). Not only are British youth represented as a social group 'at risk' from harms posed by child abusers and paedophiles (e.g. Jenkins 1992; Hay 1995; Critcher 2002), but they are also identified as a *source* of risk (e.g. Cohen 1972; Hay 1995). Long-term efforts to regulate British youth over the past decade have manifested in moral-legal regulatory apparatuses institutionalized to counteract 'anti-social behavior'. We conceptualize these mechanisms of regulation in terms of governmental and extra-governmental attempts to responsibilize youth conduct in public spaces by encouraging certain modes of dress and behavior. By explicating the ways that moral regulation is currently enacted in relation to British youth, we conceptualize the events that followed the ban of hooded tops by representatives of the Bluewater Shopping Centre.

In 2003, the Home Office introduced the Anti-Social Behaviour Act (ASBA). Applicable to England and Wales, the ASBA facilitated the regulation of 'anti-social behaviors' through the deployment of ASBOs and 'Acceptable Behaviour Contracts' (ABCs). The Home Office defines ASBOs as

> civil orders that exist to protect the public from behaviour that causes or is likely to cause harassment, alarm or distress. An Order contains conditions

prohibiting the offender from specific anti-social acts or entering defined areas and is effective for a minimum of two years.

(Home Office 2003: 9)

Whereas the purpose of ASBOs is to act on the conduct of moral transgressors after the fact, ABCs are pre-emptive, non-legally binding agreements between offenders and police. The Home Office defines ABCs as

> an intervention designed to engage the individual in recognising their behaviour and its negative effects on others ... An ABC is a written agreement between an anti-social behaviour perpetrator and their local authority, Youth Inclusion Support Panel, landlord or the police ... ABCs are not legally binding, but can be cited in court as evidence in ASBO applications or in eviction or possession proceedings.

Together, ASBOs and ABCs act as a two-step prohibition (Simester and Hirsch 2006). Despite the fact that neither ASBOs nor ABCs are exclusively applicable to youth, their primary target is youth transgression, which, Crawford (2007) argues, follows the logic of de-differentiation insofar as all youth are problematized as probable sources of harm. The ASBA is also designed to enable spatial regulation – Section 30 of the ASBA invokes the notion of dispersal zones and orders. Crawford and Lister (2007) describe how dispersal orders are used to target youth simply on the basis of their presence in particular urban spaces (e.g., shopping centres). Millie (2008) comments on how ASBOs are used to regulate disparate forms of activity, which means there is no clear-cut definition of anti-social behavior. The application of ASBOs, argues Millie, is often based on aesthetics.

When New Labour introduced the Crime and Disorder Act (CDA) of 1998, government rhetoric problematized simultaneously the behaviour of youth and the existing institutional measures to counteract youth irresponsibility.

> An excuse culture has developed within the youth justice system. It excuses itself for its inefficiency, and too often excuses the young offenders before it, implying that they cannot help their behaviour because of their social circumstances. Rarely are they confronted with their behaviour and *helped to take more personal responsibility for their actions*. The system allows them to go on wrecking their own lives and disrupting their families and communities.
>
> (Home Office 1997: Preface, emphasis added)

The institutionalization of the CDA signified a wider ideological shift in the regulation of British youth from a 'minimum intervention' approach that predominated in the 1990s to a preventative 'early intervention' approach (see Crawford 2009; Squires 2008). As Bottoms and Dignan (2004) explain, the reason for this shift was the perceived failures of the Conservative Party's so-called 'new-orthodoxy' that prevailed among youth justice workers in the period 1985–97. The 'new orthodoxy' adopted two discernable governing principles: first, a retreat from carceral strategies based on the belief that institutionalization and the 'official processing of juvenile delinquents' (ibid.: 33) was both harmful to youth and conducive to establishing more long-term criminal tendencies in young offenders; second, the endorsement of the 'age-crime curve' (see Rutherford 2002) – an assertion that the majority of young offenders naturally 'grow out of crime' over time. The CDA was facilitated by the Audit Commission's report on the youth justice system, which found that much of the £1bn spent annually on processing young offenders 'was wasted through lengthy and ineffective court procedures' (Muncie 1999: 150). The Commission recommended a shift to preventative policy, concluding: 'the present arrangements are failing young people – who are not being guided away from offending to constructive activities' (Audit Commission 1996: 96). Jones (2001) argues that the 1996 audit influenced the rise to prominence of ASBOs as a mechanism of legal regulation in England and Wales.

For Coleman (2005), ASBOs and ABCs converge under the auspices of 'entrepreneurial urbanism': hybrid public/private regulatory projects negotiated between businesses and state agencies that wield control over the 'normative-cultural dimensions' extending beyond criminality (ibid.: 133). When youth skateboarders dodge the gaze of cameras, or when working-class youth gather outside malls, these actions are met with fines, bans, and curfews. It is at the antagonistic intersection of entrepreneurial urbanism and youth cultural expression that the problematization of hoodies articulated (Crawford, 2008; Pearson, 2006; Burney 2005; Walsh 2002). Even though ASBOs are mechanisms of legal regulation, they depend on extra-governmental partnerships to be applied. State agencies must extend themselves through public/private partnerships and spaces (Crawford 2006; Button 2003; Raco 2003). Bluewater is an example of private regulation in a quasi-public space, which leads to post hoc forms of state agency regulation in the application of ASBOs (see Wakefield 2008; Crawford 2008).

Problematizing hoodies and the Bluewater ban

In this section, we explain how volatile moralization emerged where long-term regulatory efforts aimed at youth were perceived to be in a state of breakdown. We draw from two data sources. The first data source consists of newspaper stories in the mainstream newspaper media. We sampled six of the most widely circulated national newspapers in Britain: *The Times*, *Guardian*, *Express*, *Daily Mail*, *Sun*, and *Mirror*. These sources were sampled to include coverage in quality broadsheets, middle-of-the-road tabloids, and redtop tabloids (Critcher 2003). We do not present a detailed content or discourse analysis but, rather, illustrate how the dominant discourse in the mainstream press and political debate was countered in the context of a web of media relations and social activism. Legislation was enacted even in the absence of consensus, which is important to analyses of moralization of youth because it demonstrates how folk devils and their supporters fight back and how these counter-claims can be reversed.

Primary definition

On 12 May 2005, the day following the Bluewater ban, the *Express* ran front-page coverage under a headline reading, 'Shopping centre bans hoody yobs: Britain's biggest mall has had enough of menacing gangs'. The article frames the Bluewater ban in the wider context of a moral decline in youth behavior: 'prowling gangs of "hoody" hooligans who plague our high streets and malls'; 'yobs who deliberately strike fear by skulking behind hooded tops'; and 'gangs of thugs have plagued the venue ... making shopping a terrifying experience'. The following day, the *Mirror* (13 May 2005) proclaimed that 'the sight of youths kitted out in [hoodies] strikes fear in law-abiding citizens'; 'in their Grim Reaper-style headgear, "hoodies" have become the reviled and feared bogeymen of modern Britain'. The *Daily Mail* invoked the imagery of 'the feral gangs who rule our streets' (18 May 2005) to characterize youth who don hooded tops in public space. And the 'hoodies' signifier was adopted to denote a range of deviance and crime: '"Hoody" thug mugs pregnant woman in front of shoppers' (*Daily Mail*, 15 June 2005), 'Evil hoody battered me black and blue' (*News of the World*, 15 May 2005), 'Fond farewells ... And then a vicious attack by hoodies' (*Express* 18 May, 2005), and '"Hoodies" rampage on train' (*Sunday Mirror*, 12 June 2005).

Following the Bluewater ban, Prime Minister Tony Blair and his deputy, John Prescott, laid claim to the problematic nature of youth behaviour. Speaking in support of the ban, Blair argued that 'People are rightly fed-up with street corner and shopping centre thugs' (*Express* 13 May 2005), and he openly supported the banning of hooded tops (*Guardian*, 12 May 2005). Prescott, too, endorsed the ban, reinforcing his support by recollecting a personal encounter with a group of 'hoodies' when he was surrounded and 'menaced' at a motorway service station; he reported that it was 'very intimidating' to be confronted by 'ten people wearing hoods – you know, these covers with hoods on' (*Express*, 13 May 2005). The claims made by Blair and Prescott were articulated in the context of an established governmental discourse concerning anti-social behavior invoked in government rhetoric since the introduction of the ASBA.

Deviance amplification

Emerging from the initial problematization of hoodies, newspaper coverage amplified the severity of the problem by linking hoodies to a range of crimes. For instance, under a headline reading, 'Hunt for hoodies', the *News of the World* reported that 'a teenager may be blinded in one eye after an unprovoked attack by hoodies' (10 July 2005). When Phil Carroll, a building site engineer, was attacked outside his house and left 'fighting for his life' in a coma (*Daily Mail*, 18 May 2005), newspaper coverage identified a 'feral, drunken and abusive hoodie gang' as the culprit. Three days later, the *Daily Mail* ran a front-page story about Alan Irwing, a 72-year-old pensioner who was beaten to death on his doorstep, adding: 'the area had been plagued by gangs of youngsters wearing 'hoodies'''. In the span of two months, the repertoire of deviance attributed to hoodies included the rape of an 11-year-old girl (*The Times*, 18 June 2005), underage drinking and sex (*Mirror*, 16 May 2005), murder (*Daily Mail*, 21 May 2005), 'binge-drinking' (*Express*, 13 May 2005), and, somewhat contradictory, a '"Hoodies" nude riot' (*Express*, 2 July 2005).

The escalating coverage on hoodies exemplifies what Hall *et al.* (1978) conceptualize as a signification spiral, which designates the symbolic escalation of harm posed by deviants through a process that inflates the volume and magnitude of deviance attributed to signifying categories. This signification spiral is demonstrated by the newspaper media's conflation of hoodies and 'happy slapping': an ambush-style physical attack – sometimes a slap, but variously a punch, stab, or attack with a weapon, possibly in conjunction with a robbery – which is recorded on a hand-held video device for the amusement of the attackers or distribution via the Internet and mobile telephony networks. Happy slapping entered the inventory of deviance through the claims-making activities of primary definers and 'experts'. The Deputy Prime Minister, recounting his confrontation with a gang of 'hoodies', proclaimed: 'not only did they come with these kinds of uniforms but they had a movie camera to take a film of any such incident' (*Express*, 13 May 2005). The 'expert' opinions of crime-control officers were drawn upon in efforts to link happy slaps to hoodies:

> Police have now identified so-called 'hoody' culture as a major concern, as yobs lurk in our streets and shopping malls with their faces hidden behind hoods and baseball caps ... innocent members of the public are being targeted in the latest craze for 'happy slapping' in which children randomly attack complete strangers just for fun.
>
> (Sunday Express, *22 May 2005*)

According to Hall *et al.* (1978), signification spirals precipitate the symbolic amplification of deviance across certain 'thresholds' of societal tolerance. Primary indicators of threshold breach in the hoodies discourse came in the form of increasing calls for regulatory action vis-à-vis the growing perception of an 'out-of-control' situation. The repetition of nomenclature including 'feral', 'yob culture', 'running riot', and 'culture of disrespect' attests to the perception of a widespread breakdown in the behavioural code, summarized by Lord Stevens, ex-chief of the Metropolitan Police:

> After terrorism, the biggest single crime crisis facing this country is juvenile yobbery. It is a raging social cancer tearing away at Britain – but currently we are treating this terrible sickness with the moral and social equivalent of a sticking plaster ... I've been a policeman for 43 years, and have never seen such fear and helplessness about juvenile crime in our communities ...
>
> (News of the World, *22 May 2005*)

Before long, news sources called for new regulatory responses. Demands such as 'hooded thugs and happy slappers should get longer sentences than other criminals, a former senior policeman said yesterday' (*Mirror*, 23 May 2005), calls for 'compulsory national community service' (*Express*, 21 May 2005) and a 'nationwide ban' of hoodies (*Express*, 13 May 2005) followed.

The amplification of the harm posed by hoodies involved numerous converging factors. While the Bluewater ban was not the first prohibition of hooded tops or baseball caps in UK shopping precincts, previous actions in Essex, Hampshire, Cornwall, and Devon (Coleman 2005) did not lead to the level of coverage and debate that followed the Bluewater ban. One feature that was absent from earlier clothing regulations was the lack of a concerted attempt by primary definers to articulate the ban in the context of wider social problems. Although governmental claims contributed to the intensification of concern – and indicated by attempts to seek consent for their proposed expansion of regulatory measures under the auspices of the ASBA – the newspaper media further imbued the hoodies signifier with a dimension of risk.

Fighting back against primary definitions

In this section, we examine forms of contestation that emerged in opposition to the dominant hoodies discourse to empirically demonstrate how folk devils and their supporters fight back (McRobbie 1994). Sociologists of risk, such as O'Malley (2006), contend that problematization engenders contestation among targets of regulation. Such contestation often takes forms that appear unorganized (Moore, 2007), as is the case with many of the examples discussed below. Opportunities to participate in the production of media messages have increased, due in part to technological means such as the Internet and the proliferation of desktop publishing software (Downey and Fenton, 2003). The increasing array of 'interpretive agents who are constructing our view of the world' (Vattimo 2004: 17) weaken media claims to objectivity, and authoritative versions of events give way to numerous interpretations.

Problematization shifted somewhat from youth socialization to the government's youth regulation policies. We provide an illustration of a heterogeneous oppositional movement that emerged following the Bluewater ban and that gained the attention of mainstream journalists. We also draw on data from Internet news publications and forums to show how alternative media enabled marginalized communities to enter into the debate about hoodies. The influence of diverse claims in the mainstream media, oppositional claims making outside the press, and alternative media messages combined to precipitate a re-articulation of the hoodies discourse. However, it was not enough to halt the continuation of attempts to regulate youth through legislative activity.

Problematizing state typifications: counter claims and alternative frames

The *Daily Mail* has long been associated with moralization as a standard mode of reporting (Hill 2002). Following the Bluewater ban, coverage in the *Daily*

Mail, instead of individualizing moral culpability through the hoodies signifier, invoked youth transgression as a platform from which to criticize Tony Blair's government. Playing on the language of Blair's 'Reform and Respect' agenda, the *Mail on Sunday*'s 'Respect? Surely you abolished it, Mr. Blair' (22 May 2005) attributed causality for anti-social behavior to an ideological shortfall inherent to Left-liberal governance:

> The liberal Left have been on a long march through this country, destroying old-fashioned authority. They believe deference and respect are wrong and bad and repressive.

Under a headline reading, 'When will our politicians wake up to the fact that it's THEY who have done more than anyone to create this culture of yobbery?' (19 May 2005), it was argued, 'disorder and threatening behaviour are a modern plague, and whole communities are under siege from crime and yobbery'. The problematization of New Labour in the *Daily Mail* was attributed to a retreat from authoritarianism on behalf of the liberal Left that is responsible for 'the destruction of the family' (ibid.). By holding the government culpable for the erosion of 'traditional' family values, including responsibility towards others and the behaviour of British youth, the dominant discourse was countered by retaining the hoodies signifier. The newspaper subverted primary definitions to implicate New Labour as morally misaligned with public opinion.

The *Guardian* attacked the initial framing of hoodies as an attempt to draw attention away from the failure of the state's education and social order policies: 'the new concern for boys' underachievement, hoodies and chavs parallel fears of a black rap culture ... like "gangstas", the "dumbed down" are turning away from learning' (*Guardian*, 14 June 2005). At the same time, the *Guardian* remained reflexive about the role of the media: 'the latest moral panic over hoodies echoes the last one over chavs ... Manufactured moral panic, or last stand of the lost tribe of the white working class?' (ibid.). As McRobbie and Thornton (1995) contend, since the early 1990s 'moral panic' has entered the lexicon of mainstream society and media. Hay (1995) commented that the standardization of moral panics as ordinary modes of news reporting has heralded in the age of the 'reflexive moral panic'. Media opposition to the dominant discourse was buttressed by enlisting 'experts' to counter the vilifying claims. Angela McRobbie was recruited as an expert sociologist by the *Guardian* in the interests of normalizing hoodies: 'nowadays it is the norm among young people to flag up their music and cultural preferences in this way, hence the adoption of the hoodie by boys across the boundaries of age, ethnicity and class' (*Guardian*, 13 May 2005).

Perhaps sensing the opportunity to align with a growing tide of populist dissent against representations of youths, the leader of the UK Conservative Party, David Cameron, delivered a 'hug a hoodie' speech to the Centre for Social Justice on 9 July 2006. Cameron's speech sought to undermine New Labour's approach to youth regulation and presented an alternative interpretation of hooded clothing:

Because the fact is that the hoodie is a response to a problem, not a problem in itself. We – the people in suits – often see hoodies as aggressive, the uniform of a rebel army of young gangsters. But, for young people, hoodies are often more defensive than offensive. They're a way to stay invisible in the street. In a dangerous environment the best thing to do is keep your head down, blend in, don't stand out. … For some, the hoodie represents all that's wrong about youth culture in Britain today. For me, adult society's response to the hoodie shows how far we are from finding the long-term answers to put things right.

Fighting back for folk devils

McRobbie (1994:111) – once the sole torch-bearer for the defence of 'moral minorities' – acknowledges that the academic is now bolstered and even surpassed by 'a new band of experts' in the form of skilled representatives from pressure groups and voluntary organizations. Below we focus on how the dominant framing of hoodies was countered by activist groups, making no claims about the success of these attempts at fighting back. In 2005, attempts to deflect a general demonization of youth were made by organizations such as the British Youth Council (*Guardian*, 13 May 2005), the Children's Society Charity (*Mirror*, 20 May 2005) and the charity NCH (*Mirror*, 3 June 2005) who went on record to decry the ban. The British Youth Council commissioned a report that found youths increasingly alienated by negative portrayals, and it circulated a press release recommending fairer media coverage, and greater political involvement opportunities for youth. The Children's Rights Alliance for England (CRAE) also raised questions about human rights violations.

Among organized attempts to counter negative typifications of youth through the hoodies signifier, the renowned subversive artists Gilbert and George produced *Hooded*, a work of art depicting the artists standing alongside two hooded youths (*Guardian*, 23 May 2005). Two headmasters introduced attire codes including hooded tops as official school uniform (*Mirror*, 15 May 2005; 20 May 2005) – each was quoted as opposing the government-endorsed clothing bans. The most direct example of successful contestation involved the Scottish Socialist Party (SSP) and the subsidiary Scottish Socialist Youth (SSY) (see 'Young hoodies fight ban with street protest', *Express*, 2 June 2005). In response to plans by businesses of the Eastgate Centre in Inverness to follow suit with Bluewater, SSY volunteers canvassed stores in the mall and publicized a Saturday demonstration against the ban. On 2 June, the mall released a statement retracting its plans, a decision the SSY attributes to its pressure. The Lambeth and Southwark Respect Coalition – a London-based activist group – coordinated a similar action at the Elephant and Castle mall in London. Although it failed to prevent the ban, it attracted the support of local community groups and formed an alliance with the civil-liberties organization ASBO Concern.

Contestation involved the use of alternative media. While 'mass' media are regularly conceptualized as a monolith in analyses of public policy formation, it is important to consider texts that fall on the periphery of customary conceptions of the 'mass' media.

Dominant, state-sponsored claims may be countered, or bypassed, by particular efforts originating in micro, niche, or alternative media (Couldry and Curran 2002; McRobbie 1994) or through an engagement with the 'mass' media by organized groups who seek to subvert dominant discourses.

Dedicated communicative networks condensed around hoodies. The libertarian community 'libcom', for example, opened a forum dedicated to hoodies that yielded a critical discourse negotiating the politics of negative youth depictions and was subject to over 5,000 views. The popular Flikr, an online photograph-hosting site, featured a 'hoody moral panic' area where the public could upload positive photographs of hooded clothing to stimulate political discussion. The 'G-Rime' musician, Lady Sovereign, began an online 'save the hoodie' campaign, inviting viewers to sign a petition opposing the ban that Sovereign would present to the Prime Minister. This coincided with the imminent release of Sovereign's 'Hoodie' single, and the petition received over 1,500 signatures and attracted attention in the mainstream and 'alternative' media.

Collectively, these strategies of contestation managed to partially shift the onus of problematization from youth transgression to governmental regulation. However, while studies of moralization have hitherto been concerned to demonstrate how contestation may be enacted, scholars interested in moralization have not pressed further to explore state agency responses to counter claims making.

The Reform and Respect Agenda

The response of state agencies can be understood in two forms: a symbolic alignment with wider sentiments to legitimate further regulatory legislation, and the deployment of existing regulatory measures to intervene directly in the behavior of those failing to self-regulate. On 17 May 2005, six days after the Bluewater ban went into effect, New Labour's 'Reform and Respect Agenda' was announced in the Queen's Speech at the State Opening of Parliament. The Prime Minister legitimized the agenda with reference to anti-social behavior: 'It is time to reclaim the streets for the decent majority'; and later, cited in the 'Respect Action Plan': 'I am pleased that an ASBO is now a household expression – synonymous with tackling anti-social behaviour' (Home Office 2006). The agenda included 45 bills and 5 drafts that introduced new measures to regulate anti-social behaviour. In January 2006, the agenda was expanded to include additional regulatory measures, including fines for the parents of 'anti-social children', a new mandate allowing the judiciary to ban people from their own dwelling places for recidivist anti-social activity, and the introduction of 'on the spot' fines levied by patrolling police. The 'Respect Task Force' – tasked with delivering the Respect Agenda – was launched in January 2006 by Home Secretary Charles Clarke with this address:

> Tackling disrespect in our society is an absolute priority for the Government and this new task force will play a vital role in improving our communities and the lives of people in them. From bad behaviour in schools and poor parenting to binge drinking and noisy neighbours, disrespect for others can take many

forms. ... We all have the right to live our lives free from harassment. But with those rights come responsibilities, and we all need to play a part in tackling disrespect and unacceptable behaviour.

Regardless of whether New Labour acted to stimulate the hoodies discourse, the agenda's political efficacy lay in its linkage with an established discourse of anti-social behavior, and stylized representations of declining behavioral standards among the polis – youths in particular. Language employed by state spokespersons to legitimize the new legislation drew on the typifications of youth behavior in the media following the Bluewater action. While the long-term project of morally regulating youth hinges upon a call for rational risk subjects to self-regulate, the hoodies discourse is indicative of a temporary breakdown of moral regulation, whereby the agency of youth came under scrutiny and subsequent regulation.[1] Claims making by politicians and law and order officials ascribed blame to youth in terms of an 'irresponsible' retreat into a 'culture of disrespect'.

Discussion and conclusion

The individualization of harm has thus far been conceptualized in moral panic studies through the signification of 'folk devils'. The folk devil concept, as 'unambiguously unfavorable symbols' (Cohen 1972:41), fails to account for the contingency by which harm becomes attributed to individual bodies in urban spaces. The temporary inversion of the dialectic that operates in the moralization in everyday life involves a conceptual shift from individualized discourses governing responsible and ethical self-conduct to collectivizing discourses that individualize responsibility for harm (Hier 2008). The Bluewater ban opened possibilities for the articulation of familiar, cultural artifacts and the very *mise-en-scène* of urban spaces with a symbolic dimension of harm. The symbolic dimension of harm articulated with pre-existing discourses of risky behavior through media sensationalism, retaining as an element certain signifiers originating in representations of commonplace phenomena of the cultural realm (e.g., hooded clothing, groups of congregating youths). Problematization of youth behaviour thus involved the inscription of a dimension of harm into established cultural texts, which came to represent a range of risks associated with contemporary urban spaces in Britain. The hoodie emerged as a dialectical articulation of risk and harm in the context of a series of highly recognizable cultural motifs to negotiate the management of risks in localized settings.

Arguments to the effect that folk devils may contest regulatory efforts owe much to a conception of political power as the aggregate of dispersed forces. Folk devils and their supporters can and do 'fight back'; the opportunities to participate in and subvert problematization are opening up to more variegated publics. Although contestation was subverted by New Labour's 'Reform and Respect Agenda', these efforts and their ramifications for understanding moral panic should not be discounted. We have also shown that the volatility of moralization hinges upon the amenability of cultural representations to link up with pre-existing, or emergent, themes of risk (also see Hier 2008). Such representations are tied to long-term political and moral projects, and they are not simply irrational, amoral, technical, and instrumental episodic articulations.

Note

* This chapter is a revised version of a paper appearing in *Criminology and Criminal Justice*, 2011, 11, 3.
1 Existing measures, combined with those introduced under the auspices of the Reform and Respect Agenda, have been brought to bear on specific youth behaviour problematized through the hoodies signifier. To enforce this increasing array of conditions, ASBOs and ABCs are supplemented by Individual Support Orders (ISOs), Parenting Orders, Dispersal Orders and Injunctions, which Crawford (2009) argues target not only youth but also their support networks. The breaching of ASBOs and other orders results, in many cases, in immediate detention for youths. Common to each of the orders mentioned above are the imposition of restrictions on actions, movements through space, and even gestures (also see Millie 2008).

References

Audit Commission. (1996), *Misspent Youth*. London: Audit Commission.
Bottoms, A. and J. Dignan. (2004), 'Youth Justice in Great Britain', *Crime and Justice* 31: 21–183.
Burney, E. (2005), *Making People Behave: Anti-Social Behavior, Politics and Policy*. Cullumpton: Willan.
Button, M. (2003), 'Private Security and the Policing of Quasi-Public Space', *International Journal of the Sociology of Law* 31(3): 227–37.
Cohen, S. (1972), *Folk Devils and Moral Panics*. London: MacGibbon and Kee.
Coleman, R. (2005), 'Surveillance in the City: Primary Definition and Urban Spatial Order', *Crime, Media, Culture* 1(2): 131–48.
Couldry, N. and J. Curran. (2002), *Contesting Media Power: Alternative Media in a Networked World*. Toronto: Rowman & Rowman.
Crawford, A. (2009), 'Governing through Anti-Social Behavior: Regulatory Challenges to Criminal Justice', *British Journal of Criminology* 49(6): 810–31.
Crawford, A. (2008), 'Dispersal Powers and the Symbolic Role of Anti-Social Behavior Legislation', *The Modern Law Review* 71(5): 753–84.
Crawford, A. (2007), 'Criminalizing Sociability through Anti-Social Behavior Legislation: Dispersal Powers, Young People and the Police', *Youth Justice*, 9(1): 5–26.
Crawford, A. (2006), 'Networked Governance and the Post-Regulatory State', *Theoretical Criminology* 10(4): 449–79.
Crawford, A. and S. Lister. (2007), *The Use and Impact of Dispersal Orders: Sticking Plasters and Wake-Up Calls*. Bristol: Policy Press.
Critcher, C. (2009) 'Widening the Focus: Moral Panics as Moral Regulation,' *British Journal of Criminology* 49(1): 17–34.
Critcher, C. (2008) 'Moral Panic Analysis: Past, Present, Future', *Social Compass* 2(4): 1127–44.
Critcher, C. (2003), *Moral Panics and the Media*. London: Open University Press.
Critcher, C. (2002), 'Media, Government and Moral Panic: the Politics of Paedophilia in Britain 2000–2001', *Journalism Studies* 3(4): 521–35.
Downey, J. and N. Fenton. (2003), 'New Media, Counter Publicity and the Public Sphere', *New Media & Society* 5(2): 185–202.
Fionda, J. 2006. *Devils and Angels: Youth Policy and Crime*. Oxford: Hart Publishing.
Garland, D. (2008) 'On the Concept of Moral Panic', *Crime, Media and Culture* 4(1): 9–30
Goode, E. and B. Ben-Yehuda. (1994), *Moral Panics: The Social Construction of Deviance*. London: Blackwell.

Hall, S., C. Critcher, T. Jefferson, J. Clarke and B. Robert. (1978), *Policing the Crisis: Mugging, the State, and Law and Order*. London: Macmillan.

Hay, C. (1995), 'Mobilization through Interpellation: James Bulger, Juvenile Crime and the Construction of a Moral Panic', *Social and Legal Studies* 4(3): 197–223.

Hier, S. (2008) 'Thinking beyond Moral Panic: Risk, Responsibility and the Politics of Moralization', *Theoretical Criminology* 12(2): 173–90.

Hier, S. (2003), 'Risk and Panic in Late-Modernity: Implications of the Converging Sites of Social Anxiety', *British Journal of Sociology* 54(1): 3–20.

Hier, S. (2002a), 'Raves, Risks and the Ecstasy Panic: A Case Study in the Subversive Nature of Moral Regulation', *Canadian Journal of Sociology* 27(1): 33–57.

Hier, S. (2002b), 'Conceptualizing Moral Panic through a Moral Economy of Harm', *Critical Sociology* 28(3): 311–34.

Hill, A. (2002), 'Acid House and Thatcherism: Noise, the Mob, and the English Countryside', *British Journal of Sociology* 53(1): 89–105.

Home Office. (2006), *Respect Action Plan*. Ref. 272299. London: Home Office.

Home Office. (2003), *A Guide to Anti-Social Behaviour Orders and Acceptable Behaviour Contracts*. London: Home Office.

Home Office. (1997), *No More Excuses: A New Approach to Tackling Youth Crime in England and Wales*. Cm. 3809. London: The Stationery Office.

Hunt, A. (2003), 'Risk and Moralization in Everyday Life', in R. Ericson and A. Doyle (eds), *Risk and Morality*, pp. 165–92. Toronto: University of Toronto Press.

Hunt, A. (1999), *Governing Morals: A Social History of Moral Regulation*. Cambridge: Cambridge University Press.

Hunt, A. (1997) 'Moral Panic and Moral Language in the Media', *British Journal of Sociology* 48(4): 629–48.

Jenkins, P. (1992), *Intimate Enemies: Moral Panics in Contemporary Great Britain*. New York: Aldine de Gruyter.

Jones, D. (2001), '"Misjudged Youth": A Critique of the Audit Commission's Report on Youth Justice', *British Journal of Criminology* 41(2): 362–80.

McRobbie, A. (1994), 'Folk Devils Fight Back', *New Left Review* 203: 107–16.

McRobbie, A. and S. Thornton. (1995), 'Rethinking "Moral Panic" for Multi-mediated Social Worlds', *British Journal of Sociology* 46(4): 559–74.

Millie, A. (2008), 'Anti-Social Behavior, Behavioral Expectations and an Urban Aesthetic', *British Journal of Criminology* 48(3): 379–94.

Moore, D. (2007), *Criminal Artefects: Governing Drugs and Users*. Vancouver: University of British Columbia Press.

Moore, D. and M. Valverde. (2000), 'Maidens at Risk: "Date Rape Drugs" and the Formation of Hybrid Risk Knowledges', *Economy & Society* 29(4): 514–31.

Muncie, J. (1999), 'Institutionalized Intolerance: Youth Justice and the 1998 Crime and Disorder Act', *Critical Social Policy* 19(2): 147–75.

O'Malley, P. (2006), *Risk, Uncertainty and Government*. London: Glasshouse Press.

Pearson, G. (2006), 'Disturbing Continuities: "Peaky Blinders" to "Hoodies"', *Criminal Justice Matters*, 65(1): 6–7.

Raco, M. (2003), 'Remaking Place and Securitising Space: Urban Regeneration and the Strategies, Tactics and Practices of Policing in the UK', *Urban Studies* 40(9): 1869–87.

Rohloff, A. (2008) 'Moral Panics as Decivilizing Processes: Towards an Eliasian Approach', *New Zealand Journal of Sociology* 23(1): 66–76.

Rohloff, A. and S. Wright (2010). 'Moral Panic and Social Theory: Beyond the Heuristic', *Current Sociology* 58(3): 403–19.

Rutherford, A. (2002). *Growing out of Crime: The New Era* (2nd ed.). Winchester: Waterside.

Simester, A. and A. von Hirsch. (2006), 'Regulating Offensive Conduct through Two-step Prohibitions', in A. von Hirsch and A. Simester (eds), *Incivilities: Regulating Offensive Behavior*, pp. 173–94. Oxford: Hart Publishing.

Squires, P. (2008), 'The Politics of Anti-Social Behavior', *British Politics* 3(3): 300–323.

Thompson, K. (1998), *Moral Panics*. London & New York: Routledge.
Thornton, S. (1994), 'Moral Panic, the Media and British Rave Culture', in A. Ross and T. Rose (eds), *Microphone Fiends: Youth Music, Youth Culture*, pp. 176–92. London: Routledge.
Ungar, S. (2001) 'Moral Panic versus the Risk Society: The Implications of the Changing Sites of Social Anxiety', *British Journal of Sociology* 52(2): 271–92.
Vattimo, G. (2004), *Nihilism and Emancipation: Ethics, Politics and Law*. New York: Columbia University Press.
Waiton, S. (2008) *The Politics of Antisocial Behavior: Amoral Panics*. London: Routledge.
Wakefield, A. (2008), 'Private Policing: A View from the Mall', *Public Administration* 86(3): 659–78.
Walsh, C. (2002), 'Curfews: No More Hanging Around', *Youth Justice* 2(2): 70–81.
Young, J. (2009), 'Moral Panic: Its Origins in Resistance, Ressentiment and the Translation of Fantasy into Reality', *British Journal of Criminology* 49(1): 4–16.
Young, J (1971) *The Drugtakers: the Social Meaning of Drug Use*. London: McGibbon & Kee.

Newspapers

Express

Express, (2005, May 21) 'Slapping craze must end'. *Express*, Leader column, p. 12.
Express, (2005, July 2) 'Hoodies' nude riot'. *Express*, p. 31.
Fagge, N. (2005, May 12) 'Shopping centre bans hoody yobs: Britain's biggest mall has had enough of menacing gangs'. *Express*, pp. 1, 7.
Fagge, N. and Chapman, J. (2005, May 13) 'Ban hooded thugs from our streets'. *Express*, pp. 1, 4.
Knapp, M. (2005, May 22) 'Living in fear of ferals'. *Sunday Express*, p. 31.
Moriarty, R. (2005, May 18) 'Fond farewells ... and then a vicious attack by hoodies'. *Express*, p. 2.
O'Kane, R. (2005, June 2) 'Young hoodies fight ban with street protest'. *Express*, p. 32.

The Times

Sulaiman, T. (2005, June 18) 'Girls' rape "filmed by teenagers on mobile"'. *The Times* (London), p. 2.

Daily Mail

Ginn, K. (2005, June 15) '"Hoody" thug mugs pregnant woman in front of shoppers'. *Daily Mail*, p.13.
Hitchens, P. (2005, May 22) 'Respect? Surely you abolished it, Mr. Blair'. *Mail on Sunday*, p. 2.
Seamark, M. (2005, May 18) 'The feral gangs who rule our streets'. *Daily Mail*, p. 1.
Taylor, B. (2005, May 21) 'Beaten to death on his doorstep'. *Daily Mail*, p. 1.

Mirror

Gallagher, P. (2005, May 20) 'Buys in the hood: massive surge in business at shops mall that outlawed hoodies'. *Mirror*, pp. 8–9.
Harper, J. (2005, May 15) 'Head: hoodies for school uniform'. *Sunday Mirror*, p. 40.
Lakeman, G. (2005, May 20) 'Hoodie two-shoes'. *Mirror*, p. 9.
Roberts, B. (2005, May 23) 'Reclaim our streets: hoodies jail plea'. *Mirror*, p. 28.
Roberts, B. and V. Allen. (2005, May 13) 'Reclaim our streets: hoodies and baddies'. *Mirror*, pp. 8–9.

Mackay, C. (2005, May 16) 'Battered to death: thugs use planks in birthday beating'. *Mirror*, Scottish Edition, p. 24.
Mirror, The. (2005, June 3) 'Now head bans kids in hoodies'. *Mirror*, p. 7.
Sunday Mirror. (2005, June 12) '"Hoodies" rampage on train'. *Sunday Mirror*, p. 28.

Guardian

Ainley, P. (2005, June 14). 'Open your arms'. *Guardian*, available at www.guardian.co.uk/education/2005/jun/14/furthereducation.socialexclusion (retrieved August 5, 2010).
Guardian (2005, May 12). 'Blair pledges crackdown on yobs'. Available at www.guardian.co.uk/uk/2005/may/12/politics.society (retrieved August 5, 2010).
Kennedy, M. (2005, May 23) 'Hoodie art unveiled Gilbert and George's new fashion statement'. *Guardian*, Home Pages, p. 1.
McLean, G. (2005, May 13) 'In the hood: on the meaning of the hoodie'. *Guardian*, G2, p. 2.
White, M. (2005, May 13) 'PM attacks yob culture and pledges to help bring back respect'. *Guardian*, available at www.guardian.co.uk/politics/2005/may/13/ukcrime.immigrationpolicy (retrieved August 5, 2010).

News of the World

Hamilton, M. (2005, May 15) 'Evil hoody battered me black and blue'. *News of the World*, Exclusive, p. 1.
News of the World. (2005, July 10) 'Hunt for Hoodies', p. 1.
Stevens, Lord. (2005, May 22) 'Lord Stevens has the cure for yobs'. *News of the World*, Leader, p.1

11

DRUNKEN ANTICS

The gin craze, binge drinking and the political economy of moral regulation

Chas Critcher

Introduction: opening time

Moral panic analysis is back in fashion. In just the last few years, we have seen a magisterial review (Garland 2008), a theoretical incursion by new recruits (Rohloff and Wright 2010) and a case study of British press reaction to East European immigrants (Mawby and Gisby 2009). My own recent contribution (Critcher 2009) sought to explore the implications of contextualizing moral panics as extreme instances of more routinized practices of moral regulation, a concept developed by Canadian sociologists, notably Hunt (1999) and Hier (2002). In that article, I used a wide range of illustrative examples in a necessarily superficial way. In this chapter, I explore and extend some of the new ideas being suggested in current debates through an empirically based case study of alcohol regulation.

The case of alcohol regulation was intentionally sought out. I was conscious that my previous work (Critcher 2003) had failed to acknowledge that, as Hunt (1999) points out, the three most long-established targets of moral regulation have been sex, gambling and drink. A remedy for this deficiency was to examine what in Britain has been a sustained furore over the last seven or eight years concerning a problem characterized as 'binge drinking'. This was an obvious test case for exploring the relationship between moral panic and moral regulation. The case study might confirm that moral regulation is a continuum, with moral panics at one end and ethical self-formation at the other, as I had earlier suggested. Additionally such a case study might reveal new insights about the wider processes involved.

Our understanding of moralization processes is currently limited by the geographical and historical restrictions of the moral panic literature. Debates about a whole range of contemporary phenomena, from the role of the mass media to technologies of governance under neo-liberalism, can benefit from comparison with previous historical periods only when these factors were different in kind or absent altogether. To supplement the case study of twenty-first-century binge drinking, I wanted another case study from the past when alcohol consumption emerged as a social problem and an attempt was made to mount a moral panic about it. This was easy to find in the 'gin craze' of early eighteenth-century England. The three hundred years separating the two episodes became an advantage, since neither was affected by the temperance campaigns of the nineteenth century. When I first set out to research the well-documented literature, I had no idea to what extent or in what ways the two might be compared. Nor could I anticipate how they might contribute to elaborating the relationship between moral panics and moral regulation.

This chapter reports the outcome of this process. It opens with two similarly structured narrative accounts of the gin craze and then of binge drinking. Next, I follow three slightly different ways of comparing the two: a naïve reading of their similarities and differences, an assessment of their status as moral panics and an analysis of their significance to the process of moral regulation. The conclusion develops a series of observations about the political economy of the moral regulation of pleasure under liberal modes of governance.

The gin narrative: raising spirits up

In the early eighteenth century there occurred what historians call the 'gin craze', although the phrase was not used at the time. It has an orthodox interpretation (George 1951; Rudé 1971). A sudden eruption of gin drinking in London had dramatic effects upon the health and productivity of the capital's lower classes. Legal action was necessary to curb the threat, though it took until 1751 for parliament to pass a really effective law. After that, gin consumption was controlled. Warner (2002) amongst others has provided a quite different interpretation of the causes of increased gin drinking, the threat it posed, the people who campaigned against it, the reasons why it was so difficult to control and the forces that finally decreased its consumption. Only a brief review of this complex and historically dense issue can be conducted here, sufficient for our purposes. Our discussion focuses in turn on the rise of gin; the levels, places and styles of its consumption; the campaigners against it; and the legal measures passed to control it.

Context

The 'gin craze' lasted from 1720 until 1751. It began when, for the first time in England, spirits became cheap and widely available. In the later years of the seventeenth century and the early years of the eighteenth century, governments passed laws designed to stimulate home production of spirits. A parliament dominated by the landed interest was motivated to provide a new outlet for surplus grain. These laws prohibited the importation of foreign wines and spirits, broke the monopoly of the London Distillers Guild and permitted spirits to be retailed on unlicensed premises, comprising an 'almost unremitting parliamentary promotion of the distilling industry' (Davison 1992: 25). The distilling trade had been effectively deregulated (Austin 1985).

Made from the most inferior grain and tasting foul, gin had to be flavoured with fruits to become palatable. The name gin had come from Holland, where it was known as 'genever', a term corrupted to first 'Geneva' and then just gin. The Dutch version, flavoured solely with juniper, was imported and thus expensive. English gin was crude, nasty and extremely alcoholic. Cheaper to produce than beer, it was also taxed at a much lower rate. All it needed was a market.

In London in the early eighteenth century, low population growth and relatively high wages left the working poor with marginal disposable income. For people whose lives were otherwise 'hard, brutal and violent and a constant struggle against disease, high mortality and wretched economic conditions' (Rudé 1971: 84), gin had clear attractions.

Consumption levels and styles

In Georgian England, 'hard drinking was endemic among both sexes and in all ranks of society' (Porter 1985: 386). Supplies of drinking water were often contaminated. Alcohol provided nourishment, helped digestion and blocked out pain. It suffused work and social life. Persons of substance, including politicians and aristocrats, were habitually drunk. In this context gin production and consumption expanded. Annual amounts increased dramatically: 0.5 million gallons in 1690, 2.5 million in the 1720s, 7 to 8 million in the 1740s. In the 1760s it declined to 2 million, its level for another 20 years. Often drunk in addition to, rather than instead of, beer, gin could get you drunk cheaper and faster. 'Spirits weren't just stronger versions of wine or beer; they were different in kind, more destabilising, more dangerous' (Dillon 2002: 4).

Class, gender and region defined gin drinkers: the working poor, often women, mainly in one city: 'gin did not constitute a serious threat outside London' (Warner 2002: 40). By 1750 London would be the largest city in Europe. It population of 765,000 was a tenth of the population of England and Wales. It had more people, more money and less inhibition than the rest of the country. Many of gin's retailers and consumers were female. Gin took as its symbol 'Madam Geneva', otherwise known as 'Mother Gin'. London gave single women unusually wide employment opportunities outside domestic service. Selling gin had three attractions: it required little capital, did not involve belonging to a traders' organization and women were not excluded. The gin craze was a rare historical moment when 'men and women are found drinking side by side, and, in the process, inhabiting and constructing the same social world' (Warner and Ivis 2000: 86). However, the participation of women was a source of censure, especially when they were wives or mothers.

Moral campaigners

Concern over gin was first articulated in the late 1720s. In a 1728 newspaper article the chairman of the Westminster Bench of Justices complained that gin induced violent language and behaviour. A 1736 petition of Middlesex magistrates lamented that gin was undermining the health and morals of London's populace. Behind these surface objections were deeper, less disinterested ones: the loss of pliable labour, resentment at the poor becoming consumers and fear of disorder. However, opponents of gin were not anti-alcohol, often endorsing extensive beer drinking. They objected specifically to gin as an alien and malign influence.

The Middlesex magistrates assiduously alerted the authorities about the gin problem. Friends and allies included physicians and extant religious campaigns like the Societies for Reformation of Manners and the newer Society for Promoting Christian Knowledge. This alliance, 'an articulate and resilient group of middling-order Londoners' (Borsay 2007: 3), produced pamphlets throughout the 1720s decrying the evils of gin and demanding government action.

Their campaign strategies were sophisticated. Circumventing producers, aiming instead at retailers, they deployed a whole battery of arguments, both moralistic and mathematical. Warner (2002: 103) identifies this as a new and distinctively modern strategy, 'laying the groundwork for a new type of advocacy in public life'. This new type of argument also found a new kind of outlet. Press licensing had been abolished in 1695, permitting the emergence of the modern press. The first daily newspaper, the *Daily Courant*, appeared in 1702. Borsay (2007: 3) concludes that 'the Gin Craze was ... a media-driven crisis'.

It was also underwritten by some ancient prejudices of class and gender. The class bias aimed 'to effect a general reformation of the manners among the lower classes' (Warner 2002: 111). The gender bias sought to restore women to their place in the natural order of things from which the attractions of gin had lured them. 'Knocking back drams outside the pawnbrokers' shop, a woman discarded all the standards of behaviour which society had set out for her: her obedience, her humility, even her chastity' (Dillon 2002: 210). Anti-gin propagandists claimed that gin-swilling mothers and nursemaids were neglecting children and thus the next generation of soldiers, sailors and labourers. Solving the gin problem would restore the hierarchies of class and gender. The solution lay in changing the law.

Laws and policies

Between 1729 and 1751, eight acts of parliament were passed to control gin consumption. The first Gin Act in 1729 used fiscal measures: the excise tax on gin was raised and publicans were required to pay an increased licence fee to retail spirits. Without effective means of enforcement, the Act failed to control gin sales in local shops or on the streets. In 1733 a new law encouraged informers. If a conviction was secured, the informer would receive half of the £10 fine. However, those convicted were often unable or unwilling to pay the fine.

Two Acts had been ineffective. There the matter might have been allowed to lie. But, led by the Master of the Rolls, Sir Joseph Jekyll, the same alliance of moralising individuals and organizations, aided by the Middlesex justices producing yet another scathing report on the effects of gin, launched a fresh campaign 'of broadsides, pamphlets and articles in the periodical press' (Davison 1992: 29). Similar concerns were voiced about gin threatening 'public health, public morals and public order' (Davison 1992: 32).

The result was the Gin Act of 1736, 'one of the most sweeping pieces of social legislation passed during the first half of the century' (Davison 1992: 33). The tax and price of licences were both increased yet again. Those failing to pay fines for illegal selling would be jailed. Few publicans could afford the £50 licence. They were now open to denunciation by informers with enhanced prospects of reward. The outcome was a temporary dip in gin consumption, but hostility to informers was widespread. Anticipating possible riots, the government put troops on the streets when the Act came into force. The informers' poor character and dubious role eventually discredited the whole system, juries declining to convict solely on their evidence. Two amendments in 1737 and 1738 tried to protect informers but could not prevent sporadic riots. In the meantime gin consumption reached an all-time high in 1740. Unable to enforce the Act, the government allowed it to lapse.

A sixth Act was passed in 1743, returning to fiscal control. Excise and licence fees were raised but remained at affordable levels. A 1747 Act increased the tax and licence fee yet again. Finally, in 1751, following yet another propaganda campaign, a new Gin Act was passed. Austin (1985: 324) stresses its comprehensive scope. Taxes and licence rates were reset. Only publicans of substance could retail spirits. Prisons and workhouses would no longer dispense gin. The net effect was to control gin by separating production and consumption and shifting the onus from prohibition to licensing.

The 1751 Act was apparently the ultimate victory for reformers, but Warner (2002) argues that other factors depressed gin consumption. Wages were being driven down by a combination of rapid population growth and poor harvests. The working poor could no longer afford gin. A shortage of grain provoked a two-year ban from 1758 to1760 on its use in distilling. Beer was also improving in quality and durability.

These legal measures were expressly designed to eliminate street sales of gin and control its consumption on licensed premises. Taxes, licensing and informers were all used in various combinations but without any great success. Historians (Clark 1988) usually stress the virtual impossibility of enforcing an unpopular law with only limited resources. Davison argues that the government chose not to enforce the law. It was rigorously applied during 1737, when the threat of disorder was at its height. Otherwise, governments basically remained indifferent to the problem. 'During this period, economic and fiscal policy were the two most important domestic objectives of the state, and a social policy which was at odds with either of these was likely to fail' (1992: 44).

The binge drinking narrative: one for the road

The term 'binge drinking' entered public discourse some time in 2003. Analysts prefer the more precise term of 'heavy sessional drinking'. Such activity expanded during the 1990s, when alcohol consumption doubled amongst those aged under 24. It peaked at the end of the 1990s and is already declining by the time the problem has been recognized and labelled. As with the gin narrative, we cover in turn: the context; consumption levels and styles; moral campaigners; and legal measures.

Context

The problematic relationship between British young people and alcohol had already been evident in three episodes at the end of the twentieth century, featuring in turn lager louts, rave/ecstasy and alcopops. First, a Home Office study published in 1989 revealed that rural areas were experiencing drink-related violence at weekends. The definition and commentary on the problem were led by organizations representing senior police officers (Measham and Brain 2005).The media coined the term 'lager lout'.

Second, in the late 1980s came illegal raves and ecstasy consumption. Raves were held in disused air hangars, barns or in the open air in the countryside. Ecstasy and other drugs were consumed instead of alcohol. The eventual solution to this problem was to move music events, and thus drugs, back into clubs, which were simultaneously granted longer licensing hours (Critcher 2003). The right had been conceded to experience psychotropic highs without constant police interference.

Third, as a conscious attempt to attract young people back to alcohol, brewers introduced in the mid 1990s new kinds of soft drink laced with spirits. Known as alcopops, they proved controversial because they were seemingly aimed at very young consumers. Brewers were forced to revise their marketing techniques but had learned how to soften spirits to enable drinkers, especially young women, to get drunk quickly.

Binge drinking continued this narrative of young people in search of drugs to enhance pleasure. Two features of the economic context would prove vital. First was the clear shift in patterns of alcohol consumption. Overall consumption was falling. More people were drinking at home than in pubs and clubs. Wine was displacing beer and lager. Discounted supermarket prices were making significant inroads into the retail market. The drinks industry needed to find ways to recover old markets and discover new ones. Second was the slow decline of city centres as the focus for shopping and leisure. Shopping malls, supermarkets, leisure complexes comprising cinemas, bowling alleys and restaurants – all attracted people away from city centres, which consequently needed to be rejuvenated. Binge drinking would offer a solution to the economic problems of both the drinks industry and city centres. There was also a political factor. The New Labour government was committed to deregulating the alcohol retail trade by abolishing restrictions on licensing hours. This project fitted uneasily with reducing excessive drinking.

Consumption levels and style

The term 'binge drinking', originally referring to lengthy bouts of drinking by alcoholics, had been redefined to refer to apparently excessive amounts of alcohol consumed on one occasion. The Prime Minister's Strategy Unit defined binge drinking as consuming more than twice the recommended daily intake of 6 units for females (3 pints of beer, cider or lager, or 6 glasses of spirits or wine); and 8 units for males (4 pints of beer, cider or lager, or 8 glasses of spirits or wine). As Hayward and Hobbs (2007) point out, most young people out on the town at the weekend would qualify as binge drinkers.

Academic commentators lament the phrase, its pseudoscientific definition and negative connotations. However, there is no denying that such activity has been on the increase in Britain.

The Strategy Unit concluded that there were nearly six million 'binge drinkers' in Britain. The group comprised 15% of all adults, 75% of women and 84% of men aged 15–24. Alcohol intake increased throughout the 1990s, peaking at the end of the century and slowly declining into the next. Though below several other European nations in the league table of alcohol consumption, 'Britain is experiencing a level of heavy drinking that has not been evident since the nineteenth century' (Plant and Plant 2006:149).

Age is the key factor in binge drinking, which starts early. Half of English 16-year-olds have been seriously drunk at least once. Binge drinking declines dramatically beyond age 30, but slowly reappears after 40. Amongst 18- to 24-year-olds only one-quarter of women and one-sixth of men say they never binge drink (Institute of Alcohol Studies 2007). Female drinking is distinctively British, with an 'unprecedented rise in heavy drinking among young British women' who 'drink heavily and become loudly and conspicuously drunk' (Plant and Plant 2006: 44). Overall, the statistics suggest that Britain has higher than average rates of: total alcohol consumption; drinking amongst young adults and especially teenagers; women and especially young women drinking; and the proportion of drink consumed in intense bouts or binges.

Explaining these trends, Measham and Brain (2005) identify a 'new culture of intoxication', brought about by four developments over the last twenty years. The first was the reversion to heavy drinking after the period when ecstasy displaced alcohol. Second was the 'recommodification of alcohol' by an industry anxious to recapture the youth market. The strategy involved product innovations, in the 1990s 'high strength bottled beers, ciders, lagers and fortified wines' and then 'second generation ready-to-drink spirit mixers, flavoured alcoholic beverages and "buzz" drinks containing legal stimulants'. After 2000 came 'shots or shooters' (ibid.: 267), which are 'small glasses containing mixtures of spirits and liqueurs, mostly consumed in one swallow and costing £1–2' (ibid.: 279). Alcohol was being marketed in terms of lifestyle: traditional pubs gave way to bars and clubs. The third development was a cultural shift towards drunkenness as a desired state. Young interviewees emphasized their determination to get (safely) drunk. The fourth development was the redefinition of alcohol's place in a 'post-industrial consumer society and a culture of consumption' (ibid.: 275).

The problem with binge drinkers is that they are 'often badly behaved and do not conform to discourses of polite, civilized and cosmopolitan urbanity' (Jayne *et al.* 2006: 461). The consequence is violence and disorder:

> the overwhelming evidence available from major cities and smaller urban centres alike is that increases in the number (and especially density) of licensed premises, their total capacities and terminal trading hours contribute to an increase in assaults and public order offences.
>
> *(Hobbs et al. 2005: 168)*

The threat to public order posed by binge drinking has become the main focus of concern for moral campaigners.

Moral campaigners

New Labour aimed for a coherent alcohol policy when it assumed power in 1997. Binge drinking was publicly defined as a prime target. An opinion poll in 2001 suggested that two-thirds of the public regarded binge drinking as a 'major' problem (Measham and Brain 2005). Policy development passed to the Prime Minister's Strategy Unit. This produced in 2003 an *Interim Report* of evidence, and an *Alcohol Harm Reduction Strategy for England* in 2004. These calculated the annual costs of binge drinking: to the health service at £1.7 billion, with £95 million spent on specialist treatment, over 30,000 annual hospital admissions and up to 20,000 premature deaths. Alcohol-related crime was costing £7.3 billion; 360,000 incidents of domestic violence were alcohol related (Plant and Plant 2006).

In February 2005 the Prime Minister called binge drinking the 'new British disease'. Minister Tessa Jowell issued a press release which contrasted 'the law-abiding majority' enjoying 'the pleasure of a quiet night out' who deserved to 'be treated like the adults' with 'the freedom they deserve' and who should have 'the right to a drink after 11pm' with 'yobs' causing 'alcohol-fuelled disorder' who merited 'tough treatment' (cited in Measham and Brain 2005: 280).

The peak of press concern seems to have been in 2005. Media treatment was suffused by the controversy over licensing hours. Graphic pictures of late-night drunkenness in city centres were frequently shown on television. In the (right-wing, mid-market) *Daily Express* (Critcher 2008), politicians were the main definers of the issue, followed by the control culture (judges and police), medical experts, the brewers and then campaigners. The names of the pressure groups do not always reveal their interests. 'Alcohol Concern' is a federation of agencies tackling alcohol abuse, part funded by government; the 'Institute of Alcohol Studies' is sponsored by the main British temperance organization; and the 'Portman Group' was set up by the drinks trade to encourage 'responsible' marketing and consumption.

Overall, binge drinking may be an instance of what Goode and Ben-Yehuda (2009) call 'elite engineered' panics. A long-term concern of the police was taken up by a powerful government department, the Home Office, and became a live issue for New Labour politicians. Or perhaps the sequence was the other way round. Whatever the detail, the ultimate source of moral concern and action about binge drinking was the state apparatus.

Laws and policies

New Labour's Licensing Act of 2003 aimed principally to deregulate licensing hours and also 'to reduce crime and disorder, reduce alcohol misuse, encourage tourism and assist self-sufficient rural communities' (Yeomans 2009: 1.1). Licences for alcohol could be extended up to twenty-four hours on application. Controlling provisions included on-the-spot fines for serving underage drinkers and the declaration of 'alcohol disorder zones' in troublesome areas, with bars and clubs charged for additional policing.

The police already had sufficient powers to deal with public drunkenness, had they chosen to use them. The Police and Criminal Justice Act 2001 had 'increased the power of the police to confiscate alcohol if consumed in a public place, imposed a "positive duty" on licensees not to sell alcohol to underage drinkers and authorized police forces to carry out "test purchasing" of alcohol by children' (Yeomans 2009: 5.5).

This apparently robust legal framework failed to control binge drinking. Analysts offered two explanations. One was the undue influence of the drinks trade. Plant and Plant claim that the drinks trade intervened to tone down the Strategy Unit's Report, confirming that 'industry influence appears to dictate the main shape of UK policy and renders it largely ineffective' (2006: 150). Really tackling binge drinking required controlling the drinks industry and its fostering of excessive drinking in the night-time economy, which the government refused to contemplate. The second explanation stressed how the police had ceded control of the night-time economy to the private sector: bouncers, not police officers, would intervene to control drunken antics. Hobbs *et al.* have argued that the state 'refrains from utilizing the full range of preventive measures and police powers for the licensing, regulation and management of the night-time economy' (2005: 173). They claim that in Manchester city centre on Friday and Saturday night you will find 75,000 and just 30 police officers, but over 1000 bouncers. Proper enforcement of the law would require a huge police presence and mass arrests, straining police resources. So all but the most extreme behaviour is tolerated on the streets whilst bouncers maintain order inside clubs and exclude those whose behaviour is unacceptable.

Comparison: instilling ideas

Comparing the gin craze with binge drinking is not a new enterprise (Borsay 2007, Herring *et al.* 2008). Focusing on differences and similarities, we need to group rather than just list the points. Emphasized here are three topics: how the issue was constructed; the claims makers involved in its construction; and the types of remedial measures adopted.

Similarities

In defining gin and binge drinking as issues, there was great emphasis on the ease, speed and cheapness with which people could get drunk. The fundamental objection was to drunken disorder on city centre streets. The issue was highly gendered. Men were accused of criminal behaviour, often violent. Females were accused of deserting childcare responsibilities (gin) or demeaning their sexuality (binge). Drunken women on the streets scandalized opinion in the 1730s and in the 2000s.

In both cases, claims making was enhanced by newspaper coverage portraying and indicting the behaviour for those otherwise unaware of it. Public opinion was constructed by enraged sectors of the middle class but popular feeling was indifferent or tacitly tolerant. The media did not lead the campaign but reflected the views of moralistic campaigners with wider agendas. Claims makers offered statistical calculations of the damage wreaked by alcohol as well as emotive denigration of drinkers, including vivid, visual images of public disorder and social disintegration.

Measures adopted extended the powers of state officials to immediately apprehend offenders. In the gin craze the use of paid informers, designed to exert control, instead provoked minor disturbances and occasional riots. Action against binge drinkers – such as on-the-spot fines or alcohol-free zones – seem ineffective compared with enforcing existing legal powers. In both cases the power of the state could be increased in principle, but proved difficult to realize in practice.

Differences

The political contexts differed, especially government priorities. During the gin craze Britain was, paradoxically, a stable country with fragile institutions: 'even the slightest threat to the status quo was a source of enormous alarm to the nation's governing class' (Warner 2002: 7). 'New' Labour aimed to create a new moral order, based on rights and responsibilities, with great hostility towards those threatening it. The issues varied by geography and generation. The gin problem was confined to London but binge drinking is a problem in all towns and city centres. Gin drinking was an issue between classes; binge drinking is an issue between generations. The gin issue provoked an objection to a specific type of alcoholic drink rather than to drunkenness. Binge drinking provoked a critique of excessive drinking, whatever the type of drink involved.

The deleterious effects of excessive alcoholic consumption were stressed for both gin and binge drinking, but with different emphases. Gin harmed the health of the nation and future generations. Binge drinkers damaged their own health. Claims makers about gin were moral, and especially Christian, reformers but for binge drinking more prominent critics were law-enforcement agencies supported by anti-alcohol groups. Claims about gin were largely uncontested because brewers and distillers were politically disorganized. By the time of binge drinking the trade is highly organized, public-relations conscious and allegedly very influential on government policy. Measures adopted differed because the absence of a police force stymied attempts to suppress the gin trade, whereas the police have been crucial to the definition of binge drinking. Government acted reluctantly over gin but it has been the prime mover on binge drinking.

A grasp of these basic similarities and differences can support more sophisticated comparison in terms of moral panic and moral regulation.

Moral panic: trouble brewing

Warner (2002) has argued that the gin craze exhibits a dynamic common to all drug scares, of which it was probably the first. There emerges a new, cheap and widely available drug which is stronger and more dangerous than its predecessors. It is consumed by marginal members of society whose lifestyle is seen to invite deviant behaviour. Vulnerable people, especially women and children, become direct or indirect victims. Production and consumption are located in identifiable areas of the city or in dens of inequity, contrasted with the calm of rural or suburban life. Experts provide scientific evidence about the drug's prevalence and dangers and it is agreed that extreme legislative measures must be taken to solve the problem.

This list bears an uncanny resemblance to that originally identified by Cohen as characteristic of a moral panic:

> Societies appear to be subject, every now and then, to periods of moral panic. (1) A condition, episode, person or group of persons emerges to become defined as a threat to societal values and interests; (2) its nature is presented in a stylized and stereotypical fashion by the mass media; (3) moral barricades are manned by editors, bishops, politicians and other 'right-thinking' people; (4) socially accredited experts pronounce their diagnoses and solutions; (5) ways of coping are evolved or (more often) resorted to; (6) the condition then disappears, submerges or deteriorates and becomes more visible.
>
> *(Cohen 2002: 1, numbers added)*

The gin craze and binge drinking can be compared in terms of this model. In the gin craze 'for the first time in history, the mere drinking of an alcoholic beverage became stigmatized' (Austin 1985: 11). This has led some analysts to suggest that it was 'an early – perhaps the first – drink-related "moral panic"' (Borsay 2007: 2). The same writer explicitly compares the gin craze and binge drinking as moral panics, seeing similarities in: the definition of crisis (Cohen's stage 1); the crucial role of pressure groups and the media (stages 2–4); and the expression of generalized anxieties about social change. New laws were also passed to remedy each problem (stage 5). However, Borsay emphasizes that the model cannot account for the massive historical changes between the two episodes, such as attitudes to alcohol and gender, the power of the drinks industry and the pervasiveness of the mass media system.

Warner, Birchmore-Timney and Ivis (2001) examined whether the press endorsed a moral panic about gin. They analysed the content of ten periodicals for the key periods around the Acts of 1736 and 1751. Most items in the first period (70 percent) were about crimes or prosecutions related to gin; in the second period the same percentage were about the proposed new law. Coverage showed some evidence of moral panic. Peaks of coverage followed campaigners' concerns rather than consumption patterns. However, there was little evidence of the kinds of sensationalism and moralizing typical of the modern press. This they attribute to lack of interest in social problems amongst the political elite and the inexperience of a press still reliant upon official news sources. They suggest that during the gin craze, even at the height of the moral panic in 1736, the press played a secondary role. It reflected the campaigners' concerns without endorsing them.

Thanks to some recent collations of historical studies, we are now much better able to place the gin craze amongst some other emergent types of moral panic, notably about crime. This wider project is to meet 'the demand for sensitive comparative analysis of moral panics over a relatively long period, using the concept flexibly as a heuristic device to consider changes in the public sphere and news media, particularly their role in governance and legislative outcomes' (Lemmings 2009b: 249). The moral panics model is apparently proving useful to historians.

Contemporary analysts of binge drinking are more circumspect about applying the moral panic model. Plant and Plant (2006: 28) pose the question directly: 'Is the campaign about "binge drinking" and the problems associated with heavy drinking just a "moral panic"?' Despite familiar cycles of media concern, exaggeration and outrage, they conclude that because something real was happening 'there is ample justification for media interest and public concern'. Others have different reservations. Binge drinking is the 'latest in a long line of press campaigns to highlight and exaggerate the consequences of youth at play', particularly where sex, drink and the city coincide, but 'media coverage is more complex than captured by the concept of moral panic and consequently cannot simply be dismissed as such' (Measham and Brain 2005: 264).

Yeomans (2009: 2.6) has applied the moral panics model to the binge drinking issue in an unexpected way. He argues that reaction to the deregulatory Licensing Act of 2003 was itself a moral panic about the alleged consequences of longer opening hours. He shows how and why 'the reaction appears irrational and disproportionate to the level of threat actually posed'.

The effective academic consensus is that the moral panic framework is not helpful to the analysis of binge drinking. However, this judgement underestimates the subtlety and applicability of the model. Binge drinking was identified and labelled as a new kind of problem (Cohen's stage 1); media, moralists and experts did pronounce upon it (stages 2–4); a series of legal measures were taken to control it (stage 5). On the other hand, binge drinkers are not convincing folk devils. Otherwise ordinary, even respectable citizens, they are not defined as evil by their bingeing. The threat they pose is localized and occasional. The moral order is not at stake. There is not the sense of urgency and crisis evident in the gin craze. The difference is one of degree rather than kind: both exhibit signs of moral panic but they are clearer for the gin craze than for binge drinking.

The usefulness of the moral panic model lies in its capacity to make systematic comparisons, but it requires us to abstract cultural processes from their social, political and economic context. There is yet another way to link issues nearly three hundred years apart, as instances of the process of moral regulation.

Moral regulation: licensed trade

Any assessment of the significance of the gin craze or binge drinking inevitably raises questions about the nature of regulation and the moral impulses behind it. Both episodes qualify as projects of moral regulation in Hunt's terms. They 'involve practices whereby some social agents problematize some aspect of the conduct, values or culture of others on moral grounds and seek to impose moral regulations on them' (1999: ix). Each exhibits Hunt's five essential features: identifiable agents, a specific target, distinctive strategies, a common discourse and a struggle against competing interests. Here we look in more comparative detail at the threat to moral order, the nature of regulatory practices and the role of political economy.

Moral order

For Borsay (2007: 3), reaction to the gin issue 'was harnessed to a battery of structural anxieties that pervaded early Georgian society'. Social conventions were apparently threatened by urban growth, rising wages and family breakdown. Xenophobia was rife. Governments remained indifferent to social problems. For some Georgians, gin symbolized the fragility of their social order. As Warner argues, their 'concerns over drunkenness bore very little correspondence to actual consumption' because the reaction was more about 'larger and more intractable threats to their society and way of life' (2002: 4). Order was at stake. Whilst all classes drank heavily, the poor did so in public. 'What many upper-class critics really objected to was public drunkenness, and it was among the lower classes that public drinking was most prevalent.' (Austin 1985: 11)

The public nature of drunkenness and the threat posed to public order is also a crucial objection to binge drinking. Yeomans has argued that the controversy presupposes 'the fundamentally problematic nature of alcohol, the comparative depravity of the British and the urgent need to reform behaviour'. Reminiscent of 'ascetic Protestantism' are preoccupations with 'social order and self-control, a sense of personal or national self-repulsion and a desire to struggle against overwhelming social problems' (2009: 6.7).

It is the order of public space which is in jeopardy. Thus one goal of regulation is to restore the order on the streets which prevailed before habitual drunkenness took over. The intractability of this problem reveals much about the nature of campaigns for moral regulation and the measures they sought to introduce.

Regulatory procedures

From the agitation about gin, Davison (1992) draws four lessons: the influence of lobbies and pressure groups; the expanded role of the press; expectations that the state should intervene in social problems; and the inadequacies of existing means of law enforcement. For Warner (2001: 375), the two standout features are, first, that 'it is the first example of a sustained and systematic intervention by the state in regulating sales of alcohol'; second, 'it is the first time that statistics, both economic and epidemiological, were enlisted in an attempt to sway public opinion and influence wavering legislators', showing 'what can happen when the public health model is cast in the form of legislation and is enlisted in a crusade to reform the morals of the working poor'. The gin craze was a prototype of moral crusades to follow.

Plant and Plant argue that, for all its bluster, New Labour has actually avoided really effective means of regulating binge drinking, such as: systematic police surveillance of known trouble spots; rigid enforcement of drink–driving laws; raising the legal age for alcohol purchase and consumption; curbing advertising; outlawing happy hours; and sharply increasing taxes. If 'the main aim of alcohol policy should be to stop people drinking heavily' then it is imperative 'for UK polices to be led by evidence and not by political expediency or commercial pressure' (2006: 149).

Regulatory policies around binge drinking have been beset by contradictions. The most fundamental is that economic deregulation, releasing the consumer to pursue pleasure, simultaneously requires increased social regulation to punish inappropriate behaviour (Measham and Brain 2005). What appears to be unprecedented freedom to consume alcohol comes at the price of constant surveillance and intervention by agents of control. In their analysis of the regulatory regimes applied to new kinds of 'urban playspaces', Chatterton and Hollands emphasize the failure of the new night-time economy to police itself through bouncers and CCTV. The shift from traditional regulators (magistrates and police) to new regulators (councils and clubs) has fractured public order which new laws of increasing severity endeavour to restore. Such complex patterns constitute a challenge to theories of modes of social control in post-Fordist society so that we are well short of 'fully understanding regulatory regimes in relation to consumption and leisure' (2002: 106).

The regulatory problem is, at one level, how to enforce order on the streets when large numbers of people behave in systematically disorderly ways – a problem common to both the gin craze and binge drinking. Striking in both instances is the determination to control the consumption of alcohol whilst refusing to control its production and distribution. The reasons for that tell us much about the balance of forces behind regulatory strategies.

Political economy

These apparently moral crusades were consistently subject to pressures from the relationship between government and the brewing trade, what might be called the political economy of moral regulation. In the case of the gin craze, the political economy of the brewing industry deliberately instigated gin production and consumption. The construction of the problem was largely moralistic and yet the laws proposed, passed and unevenly implemented constantly reflected the politics of excise and the economics of grain. Even the final decline in gin drinking owed less to legal suppression than to changes in the economics of the average wage, the decline in grain surpluses and the burgeoning brewing industry. Binge drinking emerged from changes in consumer tastes, the search of brewers for new markets and the desire by local councils to rejuvenate city centres. The apparently severe legal sanctions against binge drinking belied the influence of the industry and the consequent reluctance to enforce extant legal powers. The activity is morally denounced by those whose economic and political actions have helped to create it.

Wary of excessively simplistic 'political economy' approaches, Jayne *et al.* nevertheless highlight the contradictory pressures behind the attempted regulation of binge drinking:

> This is an economy of pleasure, and the 24-hour city becomes the vehicle for economic growth, profit generation and entrepreneurialism. However, while the

financial success of drinking has stimulated further demands for its deregulation, the night time continues to be heavily influenced by Fordist concerns for tighter regulation, social control and zoning, due to lingering moral panics and fear of disorder. The city, especially at night, is shown to be contradictory – simultaneously conflictual and segregated, commodified and sanitized, saturated both by emotion (enhanced through alcohol, drugs, dance, sexual encounter) and rational elements (planning, surveillance and policing) – and such tendencies are not always easy to understand and reconcile.

(2006: 458–59)

The moral regulation of alcohol is constantly cut across by the political economy of pleasure. Extraneous interests include: the commercial benefits of the production and consumption of alcohol; its key role as a source of government revenue; the lobbying interests of the industry; and the apparently contradictory urges to deregulate the industry (production and distribution) whilst regulating drunkenness (consumption). Put simply, moral campaigns and issues are always likely to be touched by economic and political interests. More elaborately, moral regulation, at least for an issue like alcohol, is intimately bound up with economic and political regulation. The outcome cannot be anticipated in advance but, where economic and political interests pull one way and moral interests another, the struggle is likely to be an unequal one.

Conclusion: last orders

In general terms the comparative case studies have demonstrated the utility of situating moral panics as extreme instances of a generalized process of moral regulation. Had we used only moral panic analysis, we should not have been able to go much beyond saying that the gin craze seemed to be 'more of' a moral panic than binge drinking. However, had we used only the language of moral regulation, then we should not have been able to specify exactly why the reaction to the gin craze had a more consistent trajectory than that to binge drinking, notably the failure to generate sufficiently threatening folk devils. The empirical data here seem to validate the conceptual framework, confirming moral panics as 'the *volatile local manifestation* of what can otherwise be understood as the *global project of moral regulation*' (Hier 2002: 329, original emphases). But there is yet more to say. By way of further conclusions I want to make three observations, one about each of the case studies and the third about the relationship between them.

The observation about the gin craze is that this may have been the first modern moral panic (Nicholls 2003), much more successful than earlier attempts to regulate sexuality (Dabhoiwala 2007). It is modern in several senses. It is not about religious dissidents or foreign spies, as many seventeenth-century panics were. The folk devils were not heretics or traitors but ordinary lower-class Londoners. Their transgressions were less against Church or monarchy than against sobriety and public order. The objections came less from the state than from the upper middle class of London society who assumed the role of moral entrepreneurs. They adopted recognizably modern propaganda tactics: not only the broadsheet and the pamphlet but scientific assertion and statistical data. If not always unconditionally supportive, the emergent London press reported and voiced their concerns. The solution to the problem was legislation, even though a properly effective law required thirty years and seven attempts.

As recent historical accounts (King 2003) have shown, crime was simultaneously emerging as an object of moral panic and moral regulation. Attempts to regulate gambling and commercial sex would not be far behind. The gin craze, then, is more than a convenient historical case study; it reveals for the first time the complex relationships between modernity, moral regulation and moral panic (Lemmings, 2009a). Not the least factor here is the emergence of a recognizably modern public sphere (Lake and Pincus 2006).

Nearly three centuries later, binge drinking prompts a rather different observation: the contradictions in late modernity of the governance of pleasure. Critics of binge drinking and advocates of 'responsible' drinking seem consistently to miss the point about alcohol. People (in Northern Europe, at least) drink alcohol as much for the effect as the taste. Alcohol becomes the drink of choice because it provides a form of release. It relaxes and disinhibits, the more of it you drink.

As O'Malley and Valverde have pointed out, 'Governmental discourses about drugs and alcohol, in particular, tend to remain silent about pleasure as a motive for consumption' (2004: 26). This is true for the public debate about binge drinking. Perhaps the objection is less to drink, or even being drunk, than to the place and style of drunkenness. Those who drink themselves into a stupor at home might risk their own health but do not disrupt order on the streets. So exhortations to drink 'responsibly' imply that we should drink only limited amounts so that we do not get 'too' drunk. Excess, which is deplored, is in actuality the whole point. Judged from the viewpoint of New Labour, pleasure is to be enabled by economic deregulation but disabled by moral regulation.

The observation about the relationship between the two case studies is that this curious concoction of political expediency, commercial calculation and moral rectitude appears in each case study, albeit in different forms. In both instances attempts to mount a moral panic and instigate moral regulation encountered political and economic interests which the strategies of moral entrepreneurs had to incorporate. Moral regulation is subject to political economy, defined in its simplest terms as 'the relations between politics and economics' (Caporaso and Levine 1992: 7). For our case studies this meant analysing: the balance of political forces (government, state agencies, pressure groups, commercial lobbying); the balance of economic forces (wholesale and retail industries, tax revenues, employment generated); and, crucially, the balance between economic and political forces at moments of policy formation. It is not simply that political or economic forces affect moral regulation. It is that, dependent on the issue and the historical conjuncture, the moral regulation of pleasure – not only alcohol but also gambling and sex, as well as the mass media – may be structured by political economy.

This is not, however, the final lesson from our case studies. They have shed light on the basic process of moral regulation. For many observers (for example Hackley *et al.* 2008), British government policy about alcohol at the turn of the century appeared to be contradictory. The compulsion towards economic deregulation seemed to be at odds with the urge towards moral reregulation. But from another point of view (Rose 1999) this is not at all inconsistent. It is integral to a new form of governance under 'advanced liberalism', based upon the 'the self-organizing capacities of natural spheres of the market, civil society, private life, individual'. Freedom to consume is not opposed to but dependent on the exercise of self restraint, producing 'a twin process of autonomization plus reponsibilization – opening free space for the choices of individual actors whilst enwrapping these autonomized actors within new forms of control' (p. xxiii.).

The belief that the individual has a right to consume alcohol on licensed premises at any time of the day or night is fully compatible with the exhortation to drink it 'responsibly'. Rose calls the whole cultural process of which this is an example the 'ethicalisation of existence' (1999: 264). This is a radical Foucauldian inversion of the original formulation of moral regulation as the nation-state having 'a project of normalizing, rendering natural, taken for granted, in a word "obvious", what are in fact ontological and epistemological premises of a particular and historical form of social order' (Corrigan and Sayer, 1985: 4). Historically the reaction to gin may have approximated more to the model of Corrigan and Sayer, whilst that to binge drinking is closer to Rose's paradigm. Thus we began with a straightforward comparison between two case studies of social reaction to excessive consumption of alcohol and have ended with basic controversies about historical variations in modes of governance and moral regulation. Quite a bender.

References

Austin, G.A. (1985) *Alcohol in Western Society from Antiquity to 1800:a Chronological History*, Santa Barbara: ABC-Clio Information Services.
Borsay, P. (2007) 'Binge drinking and moral panics: historical parallels', *History and Policy* Paper no. 62, www.historyandpolicy.org/papers/policy-paper-62.html
Caporaso, J.A. and Levine, D.P. (1992) *Theories of Political Economy*, Cambridge: Cambridge University Press.
Chatterton, P. and Hollands, R. (2002) 'Theorising urban playscapes: producing, regulating and consuming youthful nightlife city spaces', *Urban Studies*, 39: 95–116.
Clark, P. (1988) 'The "Mother Gin" controversy in the early eighteenth century', *Transactions of the Royal Historical Society*, 38: 63–84.
Cohen, S. (2002) *Folk Devils and Moral Panics*, 3rd edition, London: Routledge.
Corrigan, P. and Sayer, D. (1985) *The Great Arch: English State Formation as Cultural Revolution*, Oxford: Basil Blackwell.
Critcher, C. (2003) *Moral Panics and the Media*, Milton Keynes: Open University Press.
Critcher, C. (2008) 'Moral panics: the case of binge drinking', in B. Franklin (ed.) *Pulling Newspapers Apart*, London: Routledge.
Critcher, C. (2009) 'Widening the focus: moral panics as moral regulation', *British Journal of Criminology*, 49 (1): 17–35.
Dabhoiwala, F. (2007) 'Sex and societies for moral reform', *Journal of British Studies*, 46 (2): 290–319.
Davison, L. (1992) 'Experiments in the social regulation of industry: gin legislation 1729–51', in L. Davison, T. Hitchcock, T. Kerrin and R.B. Shoemaker (eds) *Stilling the Grumbling*

Bee Hive: the Response to Social and Economic Problems in England 1689–1750, New York: St. Martin's Press.
Dillon, P. (2002) *The Much-lamented Death of Madame Geneva*, London: Review.
Garland, D. (2008) 'On the concept of moral panic', *Crime, Media, Culture*, 4 (1): 9–30.
George, D.M. (1951) *London Life in the Eighteenth Century*, London: London School of Economics and Political Science.
Goode, E. and Ben-Yehuda, N. (2009) *Moral Panics: the Social Construction of Deviance*, Chichester: Wiley-Blackwell.
Hackley, C., Bengry-Howell, A., Griffin, C., Mistral, W. and Szmigin, Z.(2008) 'The discursive constitution of the UK alcohol problem in Safe, Sensible, Social: a discussion of policy implications', *Drugs: education, prevention and policy*, 15 (1): 61–74.
Hayward, K. and Hobbs, D. (2007) 'Beyond the binge in "booze Britain": market-led liminalization and the spectacle of binge drinking', *British Journal of Sociology*, 58 (3): 437–56.
Herring, R., Berridge, V. and Thom, B. (2008) 'Binge drinking today: learning lessons from the past', *Drugs: Education, Prevention and Policy*, 15 (5): 475–86.
Hier, S. (2002), 'Conceptualizing moral panic through a moral economy of harm', *Critical Sociology*, 28: 311–34.
Hobbs, D., Winlow, S., Hadfield, P. and Lister, S. (2005) 'Violent hypocrisy: post industrialism and the night-time economy', *European Journal of Criminology*, 2 (2): 161–83.
Hunt, A. (1999) *Governing Morals: a Social History of Moral Regulation*, Cambridge: Cambridge University Press.
Institute of Alcohol Studies (2007) *Binge Drinking – Nature, Prevalence and Causes*, IAS Factsheet, St Ives: Institute of Alcohol Studies.
Jayne, M., Holloway, S.L. and Valentine, G. (2006) 'Drunk and disorderly: alcohol, urban life and public space', *Progress in Human Geography*, 30 (4): 451–68.
King, P. (2003) 'Moral panics and street crime 1750–2000: a comparative perspective', in B. S. Godfrey, C. Emley and G. Dunstall (eds) *Comparative Histories of Crime*, Cullompton: Willan Publishing.
Lake, P. and Pincus, S. (2006) 'Rethinking the public sphere in early modern England', *Journal of British Studies*, 45 (2): 270–92.
Lemmings, D. (2009a) 'Introduction: law and order, moral panics, and early modern England', in D. Lemmings and C. Walker (eds) *Moral Panics, the Media and the Law in Early Modern England*, Basingstoke: Palgrave Macmillan.
Lemmings, D. (2009b) 'Conclusion: moral panics, law and the transformation of the public sphere in early modern England', in D. Lemmings and C. Walker (eds) *Moral Panics, the Media and the Law in Early Modern England*, Basingstoke: Palgrave Macmillan.
Mawby, R.C. and Gisby, W. (2009) 'Crime, media and moral panic in an expanding European Union', *The Howard Journal*, 48 (1): 37–51.
Measham, F. and Brain, K. (2005) '"Binge" drinking, British alcohol policy and the new culture of intoxication', *Crime, Media, Culture*, 1: 262–83.
Nicholls, J.C. (2003) 'Gin Lane revisited: intoxication and society in the gin epidemic', *Journal for Cultural Research*, 7 (1): 125–46.
O'Malley, P. and Valverde, M. (2004) 'Pleasure, freedom and drugs: the uses of "pleasure" in liberal governance of drug and alcohol consumption', *Sociology*, 38 (1): 25–42.
Plant, M. and Plant, M. (2006) *Binge Britain: Alcohol and the National Response*, Oxford: Oxford University Press.
Porter, R. (1985) 'The drinking man's disease: the "pre-history" of alcoholism in Georgian Britain', *British Journal of Addiction*, 80 (4): 385–87.
Rohloff, A. and Wright, S. (2010) 'Moral panic and social theory: beyond the heuristic', *Current Sociology*, 58 (3): 403–19.
Rose, N. (1999, second edition) *Governing The Soul*, London: Free Association Books.
Rudé, G. (1971) *Hanoverian London 1714–1808*, London: Secker and Warburg.
Warner, J.F. (2001) 'Can legislation prevent debauchery? Mother Gin and public health in 18th century England', *American Journal of Public Health*, 9 (3): 375–84.

Warner, J.F. (2002) *Craze: Gin and Debauchery in an Age of Reason*, New York: Four Walls Eight Windows.
Warner, J.F. and Ivis, F. (2000) 'Gin and gender in early eighteenth century London', *Eighteenth-Century Life*, 24: 85–100.
Warner, J.F., Birchmore-Timney, C. and Ivis, F. (2001) 'On the vanguard of the first drug scare. Newspapers and gin in London 1736–51', *Journalism History*, 27 (4): 178–87.
Yeomans, H. (2009) 'Revisiting moral panic: ascetic Protestantism, attitudes to alcohol and the implementation of the Licensing Act 2003', *Sociological Research Online*, 14: 2/3, www.socresonline.org.uk/14/2/6.html

12

THE ARTFUL CREATION OF GLOBAL MORAL PANIC

Climatic folk devils, environmental evangelicals, and the coming catastrophe

Sheldon Ungar

Moral panic studies has been critically reassessed in the past few years. In their totality, revisions to moral panic studies pry open virtually every aspect of moral panic, ranging from debates about definition to whether the concept should be retained or superseded. Hier (2008), for example, seeks to subsume moral panic in a broader conception of the moralization of everyday life. Critcher (2009) critically examines moral regulation and concludes that it ultimately obscures moral panic studies. In striking contrast, Waiton (2008) proffers 'a new framework of amoral panics', and Goode and Ben-Yehuda (2009) update their conventional model by seeking to rebuff skeptical approaches.

In what follows, I do not revisit these deliberations but, rather, selectively examine key issues that emerge from applying moral panic to climate change. By venturing outside the conventional range of topics – i.e., deviance and youth – I throw moral panic into relief by examining its applicability and utility in a disparate domain. But to apply the concept to something as far afield as climate change begs the question, 'What *is* a moral panic?' The conventional use of the concept invariably involves some tacit assumptions or knowledge and exemplars of past practices that help identify relevant cases and procedures for analysis. No hidden consensus operates for climate change, creating the conundrum of demonstrating that moral panic applies even as the effort is being made to evaluate its nature and utility. Given the various conceptual contortions it has been recently put through, it is not immediately obvious whether extending its range will help to focus or clarify it or simply generate a more distended hybrid.

As compared to the paradigmatic moral panic involving localized issues of youth and social control, climate change is a unique and challenging issue. It has been on the *global* agenda for more than 20 years, and the evolving series of worldwide moral panics over climate are simply unprecedented. To capture something of the progression of these far-reaching moral panics, this chapter offers a number of empirically grounded revisions to the concept. Given that climate change has been around for more than two decades, a distinction is drawn between 'low-grade' panics and episodes of volatility. Low-grade panic creation is aimed at maintaining and stoking a generalized sense of awareness and concern, effectively keeping the threat warm. These commonplace background claims are in turn punctuated by episodes of volatility – upsurges of dread-inspiring claims and actions purposively timed to correspond to planned events like the Copenhagen Conference or built around opportunistic real-world events like Hurricane Katrina.

There is a wide range of climate advocates, a term used here to encompass major claims makers, including activist scientists, political leaders, bureaucrats and environmentalists, as well as the supportive media. Where climate change commenced as an elite engineered panic led by scientists, it has gone on to encompass various interest and grass-roots groups (Goode and Ben-Yehuda 2009).[1] For the most part, these assorted advocates possess only a limited understanding of this 'post-normal science' (this is elaborated later), and hence must rely extensively on the claims made by climatologists. By implication, a distinction is made between weak and strong disproportionality. Weak disproportionality is used to describe the claims made by (lay) climate advocates who generally present the direst threats that can be *sanctioned* by the official and ostensibly consensual science of climate change; it fits the realm of social rationality (cf. Hier 2003), where claims makers strive to make threats visible to members of the public. Strong disproportionality refers to skeptical challenges to the official science itself, with allegations that climatologists are (more or less) knowingly distorting the certainty of the science and exaggerating the likely effects of a changing climate. Strong disproportionality fits the realm of scientific rationality, where debate is centered on the validity of climate science itself.

The chapter takes a biographical approach, and the argument is as follows. Initially, global warming proved to be an unwieldy issue for the creation of moral panics.[2] But after years of misdirected efforts, climate advocates were able to artfully generate an unprecedented series of global moral panics related to climate. Artfulness in this context is necessitated by a number of exceptional challenges. For one, climate advocates must *continually* orchestrate and hype concern and outrage without letting on that claims are being systematically sensationalized or distorted. They must also render fear axiomatic in the absence of the socially marginalized folk devils found in most panics. And they must reconfirm moral values without alienating the broad swath of people whose life-style is inevitably rendered suspect. Ultimately, the challenge of artfulness is revealed by the partial collapse of the climate consensus in the past few years. With the use of the Internet by skeptics to challenge the consensus, a segment of climate scientists seemingly overreacted and unleashed *moral shocks* that exposed the machinations of panic creation and undermined a good deal of the trust invested in the climate story.

Given this ongoing biography and the conceptual renovations it seems to call for, this chapter is essentially examining whether climate change is appositely analyzed as a series of moral panics. In other words, is our understanding of moral panic advanced in some demonstrable way? And in reverse, is our grasp of the marketing of climate change rendered more intelligible? It is of course easier to ask such questions than to answer them.

The challenge of risk society issues

Climate change is one of the late modern risks typically analyzed in terms of the risk society. Beck's (1992) analysis of the risk society suggests that from about the mid-1980s, new social anxieties have built up around nuclear, chemical, environmental, biological, medical and even economic issues in advanced industrial societies. Pertinent examples of these anxieties include Chernobyl, various forms of reproductive technology and biotechnology, the ozone hole, climate change, Bovine Spongiform Encephalopathy (BSE), and the economic collapse of 2009. While risks are an inevitable consequence of industrialization, Beck claims that the 'side effects' produced by late modernization are a new development. These new risks, which have steadily gained greater prominence, have a fivefold impact: they are 1) very complex in terms of causation; 2) unpredictable and latent; 3) not limited by time, space, or social class (i.e., globalized); 4) not detectable by our physical senses; and 5) are the result of human decisions (cf. Ali 1999). Essentially, the economic gains following from the application of science and technology are increasingly being overshadowed by the unintended production and distribution of 'bads'.

Just as moral panic has been subject to considerable debate, the relationship between risk and panic as sites of social anxiety is similarly contentious. In an earlier paper (Ungar 2001), I used Goode and Ben Yehuda's (2009) attributional model of moral panic to examine the conceptual intersections and divergences between moral panic and the risk society. I claimed that newer forms of social anxiety are emerging *alongside* classic panics and, drawing on McRobbie and Thornton's (1995) analysis of alternative media, suggested that panics are becoming more difficult to create. Furthermore, while disproportionality has been the central problematic of the moral panic literature, the scientific uncertainty that surrounds most risk society issues makes it more difficult to demonstrate that risks are being exaggerated.[3]

In applying their attributional model to risk society issues, Goode and Ben-Yehuda (2009: 42) contend:

> There are some supposedly threatening, dangerous or risky conditions which qualify according to the criterion of disproportion but lack the 'folk devil' element: nuclear energy, swine flu, bird flu, e coli, global warming, the shrinking ozone layer, diseases of every description, accidents, the 'military industrial complex,' and so on.

Given that Goode and Ben-Yehuda scrupulously hedge their claims throughout their text, it is curious that in *this* one instance they amalgamate so many disparate issues and make such sweeping assertions, all without evidence.[4] Their contention that the flu and other diseases lack folk devils or the element of hostility is baffling. AIDS was initially termed a 'gay plague', and the association between germs and the 'stranger'

(Jews, immigrants) is both ancient and still potent, as seen in the reaction to SARS in Toronto (Keil and Ali 2008).

Goode and Ben-Yehuda's discussion of disproportionality is also problematic. Thus, just two pages after the preceding quote, they 'agree with Ungar that with some *unspecified* conditions "it is impossible to determine the nature of the objective threat ... "' (p. 44). Similarly, in the first edition of their book they assert that 'Threats that are "future-oriented" and potentially catastrophic, such as the greenhouse effect, the earth's shrinking ozone layer, and the risk of nuclear warfare, in all likelihood, *are* impossible to calculate' (1994: 43; italics in original). The vagaries of these assertions are never examined.

In discussing fear of nuclear energy, Goode and Ben-Yehuda contend that it is not a panic because there 'is no folk devil and no sudden burst of concern' (p. 59). Leaving aside the validity of these assertions, a major problem is that they do not adequately address the question of whether *all* five of the attributes they identify – concern, hostility, consensus, disproportionality and volatility – must be present to 'qualify' as a moral panic. Is the absence of any single attribute or specific sets of attributes fatal to such a qualification? The apparent elasticity does nothing to resolve our earlier question, What *is* a moral panic? Certainly a strict application of their five attributes will disqualify climate change. Regardless, I proceed by drawing on some of these attributes, as well as a more processual approach, as the need arises.

Failure to launch: moral panic thwarted

To speak of moral panic and climate change is essentially to speak of *disproportionality*. Even though the concept of moral panic is widely unknown in the climate change field, the question of whether claims about climate are scientifically founded or sensationalized and/or distorted is not only critical theoretically, but turns out to be the fulcrum of the discourses that constitute the climate 'debate'. Unlike most moral panics ensconced in deviance, climate change is all but invisible, and scientists are the font of claims making about it. Since it was initially cast as a future-oriented threat, often focusing on effects from 2050 on, scientists had to maintain that the science was 'in' and that their models did not exaggerate or distort future climatic disasters (Oreskes 2003). Stephen Schneider, a leading climate scientist, recognized the disproportionality imperative early on: 'We have to offer up scary scenarios, make simplified, dramatic statements, and make little mention of any doubts we may have. Each of us has to decide what the right balance is between being effective and being honest' (Schell 1989).

Given this future-oriented uncertainty, *concern* about a changing climate depends on the making of convincingly spectacular claims. This is most effective if the highly variable experience of weather can be made to appear as if it is 'outside' the range of normal (Ungar 1999). The forging of *consensus* – there seems to be little agreement in the literature on the degree and inclusiveness of the consensus required – is again likely to be a product of spectacular claims compellingly made. *Hostility*, while not completely absent, tends to be toned down with risk society issues, as the usual cast of socially marginal folk devils are supplanted by less menacing constructions who scarcely give credence to or stand in for threatening claims (Ungar 2008). This diminished sense of villainous others makes it more imperative to fashion a sensationalized sense of threat itself. Finally, while episodes of *volatility* transpire, many risk society issues, including climate change, AIDS, nuclear power and the military industrial complex, are enduring problems with unique biographies. Hence, there is likely to be considerable variation over time in the extent to which threats are propagated or exaggerated.

Moral panic creation is a gambit, an artful enterprise where putative audiences are presented with and, ideally, accept *without seeing through* volatile discourses that sensationalize or distort the reality they purport to describe. The marketing of the risk should afford audiences only a superficial view of the condition so that they buy into claims that may be out of proportion with reality. Fear mongering, in other words, should be as close to invisible as possible. At the same time, the hunt for folk devils who can be held morally responsible for the risk should cast up nominees who are the most vulnerable and have the fewest resources to ward off efforts to malign them. The use of such ploys has become problematic in the realm of deviance, as moral panic is now widely recognized as a standard way of exaggerating threats. To compound the difficulties, folk devils *may* fight back, using an ever-widening range of media to expose and foil efforts to demonize them (McRobbie and Thornton, 1995; deYoung, Chapter 8 this volume).

Climate advocates initially fumbled the issue. The Greenhouse summer of 1988 put global warming on the map, as concatenating physical impacts were felt by the person in the street. Record-breaking heat in North America was coupled with a crop-destroying drought and the fire in Yellowstone National Park. With fortuitous timing, the threat of global warming was sensationalized that summer by climate advocates at the Toronto World Conference on the changing atmosphere (Ungar 1992). But the incipient moral panic built on metaphors of the 'heat trap' and a 'manmade hell on earth' was ineptly undone when James Hansen, probably the leading scientific spokesperson, asserted that he was '99% certain' that the heat of that summer was due to global warming. This claim, at a time when climate scientists freely admitted that their models were primitive, garnered widespread public criticism of Hansen and undermined any possible consensus. At the time, scientists strenuously denied inferences that tried to link observed events with global warming, and this dissociation extended to the media (Ungar 1999).

Climate change has long been regarded as a tricky issue to market. Its liabilities include the complexity and uncertainty of the science, the original formulation of consequences as future oriented and hence mostly relevant to our grandchildren, and the less-than-menacing cast of folk devils. Thus preliminary attempts to create surges of concern about a changing climate were largely thwarted. Advocates had to learn to simplify the topic and find mundane metaphors that would resonate, reverse the future orientation and identify current manifestations of catastrophic climatic impacts, and forage around for plausible *and* vulnerable folk devils (Ungar 1998).

From the late 1990s through most of the first decade of the new century, the marketing problems of climate are, by and large, surmounted, spawning a series of global moral panics. Climate change and an attendant sense of doom now float in the air we breathe. As happened with nuclear panics, evidence suggests that many children fear for the future, due to the climate threat hammered home in public schools (Kunstler 2005). CO_2, a greenhouse gas vital to life on the planet, has been transmuted into a 'pollutant' by both the EPA and the US Supreme Court, with the latter obligating the EPA to legislate control of greenhouse gases.

The impact of climate scares also is now plainly visible in the South. At the Copenhagen Conference in 2009, leaders of many Southern nations were sufficiently fearful of droughts, floods and rising sea levels that they pressed for a stronger regime to replace the Kyoto Accords (McKibben 2010). This is an explicit reversal of their prior opposition to acting on the issue. But the most striking evidence of the inroads made by climate change advocates is that they have rendered the impossible possible: nuclear power, long moribund and dreaded in a post-Chernobyl world, is being rehabilitated because it is not a source of CO_2 (e.g., Bickerstaff et al. 2008).

This 20-year world-wide progression of moral panics is unprecedented. It is also puzzling, given the limits of global warming as a saleable social problem. Clearly, detailed and systematic studies of particular cases are required to determine *how* these panics were effectuated. Here I merely outline their development and indicate some of the factors and processes that may account for these successes – or in fact hindered them.

The artful creation of global moral panics

The creation of the Intergovernmental Panel on Climate Change (IPCC) was a consummate decision. By establishing an international body of scientific experts, climate science was provided with the trappings of authority that were seemingly beyond reproach. The bargaining and compromises that went into the four IPCC reports (1990, 1995, 2001, 2007)[5] are not settled. The uncertainties and complexities endemic to this post-normal science are buried in the entrails of these largely unread and unreadable tomes that run to thousands of pages. Over time, the IPCC has moved beyond the 99 percent quandary posed by Hansen and holds that the anthropogenic origins of climate change and its dire consequences are clear and undeniable. The 2001 report put the notorious 'hockey stick' on its cover, implying that the current warming is historically unparalleled. While the reports contain a wide range of future scenarios, their public staging by advocates ignores the scientific hedging and focuses instead on the worst-case scenarios.

Both before and after the start of the Iraq war, the US media muted criticism of the Bush administration, covering political sound bites but making little attempt to evaluate them (Rutherford 2004). The upshot was that the *New York Times* eventually criticized itself for not being adequately critical of the administrations' claims (Rosenthal 2004). For the most part (some exceptions are discussed below), the advocates who render the climate threat visible in various public arenas have played a similar accommodating role. Overall, they have fostered moral panic by dutifully echoing the IPCC, which is cast as an unimpeachable resource. Global claims makers mostly convey a stream of asymmetric and skewed claims, an unqualified inventory of the most terrifying ecological tipping points found in the reports (Weingart, Engels, and Pansegrau 2000). Since they are drawing on the IPCC as the ultimate arbiter of truth, they predictably assert that they are not distorting reality, just relaying the dire threats made manifest by the best available science.

The prevailing gospel is that climate change represents the greatest threat to humankind. We are facing a planetary crisis, replete with apocalyptic predictions about melting glaciers, rising sea levels, large increases in the frequency and severity of extreme weather events, and so on (Kolbert 2009). The cover of *Time Magazine* for April 3, 2006, put it succinctly: 'Be Worried. Be Very Worried'. After years of failed attempts to find compelling and shocking metaphors, climate change is now embodied in the iconic and potent images of calving ice sheets. The 2007 report of the IPCC contains the jaw-dropping claim that the thousands of Himalayan glaciers will disappear by 2035, removing the 'water towers' essential to the population of the Asian subcontinent.[6] Since this last report, scientists routinely claim that deleterious climatic changes are actually occurring far more rapidly than predicted by the worst-case scenarios (McKibben 2010).

Al Gore, the public face of the hell that awaits us, can be forthright: 'Nobody is interested in solutions if they don't think there's a problem. Given that starting point, I believe it is appropriate to have an over-representation of factual presentations on how dangerous [global warming] is, as a predicate for opening up the audience to listen to what the solutions are' (Revere 2006). Indeed, the IPCC reports can be exploited to provide cover for spurious claims on the dangers of warming. Thus, a British High Court Judge ruled that Gore's film, *An Inconvenient Truth*, which comes with the imprimatur of the IPCC, contains nine scientific errors and cannot be shown in schools without teachers pointing out the problematic sections (BBC 2007).[7] In the context of thousands of scientific papers published on climate and the huge array of communication channels around the globe, questions about scientific validity and error, journalistic balancing, exaggerated claims, and the public understanding of the issue are potentially overwhelming and can be addressed only by using very specific and limited sources. Representative samples do not mesh well with the crushing overload found on the Internet. By implication, advocates often have a free hand to present outlandish claims.

Taking this a step further, it can be hypothesized that when it comes to the *social rationality* through which risks are made 'visible' to the lay public (Hier 2003), the substantive or deep content of articles matters less than the sheer ubiquity of the cues they provide on the surface, particularly in their headlines or the accompanying 8-second sound bites or story leads. Boykoff and Boykoff (2004) are vexed by the amount of 'balancing' – coverage of *both* the IPCC consensus and climatic skeptics – found in some of the US prestige press. But considerable evidence suggests that only a tiny proportion of readers peruse and process information at such depths (Eliasoph 1998; Ungar 2008). The Boykoffs are doubtlessly committing the mistake of self-generalization, taking the *scientific rationality* of experts or erudite readers as typical rather than exceptional.

In contrast, Van Dijk (1988) focuses on the import of headlines, suggesting that they serve as retrieval cues to activate the relevant regimes of truth underlying public knowledge. So multifarious are the headlining impacts ascribed to climate change that it has become the universal environmental tag, with an imprint on seemingly everything. Shoppers must tote reusable bags, eating habits are scrutinized (the obese have been slammed for contributing to climate change by eating too much), and heating and air conditioning, driving and flying are all targeted as guilt-laden sources of CO_2. Predictions as fanciful as increases in the populations of wild cats and decreases in the size of birds may raise doubts among all but the most credulous climate supporters. However, given the increasing political and public concern about global warming through the first decade of this century, one must conclude, at least tentatively, that the bizarre linkages to everything have served to reinforce the climate juggernaut rather than render it implausible. It's as if this flood of captioned disasters keep sounding 'clicks' on the fear meter rather than adding to an inventory of the unbelievable. Thus far it seems that threat inflation has not given way to threat exhaustion.

In this regard, moral panics related to a changing climate have a twofold aspect. On the one hand, there is an ongoing succession of 'low-grade claims making aimed at maintaining a generalized sense of awareness and concern'. These fairly ubiquitous background claims over the past two decades are punctuated by episodes of volatility – eruptions of dread-inspiring claims and activities purposively timed to correspond to multinational events like the Rio and the Copenhagen Conferences or the unveiling of an IPCC report. Certainly the Copenhagen Conference brought a host of new and menacing scientific findings, essentially a daily dose of jeopardy. Beyond constant reminders that the past decade was the warmest on record, coupled with extensive coverage of the world-wide loss of glaciers and ice sheets, street-theatre events in Copenhagen and many other cities around the globe included ominous 'TckTckTck' banners and activists brandishing alarm clocks to epitomize how time is running out (McKibben 2010). In this instance, the hunt for morally reprehensible folk devils redounded on Canada. It became the prime target, as the tar sands are now deemed to be the single most egregious source of CO_2. Waffling by the federal government led David Miller, Mayor of Toronto, to assert that 'Like most Canadians, I'm embarrassed. I'm embarrassed that our government continues to be one of the biggest obstacles to reaching agreement' (Cryderman 2009).

The successful promulgation of volatile episodes of moral panics is all the more remarkable, given that climatic folk devils are far from the monstrous representations conventionally found in the realm of deviance. As with other risk society issues, blame is typically diffused among diverse candidates that include governments, corporations, and scientists (Ungar 2001). Rather than being depraved, they are more likely to be seen as vacillating, inept or ignorant. They typically have extensive resources to fight back with: street gangs cannot mount campaigns comparable to those undertaken by Shell Canada, and despite accusations of profiteering from the tar sands, people ultimately need oil, and hence the companies that supply it. Often these prospective folk devils have the capacity to simply ignore their accusers. Certainly Stephen Harper of Canada excels in standing apart from the fray. His political fortunes have not suffered by his being grouped into the 'Three Climate Stooges'; nor did the fortunes of the other stooges – George Bush and John Howard of Australia.

Moral panics usually go much deeper than the ostensible risk itself, expressing anxieties over broader social problems, including the direction of social change. In this regard, the vast array of environmental problems that beset us have become encapsulated and subsumed in the climatic threat. The late 1980s saw the environment move to the top of the public agenda, and environmentalists put climate at the top of their agenda and organized the bulk of their activities around it (Dunlap and Scarce 1991). At the extreme, especially among those dubbed 'climate evangelicals', environmental problems are regarded as nature's response to globalization and unrestrained consumption. In this context, they frequently try to craft CO_2 into a 'folk devil'. But this creates additional fallout, since there are both naturally occurring CO_2 which is essential to life, and the anthropogenic emissions blamed for climate change. Hence, when climate advocates rummage around for the 'sources' of CO_2, they encounter a particularly unenviable target: the clear majority of Westerners, who blithely emit 'luxury emissions' of CO_2, in sharp contrast to much of the rest of the planet, who struggle to pull off 'survival emissions'. Of course, only the politically tone deaf would spotlight such a broad moral culpability, with its attendant demands for personal and societal transformation. Efforts to moralize supposedly unsustainable life-styles amount to strategic suicide, and this part of the story must be air-brushed to avoid public reactance. For the most part, this seems to have been accomplished. Poll results generally reveal fairly high levels of public concern, yet people have little knowledge of how to reduce their own emissions and are unwilling to make much more than trivial life-style changes (Kunstler 2005). The upshot is the extraordinary amount of energy that has been devoted to the replacement of plastic bags with reusable ones, a feel-good enterprise with no bearing on planetary warming.

Moral shock and the undermining of the climate story

The preceding discussion provides a skeletal account of the climate story in public arenas, suggesting that the threat has become ingrained in public discourse and serves as the universal environmental tag. Indeed, modifying Foucault (1980: 131), it can be contended that climate change, as a relatively new social problem that is not yet melded into invisible background truths, has become part of a 'coercive' regime of truth. Political leaders of all stripes are compelled to pay lip service to it. Oil and auto companies that originally opposed the problem have jumped onboard and excel at ads promoting the green steps they are taking. There have also been allegations by mainstream scientists who dispute the IPCC consensus that they are being silenced.[8]

However, percolating below the surface is a vituperative 'debate' pitting conventional scientists who are largely in the IPCC fold against climate skeptics (Hulme 2009). As compared to our proceeding account of the prevailing climate story, most aspects of this secondary discourse are flipped on their head. The former story falls within the realm of social rationality, where risks are made visible and interpretable as lay knowledge (Hier 2003). The latter debate concerns scientific rationality, with its techno-scientific claims making by putative experts. As previously observed, while the validity of the IPCC consensus has not gone unchallenged in public arenas, it has for the *most* part been taken for granted, even cosseted. In contrast, skeptics directly contest the validity of the IPCC reports themselves. In challenging the 'reality' of climate change, they rely on the Internet, a medium in which they are not subject to what they perceive as silencing by both the media and the peer review process. Here there is little concurrence, and the media echo chambers have been subverted by strident disagreements and rancorous name calling.

In this context, the 'story' is no longer controlled by climate advocates, and their use of moral panic to present the climate risk has gradually become more visible, especially as attempts to vilify and mute skeptics have increased. Add to this an accumulation of critical findings and errors, as well as the scandal known as Climategate, and small circles of scientists have artlessly precipitated what amounts to *moral shocks*. Through their less-than-professional handling of the skeptical challenge, these scientists are widely seen as having engaged in specific and blatant moral betrayals, breaching core scientific protocols that are deemed central to the validity of the whole enterprise. So unexpected and flagrant were their actions that they jumped the barrier from the Internet to the mainstream media and therein exposed the stratagem of moral panic creation and partially undermined the trust invested in the IPCC and the climate story.

In dealing with the realm of scientific rationality, it is notable that climate change has been labeled a charter example of post-normal science. The latter fits nicely with the risk society, as it applies to risks that entail 'great complexity, uncertain facts, disputed values, high stakes, and a seemingly urgent need for action' (Bray and von Storch 1999; Hulme 2009). Post-normal science is a radical departure from how science is presented in the realm of social rationality. Where the latter embraces the view that the science is settled and commands broad agreement, the former focuses attention on what is unknown, or at best uncertain. The IPCC reports provide *some* recognition of the post-normal nature of climate science, but this is not publicized. As might be expected, in their disputes over the standing of climate science, advocates and skeptics diverge along post-normal fault lines. Skeptics formulate their assorted claims around the uncertainties, while advocates are primarily driven by a sense of urgency. The upshot is that skeptics hone in on disproportionality, while advocates focus on maligning and silencing skeptics, since they hold that immediate action on the issue is imperative.

The gaps between the in-depth reports of the IPCC and their public staging represent a *weak* form of disproportionality, since claims made in public arenas are largely drawn from what are *deemed* to be authoritative scientific truths.[9] Social rationality is expounded through asymmetric and skewed discourses that rely on the worst-case scenarios officially sanctioned by the IPCC. Whatever the reasons proffered for such biased appropriations – usually reference is made to desperate attempts to scare people into action – they are dubbed weak disproportionality because, in enlisting the most sensational and spectacular claims within the IPCC orbit (cf. Hier 2008), they fall short of the more extreme 'inventions', 'fabrications' and 'irrationalities' that

Goode and Ben-Yehuda (2009: 44–46) list as indicators of disproportionality. Consistent with the latter, a *strong* form of disproportionality is imputed by skeptics, as they target the scientific rationality of the IPCC reports themselves, contending that these range from orchestrated guesswork to outright sham. In what follows, I provide a cursory outline of key skeptical challenges to the IPCC process which ultimately redound on the moral shock of Climategate.

Since skeptics were excluded from most public forums and were thus reliant on the Internet, their founding efforts amounted to little more than a side show. They typically employed a shotgun approach that still mostly missed the mark. Skeptics tended to latch onto any possible weakness and then hammered away at it, fostering the impression that the reality of global warming was contingent on this single concern. Once the issue was 'resolved', they shifted to a new 'anomaly' and repeated the process. The numerous 'issue networks' that surfaced among them allowed for the nearly infinite reiteration of similar claims, creating a density that can generate an overwhelming sense of (un)reality among those who traverse them (Rogers 2002).

It was not until 2003 that the skeptics broke through. Soon and Baliunas (2003) asserted that temperatures during the Medieval Warm Period (MWP) exceeded the extremes found in the twentieth century, reversing the claims made by the IPCC that the late twentieth century is the warmest period on record. While their work has been termed 'fundamentally unsound' (Mann *et al.* 2003), efforts to tackle this 'past blindness' underscore the generalized state of uncertainty surrounding post-normal science. This is more than an academic debate, as the standing of the MWP has implications for evaluating the current warming, including the role of anthropogenic factors, the validity of the hockey stick model discussed below, and the significance of thinning Arctic sea ice. Some skeptics make the dodgier allegation that mainstream scientists have tried to obscure the MWP so as to prop up the view that current temperatures are unparalleled.

Skeptical challenges extended to Mann *et al.*'s (1998) work on the 'hockey stick', which figured prominently in the Third Assessment Report of the IPCC. The hockey stick graph of reconstructed temperature variations in the Northern Hemisphere over the past 1,000 years suggests that temperatures were relatively stable during the period A.D. 1000 to 1900. But following this flat part that forms the shaft of the stick, temperatures rise dramatically, especially in the last 25 years, creating the blade of the stick. After years of fruitless requests for the original data used by Mann *et al.*, McIntyre and McKitrick (2003) were finally granted access. Their re-analysis raised sufficient doubts that further investigations were undertaken by the National Research Council and other agencies. These reported mixed findings (both sides claimed vindication), though it is notable that the 2007 report of the IPCC effectively dispenses with the hockey stick.

Skeptics have also attacked the validity of climate models. It is these models that provide estimates of how much current warming is due to anthropogenic effects and how much is due to natural processes (Oreskes 2007). Skeptics dismiss these models altogether, claiming that their parameters have been 'tweaked' to reproduce past data. They are deemed non-scientific, since they generate a range of future scenarios rather than make specific predictions that are subject to falsification. IPCC scientists concede that the models are heuristic devices, but also note that skeptics uphold an outmoded model of 'normal' science, while ignoring the fundamental physical laws that modelers draw on. In other words, the models are not arbitrary creations that have been configured simply to fit past data. These scientists fall back on two further expedients: the claim that there is an overriding scientific consensus, a consensus that can survive the rejection of climate models because 'models are only one part of the argument – one line of evidence among many' (Oreskes 2007).

While climate advocates belittle these skeptical thrusts, this is seemingly belied by their augmented efforts to pigeonhole them as folk devils. Corresponding with the critical inroads made by skeptics, advocates not only hunt for more opprobrious names, but mount *ad hominem* attacks on their motives and attempt to silence them (cf. Ungar and Bray 2004). 'Skeptic' of course was an inept designation to begin with, as scientists *ought* to be skeptical and, once upon a time, could don that label as a badge of honor. Advocates have assayed other unfavorable appellations, including contrarians, traitors, and defectors; they ultimately settled on climate 'deniers', a label that draws unseemly associations with holocaust deniers.

Beyond such name calling, advocates also began to make inquisitional assertions that, in conjunction with the Climategate scandal, culminate in moral shocks. Under the auspices of the supposed consensus, calls have been made to silence skeptics and other mavericks who won't buy in to the emergency.[10] Al Gore refuses encounters with skeptics. Robert Kennedy Jr. denounced them as 'villainous enemies of America and the human race' and averred, 'This is treason. And we need to start treating them as traitors.' David Suzuki, Canada's foremost environmental spokesperson, has asserted on several occasions that recalcitrant politicians should be jailed. James Hansen dubbed coal cars 'death trains' and suggested that the CEOs of fossil fuel companies be put on trial for 'high crimes against humanity and nature' (Kolbert 2009). There have been calls to strip television meteorologists who are 'deniers' of their American Meteorological Society certification (Kaufman 2010). Skeptics have even been compared to advocates of Islamic terror; by implication, it is suggested that they be denied media access.

So long as these indictments were confined to the Internet and specialty journals catering to activists, they hardly impacted on the public rationality surrounding climate change. Since so much of the media served as little more than scientists' stenographers, there was little seepage or censure of even the most outlandish pronouncements. Still, some channels did open or broaden, and these are nicely illustrated by the mediating role assumed by Roger Pielke Jr. A professor of environmental studies, he published *The Honest Broker* (2007), which aptly described his standing in the field. He has taken on the luminaries of climate science, writing on his blog, for example: 'Hansen invokes religious terms, characterizing himself and Schneider as witness and preacher, respectively. Both are evangelists who hold science as an ascendant authority.'[11] But, unlike the silencing of skeptics, these luminaries debate him on his blog. The latter includes respectful *and* respected criticisms of the IPCC and other reports. The same holds for his handling of leading skeptics. Scientists can ignore Pielke only at their own peril, and he is frequently cited in the mainstream media, providing a conduit between it and the Internet.

On his blog, Pielke called the 2009 Annan Report, with its claim that climate change will kill 300,000 a year, a 'methodological embarrassment' and 'a poster child for how to lie with statistics'. Just how much his honest brokering provided an opening for others is difficult to say. Certainly scientific anomalies have been accumulating. In particular, we have not seen any of the predicted warming since at least 2000, and perhaps 1995. In any case, the chorus of questioning voices became especially loud from 2008 on. Dissent over aspects of climate science has conspicuously surfaced in peer-reviewed journals, major conferences, a variety of reports, and increasingly in the media. Considerable attention is now devoted to exposing the shortcomings of the IPCC process. The extent of the rising outspokenness is indicated by challenges coming from German scientists, who have hitherto been quiescent.[12]

If skeptical ideas were no longer confined to a parallel universe, the major cross-over follows from the scandal that came to be known as Climategate.[13] The hacking of a server in November 2009 at the University of East Anglia's Climatic Research Unit resulted in the release of thousands of emails and other documents. While most of the leaked information dealt with mundane matters of research, there were selected disclosures that seemed particularly compromising. A number of emails suggested that scientists might be manipulating data. Examples included reference to a 'trick' used in key graphs on tree rings, comments on manipulating computer codes, the nuisance posed by the MWP, which ought to be wiped away, and questions of how to manage the embarrassing absence of any measurable warming over the past decade. There were discussions about suppressing dissenting scientific papers, the withholding of data, and plots to remove troublesome journal editors. Disparaging comments about researchers who strayed from the official line, including the 'cheering news' of the death of one detractor, also surfaced. And perhaps most important, much of the original data used to measure temperatures over time were (somehow) lost.

To make matters worse, Climategate intersected with an error in the 2007 IPCC report. According to the latter, the Himalayan glaciers could disappear by 2035, with disastrous consequences. Skeptics, who undoubtedly scrutinize these reports line by line, discovered that this prediction came from a non-peer-reviewed and essentially speculative report put out by the World Wide Fund for Nature (WWF). Both the IPCC and WWF soon acknowledged this oversight and dismissed it as a minor lapse in a huge undertaking. But critics observed that this was not minutia, and followed up with additional charges that the IPCC reports rely far too much on 'gray literature' rather than peer-reviewed research.[14]

While most of the critical forays of skeptics have garnered minimal media attention, Climategate and 'Glaciergate' occasioned a frenzy of media coverage, particularly in Britain. They also unleashed what we have called moral shocks. Scientist are a comparatively honored and privileged group of experts who, in exchange for their distinctive status and opportunities, are expected to adhere to the basic norms and standards that underlie their role as guardians of truth. In the realm of social rationality, scientists must be *seen* as believing in and upholding the idealized normative values of their profession. But Climategate revealed specific and flagrant betrayals of the moral trust invested in them. They displayed a level of sordid and thuggish behavior that one might expect to find among the folk devils commonly thrown up in the ambit of deviance. But scientists are – or are supposed to be – superior in *this* regard, and their betrayal was a moral shock comparable to that of Catholic priests who sexually molested children in their charge.

Several investigations of Climategate agreed that no fraudulent activities were entailed (e.g., Satter 2010). But terming it a 'pinprick' hyped up by the media did little to defuse the consequences. The scandal created a perception of impropriety, revealing a shabby underside to climate research that so violated expectations about scientists' (idealized) activities that it rendered the question of fraud secondary. The investigations were accorded little confidence, as well. With partisan scientists investigating partisan scientists, the reports had about the same degree of believability found when police investigate police or bishops investigate priests. For years, skeptics have routinely used whichever of their criticisms was in vogue to declare the death of global warming. These pronouncements were obviously premature and misguided, but the effects of their opposition, culminating in Climategate, are reflected in poll results from the US, Britain and Germany. In all three nations, there have been significant and substantial drops in those who believe global warming is occurring.[15] In the US, the view that the threat of global warming is 'generally exaggerated' jumped from about one-third to 50 percent in less than two years (Newport 2010).

Conclusion

Is this moral panic? A number of renovations were required to apply the concept to climate change. Volatility has been a defining characteristic of moral panic, which is not surprising, given its roots in deviance. But to capture the combination of an extended climate biography as well as specific flurries of activity, a distinction was drawn between low-grade panic creation, on the one hand, and volatile episodes, on the other. On the face of it, this distinction could also be applied to nuclear power and emerging diseases. That climate change is not just an issue of concern but has remained near the top of the (global) public agenda for so long is utterly improbable and requires much more detailed examination than found here. It is essential in this regard that theoretical accounts of panic formation be able to explain not only successful efforts, but serial successes – and failures. Critcher (2006: 12) observes that 'the effects of moral panics vary enormously', with some being little more than symbolic endeavours. Climate change is neither an epiphenomenon nor simply symbolic, and one might reasonably ask why bother to further apply or develop the concept around such minimal occurrences.

Climate change is a post-normal science, and to adequately deal with this I have differentiated between weak and strong disproportionality. The former appears to best fit the realm of social rationality, where claims makers are seeking to make threats visible in public. Climate advocates in this context rely on the authority of science, but tend to sensationalize it by presenting the direst threats that can be scientifically warranted. Strong disproportionality, in contrast, is linked to the realm of scientific rationality, where the concern is to establish and document the validity of climatic science. While the totality of the science and its fundamental predictions, i.e., the 'big questions', remains mired in uncertainties, it is feasible to contend that aspects or components of it are exaggerated or distorted. Even in this narrower sense of disproportionality, considerable ambiguity remains.

While moral panics are generally regarded as inherently conservative, in this instance they are being used as a vehicle by, broadly speaking, liberal organizations and groups. Conservatives, particularly in the US, have provided much of the opposition, based on the fear of increasing government control over the economy and people's personal lives. A clear indicator of this division turns on the question of whether people should be free to purchase gas-guzzling SUVs or the state should constrain their choices through taxes or other methods. This distinction is replayed in the gap between people's beliefs, on the one hand, and practical exigencies and their life-style entitlements, on the other. Offshore drilling and recovering oil from the tar sands are the target of liberal moralization, yet the bottomless appetite for oil and the problems associated with importing it from foreign sources mean that neither of these is likely to be prohibited in the future. Moralization, perhaps, may be closer to symbolic than actual politics.

The present analysis points to one additional radical departure in the creation and management of moral panics. Where McRobbie and Thornton (1995) presciently examined the role of alternative media in allowing folk devils to fight back, the current levels and forms of contestation are far more sweeping and immoderate. Climate skeptics, who often seem pleased to act as folk devils by choice, are so methodical in their hunt for errors in the IPCC and other reports that essentially *no* statement goes unchallenged. Were this peer review, it would render all papers unpublishable. When this is combined with the use of the Internet, even the most frivolous criticisms are endlessly reiterated, potentially acquiring a sense of authenticity by the sheer weight of repetition. In the case under examination here, as skeptics made a few critical inroads, advocates followed with some artless responses. Between name callings, efforts to crush dissent, a few errant calls for inquisitions, and finally scandals, they unleashed moral shocks and engendered doubts about the climate story which started to migrate from the Internet to the mainstream media. As for where this story will head, especially as more conventional scientists are themselves employing blogs to question aspects of the ostensible consensus, will be of intense interest both practically and in terms of our grasp of where long-term moral panics might be heading.

Notes

1 Much of the action around climate change has taken place in cities and small towns, especially as national governments have often defaulted, due to potential economic costs.
2 Americans mostly use global warming, while Europeans speak of climate change. I use the two interchangeably.
3 This paper drew a direct rebuttal from Hier (2003), who contends that we are actually witnessing converging sites of social anxiety, coupled with a sharp increase in panic formations.

4 They do present some limited evidence related to Chernobyl (p. 83). Of course this evidence is obtained about 20 years after the event and not in advance, as is the case with climate change or threatening viruses. The single case of Chernobyl hardly makes the case.
5 Government appointees who are not scientists must also sign on to reports, but the fact that the consensus hammered out by the IPCC includes such non-scientific stakeholders is widely unknown. These reports and other special reports can be found at the IPCC website, www.ipcc.ch/
6 As discussed later below, this claim turns out to be an exaggeration that the IPCC was forced to recant.
7 A Google search reveals that the mainstream media devoted precious little coverage to this ruling.
8 See, for example, http://coast.gkss.de/staff/zorita/. All sides complain of silencing, including scientists such as Hansen, who contends that the Bush administration silenced him and tried to downplay the climate threat on government websites. My own discussions with scientists in Canada and Europe indicate that dissenters from the IPCC consensus feel intimidated and often compelled to maintain an unhappy silence.
9 As with the prior example of the Gore film, public statements using the IPCC or other scientific findings may entail fundamental distortions or outright fabrications. There is far too much claim making out there for anything but the most superficial fact checking. Skeptics focus their critical activities on the IPCC and other prominent scientific reports and findings.
10 In reference to research disputing the link between warming and malaria, Pielke observes on his blog: 'Hopefully, the new study will mark a new era in the climate debate where it is accepted among the mainstream scientific community to raise challenges to unsupportable claims made to support action, rather than seeing them go unquestioned because of the perceived delicate politics of the climate issue.'
11 http://rogerpielkejr.blogspot.com/
12 See, for example, http://coast.gkss.de/staff/zorita/ I should note here that I know Ed Zorita and he is very much a mainstream scientist who has become somewhat disenchanted with the activities of some climate scientists.
13 Climategate and Glaciergate are too recent for peer-reviewed studies to have appeared. In their absence, there are masses of newspaper reports and blogs on both sides of each issue. It is not clear how to cite coverage at this point without introducing bias.
14 See, in this regard, http://nofrakkingconsensus.blogspot.com/2010/04/ipcc-reliance-on-grey-literature-30.html
15 See, for example, http://www.spiegel.de/wissenschaft/natur/0,1518,685946,00.html

References

Ali, H. (1999) 'The search for a landfill site in a risk society', *Canadian Review of Sociology and Anthropology* 36(1): 1–19.
BBC (2007) 'Gore climate film's nine "errors"', October 11: http://news.bbc.co.uk/2/hi/uk_news/education/7037671.stm
Beck, U. (1992) *Risk Society: Towards a New Modernity*. London: Sage.
Ben-Yehuda, Nachman. (2009) 'Moral panics – 36 years on', *British Journal of Criminology* 49(1): 1–3.
Bickerstaff, K., Lorenzoni, I., Pidgeon, N.F., Poortinga, W. and Simmons, P. (2008) 'Reframing nuclear power in the UK energy debate: Nuclear power, climate change mitigation and radioactive waste', *Public Understanding of Science* 17(2): 145–69.
Boykoff, M. and Boykoff, J. (2004) 'Balance as bias: Global warming and the US prestige press', *Global Environmental Change* 14(2): 125–36.
Bray, D. and von Storch, H. (1999) 'Climate science: An empirical example of post-normal science', *Bulletin of the American Meteorological Society* 80: 439–55.

Critcher, C. (2009) 'Widening the focus: Moral panics as moral regulation', *British Journal of Sociology* 49(1): 17–34.
Critcher, C. (2006) *Critical Readings: Moral Panic and the Media*. Buckingham, UK: Open University Press.
Cryderman, K. (2009) 'Toronto's Mayor Miller "embarrassed" for Canada', *National Post*, December 11: N1.
Dunlap, R. and Scarce, R. (1991) 'The polls – poll trends: Environmental problems and Protection', *Public Opinion Quarterly* 55(4): 651–72.
Eliasoph, N. (1998) *Avoiding Politics: How Americans Produce Apathy in Everyday Life*. Cambridge: Cambridge University Press.
Foucault, M. (1980) *Power/Knowledge: Selected Interviews and Other Writings*. New York: Pantheon.
Goode, E. and Ben-Yehuda, N. (2009) *Moral Panics: The Social Construction of Deviance*, 2nd edition, Chichester: John Wiley.
Goode, E. and Ben-Yehuda, N. (1994) *Moral Panics: The Social Construction of Deviance*. Cambridge, Mass: Blackwell.
Hier, S.P. (2008) 'Thinking beyond moral panic: Risk, responsibility and the politics of moralization', *Theoretical Criminology* 12(2): 173–90.
Hier, S.P. (2003) 'Risk and panic in late modernity: Implications of the converging sites of social anxiety', *British Journal of Sociology* 54(1): 3–20.
Hulme, M. (2009) *Why We Disagree about Climate Change: Understanding Controversy, Inaction and Opportunity*. Cambridge: Cambridge University Press.
Kaufman, L. (2010) 'Among Weathercasters, Doubt on Warming', *New York Times*, March 29: www.nytimes.com/2010/03/30/science/earth/30warming.html
Keil, R. and Ali, S.H. (2008) '"Racism is a weapon of mass destruction": SARS and the social fabric of urban multiculturalism', in S.H. Ali and R. Keil, (eds.) *Networked Disease: Emerging Infections in the Global City*, Chichester: John Wiley.
Kolbert, E. (2009) 'The catastrophist: NASA's climate expert delivers the news no one wants to hear', *The New Yorker*, June 29: 39–45.
Kunstler, J.H. (2005) *The Long Emergency: Surviving the End of Oil, Climate Change and other Converging Catastrophes of the Twenty-first Century*. New York: Grove.
McIntyre, S. and McKitrick, R. (2003) 'Corrections to the Mann et al. Proxy data base and Northern Hemisphere average temperature series', *Energy and Environment*, 14: 751–71.
McKibben, B. (2010) 'Heavy Weather in Copenhagen', *New York Review of Books*, March 11: 32–34.
McRobbie, A. and Thornton, S. (1995) 'Rethinking "moral panic" for multi-mediated social worlds', *British Journal of Sociology* 46(4): 559–74.
Mann, M., Bradley, R. and Hughes, M. (1998) 'Global-scale temperature patterns and climate forcing over the past six centuries', *Nature* 392: 779–78.
Mann, M., Amman, C., Bradley, R., Briffa, K., Jones, P., Osborn, T., Crowley, T., Hughes, M., Oppenheimer, M., Overpeck, J., Rutherford, S., Trenberth, K. and Wigley, T. (2003) 'On past temperatures and anomalous late-20th Century warmth', *Eos*, 84: 256.
Newport, F. (2010) 'Gallup: Americans' global warming concerns continue to drop', *Gallup News*, March 12: http://wattsupwiththat.com/2010/03/12/gallup-americans-global-warming-concerns-continue-to-drop/.
Oreskes, N. (2007) 'The scientific consensus on climate change: How do we know we're not wrong?', in J. DiMento and J. Doughman (eds.) *Climate Change: What It Means for Us, Our Children, and Our Grandchildren*. Boston: MIT Press.
Oreskes, N. (2003) 'The scientific consensus on climate change', *Science* 306: 1686–89.
Pielke, R. (2007) *The Honest Broker: Making Sense of Science in Policy and Politics*. Cambridge: Cambridge University Press.
Revere, A. (2006) 'An interview with accidental movie star Al Gore', *Grist Magazine*, May 9: www.grist.org/article/roberts2/
Rogers, R. (2002) 'Operating issue networks on the Web', *Science as Culture* 11: 191–213.

Rosenthal, J. (2004) 'What belongs on the front page of the New York Times?', *New York Times*, February 4: A1.

Rutherford, P. (2004) *Weapons of Mass Persuasion: Marketing the War Against Iraq*. Toronto: University of Toronto Press.

Satter, R. (2010) '"Climategate" scientists vindicated in investigation', *Globe and Mail*, March 31: T1.

Schell, J. (1989) 'Our fragile earth', *Discover*, December: 45–48.

Soon, W. and Baliunas, S. (2003) 'Proxy climatic and environmental changes of the past 1000 years', *Climate Research* 23: 89–110.

Ungar, S. (2008) 'Ignorance as an under-identified social problem', *British Journal of Sociology*, 59(2): 301–26.

Ungar, S. (2001) 'Moral panic versus the risk society: The implications of the changing sites of social anxiety', *British Journal of Sociology* 52(2): 271–91.

Ungar, S. (1999) 'Is strange weather in the air: A study of US national news coverage of extreme weather events', *Climatic Change*, 41(2): 133–50.

Ungar, S. (1998) 'Bringing the issue back in: Comparing the marketability of the ozone hole and global warming', *Social Problems* 45(4): 510–27.

Ungar, S. (1992) 'The rise and (relative) decline of global warming as a social problem', *Sociological Quarterly* 33(4): 483–501.

Ungar, S. and Bray, D. (2004) 'Silencing science: Partisanship and the career of a publication disputing the dangers of secondhand smoke', *Public Understanding of Science* 13: 1–19.

Van Dijk, V. (1988) *News as Discourse*. Hillsdale, CA: Lawrence Erlbaum.

Weingart, P., Engels, A. and Pansegrau, P. (2000) 'Risks of communication: Discourses on climate change in science, politics, and the mass media', *Public Understanding of Science* 9: 261–83.

Waiton, S. (2008) *The Politics of Antisocial Behavior: Amoral Panics*. London: Routledge.

13

WHEN HARM IS DONE

Panic, scandal and blame[1]

Graham Knight and Juliet Roper

Introduction

> Things go wrong and harm is done ...

On Tuesday, May 29, 2007 a worker employed by VirCom EMS disconnected the electricity supply to the home of the Muliagas, a Samoan family living in the Mangere district of south Auckland, New Zealand. VirCom EMS was acting as a subcontractor for Mercury Energy, an electricity supply company, which had authorized the disconnection because the Muliagas were in arrears in the payment of their electricity bill, and the overall amount owing had been increasing despite partial payments having been made. As a result of the disconnection, the oxygen machine used by Folole Muliaga ceased functioning, and fewer than three hours later she died, despite the efforts of paramedics who had been called to the house because of her deteriorating condition. The death of Mrs. Muliaga, who was normally described in the media as a 44-year-old mother of four, subsequently became a major news event and contentious public issue in New Zealand as the various actors involved in the situation sought to represent and justify themselves, their actions and points of view. The *dramatis personae* included not only representatives of the Muliaga family, VirCom EMS and Mercury Energy, but also the latter's parent company, Mighty River Power, the Prime Minister, the minister responsible for state-owned enterprises (SOEs), the police, media columnists expounding on the meaning of the tragedy, local community members, and even an official representing the electricity workers' union.

The situation that unfolded bore many of the features of a social drama in which a breach in the routine practices and expectations of everyday life set in motion processes of institutional and communicational resolution (Turner 1974; Cottle 2006). In this chapter, we focus primarily on the first two weeks after Mrs. Muliaga's death.

This was the 'salience period' (Hood 2002) in which a distinction can be drawn between the institutional and communicational responses to Mrs. Muliaga's death. The institutional response took the form of a police investigation, which concluded that there were no legal grounds to lay charges; the communicational response took the form of extensive media coverage in which there was some contention between the viewpoints of the central actors involved in the tragedy. We focus primarily on the communicational response in order to examine the definitional process in which some resolution began to be brought to the situation, and its dramatic impact began to be reduced. We make two main arguments. The first is that while the response to Mrs. Muliaga's death, particularly in the media, bore the marks of a scandal rather than moral panic in the conventional sense, it can also be seen as akin to a 'good' moral panic in that the actions of the powerful were subject to critical popular scrutiny and blame attribution. The second argument is that, despite this focus on the actions and culpability of elite actors, the drama was resolved communicatively in a way that framed the meaning of her death in ideologically narrow terms.

Conceptualizing harm

Harm takes many forms, but in its most general sense it involves the loss of something valued through the actions of another. This can be symbolic or material, an object or a capacity, a condition or an opportunity. Seen in this way, harm is also paradoxical. In one sense, it is part of the normal experience of everyday life that, in the abstract, can be expected and calculated in terms of its probability and effects: loss is routine. At the same time, we take harm to be abnormal, an aberration, a rupture in the expectations and experience of everyday life: loss needs to be accounted for. To make sense of this paradox we can use Luhmann's (1995) distinction between normative and cognitive expectations. To say that harm is an aberration is to say that it contravenes normative expectations: harm should not happen, and its occurrence is assumed to be illegitimate and in need of the kind of explanation that concerns questions of validity and justification. A normative orientation to the contravention of expectations is directed to the immediate past and it entails the attribution of responsibility and blame as ends in themselves. Normative thinking is about judging others, settling accounts, and denouncing illegitimate conduct and those responsible for it. By contrast, when we simply anticipate that harm is likely to occur somewhere at some point, we are thinking in terms of cognitive expectations of future possibilities based on past experience or knowledge. To think in terms of cognitive expectations is to think in terms of contingency and the ways that it can be managed or controlled. Cognitive thinking is open to learning based on a more or less dispassionate assessment of problematic events; it is oriented to finding solutions and improving performance rather than finding fault, denouncing wrongdoers, or expressing nostalgia for a past golden age. Normative thinking sees the world in terms of conformity and transgression; cognitive thinking sees it in terms of success and failure.

Response to harm normally involves a mixture of both normative and cognitive orientations. The former tend to predominate in the initial response to harm, while cognitive orientations become stronger over time as emotions begin to subside. What this indicates is that harm consists in more than simply a single, self-contained event in which loss occurs. It consists, rather, in an event situation that unfolds and realizes itself over time as some form of resolution takes shape. How this occurs depends on a multiplicity of factors, including the identities and visibility of victims and perpetrators, whether harm was inadvertent or intentional, whether it was a sole occurrence or part of a series of similar events, and the resonance that the event situation acquires in the public sphere.

To understand the situational nature of harm it is useful to distinguish the immediate event, on the one hand, and the salience period that ensues as responses to the initial event enlarge and intensify its meaning and implications, on the other. In the immediate event of harm there is an imperative to give the situation a categorical meaning. A distinction can be made here between fiascos and tragedies. The concept of fiasco has been used mainly to understand failures in the formulation and implementation of organizational policies and procedures that become evident in the public sphere and result in extensive forms of communicational crisis management (Bovens et al. 1999). Fiascos result when an initial problem is compounded by a series of subsequent failures and errors that ensue as a result of attempts to control the initial problem. While the policies and procedures of VirCom EMS, Mercury Energy and Mighty River Power became a primary focus of public discourse around the death of Mrs. Muliaga, the precipitating event was not a fiasco but a tragedy. The critical feature of fiascos is that harm is largely symbolic: it is status, reputation and credibility that are the principal objects of loss. Tragedies, conversely, result when harm has definite material consequences: the loss of life, health, livelihood or other material value. Unlike fiascos, which have an ironic aspect to them, tragedies are marked by gravity and seriousness. Although they occur as unintended side effects, tragedies nonetheless imply transgression or violation rather than simply failure, and it is this normative dimension that makes tragedies into a particularly compelling kind of social drama. The gravity of tragedies tends to draw the observer into a close emotional relationship, at least initially when the impact is strongest. Although tragedies set in train a sequence of events and developments, it is the initial disruption of normality that acquires focal prominence. Subsequent developments acquire their meaning in relation to the initial event. If these too go awry, then tragedies can take on the dimensions of a fiasco, but this never applies to the initial, tragic event itself, only to the way it is subsequently processed institutionally and communicatively.

The gravity of tragedies accentuates the imperative for explanation and accountability. The critical issue here is whether or not they are defined as accidental. In the case of tragic accidents, causation is attributed to the aleatory nature of fate: no further explanation is possible. Tragedies that are not deemed accidental, that are seen as events or situations attributable to human agency, acquire a strong normative character as transgressions or violations, and this 'normativizes' the kind of explanation and accounting that is called for. This normativization of causality stems not only from the sense that a transgression or violation has occurred, but also because non-accidental tragedies are seen as potentially symptomatic of broader problems that may result in a recurrence of the tragic event at a later point. The imperative for the kind of explanation that relates events to human motivation and agency is a precondition for the possibility of taking remedial action to forestall the possibility of recurrence. Treating problematic events as symptomatic reinforces the imperative for explanation and accounting in terms that are amenable to subsequent control.

Social reaction to tragedy can take different forms, of which moral panics and scandals are two of the more dramatic. Panics and scandals share a number of features in common. Both are phenomena that are realized in the public sphere as forms of what Cottle (2006) calls 'mediatized rituals,' whose narrative ingredients and combination tend to be standardized and formulaic. In this respect, panics and scandals are both forms of discourse, ways of narrating and making sense of real-world events by means of framing – selecting, evaluating and articulating what is relevant to a more or less coherent, ongoing account (Critcher 2008). The media, in particular, can play a central role in this discursive process by broadcasting or amplifying the elements of a panic or scandal, which then loop back into the event situation and produce further reaction and development (Garland 2008). As a result, scandals and panics unfold in a contingent fashion, despite the ritualistic manner of media representation (Hier 2008). There is no guarantee that either will take a definite course of development, have a particular life span, or result in any specific lasting change. In fact panics and scandals have been seen as an indirect reaction to broader changes occurring in the normative and institutional orders, and as a means of localizing these changes in a concrete way congruent with individual structures of relevance (Hall *et al.* 1978; Tomlinson 1997).

Scandals resemble panics in that they involve a sense of alarm, anxiety and concern at the turn of events (Garland 2008). This often translates into feelings of hostility, anger and disdain for those held responsible for causing the problem and/or for failing to prevent or repair it. The contingent nature of panics and scandals means that the dimensions and targets of blame can proliferate, and its attribution can become dispersed and diffuse. While the attribution of blame may be concentrated consistently on certain targets, the institutional processing of problems as well as the media narratives that accompany this processing usually lead to the apportionment of responsibility and blame along different lines and among different actors. Once causality is cast in terms of human agency, responsibility and blame, it becomes contentious. Blame carries a threat to self-interest in various ways, such as status impairment, loss of credibility and the trust of others, the prospect of legal liability and sanctions, as well as the demands on time and energy that blame entails. Actors caught in the spotlight of public and media attention find it difficult to resist engaging in what Hood (2002) calls the 'blame game.' Those who are caught up in the attribution of blame normally seek to extricate themselves in various ways, such as denial of involvement, malice or harm; blame shifting onto other actors inside or outside the existing field of vision; blame displacement onto other dimensions of the situation for which one cannot be held responsible; and attempts to identify and emphasize silver linings that may arise when harm is done. When actors compete to manage the intensity and ecology of blame, causal chains become more complex as the attribution of responsibility is expanded and dispersed in different directions.

Panics and scandals are also ways in which tragic or harmful events are viewed as symptomatic of a larger threat of normative disorder (Garland 2008). Panics and scandals are expressions of volatility not only in the reaction of the audience but also in the structural and normative conditions that have allowed things to go wrong. The precipitating event is never seen as fully self-enclosed and bounded, but is taken as an example of something problematic that could easily get out of control, if it has not already done so. In this respect panics and scandals subsume the present under scenarios of the future by introducing, at least implicitly, the idea of risk, i.e., the possibility that harm will recur and become worse if control is not restored. The notion of a loss of control makes intervention imperative, and the message that something must be done to put things right is a constant theme in most panics and scandals. The imperative of intervention means that panics and scandals are open to politicization and strategic manipulation, and in this respect they are, as Garland (2008) argues, 'productive' situations. Attempts to exploit panics and scandals for strategic purposes, however, occur in a situation that is both competitive, as different actors seek to realize comparative advantage and minimize setbacks such as blaming, and reflexive, as various interventions interact with one another in unforeseeable ways. The process of moralization (or normativization) that is at the heart of panics and scandals is, in the final, analysis volatile and unpredictable (Hier 2008). Ironically, however, this only intensifies a sense of urgency about intervention, control and reform.

Despite these commonalities, panics and scandals also differ. While they share a similar mix of emotions, for example, the relative weight of these varies to some extent. Panics tend first and foremost to frame alarm in terms of fear and hostility, while scandals are more likely to provoke an initial reaction of outrage and disdain. In the case of panics, these emotions are directed at a transgressor who is seen to be close by, and a major part of what provokes alarm and uncertainty is the relative lack of social distance between folk devils, their victims and their audience – it is not incidental that in its original sense scapegoating involved geographical expulsion. With scandals, there is less sense of proximity and immediacy. The transgressor is generally more remote, and this distance allows the audience, which may itself feel symbolically victimized, to develop a more voyeuristic relationship to the situation and those being blamed. The primary emotions that panics comprise also speak to the way that normative breaches touch on matters of safety, security and certainty. Panics are expressions of doubt and danger. Scandals, on the other hand, pertain primarily to sentiments of unfairness, injustice, and even incompetence rather than safety and security. The aspect of doubt is more muted, and the erosion of trust that scandals create is experienced in a less immediate way. Scandals express the threat to normative regulation represented by amorality and unmitigated self-interest.

These differences in emotional inflection and social distance stem largely from the principal way in which panics and scandals diverge, namely the locus of hostility and blame. In the case of panics, primary hostility and blame tend to be directed down the social hierarchy at those who are deemed morally and symbolically inferior. Criminals, deviants, immigrants, the socially marginalized and others who represent the threat of a world out of control are the staple folk devils that moral panics target

(Critcher 2008). Scandals, on the other hand, tend to target those at or close to the top of the social hierarchy who wield symbolic, material, political or some other form of institutional power (Lull and Hinerman 1997). Scandals are primarily about the transgressions of the powerful, whose status makes them the object of scrutiny and fascination by virtue of the advantages they enjoy in comparison to the public at large. In contrast to panics, which involve an impulse to expel or confine the folk devil, scandals provide an opportunity to reduce social distance by bringing the powerful down to earth, where they are symbolically and momentarily exposed and denounced, stripped of their privilege, and forced to account for themselves.

Paradoxically, however, what distinguishes scandals and panics also aligns them together. In response to developments in and criticisms of the theory of moral panics and folk devils, Stanley Cohen (1999, 2002) draws a suggestive distinction between 'good' and 'bad' moral panics. Most research on panics has focused on the latter, viz., collective alarm at and hostility towards threats of menace from below − deviants, criminals, undocumented migrants, elements of the masses behaving badly − and has been concerned politically to discriminate between elite engineered panics and those that arise spontaneously from popular anxiety and concern. Good panics, on the other hand, are attempts to overcome 'barriers of denial, passivity, and indifference that prevent a full acknowledgement of human cruelty and suffering' (Cohen 1999: 590). Although Cohen does not explicitly equate this with media and public attention to the actions (or inactions) of the powerful, it is a reasonable inference that good panics, like scandals, strive more insistently to put the powerful and their conduct in the spotlight of accountability, blame and redress. Scandals and good panics are dramas where the social gaze is lifted up the social hierarchy, more so than down; they are situations in which moralization is used as a form of counter-power. As such, however, they are potentially threatening to powerful interests in ways that bad panics are not.

Who's to blame?

> Debate has ... raged throughout New Zealand, as the public and politicians sought to establish who was to blame for the tragedy.
>
> (New Zealand Herald 2007c)

In reality, elements of both panics and scandals are evident in the way that situations of harm evolve. Which elements become preponderant depends chiefly on the way that causal chains develop − how simplified or complicated they become, the direction in which they travel, the intensity with which blame is attributed and contested − and where responsibility for causing harm is ultimately laid. There were several possibilities for the attribution of blame for the death of Mrs. Muliaga: the employee of VirCom EMS who disconnected the power supply; VirCom EMS itself as his employer; Mercury Energy, which had subcontracted and authorized the disconnection; Mighty River Power as Mercury Energy's parent company, responsible for setting organizational policy; and the New Zealand government, which was responsible for the policies governing SOEs such as Mercury Energy and Mighty River Power.

Even the victim herself and members of the family at home at the time of the disconnection were potential candidates for blame attribution. The Muliagas were an immigrant family whose first language was not English. They had previously had difficulties paying their electricity bill, and were in arrears again. As is common in situations of inadvertent harm, initial accounts of what happened at the time of the disconnection were also contradictory. Mrs. Muliaga was seriously ill – hence the use of an oxygen machine – and she had recently been released from hospital with a poor prognosis. The Muliagas claimed that the contractor had been informed of her poor condition and dependence on the oxygen machine, but had ignored the information and proceeded with the disconnection. The CEO of Mighty River Power, on the other hand, claimed that the contractor had not been told about Mrs. Muliaga's condition (New Zealand Herald 2007a).

Where, then, did blame finally travel? What happened in the immediate aftermath of Mrs. Muliaga's death followed what has become a typical pattern in both official and popular reaction to instances of serious harm. Developments split along two paths: institutional and communicational. On the one hand, the legal system intervened in the form of a police investigation to determine if there were grounds to lay criminal charges. On the other hand, representatives of the Muliaga family, senior politicians (including the Prime Minister, the Minister responsible for SOEs, and representatives of opposition parties), media commentators and the three companies involved intervened discursively to establish a definition of the situation, its impact and implications. In both cases, developments began with an accent on the normative aspects of Mrs. Muliaga's death, only for this to be subsumed by procedural considerations and processes redolent of a more cognitive orientation to problem resolution. Although both lines of response evolved in a similar way, their separation imposed important constraints on the range of debate that ensued, and demonstrated how the transformation of harmful events into social issues can impose limits on what are regarded as valid topics for extrapolation and discussion when things go wrong. Harm may threaten to undermine the legitimacy of powerful institutions and organizations, but these threats are typically contained by ideological assumptions about what the issues already are.

Separation of the institutional and communicational responses to Mrs. Muliaga's death represented a temporal and conceptual distinction between event and issue. The event, as a particular occurrence, belonged to the past, and legal intervention in the form of the police investigation reinforced its particularity and self-containment. 'Eventalization' means defining a strip of social action in terms of its singularity and exceptionality (Foucault 1977). The effect of legal intervention of this kind is to sequester the process of determining causality and the possibility of legal culpability in a way that is removed, to a large extent, from the public sphere. Procedures for police investigations normally adhere to a high level of secrecy in which information disclosure is determined by strategic, organizational considerations. In this case, in fact, the media defined the police as being particularly 'tight-lipped' about their investigation, despite criticisms of 'racism and insensitivity' from a representative of the Muliaga family about how it was being conducted (New Zealand Herald 2007c).

Police and other agencies of the legal system have the right to exercise considerable control over the nature and extent of public communication, and this tends to be restricted to empirical rather than normative aspects of how the situation is evolving. The police do not per se pass judgment; their intervention is about deciding whether or not the normative can be transformed and processed legally. More importantly, actors involved in the situation, particularly those facing investigation and the possibility of sanction, can use this procedural secrecy and opacity as a way to limit their own communicational activity when pressed to speak – in the public sphere, *sub judice* often means no comment. The relative sequestration of police intervention and its focus on empirical evidence acts to relieve those in the spotlight of blame from having to communicate extensively in the public sphere about the problem and their role in it. Police intervention conforms to the codes of the system rather than the lifeworld (Habermas 1984). In systemic spheres social interaction is realized through media such as money, institutional authority and law. These media act as what Habermas (1984) calls 'relief mechanisms.' They free actors from the time- and energy-consuming necessity of deliberating over the terms, meaning and validity of conduct by objectifying meaning and value in ways that can be taken for granted for purposes of decision making.

The police investigation into Mrs. Muliaga's death lasted for two weeks, at which point the police announced that there were no grounds to lay charges, a finding that was then passed on to the coroner's court for further institutional processing. In the intervening period the second, communicational line of response had quickly expanded and intensified. Despite contradictory accounts of what happened when the power was disconnected, the focus of attention moved quickly on to Mercury Energy and Mighty River Power. The VirCom EMS contractor who had carried out the disconnection and VirCom EMS itself figured only peripherally in the media coverage. The former remained unnamed, and was only ever identified speculatively in an opinion column as a possible 'African refugee' who was under 'extraordinary emotional pressure' (O'Sullivan 2007). VirCom EMS's chief executive issued a statement to the effect that the company operated on 'written instructions' from Mercury Energy, it was conducting its own internal inquiry into what had happened and no further comment would be appropriate, in view of the police investigation (New Zealand Herald 2007a).

In the media at least, blame bypassed those actors closest to the circumstances of Mrs. Muliaga's death and moved quickly on to Mercury Energy and its parent company. The power companies had begun to respond publicly to the event itself as well as to claims by others that they were at fault not only for Mrs. Muliaga's death but also their response to it. The companies' initial response conformed to classic crisis management techniques. When faced with allegations that they had acted improperly and irresponsibly, they denied that they were to blame and asserted that they and their contractors had followed normal procedures. This procedural resort to denial of responsibility served only to create a credibility problem, as well as a performance problem for Mercury Energy and its parent. Within days of Mrs. Muliaga's death there was a demonstration outside Mercury Energy's headquarters, with 'angry' protesters denouncing the company for its 'heartless' actions (Dominion Post 2007a). But the key intervention that focused blame on the companies and their corporate culture was from the then Prime Minister, Helen Clark. Clark was described as 'horrified' and 'outraged' at Mercury Energy's stance (Dominion Post 2007d). Clark described the company as 'callous,' claimed that its actions created a 'heartless' image of New Zealand around the world and called on it to stop making excuses and take responsibility for the situation (Dominion Post 2007d; O'Sullivan 2007). She visited the family personally to express her condolences, and while she was there she snubbed executives from the power companies who were also present. She also cut short the claim that the contractor had not been informed of Mrs. Muliaga's medical condition by asserting publicly that Mercury Energy had confirmed that the contractor had seen that Mrs. Muliaga had a breathing tube inserted in her nose when he was at the house. Clark capped this move to the concentrate blame by calling for advice 'on toughening up the regulations that cover the electricity industry, saying voluntary guidelines and protocols based on "goodwill" were clearly not working' (New Zealand Herald 2007b). Other politicians became involved as well. Representatives of the opposition decried the situation, and the minister responsible for SOEs, in comments made the day before the findings of the police investigation were announced, criticized Mercury Energy for having failed to communicate effectively with its board of directors and parent company in the immediate aftermath of Mrs. Muliaga's death, and accused it of having been insensitive and self-preoccupied in its response to the situation.

The reputation and success of SOEs like Mercury Energy that compete with private sector companies are subject to both consumer pressure in the marketplace (concern was expressed that Mercury customers might switch to other suppliers) and political pressure from a government that is accountable for its policies and performance at the ballot box. Reaction to the situation on the government's part was interesting, however, because it focused as much if not more on the power companies' credibility deficit as on their performance deficit. Once the institutional response to Mrs. Muliaga's death was set in motion, the government too was no longer in a position to speak openly about culpability and blame, as this could compromise the police investigation and any further legal action that might flow from it. In fact at one point the minister responsible for SOEs cautioned against jumping to conclusions about Mrs. Muliaga's death until the police investigation had been completed. Critical reaction by the government shifted, then, to the companies' communicative action in response to the situation. The effect of this was to reset the stage of controversy in communicational terms.

As the political winds began to shift against Mercury Energy and its parent, the companies began to change tack and stopped denying blame by claiming that routine procedures had been followed. Three days after Mrs. Muliaga died, senior officials from Mercury Energy and Mighty River Power paid a visit to the family. The group followed Fa'a Samoa protocols, and made a donation of $10,000 towards funeral expenses. The CEO of Mighty River Power stated that 'We are deeply grateful to the family that we were able to express our feelings to them and the spirit of forgiveness [sic] with which we were received' (Mercury Energy, 2007). The following day the CEO of Mercury Energy, Carole Durbin, publicly apologized to the family for the company's part in the tragedy:

> I am here to say sorry publicly to the family and to apologise to the community for our part in this tragedy. Mrs Muliaga died so clearly something went wrong. In the meantime you can be assured that our management advised me that all disconnections have been suspended indefinitely from last Wednesday. No one should ever die because they can't pay a power bill.
> (Mighty River Power 2007a)

It is striking that this statement offered an apology rather than simply an expression of regret, particularly in light of the fact that the police investigation was still ongoing. Apologies entail a greater degree of normative liability than expressions of regret, as they implicate the speaker in responsibility for controversial actions. Although apologies involve greater risk than statements of regret, they also function as a symbolic offer of reconciliation (Tavuchis 1991). In this respect what made the apology, and the shift in communicational strategy of Mercury Energy and Mighty River Power, possible was the fact that the companies were not only being pushed by their political masters to assume responsibility, but also being pulled there by the reaction of the Muliaga family itself. Although representatives of the family (a lawyer and relative) were calling publicly for corporate accountability and compensation, the immediate family was portrayed in the media as being gracious in its reaction. When company officials finally visited the family home, members accepted their 'show of remorse' and offered them drinks (New Zealand Herald 2007b). The phrase 'forgiveness and reconciliation' recurred in the press coverage – in one instance attributed to the Prime Minister – to describe the mood at Mrs. Muliaga's funeral (The Press 2007; Dominion Post 2007b). The openness of the family to reconciliation reduced some of the risk associated with apology and created an opportunity to begin to finalize the past and move the situation elsewhere. As a gesture of reconciliation, apologies act as a turning point by opening up new lines of communication and discourse.

In the salience period after Mrs. Muliaga's death the situation developed in a way that was more characteristic of scandal or good panic rather than conventional bad panic. The locus of blame moved upward, to senior officials of Mercury Energy and its parent company. The media generally sought to dispel any residual sense that the Muliagas themselves were to blame for the tragedy or their straitened circumstances. Mr. Muliaga, it was noted, had a job, albeit one that paid poorly; Mrs. Muliaga was no longer able to work because of her medical condition; and the family had made a genuine effort to make payments on their electricity bill. Whether disconnection had directly caused Mrs. Muliaga's death would have to be a matter for the coroner to rule on at a later point, but it was clear that if a choice had to be made between the family and the power companies as to where primary blame lay, it was with the latter. At the same time, blame did not travel in any significant way from the economic and into the political realm. Helen Clark's unequivocal criticism of the power companies left them politically isolated at the same time that it helped to insulate the government from direct responsibility. Clark's response was derided by opposition politicians as an attempt to gain political mileage from the situation in light of her government's low rating in the opinion polls, and her attempt to distance the government from its own enterprises did receive some criticism (Espiner 2007). But the conclusion drawn from the latter was that expectations that SOEs function on the basis of both social responsibility and profit maximization were untenable (Dominion Post 2007c). Sensing this contradiction, the government made appropriate noises about the need to re-examine the policy of requiring SOEs to operate solely on the basis of profit maximization, particularly in the case of an essential service such as electricity.

From tragedy to risk: the resolution of a social drama

Carole Durbin's apology to the Muliaga family and the community was, however, a qualified one. Her words were crafted in a way that claimed only partial responsibility, highlighted the companies' actions to prevent any recurrence, and reminded the audience that the power bill had not been paid. The statement of apology already gave a hint of where the companies would take the situation, namely in the direction of preventive measures. At this point the public identity or meaning of Mrs. Muliaga's death began to be transformed from an event into an issue that carried broader implications about managing future contingencies. This provided the two companies, as well as the government and the electricity industry as a whole, with an opportunity to begin to repair the damage to their reputation that had resulted from Mrs. Muliaga's death. In the public sphere, the meaning of Mrs. Muliaga's death became less a question of its causation as a specific event, and more a matter of what could be done, what lessons could be learned, to prevent similar harm from occurring in the future. At the communicational level as well as the institutional, a normative orientation was yielding to a cognitive one. The past was being subsumed under the future, and normative questions were being displaced by procedural ones.

Less than two weeks after Durbin's apology the government announced more stringent guidelines for electricity disconnections. The CEO of Mighty River Power admitted that Mrs. Muliaga's death had raised important issues about corporate practices, and announced that Mercury Energy was reviewing its internal processes and procedures to improve safeguards for customers with medical dependencies or financial difficulties from having their electricity supply disconnected. He affirmed that the company was 'committed to working with government regulatory and welfare agencies to develop improved procedures so that we can identify and assist more vulnerable customers more effectively' (Mighty River Power 2007b). The event of Mrs. Muliaga's death had now become the issue of future risk prevention for those deemed more vulnerable. Risk mediated the transformation of a communication strategy oriented to immediate crisis management, which had only exacerbated an already serious situation, into one of longer-term issues management. What mattered now was not why or how Mrs. Muliaga had died, but what could be done to reduce the possibility of a similar event happening again. From being at the centre of the controversy, the normative aspects of the situation had now become the taken-for-granted assumption on which measures to improve procedures for the future were implicitly based; instrumental risk control trumped moral evaluation (cf. Cohen 1999: 591). What mattered, in the companies' view, was affirming publicly that they had learned from the past and that something would be done. Amends would be made by cognitively re-organizing the future for the benefit of others. Promoting a cognitive orientation, in other words, became the appropriate way to display normative consideration: better procedures will reduce the threat of recurrence and allay any fear or alarm that might otherwise persist about the future.

In a sense, then, this cognitive re-orientation was not about improving service so much as about considering measures to ensure that normal practices would be less likely to be disrupted by problematic events. It was about learning, deliberating, and implementing better ways to stabilize and normalize what was already considered normal. Although the event had been transformed into an issue, the issue still remained anchored in the anticipation and control of events. Just as the normative remained the assumption underlying a cognitive concern for better procedures, so the harmful event remained the underlying focal point of issue management. Although the event was finalized both institutionally (the police investigation) and communicatively (Clark's intervention and Durbin's apology), it remained an integral, albeit transformed or sublated, aspect of the issue. The effect of this was to determine how the issue was extrapolated out of the event and framed in the public sphere in a way that had important ideological implications.

The framing of issues is a communicational process that has three principal elements: the definition or thematization of the problem, a causal explanation of why and/or how it arose, and a view about what remedies can best correct the situation in the present and prevent any future recurrence (Entman 1993). In practice these three dimensions are often contested by participant stakeholders who have different, often conflictive interests that are reflected in the kinds of framing they promote or sponsor (Gamson and Modigliani 1989). When framing becomes contentious, the three dimensions are usually worked out recursively rather than in a linear, sequential fashion. Initially, the strong emotional reaction to instances of harm means that thematic and causal framing become fused in strongly normative terms – denunciation of the event and those deemed responsible and culpable. Certain actor(s), in this case the power companies, were targeted as blameworthy. As targets of blame, their stakes in the situation became intensified as a result of the threat to their reputation, legitimacy and legal status that the finger pointing implied. Given that causal framing quickly became institutionally sequestered and 'cognitivized' in the form of the police investigation, and the initial attempt to manage the crisis through denial and self-affirmation on the power companies' part failed, remedial framing offered the most strategic way for both the government and the two companies to attempt to take control of the way the controversy was being publicly framed. This could then be used retroactively to re-shape the definitional or thematic framing by subsuming the event of Mrs. Muliaga's death under the broader issue of future risk prevention that offered them an opportunity to re-establish credibility.

The ideological effect of this was to narrow the way in which an event of harm came to signify a broader issue. Although some of the initial voices of concern over Mrs. Muliaga's death had highlighted the matter of the cost of electricity as an essential service, particularly for those with limited economic resources, this aspect of the situation was not taken up for development and elaboration in subsequent discussion, which was dominated by the companies' and government's framing in terms of the risk of individual harm from disconnection of electricity supply, and the measures that would prevent this. The affordability of electricity and the manner of its provision as an essential public service were never really developed arising out of Mrs. Muliaga's death. Questions concerning the affordability and provision of essential services are social and political rather than purely individual and private in character. The type of risk they speak to represents a much broader range of issues that pertain to collective well-being and even social solidarity, rather than to the possibility of specific instances of serious or dramatic harm. They imply a much greater interventionist and steering role for public authority than simply establishing and enforcing regulatory mechanisms. To have framed the issue in terms of affordability and provision would have meant contextualizing Mrs. Muliaga and family not in terms of her death, but in terms of the structure of social inequality that make access to essential services precarious for many people.

To have extrapolated the issues of affordability and provision out of Mrs. Muliaga's death would have required a socialized rather than individualized interpretation of the situation. This would have run counter to the government's own commitment to a neo-liberal ideology of SOE management in which profit comes first and social responsibility is added on as a secondary value conceptualized in negative terms, i.e., via regulatory measures designed to avoid the risk of further harm. For the government and the power companies it owned, the affordability and provision of an essential service like electricity presented a much greater, long-term political problem than did allegations of irresponsibility and insensitivity over a single instance of serious harm. The individualization of risk is central to neo-liberal ideology. While the response to risk may take the form of collectively imposed measures and procedures, these only provide a regulatory framework within which individuals are faced with decisions about how to manage uncertainties they have little power to determine or control. By accentuating the social impact of market forces, neo-liberalism simultaneously weakens or eliminates institutional mechanisms for meeting social demands and enhancing social protection and care that were established in the earlier, post-World War II era of welfare state expansion. The neo-liberal assault on the welfare state occurred more rapidly and radically in New Zealand than in other developed societies (Kelsey 1997). While some reversal of neo-liberal policies has subsequently occurred, it remains strongly entrenched in governmental management of the economy. The primary mandate of Mercury Energy and its parent company remains successful market performance, not the fulfillment or enhancement of social needs – or the promotion of environmental sustainability.

Because scandal discourse entails the upward movement of blame for harm to those with power and status, it tends to conjoin the locus of causal, remedial and preventive responsibility. The overall chain of responsibility tends to be simplified in the sense that it is concentrated rather than dispersed. Panic discourse, by contrast, involves the separation of causal blame from remedial and preventive blame. The former moves downward to the socially marginalized and stigmatized and the latter two upward to those with authority, status and the capacity to reassert control, enact sanctions and regulate future risk. Because scandal discourse conjoins the different dimensions of blame, it tends to allow a speedier and more complete shift from a normative to a cognitive orientation, from a focus on denunciation to risk management, as the way that situations of harm become processed. This, in turn, tends to reinforce a procedural view of the management of harm, which is interpreted in terms of individualized probabilities rather than the social distribution of resources, opportunities and constraints. Risk management becomes a generalized logic of practice that encourages a prudential, procedural approach to calculating courses of action, whether it is suspending essential services or not paying one's bills on time.

While scandal or good panic discourse obviously contains its own political risks for those who are the locus of concentrated blame, it also offers a more streamlined way for those with decision-making authority to manage and resolve situations of harm, particularly if, as in the case of Mercury Energy and Mighty River Power, causal blame can be delegated to actors slightly lower down the hierarchy of power who have little opportunity to shift or displace blame elsewhere. There is a potential political pay-off in this. The conduciveness of this discourse to an individualized concept of risk limits its critical ideological potential. When decision making is conducted through the optic of individualized risk, it tends to be managed defensively and procedurally; the question is not so much what or what not to do – this is assumed to be relatively obvious – but how or how not to do it. A risk perspective tends to define behaviour in terms of an avoidance logic, and this is chiefly about process, procedure and reflexive learning. It comprises a cognitive orientation to expectations and outcomes that is (has to be) amenable to altering practices in order to lessen risk and increase the likelihood of harm defined in terms of failure rather than transgression or inequity.

Conclusion

Seen from the perspective of moral panics and scandals as forms of discourse for interpreting tragic situations of harm, response to the death of Mrs. Muliaga resembled the form of a scandal or good panic rather than a more conventional bad panic when understood in terms of the attribution of responsibility and blame. Although there were several possible directions in which blame could have flowed, it moved quickly in the direction of state-owned Mercury Energy, which had commissioned the disconnection of the Muliagas' electricity supply, and its parent company, Mighty River Power. Their initial reaction conformed to classic crisis-management techniques: denial of responsibility and insistence that proper procedures had been followed. This provoked negative reaction in the form of both popular protest and intervention by the Prime Minister, who was unequivocally critical of the companies' callousness and failure to take responsibility for the tragedy. This resulted in a clear change of corporate tactics, culminating in a public apology by the CEO of Mercury Energy for Mrs. Muliaga's death.

Although the apology went further than an expression of regret, it was also qualified in a way that set the stage for a shift in discursive focus away from a normatively inflected orientation, to blame attribution, towards a cognitively oriented focus on future risk management. This shift was complemented by the government's announcement of tighter guidelines governing electricity disconnections. The shift from blame to risk discourse signalled not only a change in focus from the past to the future, from a concern with culpability to a concern with procedural reform, but also an ideological narrowing of the issues that arose from the event of Mrs. Muliaga's death. Although initial reaction to her death had touched on issues of inequality, economic precariousness and the provision of essential services like electricity, these quickly faded as an individualized concept of risk became the grounds on which future preventive action was framed. Because scandal discourse concentrates the locus of causal, remedial and preventive responsibility at the top of the hierarchy of power, it enables those with the capacity to formulate and deliver solutions to risk to limit its definition in ways that also limit the scope of necessary intervention. To have framed the issues arising from the tragedy in terms of broader questions of *social* risk would, ironically, have meant framing this tragedy not in terms of Mrs. Muliaga's death, but rather, in terms of her life.

Note

1 The authors would like to thank Sean Hier for his helpful comments on an earlier draft of this chapter.

References

Bovens, M., t'Hart, P., Dekker, S. and Verheuvel, G. (1999) 'The politics of blame avoidance: defensive tactics in a Dutch crime-fighting fiasco,' in H. Anheier (ed.) *When Things Go Wrong: Organizational Failures and Breakdowns*, Thousand Oaks, CA: Sage.
Cohen, S. (1999) 'Moral panics and folk concepts,' *Paedagogica Historica*, 35(3): 585–91.
Cohen, S. (2002) *Folk Devils and Moral Panics*, 3rd edn, London: Routledge.
Cottle, S. (2006) 'Mediatized rituals: beyond manufacturing consent,' *Media, Culture & Society*, 28(3): 411–32.
Critcher, C. (2008) 'Moral panic analysis: past, present and future,' *Sociology Compass*, 2(4): 1127–44.
Dominion Post. (2007a) 'Power death family hire lawyer.' 1 June. Online. Available via Lexis-Nexis (accessed 9 September 2009).
Dominion Post. (2007b) 'A family and community mourn.' 7 June. Online. Available via Lexis-Nexis (accessed 9 September 2009).
Dominion Post. (2007c) 'SOE model is coming apart.' 8 June. Online. Available via Lexis-Nexis (accessed 9 September 2009).
Dominion Post. (2007d) 'Disconnection as a last resort.' 4 July. Online. Available via Lexis-Nexis (accessed 9 September 2009).
Entman, R. M. (1993) 'Framing: toward clarification of a fractured paradigm,' *Journal of Communication*, 43(4): 51–59.

Espiner, C. (2007) 'Key must learn to curb his enthusiasm,' *The Press*. 11 June. Online. Available via Lexis-Nexis (accessed 9 September 2009).
Foucault, M. (1977) *Language, counter-memory, practice: selected essays and interviews* (D. F. Bouchard and S. Simon, trans.), D. F. Bouchard (ed.), Ithaca, NY: Cornell University Press.
Gamson, W. and Modigliani, A. (1989) 'Media discourse and public opinion on nuclear power: a constructionist approach,' *American Journal of Sociology*, 95(1): 1–37.
Garland, D. (2008) 'On the concept of moral panic,' *Crime, Media, Culture*, 4(1): 9–30.
Habermas, J. (1984) *The Theory of Communicative Action* (T. McCarthy, trans.), Boston: Beacon Press.
Hall, S., Critcher, C., Jefferson, T., Clarke, J. and Roberts, B. (1978) *Policing the Crisis: Mugging, the State and Law and Order*, London: Macmillan.
Hier, S. (2008) 'Thinking beyond moral panic: risk, responsibility and the politics of moralization,' *Theoretical Criminology*, 12: 171–88.
Hood, C. (2002) 'The risk game and the blame game,' *Government and Opposition*, 37(1): 15–37.
Kelsey, J. (1997) *The New Zealand Experiment: A World Market for Structural Adjustment?* 2nd edition, Auckland: Auckland University Press.
Luhmann, N. (1995) *Social Systems* (J. Bednarz Jr. with D. Baecker, trans.), Stanford, CA: Stanford University Press.
Lull, J. and Hinerman, S. (1997) 'The search for scandal,' in J. Lull and S. Hinerman (eds.), *Media Scandals: Morality and Desire in the Popular Culture Marketplace*, New York: Columbia University Press.
Mercury Energy. (2007) Media release 1 June 2007. Online. Available HTTP: www.mercury.co.nz/News/news_story.aspx?id=753 (accessed 1 July 2009).
Mighty River Power. (2007a) Public statement from the Chair of Mighty River Power. Online. Available HTTP: www.mightyriverpower.co.nz/News/NewsArchive2007/Detail.aspx?id=9 (accessed 1 July 2009).
Mighty River Power. (2007b) 'Mighty River Power welcomes conclusion of police investigation.' Online. Available HTTP: www.mightyriverpower.co.nz/News/Detail.aspx?id=949 (accessed 1 July 2009).
New Zealand Herald. (2007a) 'Power cut death: Mercury – We're in the clear.' 1 June. Online. Available via Lexis-Nexis (accessed 9 September 2009).
New Zealand Herald. (2007b) 'Auckland market holds minute's silence for power-cut victim.' 2 June. Online. Available via Lexis-Nexis (accessed 9 September, 2009).
New Zealand Herald. (2007c) 'Bradford unhappy at blame falling on Muliaga family.' 13 June. Online. Available via Lexis-Nexis (accessed 9 September 2009).
O'Sullivan, F. (2007) 'Fran O'Sullivan: The buck stops where?' *New Zealand Herald*, 6 June. Online. Available via Lexis-Nexis (accessed 9 September 2009).
Tavuchis, N. (1991) *Mea culpa: The Sociology of Apology and Reconciliation*, Stanford CA: Stanford University Press.
The Press. (2007) 'Sense of forgiveness at Muliaga funeral.' 7 June. Online. Available via Lexis-Nexis (accessed 9 September 2009).
Tomlinson, J. (1997) '"And Besides, the Wench is Dead": media, scandals and the globalization of communication,' in J. Lull and S. Hinerman (eds.) *Media Scandals: Morality and Desire in the Popular Culture Marketplace*, New York: Columbia University Press.
Turner, V. (1974) *Dramas, Fields, and Metaphors: Symbolic Action in Human Society*, Ithaca, NY: Cornell University Press.

14

THE UNHEALTHY RISK SOCIETY

Health scares and the politics of moral panic[1]

Daniel Béland

Introduction

Moral panic studies has made strong contributions to sociological debates about the nature of fear and the politics of social problems in contemporary western societies (see, for example, Goode and Ben-Yehuda 2009; Critcher 2003; Thompson 1998; Critcher 2009; Hier 2008; Ungar 2001; Furedi, Chapter 6 this volume; Best, Chapter 3 this volume). Debates regarding Ulrich Beck's (1992) risk society thesis (i.e., a society in which technological and environmental risks are a major source of concern) have also impacted on the moral panic literature; scholars have argued over the enduring merit of the concept of moral panic in an era of acute environmental risk perceptions (Hier 2003; Ungar 2001 and Chapter 12 this volume).

This chapter broadens the focus of debates about risk and panic by examining health scares. Health scares are episodes of acute collective insecurity pertaining to health-related issues that erupt suddenly, are limited in their duration, and fade rather quickly. During health-scare episodes, alleged public health threats are constructed as major issues that require prudent individuals and responsible collective actors to manage risk. In such episodes, perceived health threats are the subject of constant media and political attention and speculation. Western citizens live longer and healthier lives, yet health scares continue to emerge from pervasive health concerns (Dalrymple 1998) and public awareness of environmental risks (Beck 2002).

Although health scares are episodic in nature, some collective health anxieties last longer than others. For instance, the fear of asbestos as a potential source of cancer has seemingly become a constant feature of popular health discourse. This does not mean that the intensity of collective insecurity pertaining to asbestos remains stable, however; media reports can continue to heighten the level of public concern. Importantly, analysing health scares does not involve any judgement about the 'true' or 'false' nature of the perceived health threats that actors both face and help to construct.

Moreover, only some health scares take the form of moralizing, sensational, exaggerated, and volatile political episodes known as moral panics. For instance, some health scares may not involve exaggerated media reports or the emergence of a moral discourse about the collective source of harm (i.e., blame assignment). Consequently, 'health scare' and 'moral panic' remain analytically distinct but empirically overlapping concepts.

Still, the concept of moral panic is relevant to the study of contemporary health scares largely because, in some cases at least, episodes of acute health anxieties directly intersect with moral regulation processes. Drawing on the work of Alan Hunt (1999, 2003), Sean Hier (2002b, 2008; for a critical discussion see Critcher 2009) has explained how moral panics are best conceptualized as amplified and volatile expressions of long-term moral regulation processes – regulation processes that entail ongoing configurations about risk and harm. Following Hier (2008), health scares are related to both moral regulation and risk perception. In fact, the frequent moralization of health scares backs Hier's claim that moral panic remains ever present in the so-called 'risk society' (Hier 2003, 2008). Indeed, in some contexts health scares involve the construction of 'folk devils' that are deemed at least partially responsible for disease outbreaks and other prominent health problems. This is especially the case when diseases involve person-to-person contagion and when specific ethnic/social groups are targeted in media reports. The example of the Toronto 2003 SARS outbreaks will provide ground to these claims, and to the general idea that the moral panic framework can enrich the empirical study of contemporary health scares. The targeting of Chinese Canadians and other Asian minorities during this episode suggests that the concept of moral panic sheds light on the contemporary politics of health scares, which, like moral panic (Hier 2002a), often entail assigning blame in a context of acute risk awareness.

Public health scares like the 2003 SARS outbreak can be classified as moral panics, but not all health scares fit the moral panic framework. The analysis of the 1996 BSE episode provides grounds to support this claim. By reframing the BSE crisis in economic terms, British policy-makers helped direct public attention away from the ethical issues stemming from existing state regulations. Starting from the perspective that 'blame avoidance' (Weaver 1986) is a central aspect of moral panics (Hier 2002a), the 1996 BSE crisis shows how politicians helped to avoid a potential moral panic that could have targeted them in a sustained, moralizing way.

The chapter is divided into three sections. In order to assess the relevance of the concept of moral panic to the analysis of health scares, the first two sections explore the 2003 SARS epidemic and the 1996 BSE episode, respectively. While the first case stresses that the moral panic framework can improve our understanding of specific health-scare episodes, the second case is not about moral panic in the strict sense of the term. Thus, although the concept of moral panic is helpful for understanding some health scares, case-by-case empirical investigation is necessary to assess whether a particular health-scare episode constitutes a moral panic. Comparing these two cases directly, the final section offers general remarks about the applicability of the moral panic framework to the sociological analysis of health scares in contemporary societies.

SARS

Severe Acute Respiratory Syndrome (SARS) is a respiratory infection caused by a virus unknown until the 2003 outbreaks in the City of Toronto, Canada. SARS can spread from one person to another through interpersonal contact. Moreover, SARS symptoms, such as fever, chills and malaise, are not different than those associated with pneumonia, making it more difficult for doctors to come up with an accurate and speedy diagnosis. This was especially true when SARS first emerged on the world stage in 2003. These two factors, combined with the media frenzy that surrounded it, helped transform SARS into a major health scare. Before exploring the genuine panic that surrounded the emergence of SARS as a key public health issue, it is necessary to reconstitute the events leading to the perceived SARS crisis.

In early 2003, SARS rapidly and unexpectedly spread from China's Guangdong province to affect people in no fewer than 37 countries.

> The first case of SARS outside China was reported on 26 February 2003. By 31 May the number of probable cases reached 8359, with the mortality rate outside China climbing to around 14%. However, from June this increase slowed sharply, and by July the number of probable cases had climbed by just 89 cases, to 8448, with a total of 774 deaths.
>
> *(Smith 2006: 3113)*

Although these numbers are significant, they fell far below early expectations for the anticipated spread of SARS. For instance, at the beginning of the 2003 outbreaks, experts and commentators compared SARS to the 1918 influenza pandemic, which killed about 40 million people (Smith 2006: 3114). In March 2003, the World Health Organization even issued 'a rare global alert about atypical pneumonia' (WHO 2006: 13). These remarks point to the discourse of fear surrounding SARS, which the mass media amplified throughout the outbreak period.

Painting a scary picture of a global disease that threatened people everywhere around the world, 'mainstream Western media sensationalized' (Eichelberger 2007: 1286) SARS in a strong way. In North America, cities with large Chinatowns and Asian populations, like Boston, New York City and Toronto, became the object of intense media coverage that fuelled rumours about the spreading of SARS in Chinatowns.

> In Boston and New York City false rumours of infection proliferated faster than the microbe itself. An insidious April fool's hoax surfaced on a Massachusetts Institute of Technology website warning of infected employees at a restaurant in Boston's Chinatown. Exaggerated by mouth and e-mail, rumours soon alleged that there was widespread contagion in the district.
>
> *(Schram 2003: 939)*

The mass media helped fuel these fears through reports that associated SARS with the Chinese community. On television, for example, reports about SARS often featured images of people from China and Hong Kong wearing facemasks. 'Innumerable pictures of Asians in facemasks racialized the epidemic by identifying Asian bodies as the source of contagion, contributing to their stigmatization' (Eichelberger 2007: 1288). This racialization of SARS became especially detrimental to people living in Chinatowns – urban areas that have been a source of prejudice and health fears since their emergence in the nineteenth century. As Eichelberger (2007: 1286) states, 'The historic construction of Chinatowns as disease reservoirs continues to define these communities.' This is true in the United States and Canada, where racism against people of Chinese descent has been witnessed since the arrival of Chinese railroad construction workers during the second half of the nineteenth century (Hier and Greenberg 2002; Ward 2002).

The SARS outbreaks in Toronto

More than other North American cities (e.g., Boston and New York City), Toronto witnessed escalated media attention, in part because, during the second quarter of 2003, this ethnically diverse city faced genuine SARS outbreaks that had significant consequences (Leslie 2006; Muzzatti 2005). 'Between February and September 2003 Health Canada reported 438 probable or suspect cases of severe acute respiratory syndrome (SARS) resulting in 43 deaths primarily in the Greater Toronto Area (GTA)' (Borgundvaag et al. 2004: 1342). Although less dramatic than originally expected, these outbreaks generated strong public and media reactions. Largely because of media reports depicting Toronto as a dangerous place to visit, the city lost considerable business during and after the outbreaks. This was particularly the case in the travel and tourism industry (Leslie 2006). Consequently, like in other countries, SARS resulted in disproportionate economic loss, especially considering the true – albeit limited – scope of the outbreaks. From this angle, media-induced fears consistent with the idea of moral panic had real economic and social consequences (Smith 2006: 3114).

SARS came to Toronto in late February 2003 through an elderly woman who had been contaminated during a trip to Hong Kong. This woman died soon after she returned to Canada, and her son died from the disease as well. 'Of the two patients in beds adjacent to the primary case, one spread the disease to 20 others while the other patient infected 19 individuals [...]. After the initial outbreak in late February, a second outbreak phase began in mid-May' (Salehi and Ali 2006: 375). Although the outbreaks were largely confined to the Toronto healthcare system (Salehi and Ali 2006: 376), Canadian newspapers and magazines used the language of fear, suggesting that SARS was a 'deadly' disease and a mysterious 'killer' that appeared as a major threat in the everyday lives of Canadians (Guan 2004: 8). Furthermore, the 'Hong Kong connection' in the first SARS outbreak, as well as constant media coverage, meant that Chinese Canadians soon became a target of collective fear and anxiety. For instance, just like in the United States, newspaper articles and TV reports about SARS often featured Asian-looking people wearing facemasks. 'Visual references in the media, especially those of masked Asian faces, played an equally important role in marking Chinese and Southeast/East Asian communities in the SARS crisis. [...] The media used other visual strategies to fuel SARS panic. Often, Canadian SARS reports were juxtaposed with photos taken in Asian countries. [...] While these strong, often misleading, visual images served the purpose of the media, they powerfully communicated an image of SARS a mysterious, "Oriental" disease causing further mass hysteria' (Guan 2004: 9).

During the 2003 SARS outbreaks, another media practice that helped spread fears surrounding Chinese Canadians was to repeatedly state the ethnic background and publish the Chinese-sounding names of the two first SARS victims who died in Toronto (Guan 2004: 9). Although journalists did not necessarily depict SARS as a 'Chinese problem,' their reports helped transform Chinese Canadians and other Asian-looking people into potential threats to public health that other citizens started to avoid in everyday life. During the SARS outbreaks, in a context of intense moralization that exacerbated traditional racial prejudice present in everyday life, Chinese Canadians from the Toronto area and beyond felt the weight of discrimination and even outright racism, as reports of 'public bus drivers using face masks on routes near Chinese communities and empty seats surrounding Chinese university students' multiplied (Schram 2003: 939).

A former Chinese Canadian activist quoted by Justin Schram (2003: 939) illustrates the moral panic surrounding ordinary people who suddenly became Asian 'folk devils' during the Toronto SARS outbreaks. 'Stories of stereotyping and targeting are coming at us fast and furious: Asian-Canadians being shunned in subways and streetcars; real estate agents being told not to bring Asian clients to see houses; and outright hate messages left at organizations.' From this perspective, long-entrenched racist attitudes exacerbated by the SARS outbreaks and the media frenzy surrounding them are similar to the one then witnessed in the United States, even in places where SARS did not materialize (Eichelberger 2007). In the end, like in Boston and New York City, business owners in Toronto's large Chinatown areas lost millions of dollars during the 2003 SARS outbreaks, as many people avoided these areas altogether. Interestingly, even some Chinese Canadians ended up avoiding Chinatowns, a situation that stresses the sheer scope of the fears surrounding SARS (Leung 2004).

Moreover, like in the United States, recent immigrants or people who travelled to China regularly were regarded with suspicion by other people within their own ethnic group (Eichelberger 2007). This remark points to the fact that, in North America as elsewhere, ethnic communities are internally stratified and moralized forms of blame and discrimination can take place within them, especially during health scares and episodes of panic that divide citizens and make the fear of the 'other' a characteristic of media coverage and everyday interaction. This 'othering' of illness is not a new phenomenon and, as suggested above, in North America people of Chinese descent have long been perceived as a source of public health hazards. This historical background is essential to understand the transformation of Chinese Canadians into 'folk devils' during the 2003 SARS outbreaks (Muzzatti 2005). The presence of these 'folk devils' is another aspect of this health-scare episode that stresses the analytical relevance of the moral panic framework for the analysis of such an episode.

In Toronto and beyond, the SARS outbreaks and the moral panic surrounding them hurt Chinese Canadians and other Asian populations, who became the target of intense public fears in an era of global health scares. As for Canadian politicians, they played a less prominent public role during the SARS outbreaks than their British counterparts during the BSE crisis analyzed below. As far as SARS is concerned, Canadian authorities did not face widespread accusations of trying to mislead the public and, once the outbreaks became public, they adopted a more cautious approach than some of their international counterparts. Yet, as far as the fate of Chinese Canadians is concerned, politicians could do little to reduce the climate of fear surrounding Chinatowns and the Asian populations in general. For example, during the 2003 SARS crisis, the fact that Prime Minister Jean Chrétien ate lunch in a Toronto Chinatown restaurant (Mackay 2003) represented only a symbolic gesture that did little to calm the fears central to mainstream media reports implicitly depicting Chinese Canadians as a potential threat to public health (Leung 2004) and to the existing social and moral order. Like in the United States, this type of superficial political gesture on the part of elected officials did little to help "Asian-looking" people avoid stigma or to help small businesses stay afloat during the crisis (Eichelberger 2007). Considering the key role of small businesses in Chinatowns, SARS had a devastating economic and social impact within Chinese Canadian and other Asian communities targeted during the 2003 Toronto outbreaks (Leung 2004). Exposing the flaws of the healthcare system, these outbreaks also pointed to the undeniable fact that racism can mesh with health scares to produce powerful and socially harmful moral panics in which members of specific ethnic and racial groups are targeted by the media and potentially excluded by other citizens in the name of health.

BSE

Contrary to the 2003 Toronto SARS outbreak, the 1996 British BSE crisis is difficult to categorize as a moral panic, partially because of the non-human nature of an easily avoidable threat (infected cattle) and its limited moral resonance beyond state responsibility as an issue (which began to fade when British politicians redefined BSE as a nationalist cause). After a brief description of the disease and the scientific debate over SARS in the late 1980s and early 1990s, the chapter focuses on the 1996 crisis and its aftermath.

Background

BSE belongs to a group of animal diseases known as Transmissible Spongiform Encephalopathies (TSEs).[2] TSEs have long occurred in mammalian species. 'The form of the disease in sheep is called scrapie, and it has been present in Britain and in several other countries for well over 200 years. The form of the disease in humans is called Creutzfeldt-Jakob Disease (CJD) and it has also been known for a long time' (Lacey 1994: 1). Both BSE and CJD are degenerative diseases impacting on the central nervous system of the animal or person infected. Although some cattle had may have been infected by BSE as early as the 1970s, the first cases were recorded only in 1985.³

Even though it is now clear that BSE causes CJD, no consensus over this question existed in the mid-1980s. However, at the time, a number of scientists claimed that the ingestion of the animal disease could cause CJD in human beings (Goethals et al 1998: 99).⁴ Yet, in the late 1980s, British officials depicted BSE as only an animal health concern, not a public health threat. This reassuring discourse served the perceived interests of the meat industry, which sought to preserve public confidence in British beef (Smith 2004). This initial definition of BSE as an animal health issue would have lasting political consequences as the reassuring rhetoric of British officials would later be turned against them in the context of increasingly alarming reports about the relationship between BSE and CJD (Powell and Leiss 1997: 7).

In spite of concerted state efforts to depict BSE as only an animal health issue, some measures were enacted in the late 1980s to fight the disease. This situation probably stems from the rapid increase in the number of confirmed BSE cases, which reached 867 by June 1988 (Lacey 1994: 62). The measures adopted in the summer of 1988 included compulsory notification of BSE and the slaughter of potentially infected cattle, which were 'largely predicated on the assumption that BSE was unlikely to pose a human health risk but that nevertheless the uncertainty required that some precautions be taken' (Greer 1999: 601). In November 1989, the multiplication of BSE cases in Britain led to the enactment of new measures regarding carcass disposal and the consumption of milk from infected cows.

BSE first emerged as a media issue in May 1990 and, when it became clear that '[TSEs] could jump the species barrier' (Miller 1999: 1247), the Conservative government denied once again that BSE represented a significant public health concern; the official message was that British beef was safe. In order to back that statement with a powerful yet reassuring image, Agriculture Minister John Selwyn Gummer even fed his young daughter a British beef hamburger in front of television cameras (Béland 2007). This example shows that political actors do not always attempt to spread fear; in some circumstances, they can use the media to send reassuring messages to the population when they think that it is in their interest to do so. This remark is important as far as the concept of moral panic is concerned, because it would be misleading to assume that political actors always act as moral entrepreneurs seeking to both exploit and exacerbate fear.

After several days of high-profile media exposure, the BSE issue quickly moved to the periphery of the British political agenda after the European Union enacted a measure on beef certification for BSE-free herds. The British media lost interest in an issue whose novelty and sensational appeal had rapidly declined.

The BSE crisis

In late 1995, the increasing number of CJD cases generated new media interest in BSE which peaked dramatically in March 1996, when British officials finally acknowledged that BSE could cause CJD in humans (Béland 2007). Perhaps in order to compensate for their past optimism about the disease, Conservative officials came to recognize BSE as a central public health issue. At the time, these officials faced strong attacks from the Labour Opposition, which challenged them to disclose all the scientific evidence to the public in order to restore confidence in the state.[5] Instead of downplaying potential public health hazards as they had done before, the Conservative government adopted a crisis discourse grounded in the assumption that bold actions were necessary to protect both meat consumers and the British beef industry. By then, 'the inaccurate estimate of extremely low risk had been replaced by a new officially sanctioned but equally unsubstantiated account of a much higher risk' (Forbes 2004: 353). After denying the idea of a public health threat for years, the Conservative government acknowledged it in a dramatic manner, which increased popular fears and fed overly dramatic media reports.

Indeed, in 1996 the British media played a key role in creating a health scare around BSE. For instance, on 20 March 1996 the *Daily Mirror* printed on its front page that 'MAD COW CAN KILL YOU'. This front-page story appeared on the very same day as Health Secretary Stephen Dorrell admitted publicly that ten cases of a new strain of CJD could be tied to the propagation of BSE in cattle over the last decade (Brookes 1999: 250). Over the following days, the British press focused extensively on the public health insecurity stemming from BSE. Depicting it as an excessively dangerous curse, British tabloids helped to spread acute collective insecurity about BSE, which strongly increased the awareness of British consumers about beef-related food hazards (Smith *et al.* 1997). Considering the limited number of people who actually died from the human variant of BSE (CJD), media reports proved excessively pessimistic.[6] However, although BSE was a source of acute insecurity, there was relatively little widespread panic besides the dramatic media reports mentioned above. The absence of widespread and sustained collective panic is related in part to the fact that those truly afraid of BSE could protect themselves by simply avoiding eating beef altogether. This is a crucial difference with SARS, which was about human-to-human contagion, a feature of the apparent public health threat that makes risk avoidance a potentially greater source of panic. Because it is easier to avoid eating beef than to stay away from other human beings, SARS has a greater panic potential than BSE. Additionally, in the case of BSE, nationalism came to the rescue of politicians, who used it to divert attention away from the health scare itself in the name of a patriotic struggle to save the British beef industry.

In late March 1996 the European Union (EU) considered, and then adopted, a ban on British beef. According to the Conservatives, the country's economy was under attack. 'As the crisis developed all five tabloid newspapers began to focus on the threat posed to the British beef industry from the European ban at the expense of the food health aspects' (Brookes 1999: 251). On March 21, Conservative Prime Minister John Major spoke in Parliament to strongly condemn the European attempt to institute a ban on British beef:

> Important national interests for Britain are involved in this matter. I cannot tolerate those interests being brushed aside by some of our European partners,

with no reasonable grounds to do so. The top priority of our European policy must be to get the unjustified ban on beef derivatives lifted as soon as possible and to establish a clear path for the lifting of other aspects of the wider ban. We shall continue our present efforts, although these are not enough.[7]

For the Conservatives, the nationalistic rhetoric surrounding the political push to save the British beef industry constituted an opportunity to shift the public's attention toward the seemingly irrational, biased, and unfair behaviour of other European countries. This political diversion is a major aspect of the 1996 BSE scare, which did not constitute a case of moral panic in the strict sense of the term (Béland 2007).

This discussion points to the relationship between health scares and 'the politics of blame avoidance' (Weaver 1986). In this specific case, by diverting attention away from their perceived responsibility and by stressing *economic* risks related to the EU ban, British policy-makers avoided becoming genuine 'folk devils', while helping to prevent the emergence of a sustained moral panic episode. This remark points to the fact that blame assignment and avoidance are major aspects of moral panics (Hier 2002a). Clearly, the 1996 BSE scare involved both risk assessments and moralization taking the form of blame assignment on the part of citizens. However, these elements did not converge to create a true moral panic, as politicians deflected some of the blame onto foreign nations while reframing the issue as a patriotic struggle for the country's economic survival.

Conclusion

The two case studies enable us to draw lessons about the relevance of the concept of moral panic for the analysis of contemporary health scares. First, the 2003 SARS crisis in Toronto illustrates the interest of using the concept of moral panic to study specific health scares. As suggested above, the construction of SARS as a media and policy problem involved the transformation of Chinese-Canadian and other minorities into folk devils that other people should fear in their everyday life. Furthermore, while the SARS epidemic was mainly confined to hospitals and other healthcare facilities, many citizens influenced by catastrophic media reports avoided Chinatown areas and even Asian-looking people. These remarks illustrate the atmosphere of panic surrounding the SARS outbreaks in Toronto and the fact that the concept of moral panic can apply to and shed light on contemporary health scares. As the analysis of SARS shows, this concept remains most useful even in the context of the so-called risk society, where increasingly global health anxieties are widespread.

Second, the British BSE case suggests that moral panic does not always apply to specific health-scare episodes. In fact, in contrast with what the term moral panic evokes, this episode was not really a source of widespread and sustained panic because citizens who were truly afraid of eating beef could simply stop consuming this type of meat and turn to other food sources. This is what actually occurred, as beef consumption in Britain fell by 8 percent in 1996, despite the nationalistic campaign to encourage British citizens to support the domestic beef industry (Foreign Agricultural Service 1998). Moreover, the moral content of the episode concerned the behaviour of state actors and, later, foreign countries, rather than everyday moral boundaries central to moral panics (Hier 2008). In fact, the shift to a nationalistic economic discourse during the BSE crisis helped politicians to defuse the type of blame traditionally associated with moral panics.

This volume as a whole suggests that the concept of moral panic, understood as part of broader moralization processes, can be successfully applied to a number of empirical contexts. As evidenced in this chapter, health scares is one of these contexts, as long as scholars are aware of the fact that not all health scares are moral panic episodes. While it applies to health scares like the 2003 SARS outbreaks, the moral panic framework should be used cautiously, as some health scares are not about moral panic in the strict sense of the term. This means that, in order to launch meaningful and rigorous empirical studies on global or even more localized health scares, scholars should avoid mechanically applying the concept of moral panic to all the health scares they encounter. As the above SARS case shows, students of health scares can benefit from engaging with the moral panic literature, as long as they pay close attention to the specific nature of the episode they seek to analyze, while starting from the perspective that the existence of a moral panic is an empirical question requiring systematic analysis. In other words: we need to demonstrate that a health scare is a moral panic by looking at the evidence. Ironically, keeping in mind that some health scares are not episodes of moral panic in the precise sense of the term is the best way to rigorously employ this concept in the analysis of health scares in what is known as the risk society.

Notes

1 The author would like to thank Sean Hier, Angela Kempf and Kathrin Komp for their comments as well as the Canada Research Chairs Program for its financial support.
2 This section draws extensively on Béland (2007). For an alternative account of the BSE story told in this chapter see the recollections of a former British official, Packer (2006).
3 It took almost two more years for British scientists to identify the new disease. In late October 1987 the publication of a scientific article made the British scientific community aware of BSE (Wells *et al.* 1987; see also Schwartz 2003). The question debated at the time was the possible causal link between BSE and CJD.
4 For a personal account see Lacey (1994).
5 Ms. Harriet Harman (Peckham) (1996), *Commons Hansard Debates*, London, March 20, 1996, Column 376.
6 Between 1995 and 2003, CJD claimed 139 lives in the United Kingdom. This represents an average of about 18 victims a year (Innes 2004).
7 The Prime Minister (Mr. John Major) (1996), *Commons Hansard Debates*, London, Thursday, March 21, Column 99.

References

Bartlett, D. M. C. (1999) 'Mad Cows and Democratic Governance: BSE and the Construction of a "Free Market" in the UK', *Crime, Law & Social Change* 30(3): 237–57.
Beck, U. (2002) *World Risk Society*, Cambridge: Polity.
Beck, U. (1992) *Risk Society*, London: Sage Publications.
Béland, D. (2007) *States of Global Insecurity*, New York: Worth Publishers.

Borgundvaag, B. et al. (2004) 'SARS Outbreak in the Greater Toronto Area: The Emergency Department Experience', *Canadian Medical Association Journal* 171(11): 1342–44.

Brookes, R. (1999) 'Newspapers and National Identity: The BSE/CJD Crisis and the British Press', *Media, Culture& Society* 21(2): 247–63.

Cohen, S. (1972) *Folk Devils and Moral Panics: The Creation of the Mods and Rockers*, Oxford: Basil Blackwell.

Critcher, C. (2009) 'Widening the Focus: Moral Panics as Moral Regulation', *British Journal of Criminology* 49(1): 17–34.

Critcher, C. (2003) *Moral Panics and the Media*, Buckingham: Open University Press.

Dalrymple, T. (1998) *Mass Listeria: The Meaning of Health Scares*, London: André Deutsch.

Eichelberger, L. (2007) 'SARS and New York's Chinatown: The Politics of Risk and Blame During an Epidemic of Fear', *Social Science and Medicine* 65(6): 1284–95.

Forbes, I. (2004) 'Making a Crisis out of a Drama: The Political Analysis of BSE Policy-making in the UK', *Political Studies* 42(2): 203–31.

Foreign Agricultural Service (1998) *The Continuing Effects of BSE Beef Market, Trade, and Policy*, Washington, DC, United States Department of Agriculture. www.fas.usda.gov/dlp2/circular/1998/98–03LP/bse.html [accessed on August 3, 2009].

Goethals, C. et al. (1998) 'The Politics of BSE: Negotiating the Public's Health', in Scott C. Ratzan (ed.), *The Mad Cow Crisis: Health and the Public Good*, New York: University Press, pp. 95–110.

Goode, E. and Ben-Yehuda, N. (2009) *Moral Panics: The Social Construction of Deviance* (2nd edition), Oxford: Blackwell.

Goode, E. and Ben-Yehuda, N. (1994) *Moral Panics: The Social Construction of Deviance*, Oxford: Blackwell.

Greer, A. (1999) 'Policy Coordination and the British Administrative System: Evidence from the BSE Inquiry', *Parliamentary Affairs* 52(4): 598–633.

Guan, J. (2004) 'The Racialization of SARS: A Media Analysis', in C. Leung (ed.), *Yellow Peril Revisited: Impact of SARS on the Chinese and Southeast Asian Communities*, Toronto: The Chinese Canadian National Council (National Office), pp. 7–11.

Hier, S. P. (2008) 'Thinking Beyond Moral Panic: Risk, Responsibility, and the Politics of Moralization', *Theoretical Criminology* 12(1): 173–90.

Hier, S. P. (2003) 'Risk and Panic in Late Modernity: Implications of the Converging Sites of Social Anxiety', *British Journal of Sociology* 54(1): 3–20.

Hier, S. P. (2002a) 'Raves, Risks and the Ecstasy Panic: A Case Study in the Subversive Nature of Moral Regulation', *Canadian Journal of Sociology*, 27(1): 33–57.

Hier, S. P. (2002b) 'Conceptualizing Moral Panic through a Moral Economy of Harm', *Critical Sociology*, 28(3): 311–34.

Hier, S. P. and Greenberg, J. (2002) 'News Discourse and the Problematization of Chinese Migration to Canada', in F. Henry and C. Tator (eds), *Discourses of Domination: Racial Bias in the Canadian English-Language Press*, Toronto: University of Toronto Press, pp. 138–62.

Hunt, A. (2003) 'Risk and Moralization in Everyday Life', in R. V. Ericson and A. Doyle (eds), *Risk and Morality*, Toronto: University of Toronto Press, pp. 165–92.

Hunt, A. (1999) *Governing Morals: A Social History of Moral Regulation*, Cambridge: Cambridge University Press.

Innes, J. (2004) 'Deaths from CJD up to 18 in 2003', *The Scotsman*, March 2. news.scotsman.com/topics.cfm?tid=671&id=244672004 [accessed August 3, 2009].

Lacey, R. W. (1994) *Mad Cow Disease: The History of BSE in Britain*, St. Helier: Cypsela.

Leslie, M. (2006) 'Fear and Coughing in Toronto: SARS and the Uses of Risk', *Canadian Journal of Communication* 31(2): 367–89.

Leung, C. (2004) *Yellow Peril Revisited: Impact of SARS on the Chinese and Southeast Asian Communities*, Toronto: The Chinese Canadian National Council (National Office).

Mackay, B. (2003) 'As SARS Toll Climbed, so Did Economic Cost to Toronto', *Canadian Medical Association Journal* 168 (11). www.cmaj.ca/cgi/content/full/168/11/1456-a [accessed August 4, 2009].

McRobbie, A. and Thornton, S. L. (1995) 'Rethinking "Moral Panic" for Multi-Mediated Social Worlds', *British Journal of Sociology* 46(4): 559–74.

Miller, D. (1999) 'Risk, Science and Policy: Definitional Struggles, Information Management, the Media and BSE', *Social Science & Medicine* 49(9): 1239–55.

Millstone, E. and van Zwanenberg, P. (2000) 'A Crisis of Trust: For Science, Scientists or for Institutions?' *Nature Medicine* 6(12) December: 1307–8.

Muzzatti, S. L. (2005) 'Bits of Falling Sky and Global Pandemics: Moral Panic and Severe Acute Respiratory Syndrome (SARS)', *Illness, Crisis, & Loss* 13(2): 117–28.

Packer, R. (2006) *The Politics of BSE*, Basingstoke: Palgrave.

Powell, D. and Leiss, W. (1997) *Mad Cows and Mother's Milk: The Perils of Poor Risk Communication*, Montreal: McGill-Queen's University Press.

Salehi, R. and Ali, S. H. (2006) 'The Social and Political Context of Disease Outbreaks: The Case of SARS in Toronto', *Canadian Public Policy* 23(4): 573–86.

Schram, J. (2003) 'How Popular Perceptions of Risk from SARS are Fermenting Discrimination', *British Medical Journal* 326: 939.

Schwartz, M. (2003) *How the Cows Turned Mad*, Berkeley: University of California Press.

Smith, A. P. *et al*. (1997) 'Consumer Information and BSE: Credibility and Edibility', *Risk Decision and Policy* 2(1): 41–51.

Smith, R. D. (2006) 'Responding to Global Infectious Disease Outbreaks: Lessons from SARS on the Role of Risk Perception, Communication and Management', *Social Science and Medicine* 63(12): 3113–23.

Smith, M. J. (2004) 'Mad Cows and Mad Money: Problems of Risk in the Making and Understanding of Policy', *British Journal of Political Science and International Relations*, 6: 312–332.

Thompson, K. (1998) *Moral Panics*, London: Routledge.

Ungar, S. (2001) 'Moral Panic versus Risk Society: The Implications of the Changing Sites of Social Anxiety', *British Journal of Sociology* 52(2): 271–91.

Ward, W. P. (2002) *White Canada Forever: Popular Attitudes and Public Policy toward Orientals in British Columbia* (3rd edition), Montreal: McGill-Queen's University Press.

Weaver, R. K. (1986) 'The Politics of Blame Avoidance', *Journal of Public Policy* 6(4): 371–98.

Wells, G. A. *et al*. (1987) 'A Novel Progressive Spongiform Encephalopathy in Cattle', *Veterinary Record* 121(18) October 31: 419–20.

Young, J. (1971) 'The Role of the Police as Amplifiers of Deviance: Negotiators of Drug Control as Seen in Notting Hill', in Stanley Cohen (ed.), *Images of Deviance*, Harmondsworth: Penguin.

INDEX

Aaronovitch, D., 28
ABCs (Acceptable Behaviour Contracts), 157–59, 167
Aberdeen (Scotland), 123
Acceptable Behaviour Contracts (ABCs), 157–59, 167
Acquired Immuno-Deficiency Syndrome (AIDS), 55, 59, 63–66, 192, 194. *See also* gay plague
activism: anti-prostitution, 60; anti-sex violence, 22; Christian, 27; claims-making activities of, 38; environmental, 82, 197, 201; and moralization, 18; role in moral panics, 21, 44, 53, 164; scientists', 191; social, 159; and vigilantism, 63
affective economies, 114
Afghanistan, 28
Agamben, Giorgio, 121
Ahmed, Sara, 105, 107–115
AIDS (Acquired Immuno-Deficiency Syndrome), 55, 59, 63–66, 192, 194. *See also* gay plague
alcohol: consumption, surveillance of, 184; disorder zones, 179; gendered consumption of, 177, 181; Institute of Alcohol Studies, 178; marketing of, 177; moralization of, 57, 62, 185; new British disease, 178; New Labour policy on, 178; as nourishment, 173; and pregnancy, 64; recommodification of, 177; and religion, 63, 68, 183; responsible drinking, 187; underage drinkers, 179. *See also* alcopops, beer, gin, wine
Alcohol Concern, 178
alcohol disorder zones, 179
Alcohol Harm Reduction Strategy for England, 178
alcopops, 176
Alexander, J.R., x
Ali, S.H., 227
Altheide, D., 2, 50, 93, 95, 106, 120
ambient fear, 93
American Meterological Association, 201
amoral panics, 17, 25, 29–30, 42, 156, 190
Annan Report (2009), 202
anomie, 4
anti-paedophile vigilantism, 57
anti-social behaviour 156–69, 163–67: of youth, 94, 156. *See also* ABCs, ASBOs
Anti-Social Behaviour Act (ASBA)(UK), 156
Anti-Social Behaviour Orders (ASBOs), 156–59; ASBO Concern, 164
Ampudia de Haro, F., 82
Archer, Margaret, 135, 140, 145, 148–49
Armstrong, E.G., 119
ASBA (*Anti-Social Behaviour Act*), 156
ASBOs (Anti-Social Behaviour Orders), 156–59; ASBO Concern, 164
atypical actors, 121–22, 125
audiences (of moral panics): actual, 31; potential, 31; specialized, 32
Audit Commission (UK), 159
Austin, G.A., 172, 175, 181, 183
authoritarianism, 163

Back, N., 26
bad moral panics, 213, 217, 221
Bannister, J., 95
Barson, M., 27
Bauman, Zigmunt, 93, 97, 121, 128
BBC (British Broadcasting Corporation), 101, 196
Bearfield, D.A., 126–27
Beck, Ulrich: on anxiety (social), 67; on folk devils, 129; on health scares, 233; risk society thesis, 29–30, 62–63, 97, 192, 224; on September 11, 2001 terrorist attacks, 97–98
Becker, Howard, 4, 6, 37, 59, 77, 100
beer, 173–77
Beisel, N.K., 58
Béland, Daniel, xii, 40, 154, 224–34
Ben-Yehuda, Nachman, xiii, 1–2, 6, 17–19, 20–36, 43, 107, 122, 136, 149, 190, 200; attributional model of, 9, 30, 40, 192, 224; contextual constructionism of, 17; on folk devils, 46; horizontal moral panic theory of, 87; moral panic models of, 7–8, 141, 178, 191–93
Berger, Peter, 6–7
Berridge, V., 188
Best, Joel, xii, 8, 19, 23, 37–52, 60, 94; on constructionism, 23–24; on satanism, 3; on stalking, 40
Beyond the Pleasure Principle, 91
Bhaskar, Roy, 135, 138–45, 147–49
Birchmore–Timney, C., 181
black youth crime, 68, 119. See also mugging
Blair, Tony, 160, 163
blogging: claims-making, role in, 201–204; as democratization, 44, 48
Bloyce, D. 83n6
Bluewater Shopping Centre, 156
Blumer, H., 38
Bolshevik political corruption, 27
Borenstein, S., 100
Borsay, P., 174, 179, 181, 183
Bosk, C.L., 47
Boston (US), 127
Boston Globe, 127, 131
Bottoms, A., 158
Bourke, J., 92
Bovens, M., 210
Bovine Spongiform Encephalopathy (BSE), 63, 81, 129, 132, 147, 151–54, 225, 229, 230–34
boy racers, 123–24
Brain, K., 176–78, 182, 184

Bray, D., 199, 201
Briggs, L., 119
Britain. See United Kingdom
British Broadcasting Corporation (BBC), 101, 196
British criminology, 4
British Youth Council, 164
Brookes, R., 231
BSE (Bovine Spongiform Encephalopathy), 63, 81, 129, 132, 147, 151–54, 225, 229, 230–34
bureaucratic stranger, 129
Bulger, James, 58
bullying, 120
Burney, E., 159
Burningham, K., 98
Bush administration. See Bush, George W.
Bush, George W., 59, 99, 195, 198, 205n8
Butler, R.V., 65
Button, M., 159

Cambodia, 28
Cameron, David, 163
Campos, P., 128
Canada: climate scientists, 205n8; and SARS, 226–27; shag bands in 50n4; Supreme Court, 65. See also Toronto
capital, moral, 126
capitalism, 82, 127, 137. See also political economy
Caporaso, J.A., 186
Carroll, P., 160
Catholic priests' molestation of children, 203
CCTV (Closed-Circuit Television Monitoring), 184. See also surveillance cameras
cell phones. See mobile telephony
Center for Disease Control (US), 100
Chambliss, W.J., 31
Chauncey, G., 22
chav, 163
Chernobyl nuclear disaster, 192, 195, 205
Child Growth Foundation (UK), 101
Children's Rights Alliance for England (CRAE), 164
Children's Society Charity, 164
China, 226–229
Chinatown, 226–229, 232
Chrétien, Jean, 229
Christian activism, 27
Christian moral reform, 180
cider, 177
cigarettes. See smoking

civilizing offences, 19, 71–72, 77–82
Civilizing Process, The, 73
civilizing processes, 11–12, 19: as self-restraint, 11. *See also* decivilizing processes
CJD (Creutzfeldt-Jakob Disease), 229–34
Clacton-on-Sea (UK), 31, 118
claims-makers, 149
claims-making, 1, 3, 13, 18, 21–24, 38, 45, 55, 93–94, 141, 144, 149. *See also* moral claims
Clark, Helen, 216–19
Clarke, Charles (UK Home Secretary), 165
Clarke, J. See *Policing the Crisis: Mugging, the State, and Law and Order*
climate change, 42, 47, 72, 153–54, 190–205; and civilizing processes, 80–82; and health, 100; as post-normal science, 191, 195, 199
climate change conferences, 197
Climategate scandal, 200–205
Climatic Research Unit, University of East Anglia, 202
Closed-Circuit Television Monitoring (CCTV), 184. *See also* surveillance cameras
Cohen, Albert, 4
Cohen, M., 26
Cohen, Stanley, 28, 34, 49, 55–56, 153, 213; and criteria for moral panic, 25; on critical uses of the moral panic concept, 55–56, 79; and definition of moral panic, 4–5, 20, 37, 42, 53, 120, 126, 181–82; and deviancy studies, vi, 4, 56, 119; on folk devils, 58, 88–89, 118–19, 121–23, 134–36, 142, 166; on permanent moral panic, 105; and the processual model of moral panic, 2, 30; on youth subcultures, vii, 5, 8, 18, 31–33, 37–38, 118, 156–57
Coleman, R., 159, 162
collective actors, 224
Collier, S.J., 63
Collins, Randall, 105, 110–16
Comstock, Anthony, 58, 68
communism, 27
Connelly, M.T., 51
conspiracy theories, 22, 28–29
consumer society, 177
conventional analytical orientations, 1–2, 8–18, 39, 121–127
Copenhagen Conference, 191, 195, 197
Corporate Agents, 148
Cottle, S., 107, 136, 208

conservatism, 41, 48–49
Conservative Party (UK), 158, 163, 230–32
conspiracy theories, 22, 28–29
Constructing Social Problems, 38
Contagious Diseases Act(s) (UK), 59
contextual constructionism, 8, 17–20, 23–24, 30, 33
Cooper, G., 98
Cornell, D.G., 29
Cornwell, B., 2, 24–26
Corrigan, P., 187
Couldry, N., 165
CRAE (Children's Rights Alliance for England), 164
crack babies, 133
Crawford, A., 156–59, 167
Creaven, S., 135, 142–44, 149
Creutzfeldt-Jakob Disease (CJD), 229–34
crime: criminal justice, 119, 179 data, interpretation of, 6, 31; fear of, 94; murder, 21, 27, 29, 34, 58, 116; street, 23, 31, 119; waves, 32, 39, 42, 44, 50; white collar, 127–28
Crime and Disorder Act (CDA)(UK), 158–59
Criminal Justice Act (2001)(UK), 179
crime wave panic, 32
criminalization: of drug use, 66; folk devils, 120; of marijuana, 37; of parents of obese children, 101
criminology, 5, 6, 118, 120, 123; British, 4; critical, 4; liberal, 6; radical, 4, 7, 38
Critcher, Chas, xii, 1–3, 9–11, 14n1, 22, 30, 34, 43, 54, 57, 62, 67, 97, 120, 153, 171–89, 211, 224–25; on AIDS, 59, 66, 71–72, 78–83, 150; on binge drinking, 66; on failed moral panics, 203; on folk devils, 88, 119–20, 212–13; on media, 135; on social anxiety, 105; on vigilantism, 109; on youth, 157. see also *Policing the Crisis*
critical realism, 89, 140–44; causality, concept of, 142; and dialectical materialism, 143–44; emergence, concept of 135; stratification, concept of, 135
crowds, 40, 105. *See also* spectral crowds
crusades, moral, 37–38, 69, 77, 94, 99–101, 118
Cryderman, K., 197
culture of fear, 90, 96, 98–99, 105
culture wars, ix
Curran, J., 165

Dabhoiwala, F., 186
Daily Courant, 174
Daily Mail, 159–63
Daily Mirror (UK), 28, 159–64, 231
Dalrymple, T., 224
Darwin, Charles, 91
Davies, N., 28, 41, 47
Davison, L., 172–75
day care, 8, 57, 60, 124, 125
Dean, Mitchell, 11
decivilizing processes, 12, 19, 72–79, 81–83
deconstructionism, 4, 5
Della-Giustina, J.A., 91
democracy, 45
demonology, 118
Denham, B., 119
deresponsibilization, 66
designer drugs, 51, 145
deviance: amplification, 3, 5, 128, 160; studies, 4, 6, 14; theory 4–5, 59
deYoung, Mary, xii, 60, 118–133; on folk devils, 88–89, 145–150; on satanic daycare panics, 8, 57
dialectical hegemonic constructions, 18
dialectical materialism, 143–44, 148
dialectics: and (de)civilization, 72, 77; emergentist material, 135, 144; moral, 9–10; and othering, 143; of security, 62
Dignan, J., 158
Dillon, P., 173–74
discourse: moral, 54, 63, 64, 122, 125, 225; risk, 63, 95, 120, 126, 130, 222; studies, 1
disgust: and folk devils, 115; phenomenology of, 115–16; in post-medieval morality, 73
Dishotsky, N.I., 26
disproportionality: criterion of moral panic theories, 55, 59, 105–8, 111, 191–93, 200–4; and emotion, 88, 105, 107–8; irrationality, compared with, 60; and ressentiment, 108; strong, 191, 199, 203–4; weak, 191, 199
division of labour, 4
Ditton, Jason, vii, 20
dole scroungers, 119, 122
Dominion Post (NZ), 216–18
Donovan, P., 27
Doran, Nob, 134
Douglas, Jack, 61
Douglas, Mary, 64, 69
Downes, D., 14
Downey, J., 162
Downs, A., 39
Doyle, K., 2

Dozier, R.W., 91
drug addicts, 31–32, 96, 122
drug scares, 39–40, 442, 50, 181
drunkenness, 177–86
Dunlap, R., 198
Dunning, E., 71, 77, 82, 83n1–2, 83n6
Durbin, Carole, 217–19
Durkheim, Emile, vii, 4, 7
Dworkin, A., 27, 62

Eagleton, Terry, 150
economic elites, 141
ecstasy (drug), 22, 35, 50–1, 84, 145
Eichelberger, L., 226–29
Eide, M., 3
Elias, Norbert, 11–12, 19; 71–85
elites: British, 5; economic, 141; engineered panics, 7, 141, 178, 191; political, 142, 181
emergentialism, 135, 143, 149
emergentialist material dialectic, 143–44
emotion: and affective economy, 114; collective level, 104; as contagion, 109; definition, 104; and disproportionality, 107; as effects, 115; fear as, 91, 95; as hostility, 105; individual level, 104; inside-out model of, 114; and the media, 106; and moralized behaviours, 19; naturalistic, 91; public, 110; social groups, constituents of, 108; and the spectral crowd, 108; volatility of, 105, 107. *See also* resentment, ressentiment
Engels, A., 196
environmental evangelicals, 190–210
epistemic gaze, 130
epistemic rupture, 81
Erasmus, 73
Erikson, Karl, vii, 4
Espiner, C., 218
ethical self-formation, 55, 66–67, 72, 171
ethics, 11, 55
ethnography, 109; in moral panic analysis, 112–13, 116
ethnomethodology, 110
European Union (EU), 188, 231
evil: and child pornography, 65; of folk devils, 29, 46, 122; and alcohol, 174, 182; and satanic day care panic, 124–25; language of, 10; unknown danger, characterization of, 97
existential security, 9–10, 17–18, 91
Express, 160, 178
Expression of Emotions in Man and Animals, The, 91

240 Index

family, 42, 115; destruction of, 163, 183; values, 163
FBI (Federal Bureau of Investigation), 29
Federal Bureau of Investigation (FBI), 29
Federal Bureau of Narcotics (US), 37
feminism, 22, 27, 32, 49, 51, 62
Ferguson, C.J., 27
Ferguson, R., 121
fiascos, concept of, 210
figurational approach 77, 80–84; definition, 72, 78;
Fishman, M., 44
Fletcher, J., 74, 76
Flew, T., 136
Flikr, 165
folk devils: fighting back, 12, 16, 162, 164–65; poor as, 31; youth as, 155–169
Folk Devils and Moral Panics: The Creation of the Mods and Rockers, 37, 49, 53
food: contamination, 59; Frankenfood, 128; genetically-modified, 56, 63; peanut panics, 59. *See also* BSE, obesity
football hooliganism, 35, 68, 71
Forbes, I., 231
Foreign Agricultural Service (UK), 234
forward panics, 110–12, 115
Foucault, Michel, 66–67, 72, 79, 121, 198, 214
Frankenfood, 128
Freud, Sigmund, 91
Frewer, L.J., 128
Frumkin, Howard, 100
Fry, Tam, 101
Furedi, Frank, xiii, 87, 90–103, 105–6
Futrell, R., 123
Fyfe, N., 95

Gallup Poll: on US crime, 29
Gamson, W., 219
gangs, 31, 56, 58–59, 160, 163–64, 169–70
gangsta culture, 163
Garland, David, 5–6, 20, 40, 42, 58, 134, 171, 211–12; on fear of crime, 94; on proportionality, 59, 108; on risk, 63
gay plague/disease, 64, 192
genetically-modified (GM) food, 56, 63
George, D.M., 172
Georgian England, 173, 183
Giddens, Anthony, 91, 98, 128
Gilbert and George, 164
gin: craze, 153, 172–189; consumption patterns in London, 172–73; and morality, 173–74, 185–86; tax on, 173; and women, 17–74

Gin Act, 174–76
Gisby, W., 171
Glaciergate scandal, 202, 205
Glassner, B., 105
globalization, 128, 192, 198
global warming, 82, 85, 96, 100, 191–207
GM (genetically-modified) food, 56, 63
God, 98
Goethals, C., 230
Goffman, E., 123
good moral panics, 14, 154, 213, 217, 221
Gore, Al, 196, 201, 205
governance: 43; neo-liberal, 171; moral, 157; of others, 76; of the self, 67, 72; studies, 157
Governing Morals, 54, 77
Goode, Erich, xiii, 1–2, 17–19, 20–36, 43, 107, 122, 136, 149, 190, 200; attributional model of, 9, 30, 40, 192, 224; contextual constructionism of, 17; on folk devils, 46; horizontal moral panic theory of, 87; moral panic models of, 7–8, 141, 178, 191–93
gray literature, 202
Gray, M.G., 95
greenhouse gases, 100, 195
Greenhouse summer, 194
Greer, A., 230
G-Rime music genre, 165
Grupp, S., 93
Guan, J., 227–28
Guantanamo detention center, 59
Guardian, The, 35, 159, 160, 163–64
Gusfield, J.R., 39, 44
Guzelian, C.P., 102

Habermas, J., 215
Hackley, C., 187
Hadju, D., 27
hagiology, 118
Hall, Stuart, 5–8, 32, 57–58, 88, 118–122, 126, 211; on ideology, 137, on signification spiral, 156, 161. see also *Policing the Crisis*
Hannigan, John, 98
happy hours, 184
happy slapping, 161
harm: amplification of, 161–62; avoidance, 157; and blame, 10; collective dimensions of, 10, 90, 154; concept of, 209–10; and drugs, 26; and folk devils, 107, 134–145, 149, 156; future, 145; and health panics, 63; individual dimensions of, 154; judicial conception

of, 65; libertarian theory of, 46; objectivist theory of, 23, 55; reduction, 66; and responsibilization, 9; risk society forms of, 29; social, 148; and smoking, 55; *See also* disproportionality, fiascos, risk, tragedies
harmful others, 9, 104, 143, 157–162
Harper, Stephen, 197
Harrison, B., 61
Hay, Colin, 58, 120, 157, 163
Hayward, K., 188
health scares, 40, 59, 154, 224–233
Heller, S., 27
heroin chic, 119
Herring, R., 179
heuristic of fear, 98
Hier, Sean P., xiii, 1–16, 63, 71–72, 79, 87–88, 92, 106, 109, 119, 155–70, 198, 204n3, 211; on amoral panic, 30; on folk devils, 122, 129–31, 145–46; on ideology, 137–38; on moral regulation, 10–12, 22, 43, 54–55, 83n8, 94, 120, 136, 156–57, 166, 171, 185, 190; on raves, 145; on risk theory, 9, 43, 50n9, 62, 81, 166–67, 224–27, 232–33
Higgins, P., 100
Hilgartner, S., 47
Hill, A., 168
Himmelfarb, G., 61
Hinerman, S., 213
hippies, 26, 38
HIV (human immunodeficiency virus), 64
Hobbs, T., 92
Hoeri, K., 120
Holland, 173
Hollands, R, 184
Holloway, W., 92, 128
holocaust (Jewish), 75
Holstein, J., 7
Home Office (UK), 157–58, 176; Respect Action Plan, 165
Homo Sacer, 121
homosexuals: as deviants, 58, 63; as folk devils, 59; gay plague/disease, 64, 192; resistance to moral panic of, 33, 64
Honest Broker, The, 201
Hong Kong, 227
Hooded (artwork), 164
Hood, C., 211
Hoodie (song), 165
hoodies: clothing, 155; folk devil, term for, 156–167
hooliganism: football, 35, 68, 71; youth, 118
House of Commons (UK), 232

Howard, John (Australian Prime Minister), 198
Hubbard, P., 93
Hughes, J., 71, 77, 82, 83n1–2, 83n6
Hulme, M., 198–99
human immunodeficiency virus (HIV), 64
Hume's Law, 138
Hunt, Alan, 2, 9, 13, 63, 94, 104, 121; on ideology, 136–37; on moral regulation, 18–19, 54, 71–72, 77, 171; on risk theory, 91, 157
Hunt, Arnold, 7, 90
Hurricane Katrina, 191

ideology, 125, 135; critique of, 138–40; discourse versus, 138; and media, 136
immigrants, 31–32, 49–50, 56, 66, 68, 212, 214
immigration, 49, 50, 120
Indian mutiny (1857), 68
individualizing discourses, 9, 166
Innes, J., 233n6
Innes, Martin, 3
Institute of Alcohol Studies, 177
interest groups, 27, 32, 106, 142, 149. *See also* pressure groups
Intergovernmental Panel on Climate Change (IPCC), 195–205
International Association for Ecology and Health, 100
Internet, 50n6, 161, 191, 196, 199–204; cyber-boosters, 47; cyberphobia, 133; cyberspace, 133; and media, 47, 125, 162; pornography, 10, 58; predators, 120, 126
IPCC (Intergovernmental Panel on Climate Change), 195–205
Iran-Contra scandal, 28
Iraq, 28, 195
Irvine, C., 101
Irvine, J., 105
Irwing, Alan, 160
Islamic terror, 201
Israeli Parliament, 28
Ivis, F., 173

Jasanoff, S., 129, 147
Jefferson, T., 92, 128
Jenkins, P., 33, 39, 106, 134, 157
Jewkes, Y., 25, 33
Jones, D., 159
Jones, E.E., 125
Jones, P., 119
Jekyll, Sir Joseph (Master of the Rolls), 174

Index

Katz, Jack, 105, 110, 112–116
Kaufman, L., 206
Keil, R., 193
Kelsey, J., 223
Kent (UK), 153, 155
Kilminster, R., 74
King, P., 188
Kinsey, R., 6
Kitsuse, J.I., 8, 23–24, 38, 44
Kitzinger, J., 112, 123
Knesset, 28
Knight, Graham, 3, 13, 154, 208–223
Kolbert, E., 196, 201
Kuntstler, J.H., 195, 198
Kyoto Accord, 195

labeling theory, 4–6, 37–38, 78
Labour Party (UK), 41, 156–58, 163–66, 176–79, 180, 184–86
Lacey, R.W., 229–30, 233
LaCombe, D., 2
Lacquer, T.W., 61
Lady Sovereign, 165
Laidi, Z., 97
Lake, P., 186
Lakeman, G., 169
Lakoff, A., 63
Langum, D.J., 60
law and order politics, 153, 156, 166
Lawrence, Stephen, 107
Lazarides, S., 121
Lea, J., 6–7
Le Bon, G., 108
left liberalism, 49, 56
Leiss, W., 230
Lemert, Edwin, vii, 4
Lemmings, D., 182, 186
Leslie, M., 227
Lett, Dan, xiii, 117, 153, 155–70
Levi, M., 127
Leung, C., 228–29
Levine, D.P., 186
Liazos, A., 6
libcom, 165
liberal criminology, 6
liberal-left intellectuals, 56
liberal moralization, 204
liberalism, advanced, 187
Licensing Act (2003)(UK), 179
Linders, A., 2, 24–26
London Distillers Guild, 172
Loseke, D.R., 23
Loyal, S., 73
LSD (lysergic acid diethylamide), 15, 25–26

Luckmann, T., 6–7
Luhmann, N., 209
Lull, J., 213
Lumsden, K., 123–24
Lupton, D., 93, 128
luxury emissions, 198
lysergic acid diethylamide (LSD), 15, 25–26

Mackay, B., 229
MacKinnon, C.A., 27, 62
mad cow disease. *See* BSE
Madam Geneva, 173
MADD (Mothers Against Drunk Drivers), 59, 64
magico-mythical knowledge, 74–7
mainstream media, 8, 136, 162, 199, 202–5, 229
Major, John, 233
Manis, J., 23
Mann Act (US), 60
Maratea, R., 44, 47
Marcus, G., 98–99
marijunana, 37
Marinello, M.J., 26
Marsh, R., 128
mass media, 5, 31–32, 40, 53, 59, 106–7, 135–36, 146, 171, 181, 207
Marxian theory, 5–7, 151
Master of the Rolls. *See* Jekyll, Sir Joseph
materialism, dialectical, 143–44, 148
Mattel Corporation, 128
Mattley, C., 108
Mawby, R.C., 171
McChesney, R., 136
McIntyre, S., 200
McKibben, B., 195–97
McKitrick, R., 200
McMullan, J.L., 132
McRobbie, Angela, 2, 7–8, 23, 94, 123, 145, 155, 204; on folk devils, 88, 122–23, 145, 162–65, 194; and horizontal moral panic theory; on media, 136, 141, 163, 192
Meades, James, xiv, 88–89, 134–50
Measham, F., 176–78, 182, 184
media. *See* mainstream media, mass media, multi-mediation
medico-moralization, 65
Medieval Warm Period (MWP), 200
Megan's law, 63
Meltzer, B., 107
Mennell, S., 74–76
Mental Health Foundation (UK charity), 95

Mercury Energy, 208, 210, 213–18, 220–21
Merton, R.K., 61
microphysics of power, 130
micropolitics of deviance, 129
middle ages, moral shift during, 73
Mighty River Power, 208, 210, 213–18, 221
Miller, D., 122–23
Miller, G., 7
Miller, P.G., 128
Miller, T., 128
Millie, A., 156, 158
Mitzman, A., 77
mobile telephony, 161
Modigliani, A., 219
Mods and Rockers, 1, 5, 8, 18–19, 31–34, 41–48, 55–58, 118–19, 131, 134
molestation of children by Catholic priests, 203
Moore, D., 53, 162
moral antagonism, 17, 22
moral capital, 126
moral claims, 46–7, 154
moral crusades, 37–38, 69, 77, 94, 99–101, 118
moral decline, 75, 155–56, 160
moral discourse, 7, 54, 63–64, 122, 125, 225
moral entrepreneurs: deviant definition, role in, 37, 56; interests of, 6, 10; and value reaffirmation, 22;
moralization: and anxiety, 67; as counter-power, 213; definitions, 9, 18, 53, 64; expanding, 64; and Foucault, 66; liberal, 204; medico-moralization, 65; as problematization, 66; and risk management, 157; volatile, panics as, 43, 88; volatility of, 57, 120, 154, 159, 166
moral hegemony, 18, 60–61
moral order: vertical, 17, 88
moral panic models: attributional, 30, 109, 192; horizontal, 31–33; processual, 30, 78; vertical, 30–33
moral politics, 18, 54–62, 67–68
moral regulation, 53–77; agents of, 59; and anxiety, 67; definition, 9–10; as function of moral panic, 22; moral panic, as a form of, 10–11, 18, 43, 54;
moral shock, 191, 198–204
morality: breakdown of, 58; claims, 10; and fear, 87, 90–99; grammar of, 90–103; middle-class, 26; irrelevance of in contemporary societies, 29; and religion, 46

morals versus ethics, 11
Mother Gin, 173
Mothers Against Drunk Drivers (MADD), 59, 64
mugging, 31, 58, 68
Muliaga family, 208–210, 213–222
Mulloy, D., 121
multi-mediation, 31–32
Muncie, J., 159
murder, 21, 27, 29, 34, 58, 116
music, as cultural preference, 118, 163
Musolf, G. 107
Muzzatti, S.L., 2, 54, 59, 120

National Center for Environmental Health/Agency for Toxic Substances and Disease Registry (US), 100
National Deviancy Symposia, 5
National Deviancy Conference (NDC) (UK), 37–38
nationalism, 229, 231–33
Nazi Germany, 75
NCH, 164
NDC (National Deviancy Conference) (UK), 37–38
Nead, Lynda, 68
neo-liberalism, 9–110, 171, 220
New Labour. *See* Labour Party (UK)
new-orthodoxy, 158
Newport, F., 203
News of the World, 160–61
New York, ix, 58, 226–28
New York Times, 50n1–3, 195, 206
New Zealand, 208, 213–17, 220
New Zealand Herald, 213–17
Nicholls, J.C., 185
Nietzsche, F., 61
noisy neighbours, 166
normative judgment, 54–66, 155–56
normativization. *See* moralization
nuclear panics, 195
nuclear power: and disease, 203; and the military industrial complex, 194; risks of, 29, 192, 195; technological advancements in, 128
nuclear warfare, 193

obesity, 66, 99–103, 197
oil: dependence, 100, 197, 204; industry, 198; tar sands (Canada), 204
Ortiz, A.T., 119
O'Malley, P., 162
Oreskes, N., 193, 200–1
Ost, S., 120

O'Sullivan, F., 215–16
Outsiders, 59

paedophilia, 15, 60, 66–67, 94, 99, 157; anti-paedophile vigilantism, 57
Pansegrau, P., 196
parents: and child abduction, 60; and child obesity, 101; responsibilization of, 64–65, 165;
Parkin, D., 92
Parnaby, P.F., 8
Pawluch, D., 7, 24
Paz, Jonathon, 100
Pearson, G., 35, 58, 75, 159
pedophilia. *See* paedophilia
Pentagon, 204
phenomenology, 5–6, 108, 110–13, 115
Pielke, R. Jr., 201–2, 205
Pincus, S., 186
Plant, M., 184
police, 28, 59, 100–1, 109, 176–80, 184, 203, 214–219
Police and Criminal Justice Act (2001)(UK), 179
Policing the Crisis: Mugging, the State, and Law and Order, 58, 68
political economy: of alcohol, 184–87; of genetic modification, 56; of moral regulation, 153, 171–72, 184–87
politics of fear, 90, 95, 98–99, 115
politics, moral, 18, 54–62, 67–68
pornography: anti-pornography, 22, 32, 58, 62; child, 15, 46, 58; Internet, 10; and harm, 65, 120
postmodernity, 31–32, 93
poverty, 24, 31, 133
Powell, D., 230
Prescott, John, 160
Press, The (NZ), 217
pressure groups, 145, 164, 178, 181–83, 186, 216. *See also* interest groups
Price, E.A., 2, 135
Primary Agenst, 148
Prime Minister's Strategy Unit, 177–78
privatisation of fear, 92–94
protest: against Mercury Energy, 216; of Scottish Socialist Youth, 164; in Toronto, 130;
Protestantism and alcohol, 68
public arenas, 48, 195, 198–99
public safety, 9, 127
public sphere, 75, 182, 186, 188, 210–19
punishment, 31, 62
puritanism, 45
Purvis, T., 136–37

Quattrone, G.A., 125
Queen's Speech (2005), 165
Quilley, S., 73, 82

racism, 31, 214, 227–28
Raco, M., 159
Ranulf, S., 61
rape, 21–22, 161
raves: advocates of, 50n9, 130; and ecstasy use, 130, 145–46; opponents of, 50n9; in Toronto, 8, 22, 129
realism, critical, 135, 142–45, 147, 149–50
reality-congruent knowledge, 74–75
red scare, 27
Reformation of Manners,
Reform and Respect Agenda (UK), 156, 165–67
Reinarman, C., 39–40
remoralization. 64
resentment, 88, 107–8
respectability, 18, 60–62, 66
Respect Action Plan (UK), 165
responsibilization, 64–66, 157
ressentiment, 16–19, 60–61, 70, 88, 107–8
Revere, A., 196
revisionist analytical orientations, 1–3, 12–14, 60, 120, 156
rhetoric, 45–50
Rio Conference, 197
riot, 175, 180; nude, 161
risk management, 9–10, 64, 157, 221; collective, 154; discourses of, 157; individual, 90
risk society thesis: convergence with moral panic theory, 9, 29–30, 62, 146; and Foucault, 9; and health, 224–25, 232–33; versus moral panic theory, 9, 25, 81, 96–99, 192–99. *See also* Beck, Ulrich
Roberts, Ian, 99–100
Robin, C., 92
Rogers, R., 101, 200
Rohloff, Amanda, 1–3, 14, 71–85, 168, 171
Ropeik, D., 95
Roper, Juliet, 15, 154
Rose, N., 189
Rosenthal, J., 207
Rothe, D., 2, 54, 59, 120
Royal Liverpool University Hospital, 101
Rudé, G., 172
Rutherford, A., 159
Rutherford, S., 195
R. V. Butler (1992), 65

Sacco, V.F., 39
Salehi, R., 227
Sandywell, B., 120
Sarah's law, 63
SARS (severe acute respiratory syndrom), 63, 154, 193, 206, 225–35
Satanism, 3, 27, 32
Satter, R., 203
Sayer, Andrew., 140, 142, 150
Sayer, D., 187
scandal, concept of, 212–13
scapegoats, 15, 30, 107, 110
Scarce, R., 198
Scheler, M., 61
Schissel, B., 31
Schmidt, C., 82
Schmitt, C., 121
Schneider, S., 193
Schram, J., 226, 228
Schur, E., 4, 123, 129
Scottish Socialist Youth (SSY), 164
self-restraint, 19, 61, 74–76
September 11, 2001 terrorist attacks, 28, 42, 97, 126–27
severe acute respiratory syndrome (SARS), 63, 154, 193, 206, 225–35
sexual behaviour, 11, 40
sexuality, 39, 62–64, 70
sexually-trarnsmitted diseases, 10, 59, 66, 124, 203
shag bands, 38–42, 46–50
Shakespeare, William, 127
Sheard, K., 77
Shell Canada, 197
Shepard, B., 119
signification spiral, 156
Silverman, E.B., 91
Simester, A., 156, 158
Simi, P., 123
Singer, L., 59
skeptical analytical orientation, 1–4, 13–14, 60, 190
Smith, Andre, xiv, 153, 155–70
smoking: anti-smoking campaigns, 10, 55, 62, 66, 101n2; hashish, 28, 37; passive/secondary, 65–66
snuff movies, 27
social movements, 7–8, 21, 39, 44, 49, 59, 66, 83, 142, 145, 149
social problems, 13, 17; and alcohol, 172; climate change as, 47, 195, 198; construction, 5, 18, 50, 87, 136; constructionist perspective, 38, 44; and drug use, 66; government disinterest in, 181, 183; imagined, 79; and immigration, 49; and inequality, 45; media, as a source of, 48; moral panics as, 8, 18, 20, 23, 37–51; new, 94; objectivist perspective, 23; realist perspective, 23; rhetoric, 45; and signification spiral, 156; sociology of, 7
Society for Promoting Christian Knowledge, 174
sociologists, liberal/left bias of, 49, 56
sociology of knowledge, 6–7
SOEs (state-owned enterprises)(NZ), 208, 213–18
Solomon, Tom, 101
Spector, M., 7, 23–24, 38, 44
spectral crowds, 108–11
Spencer, Dale, xiv, 87–88, 104–117, 136
spirits. *See* gin
Squires, P., 158
SSY (Scottish Socialist Youth), 164
state formation, 19, 84
state-owned enterprises (SOEs)(NZ), 208, 213–18
St Cyr, J., 123
Stevens, Lord (UK), 162
Stewart, Jon, 150n3
stigma: contests, 123, 125, 127, 129; social, 99
strangers: bureaucratic, 129; cultural, 120, 124, 146; danger, 120;
Sun, The, 159
Sunday schools, 69
Supreme Court of Canada, 65
Surgeon General (US), 64
surveillance cameras, 155
Suzuki, David, 201
Swidler, Ann, 93

tar sands (Canada), 204
Tavuchis, N., 217
Taylor, B., 169
Taylor, I., 38
TckTckTck banners, 197
Teddy Boys, 38, 58
television, 33, 106–7, 155, 226
Templeton, S.K., 101
terrorism, 42, 95–99, 106, 120, 133, 161
The New Criminology, 38
The Daily Show with Jon Stewart, 150n3
Thomas, W.I., 4
Thompson, Kenneth, vii–x, 2, 5, 9, 81, 101n2, 105, 224; on youth, 156–57

Thornton, Sarah, 2, 7–8, 23, 94, 155, 204; and folk devils, 88, 122; and horizontal moral panic theory; on media, 136, 141, 163, 192, 194
Three Climate Stooges, 198
Time Magazine, 196
Times, The (UK), 103, 159
Tiryakian, E., ix
TMSA (Transformational Model of Social Action), 135, 147–49
Tomlinson, J., 211
Tonry, M., 23
Toronto, 197; city hall, 130; raves, 8, 50n9, 129, 145–46; SARS in, 193, 225–29, 232–35; Toronto World Conference, 194
Toronto World Conference, 194
tragedies, concept of 210
Transformational Model of Social Action (TMSA), 135, 147–49
Transmissible Spongiform Encephalopathies (TSEs), 229
Trevor-Roper, H., 40
TSEs (Transmissible Spongiform Encephalopathies), 229–30
Tulloch, J., 93
Turner, M.J., 61
Turner, V., 208
Twitter, ix

UFO abductions, 49
Ungar, Sheldon, xiv, 2, 55, 98, 120, 128, 134, 147, 224; on climate change, 153–54, 190–208; on risk theory, 9, 30, 41, 62, 81–82, 96, 192–93
United Kingdom (UK): binge drinking, 57, 171, 177–79, 184; BSE panic, 81, 129, 147, 230–32; Climategate scandal, 202–3; *Contagious Diseases Act*(s), 59; gin craze, 180; hoodies panic, 155–70; House of Commons, 232; Mods and Rockers, 1, 5, 8, 18–19, 31–34, 41–48, 55–58, 118–19, 131, 134; obesity in, 101; paedophilia panics, 94; youth culture panics, 31, 38, 155–57, 161–166. *See also* Labour Party (UK), Conservative Party (UK)
United States (US): Climategate scandal, 201; conspiracy theories, 28–29; drugs panics, 26; drunk driving in, 57; implausible moral concerns, 27; news coverage in, 41; sex crime panics, 22; racism, 227–29; ritual abuse, 124; and SARS, 226–28; September 11, 2001 terrorist attacks, 126; wilding, 39

University of East Anglia Climatic Research Unit, 202
University of Wisconsin, 100

Valverde, Mariana, 53, 162
Van Dijk, V., 197
van Krieken, Robert, 77, 83n2
Vattimo, Gianni, 162
vertical moral order, 17, 88
victims, 29, 38, 45, 58, 111, 120, 127–28, 210–14
Victor, J.S., 2, 27, 42
Victorian society, 61, 68
vigilantism, 3, 76, 83n4; anti-paedophile, 57
VirCom EMS, 208, 210, 213, 215
volatility. *See* emotion, moralization
von Hirsch, A., 156, 158

Wacquant, L., 121
Waddington, I., 83n6
Waddington, P. A. J, 16, 27, 59
Waiton, Stuart, 2, 29–30, 42, 156, 190
Wakefield, A., 159
Walby, Kevin, xv, 87–88, 104–117, 136, 153, 155–70
Walker, J., 42
Walsh, C., 159
war on drugs, 45
war on terror, 42, 45
Warner, J.F., 172–75, 180–83
Watney, Simon, 16, 125, 128
Weaver, R.K., 225, 232
Weber, Max, vii, 21
Welch, M., 2, 135
welfare: neoliberal assault on, 220; scroungers, 31, 56; welfare state expansion post-WWII, 220; welfare state panics, 119
Weingart, P., 196
Wertham, F., 27
Wertrationalität, 21
Westminster Bench of Justices, 174
white-collar crime, 127–28
WHO (World Health Organization), 101, 226
Wilkins, Leslie, vii
wine, 64, 172–73, 176–77
witch hunts, 23, 40, 45, 52, 60, 131
Woolgar, s., 7, 24
World Health Organization (WHO), 101, 226
World Trade Center, 28, 127. *See also* September 11, 2001 terrorist attacks
World War II, 49, 220

World Wide Fund for Nature (WWF), 202
Wright, S., 1–3, 11–13, 16, 72, 80–81, 83, 168, 171
WWF (World Wide Fund for Nature), 202

Xenophobia, 183

Yankey, N. 2, 135
Yeomans, H., 179, 182–83
yobs, 160–63, 178
Young, Jock, 1, 3, 6, 18, 59, 61, 79; on drug taking, 1; on folk devils, 31; on moral indignation, 4–5, 107; on ressentiment, 61, 88, 107; on triggers of moral panic, 61

youth justice system (UK), 159
youth justice workers (UK), 158
youth: and alcohol, 57; alienated, 119; anti-social behaviour of, 94; British, 155–167; clothing, 155; culture, 56; deviance of, 6 feral, 155, 160–61; gangs 56, 159, 166; moral panics about, 31, 58, 61, 190; at play, 182; market, 177; and mugging, 68; rebellions, 33, 38; risky, 156; sexual behaviour of, 39; subcultures 5, 31, 118; transgressive, 31, 37, 41, 47, 118, 123

zombies, psychedelic, 26
Zweckrationalität, 21